Collins

AQA

Applied Business

AS

Malcolm Surridge   Tim Chapman   Debbie Cornelius   Stuart Merrills

William Collins' dream of knowledge for all began with the publication of his first book in 1819. A self-educated mill worker, he not only enriched millions of lives, but also founded a flourishing publishing house. Today, staying true to this spirit, Collins books are packed with inspiration, innovation and practical expertise. They place you at the centre of a world of possibility and give you exactly what you need to explore it.

Collins. Do more.

Published by Collins
An imprint of HarperCollinsPublishers
77–85 Fulham Palace Road
Hammersmith
London
W6 8JB

Browse the complete Collins catalogue at
www.collinseducation.com

20 19 18 17 16 15 14 13 12 11

ISBN 978-0-00-720140-2

Malcolm Surridge, Tim Chapman, Debbie Cornelius and Stuart Merrills assert their moral rights to be identified as the authors of this work

MIX
Paper from
responsible sources
FSC C007454
www.fsc.org

British Library Cataloguing in Publication Data
A Catalogue record for this publication is available from the British Library

Commissioned by Graham Bradbury

Cover Design by Blue Pig

Cover picture courtesy of Getty Images

Page design by Patricia Briggs

Additional design and page layout by Stephen Moulds, DSM Partnership

Project managed by Paul Stirner, DSM Partnership

Series managed by Kay Wright

Index by Julie Rimington

Picture research by Thelma Gilbert

Production by Sarah Robinson

Printed and bound by Printing Express, Hong Kong

Acknowledgements

The authors and publisher would like to thank the following for permission to reproduce photographs and other material:

ABB p260

Alamy p22, p46, p102, p106–7, p158, p172, p194/5, p198, p247, p255, p267, p268

Cadbury Schweppes p122

Collections p14 (John Wender), p127 (Liz Stares), p232 (Ray Roberts)

Corbis p10–1, p31, p34, p54, p64, p215, p286–7

Dell p36

Easyjet p63, p123

Education Photos p153

Empics p.31, p47, p56–7, p193, p248, p249, p266, p279

Holt Studios p238

Leicestershire Constabulary p84

MGA/Vivid p23

Newscast p31, p52, p102

Nestles p246

Nissan p270

Nokia p39

Panos Pictures p17 (Mark Henley)

Photofusion p49

Rex Features p17, p18, p31, p41, p60, p67, p119, p130, p142, p162, p174, p184, p206, p248, p257

Royal Mail p190, 191, 192

S&A Foods p27

Science Photo Library p254 (Andrew Lambert)

Roger Scruton p21, p27, p28, p30, p33, p51, p52, p55, p60, p125, p140, p142, p143, p154, p156, p178, p182, p190, p214, p216, p227, p238, p246, p251, p256, p265

Telegraph p285

Unilever p242–3;

United Biscuits p277

Courtesy of Warwick University p245

Every effort has been made to contact copyright holders, but if any have been inadvertentley overlooked, the publishers will be pleased to make the necessary arrangements at the first opportunity.

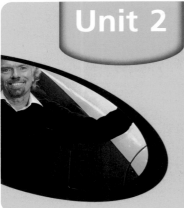

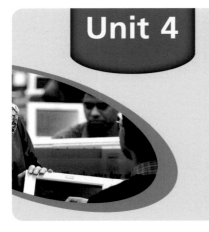

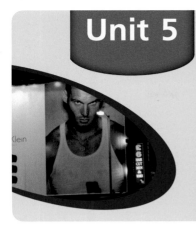

Using this book and CD-ROM

Welcome to AS Applied Business. This textbook is written specifically for students taking the AQA Applied Business awards, covering everything you will need to know for either the single or double award (see table below). If you are taking a single AS-level you will only need to complete Units 1, 2 and 3. To gain a double AS-level, you will need to complete a further three Units from 4, 5, 6 and 7, one of which must be externally assessed.

Your knowledge and understanding of the different units will be assessed either through:

■ a portfolio of work produced by you and assessed by your teacher (internal assessment)

■ a written examination lasting one hour (one and a half hours for Unit 5) that is written and marked by AQA, your awarding body (external assessment).

Applied Business AS

Setting the scene
Real-life case studies and images stimulate your ideas and help you focus on the topic. Many of the scenarios have questions to further engage you with the topic and to stimulate group discussion.

Text
Coverage of each topic is linked closely to the AQA specification of the essential knowledge-base you need to understand business.

Topic 1 — Economic conditions and competition

Setting the scene: The Bentall Centre

Located in Kingston upon Thames, 12 miles from central London, the Bentall shopping centre provides in excess of 46,000 square metres of retail space arranged over five floors. Bentall's website (www.thebentallcentre-shopping.com) provides full details about the centre and contains some virtual tours.

The Bentall centre is located close to major transport links and serves a catchment area within 30 miles of Kingston upon Thames, or within a one-hour drive. The centre attracts large numbers of people. The number of shoppers visiting the centre increased from 9 million in 1993 to 13 million in 2001.

Kingston upon Thames is a thriving town:

■ it is a university town and at the last census (in 2001) 25 per cent of Kingston's population were aged between 20 and 34 compared with the national average in England of 20 per cent

■ the average price of a detached house was £452,640 in December 2004, much higher than the average price of a detached house in England of £282,076

■ in 2003, average gross weekly pay in Kingston was £529.30 compared with average pay in England of £449.90

How do these statistics help to explain the success of the Bentall Centre? What other factors affect the success of a shopping centre?

14 — Unit 1 Investigating business

KEY TERMS

The level of economic activity in a region is a measure of the region's success in terms of employment and business activity.

Degree of competition is a measure of the number of businesses in a market relative to the number of customers. The higher the degree of competition, the greater the number of businesses compared with the number of customers.

Economic conditions

Like any businesses, the retail outlets based at Bentall Centre rely on customer confidence. If consumers are confident of their future income and prospects – because their jobs are safe or they are highly paid – then they are more likely to spend money freely and purchase products.

Kingston upon Thames is an affluent area and the rate of unemployment is usually lower than the rest of England and Wales. This suggests that the local economy is healthy, and this should benefit the shops in Bentall Centre. In general, the level of economic activity in any area – such as a town, region or country – can be measured in a number of ways:

■ the level of employment – the percentage of people of working age in paid employment

■ the average wages earned by workers

■ the number of businesses starting up compared with the number closing down

■ the level of house prices and the number of new houses being built.

Favourable changes in these measurements indicate a thriving economy, benefiting both businesses and workers. Confidence in the future will be high, and owners of businesses are likely to be expanding their operations. However, unfavourable changes in these measurements indicate a declining economy. Businesses may well be leaving the area or simply closing down. The level of unemployment could be increasing and consumer spending will probably be declining.

stop and think

Using the internet to collect relevant data, identify whether economic conditions in your area are likely to help local businesses to achieve their aims and objectives. You should be able to obtain useful information from www.neighbourhood.statistics.gov.uk and www.upmystreet.com.

The level of economic activity – at both local, national and international level – will have a significant impact on the setting and achievement of a business's SMART objectives. If economic activity is increasing, then objectives that rely on the level of demand for a product will be easier to achieve. For example, a business might have set an objective of increasing sales by two per cent in the next six months. If economic activity increases, then this objective is more likely to be achieved, and it might be revised in the future to, say, a four per cent increase in the subsequent six months.

Faced with a decline in economic activity, businesses will have to reconsider their tactics for achieving SMART objectives or they may have to revise their original expectations. Pressure is likely to be placed on employees, either because managers may introduce new working practices to improve productivity or because their job security might be threatened.

As you will see later in this unit, the degree to which employees work together as a team can significantly affect the ability of any business to cope with unfavourable economic conditions. In addition, the ingenuity and creativity of employees and the owners of the business will also contribute to the resilience of the business when faced with hard times.

stop and think

In England all business pay a local tax called the business rate. The amount each business pays in based on the size and value of its property. In 2005 these rates increased, and many small businesses were anticipating 15 per cent increases in their business rates. How might this increase affect the ability of, for example, a local newsagent to achieve its aims and objectives? What actions might it take?

Competition

In the past, British Telecom was the only business allowed to supply telephone services to domestic consumers. Today, consumers can choose from several competing providers such as OneTel and Telewest. Faced with this new competition, British Telecom has been active in developing new products and pricing schemes.

The degree of competition in a market is a significant factor affecting the ability of a business to achieve its aims and objectives. The degree of competition can be measured by the number of businesses providing similar products compared with the size of the market. For example, the market for mobile telephone ringtones has a high degree of competition as there are many businesses providing this service. Initially, this market had few competitors, with only a handful of enterprising individuals offering the service. With the arrival of polyphonic mobile telephones and companies like Jamster offering downloads over the internet, the ringtone market has opened to a wider range of providers, and each business now has to work harder to gain customers.

If the market for a product is small, it does not take too many businesses to begin trading for a high degree of competition to be present. For example, the market for ice cream on a beach in the summer can be highly competitive with just two competitors.

15 — Topic 1 Economic conditions and competition

Key terms
The specialist terminology used in the world of business is explained in simple terms.

Stop and think
These are short activities that can be done individually, in pairs or small groups that will help you to think about the issues raised by the text.

Unit	Title	How is this unit assessed
Single AS-level award		
1	Investigating business	Internal assessment
2	People in business	Internal assessment
3	Financial planning and monitoring	External test (1 hour)
Double AS-level award: you must study Unit 6 plus two units out of Units 4, 5 and 7		
4	Meeting customer needs	External test (1 hour)
5	Business information and communication systems	External test (1 hour 30 mins)
6	Developing a product	Internal assessment
7	Career planning	Internal assessment

Collins Applied Business AS for AQA is divided into seven units and each unit in this book corresponds to a unit of the AQA AS-level applied business awards. The units in this book have been divided into topics and each topic provides a manageable chunk of learning covering the subject content of an AQA AS-level unit.

Knowledge summary
This provides a quick revision of the key points covered in the text.

Quick questions
Comprehension questions designed to test your understanding of the topic you've just covered. All the answers can be found in the text.

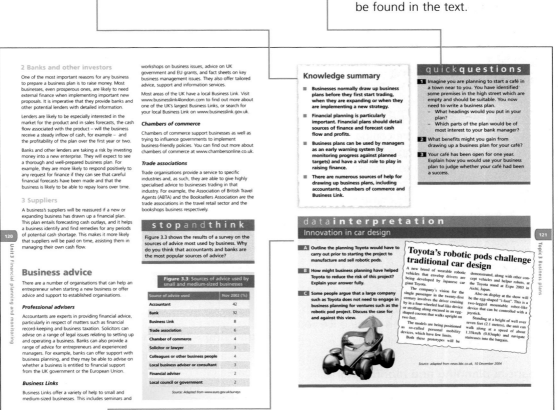

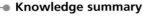

Data interpretation
These activities encourage you to extend your knowledge and skills through a variety of investigative and active learning exercises, which include internet-based research, small-scale research projects and information-gathering activities.

Using your Virtual Business CD-ROM

What's on the Virtual Business CD-ROM?

Studying business should be an active experience that will help you to develop the skills required in the workplace. The Virtual Business CD-ROM attached to this textbook will give you an interactive virtual work placement experience when used alongside your textbook studies.

Applied Business

You can work through the activities in any order you want. The activities all work in the same way – you make decisions about real-life business issues, and get feedback that compares what you have done with an ideal approach to the situation. Make sure you read the instructions on each screen.

1.1.2. AQA Unit Index:

Unit 1: Investigating business
Unit 2: People in Business
Unit 3: Financial Planning & Monitoring
Unit 4: Meeting Customer Needs
Other activities you might like to try :
Commissioning a website
Organising promotions
Running your own business

BACK TO SYLLABUS MENU

C Collins

The CD-ROM contains four games linked to the first four units of the book.

Unit 1 Investigating business: Evaluating market research

You are employed as a market researcher for a computer games company. The company has asked you to look at launching a new mass market computer game with a view to increasing its market share and raising the company profile. (It is better to try this game once you have read Unit 1 Topics 3, 4, 5 and 6.)

Unit 2 People in business: Hiring a new employee

As a junior manager at a store in a newsagents' chain, you have been asked to hire a junior shop assistant. (You may like to try this game once you have read Unit 2 Topics 5, 6, 7 and 8.)

Unit 3 Financial planning and monitoring: Managing cash flow

In the role of finance manager you must respond to different scenarios that impact on your financial plan (cash flow statement). (Reading Unit 3 Topics 7 and 8 will help you to play this game.)

Unit 4 Meeting customer needs: Providing good customer care

As the manager of a luxury hotel you will be challenged by three different customer care scenarios. You will need to use your skills to deliver good customer care to clients before, during and after their stay at your hotel. (Try this game once you have read Unit 4 Topic 9.)

There are three other activities on the CD-ROM that you may like to try:

Commissioning a website

Your company is launching a new website and you are in charge of selecting the most appropriate features to appear on the site to enable your company to make the most of its new web presence.

Organising a promotional campaign

You are in charge of making appropriate choices, based on cost and effectiveness, of suitable media channels to promote your organisation.

Run your own business

The pop business is a cut-throat industry. Make the right decisions and you'll be number 1. Make the wrong ones and you will not do so well.

Operating systems required for installing the CD-ROM

PC

Windows 98SE/2000/XP
Windows: Pentium III 600MHz or equivalent
MPC compatible sound card
800 x 600 minimum size monitor display with
16 bit colour, or higher
64MB available RAM
You will need a minimum of 90MB of free space on
your hard drive

Installation instructions:

- Insert the Virtual Business disc into your
  CD-ROM drive

- Double click on the CD-ROM drive icon inside
  My Computer

- Double click on the SETUP.EXE icon
  Follow the onscreen instructions

Mac

MacOS 9.x; Mac OS X
Mac: PowerMac G3, 350 MHz or higher
800 x 600 minimum size monitor display with
16 bit colour, or higher
2 speed CD-ROM
64MB available RAM
You will need a minimum of 90MB of free space on
your hard drive

Installation instructions:

- Insert the Virtual Business disc into your
  CD-ROM drive

- Double click on the CD-ROM drive icon inside
  My Computer

- Double click on the SETUP.OSX icon
  Follow the onscreen instructions

Good luck with your GCE AS-level studies. This book and CD-ROM provide
you with interesting, supportive and motivating learning materials that we
hope will help you to succeed in your applied business course.

SUCCESSFUL BUSINESSES ARE GOOD AT MARKETING. They are able to discover and meet the needs of their customers. They are good at getting the right product to the right place at the right time. Successful businesses also know how to make the most of opportunities that come their way. They make the most of their employees' skills.

This unit provides an introduction to business by looking at some of the key factors affecting business success. You will discover why it is important for a business to set aims and objectives. You will investigate how the external environment – such as the level of economic activity – affects the ability of a business to achieve its objectives.

Knowing what customers want is an essential ingredient of business success. This unit introduces you to the different ways in which a business can research its market. It looks at how businesses use the results of market research to meet the needs of their customers.

Finally, this unit investigates the importance of enterprise skills in building a business and the key role played by teams. Businesses need employees who can work together. They need staff who have the motivation to develop better ways of doing business. You will look at some of the ingredients needed to build an effective team and you will reflect on the enterprise skills possessed by people in business.

Investigating business

Setting the scene: what is a business?

Look up the word business in a dictionary and you will find several definitions. For example, "get down to business" refers to starting some serious work or activity, while "bad business" refers to any foolish or inappropriate action. These definitions suggest that business is an active word.

To be "in business" means that an individual or group of people have agreed a common goal and are actively working towards achieving this goal by supplying products to customers. This will be the definition of business used throughout this textbook.

business *n* **1** a trade or profession. **2** an industrial, commercial or professional operation; purchase and sale of goods and services: *the tailoring business*. **3** a commercial or industrial operation, such as a firm or factory. **4** commercial activity; dealings (esp. in the phrase do business). **5** volume or quantity of commercial activity: *business is poor today*. **6** commercial policy or procedure: *overcharging is bad business*.

Source: Collins English Dictionary

Aims and objectives

There are many different types of businesses operating in the UK. Here are some examples which show the variety of types of business:

- Oxfam International – a not-for-profit business that aims to provide solutions to poverty, suffering and injustice throughout the world

- Prontaprint – a UK business providing design, print and copying services for the general public

- Aurora's Carnival – an entertainment agency, based in Nottingham and Bristol, acting for a variety of performance artists such as jugglers, fire-eaters and jesters

- Nokia – a global business that manufactures communication products such as mobile phones.

These businesses have many differences. Oxfam doesn't aim to make a profit for its owners but strives to increase the welfare of the people it serves. It is a charity, financed by contributions from the public, and can be described as a not-for-profit business. The other businesses aim to make a profit but are different in size (number of people employed, for example) and products supplied. Aurora's Carnival is a small business that provides a service by promoting entertainment acts to the general public. Nokia, on the other hand, is a very large business that manufactures goods such as mobile telephones. However, what all of these businesses have in common is a desire to achieve their aims. They all strive for success.

To be successful any business must set itself a number of aims and objectives. An aim describes the overall goal that a business wants to achieve. Obviously

KEY TERMS

Products are goods or services. Goods are tangible products, such as mobile telephones or pizzas. Services are intangible products, such as a mobile telephone service or a pizza delivery service.

A **business** is an individual or group of people who have agreed a common goal and are working towards achieving this goal by supplying products to customers.

SMART objectives are practical objectives that are capable of being monitored and achieved. SMART is an acronym, standing for specific, measurable, achievable, relevant and time specific.

individual aims vary from business to business, but these are some typical aims of businesses.

Survival – staying in business by earning enough money from customers to meet all of the business's expenses. A new business might aim to make enough money to cover its costs during its first two years.

Meeting stakeholder needs – considering the needs of the different people involved in the business. For example, a business might aim to repay bank loans on time, pay its employees a decent wage, keep customers satisfied and pay suppliers on time.

Maximising sales revenue (income) – an ambitious aim in which a business seeks to generate as much income as it can from customers. For example, an airline business might aim to maximise revenue by selling empty seats at a low price, thereby ensuring that all seats on the flight generate some revenue.

Maximising profit (surplus) – a very ambitious aim in which a business seeks to make the gap between income and expenditure as large as possible. A business might maximise profit by keeping expenses as low as possible while still keeping customers happy.

Growth – increasing the size of the business year by year. For example, a new business might aim to double its sales by the end of its third year of trading.

Aims help businesses to measure whether or not they have been successful. If a business achieves or exceeds its aims, then it is successful. If an aim is not achieved, then a business will need to think about the way it is carrying out its operations.

In order to help achieve their aims, business managers and owners set themselves objectives. Objectives are the steps that a business needs to take in order to achieve its overall aim.

SMART objectives

Business objectives need to be SMART objectives. SMART is an acronym which stands for specific, measurable, achievable, relevant and time specific.

Specific

Objectives should have a precise description. For example, a fast food restaurant might set an objective of serving at least 70 per cent of single-order customers within a minute of the order being placed.

Measurable

An objective must be capable of being measured so that managers can assess whether it has been achieved. For example, a supervisor within the fast food restaurant could measure service times during a typical one-hour period and record the number of times single-order customers were served within a minute of placing their order.

Achievable

An objective should not be beyond the reach of the organisation and individual employees. For example, the manager of the fast food restaurant needs to assess whether it is feasible for employees, if they work efficiently, to serve single-order customers within a minute of the order being placed.

Relevant

An objective should help to achieve the aims of the organisation. For example, by setting an objective to serve customers quickly, the fast food restaurant hopes to increase its profits by attracting and serving more customers. It might encourage its employees to work towards this objective by offering bonuses for staff who achieve reductions in serving time.

Time specific

An objective should have specified start and finish dates. For example, the manager of the fast food restaurant might tell the employees that they have one month to achieve the one-minute service time objective.

What this unit covers

This unit helps you to understand how various factors affect the success of a business. These include:

■ factors outside the direct control of the business – the business's external environment

■ marketing activities carried out by the business

■ the enterprise skills possessed by the owners and employees of a business

■ the ability of the business's employees to work together in teams.

Economic conditions and competition

Setting the scene: The Bentall Centre

Located in Kingston upon Thames, 12 miles from central London, the Bentall shopping centre provides in excess of 46,000 square metres of retail space arranged over five floors. Bentall's website (www.thebentallcentre-shopping.com) provides full details about the centre and contains some virtual tours.

The Bentall centre is located close to major transport links and serves a catchment area within 30 miles of Kingston upon Thames, or within a one-hour drive. The centre attracts large numbers of people. The number of shoppers visiting the centre increased from 9 million in 1993 to 13 million in 2001.

Kingston upon Thames is a thriving town:

- it is a university town and at the last census (in 2001) 25 per cent of Kingston's population were aged between 20 and 34 compared with the national average in England of 20 per cent

- the average price of a detached house was £452,640 in December 2004, much higher than the average price of a detached house in England of £282,076

- in 2003, average gross weekly pay in Kingston was £529.30 compared with average pay in England of £449.90

How do these statistics help to explain the success of the Bentall Centre? What other factors affect the success of a shopping centre?

Economic conditions

Like any businesses, the retail outlets based at Bentall Centre rely on customer confidence. If consumers are confident of their future income and prospects – because their jobs are safe or they are highly paid – then they are more likely to spend money freely and purchase products.

Kingston upon Thames is an affluent area and the rate of unemployment is usually lower than the rest of

England and Wales. This suggests that the local economy is healthy, and this should benefit the shops in Bentall Centre. In general, the level of economic activity in any area – such as a town, region or country – can be measured in a number of ways:

- the level of employment – the percentage of people of working age in paid employment
- the average wages earned by workers
- the number of businesses starting up compared with the number closing down
- the level of house prices and the number of new houses being built.

Favourable changes in these measurements indicate a thriving economy, benefiting both businesses and workers. Confidence in the future will be high, and owners of businesses are likely to be expanding their operations. However, unfavourable changes in these measurements indicate a declining economy. Businesses may well be leaving the area or simply closing down. The level of unemployment could be increasing and consumer spending will probably be declining.

s t o p a n d t h i n k

Using the internet to collect relevant data, identify whether economic conditions in your area are likely to help local businesses to achieve their aims and objectives. You should be able to obtain useful information from www.neighbourhood.statistics.gov.uk and www.upmystreet.com.

The level of economic activity – at both local, national and international level – will have a significant impact on the setting and achievement of a business's SMART objectives. If economic activity is increasing, then objectives that rely on the level of demand for a product will be easier to achieve. For example, a business might have set an objective of increasing sales by two per cent in the next six months. If economic activity increases, then this objective is more likely to be achieved, and it might be revised in the future to, say, a four per cent increase in the subsequent six months.

Faced with a decline in economic activity, businesses will have to reconsider their tactics for achieving SMART objectives or they may have to revise their original expectations. Pressure is likely to be placed on employees, either because managers may introduce

new working practices to improve productivity or because their job security might be threatened.

As you will see later in this unit, the degree to which employees work together as a team can significantly affect the ability of any business to cope with unfavourable economic conditions. In addition, the ingenuity and creativity of employees and the owners of the business will also contribute to the resilience of the business when faced with hard times.

s t o p a n d t h i n k

In England all business pay a local tax called the business rate. The amount each business pays in based on the size and value of its property. In 2005 these rates increased, and many small businesses were anticipating 15 per cent increases in their business rates. How might this increase affect the ability of, for example, a local newsagent to achieve its aims and objectives? What actions might it take?

Competition

In the past, British Telecom was the only business allowed to supply telephone services to domestic consumers. Today, consumers can choose from several competing providers such as OneTel and Telewest. Faced with this new competition, British Telecom has been active in developing new products and pricing schemes.

The degree of competition in a market is a significant factor affecting the ability of a business to achieve its aims and objectives. The degree of competition can be measured by the number of businesses providing similar products compared with the size of the market. For example, the market for mobile telephone ringtones has a high degree of competition as there are many businesses providing this service. Initially, this market had few competitors, with only a handful of enterprising individuals offering the service. With the arrival of polyphonic mobile telephones and companies like Jamster offering downloads over the internet, the ringtone market has opened to a wider range of providers, and each business now has to work harder to gain customers.

If the market for a product is small, it does not take too many businesses to begin trading for a high degree of competition to be present. For example, the market for ice cream on a beach in the summer can be highly competitive with just two competitors.

In a highly competitive market, it is likely that a business will:

- find it difficult to charge a higher price than its competitors

- be tempted to reduce its prices in order to attract customers

- need to monitor what its competitors are offering in terms of product range and quality

- want to offer new products or a better service in order to distinguish itself from competitors

- face a high degree of uncertainty, as the success of the business will partly be determined by the actions of its competitors.

Faced with a high degree of competition, any business can find it difficult to achieve SMART objectives. The extent to which objectives are achievable will depend on the speed at which a business acts compared with the responses of its competitors. While it might be tempting for a business to set very modest objectives – ones that can be easily achieved – this is likely to instil a culture of "anything goes". Ultimately, this business is likely to fail. Instead, successful businesses manage their competitive environment by adopting one of these approaches:

- concentrate on a section of the market that no other business has focused on and meet its needs – for example, by specialising in supplying expensive but unique products

- copy the activities of the most successful business in the market, but don't threaten the dominant business

- be aggressive and try to dominate the market by offering what the majority of customers want in a way that is superior to competitor offers.

Knowledge summary

- The level of economic activity within a region is indicated by the level of employment, average wages, the growth in the number of businesses and changes in house prices.

- The higher the level of economic activity, the more likely it is that businesses will achieve their aims and objectives.

- The degree of competition within a market is determined by the number of businesses in the market (as this increases, the degree of competition increases) and the number of customers in the market (as this reduces, the degree of competition increases).

- Successful businesses manage their competitive environment by either following the practices of the dominant business, becoming the dominant business or focusing on a specialist area of the market.

data**interpretation**
The UK coffee bar market

Until the 1990s the coffee bar market in the UK was made up of independent, family-owned businesses. In 1995 the Seattle Coffee Company opened its first coffee bar in the UK. The Seattle Coffee Company was later purchased by Starbucks, which is currently the dominant firm in the UK branded coffee bar market after a period of aggressive expansion.

Caffe Nero is a relatively new entrant into the branded coffee bar market. It has not wanted to expand too rapidly, only purchasing new retail sites when good locations became available and company profits allowed.

This is an extract from Caffe Nero's 2004 annual report:

> With the UK branded market expected to reach £1 billion in the next few years, three brands have emerged in pole position to take advantage of this growth: Caffe Nero, Starbucks and Costa Coffee. Indeed, the branded market has already consolidated, such that the above three players now control approximately 57 per cent of the market. Two of these three, Caffe Nero and Starbucks, are gaining market share faster than any other brand in the coffee industry. Caffe Nero currently has 11 per cent of the UK branded market, having gained 4.3 per cent market share over the last three years. This underlines the fact that the UK retail coffee market seems to have divided into two parts: a European offering where Caffe Nero leads the way and a North American offering where Starbucks currently has top billing.

Some experts believe that the market is becoming saturated, and that too many branded coffee bars have been created with too few customers wanting to buy their drinks.

A Using the information above, describe the degree of competition in the UK coffee bar market.

B Explain how Caffe Nero seems to have managed its competitive environment.

C How might independent coffee bars ensure their long-term survival? Justify your answer.

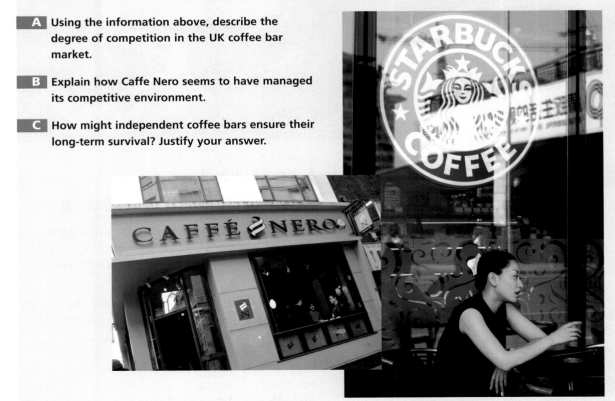

Legal, social and ethical issues

Setting the scene: the costs of recycling

Old cars that can no longer be driven are valuable as they contain a high proportion of recyclable materials which can be extracted by scrap yards. These materials are sold on to manufacturers in the UK and, increasingly, developing countries such as China. However, old cars also contain materials such as plastics, rubber and oil that can't be recycled, do not degrade and which can harm the environment.

In 2000, European Union legislation was passed imposing restrictions on the recycling of cars. This legislation, designed to improve the environment, has had an impact on consumers, scrap yards and car manufacturers. This news story illustrates some of the issues.

How has European Union legislation affected scrap yards and car owners in the UK? Should manufacturers make cars more recyclable? How might any move to make cars more recyclable impact on the price of new cars?

Bangers and cash

Clapped out old cars fetch millions of pounds as scrap metal every year, so why are owners breaking the law by abandoning their old bangers at the side of the road? Any scrap yard would take the car, but they tend to charge £50 for the privilege. So owners are tending to defy the law and abandon their old cars instead.

Since February 2004, when scrap yards had to start investing in specialised treatment facilities, a third of the UK's scrap yards have shut down. It costs around £50 to "de-pollute" a car. Both the scrap yards and green campaigners lay the blame at the car manufacturers' door, calling on them to make cars more recyclable.

Source: news.bbc.co.uk, 31 January 2005

KEY TERMS

Legislation comprises the laws set by governments and international bodies such as the European Union. For example, there is a raft of legislation setting out consumer rights.

Self-regulation is the practice by which industry bodies draw up codes of conduct to regulate the actions of businesses operating in that industry. For example, the Advertising Standards Authority has policies and rules that govern the advertising industry.

Social and ethical values express a person's (or an organisation's) sense of right and wrong and encapsulate their beliefs and concerns. For example, some people feel its is ethically wrong to test products on animals and refuse to buy products that are developed in this way.

Legal and self-regulatory issues

Businesses must comply with legislation intended to protect the rights of UK citizens. They also need to respect and respond to the values and beliefs held by consumers.

Laws are passed to protect the rights of people. In the business world, there is a range of laws intended to protect transactions between businesses and customers. These laws apply whether a business's customers are members of the public or other businesses. For example, there is legislation to ensure that customers have a legal right to receive the goods they have paid for. Legislation also protects dealings between the owners of a business and its employees. For example, there are laws that make it illegal for the owner of a business to discriminate against some of the business's employees.

Legislation also restricts the activities of businesses. This is necessary to protect the welfare of society. For example, there is legislation that restricts the use of hazardous materials by industry. This is designed to protect the health of consumers and the general public. Without this legislation, manufacturers might be tempted to use less expensive but unsafe materials in order to reduce their costs and increase their profits.

Many industries adopt voluntary codes of practice to protect the public and consumers. This practice is known as self-regulation. These self-imposed restrictions are intended to protect the image of the industry, ensure fair competition and raise customer confidence in the industry.

At the beginning of 2004, for example, the UK mobile telephone service industry established a code of practice for the self-regulation of new forms of content on mobile telephones. With the arrival of fast telecommunications and sophisticated colour screens, the industry felt it necessary to establish a number of ground rules to ensure fair competition and to protect consumers. As this extract shows, the code of practice is designed to regulate content transmitted over the mobile telephone network.

Internet content

Mobile operators will ... offer parents and carers the opportunity to apply a filter to the mobile operator's internet access service so that the internet content thus accessible is restricted. The filter will be set at a level that is intended to filter out content approximately equivalent to commercial content with a classification of 18.

Illegal content

Mobile operators will work with law enforcement agencies to deal with the reporting of content that may break the criminal law.

Taken together, laws and self-regulatory codes of practice impact on the ability of a business to achieve its aims and objectives. They act as constraints on the activities of the business. For example, a theme park business will be required to maintain its rides to very

high standards. These maintenance costs increase overall running costs, making it harder to achieve a certain level of profit. Without any legal restrictions, theme park owners might carry out a lower standard of maintenance.

stop and think

Does this news report indicate that legislation is needed to protect rollercoaster ride customers? Explain your view.

Rollercoaster risk

Amusement park rides may be the cause of unexplained head, neck and back injuries seen in accident and emergency departments, doctors have warned. Some rides reach G-forces exceeding those experienced by space shuttle astronauts.

The risk of injury is small, but US researchers warn that as the competition increases to build faster, more thrilling rides, the number of injuries and even deaths will rise.

Source: news.bbc.co.uk, 10 January 2002

stop and think

Visit the Trading Standards website at www.tradingstandards.gov.uk and go to the business section of the site. This site provides information on consumer protection legislation affecting businesses. Use this website to find out and explain two ways in which consumer protection legislation would affect the running of any business that sells food.

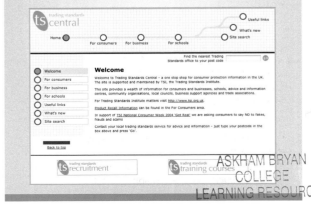

Social and ethical values

The success of a business partly depends on its ability to supply products that meet the needs of customers. If customers change their attitudes, then demand for particular products could also change. Fashion is a good example. If a particular type of clothing goes out of fashion, the demand for the products will fall dramatically. Businesses supplying the products will either have to start producing alternative, more fashionable, goods or suffer reduced incomes.

There are numerous factors affecting the demand for a product. These include the social and ethical values held by consumers, and these values can play a significant part in determining what is and is not currently fashionable and desirable. Social and ethical values describe the current concerns of people within a social group. The cutting in the "stop and think" exercise below describes some of the values that are important to teenagers living in the United Kingdom.

Businesses can take advantage of changing social and ethical values by providing products that are sympathetic towards their customers' concerns. This can extend to the ways in which products are produced or the materials used in the manufacturing of goods. By being aware of their customers' social and ethical concerns, businesses are more likely to set SMART objectives that are capable of being achieved.

Businesses need to be aware of current social concerns. If a business is supplying products that are connected to a current social or ethical issue – for example, if products are using genetically modified food sources – then it should establish whether or not its customers (both current and potential) share these values. If they do, then the business should demonstrate that its products meet certain minimum standards and are suitable for use by its customers. If they do not, then the business should not waste time and resources attempting to develop products that are likely to offend its potential customers.

stop and think

Teenagers becoming more aware

Teenagers are among the most politically active and socially aware ever, according to research. Six out of every 10 value brands highly but 85 per cent said they should be "socially responsible", putting ethical values above financial value.

However, such ethical awareness did not mean teenagers were no longer active consumers or brand-followers. While they can understand the importance of sourcing goods ethically and not using sweat-shops and so on, kids still may want to go out and buy a pair of Nike trainers.

Source: news.bbc.co.uk, 31 March 2005

Does the news article (left) reflect your own social and ethical values or those of your friends? Do your social and ethical values affect the products you purchase?

Knowledge summary

- Laws protect transactions between businesses, their employees and their customers.

- Legislation can constrain the activities that businesses are allowed to carry out and can increase the cost of operations.

- Social and ethical values shape consumers' beliefs and concerns and help to determine attitudes towards products.

- Businesses should ensure that their products are sympathetic towards the social and ethical values held by their current and potential customers.

1 Identify how (a) newsagents and (b) restaurants might be affected by UK consumer legislation. Visit www.tradingstandards.gov.uk to obtain information to answer this question.

2 Explain why the computer game industry might need a self-regulatory code of practice.

3 Explain why (a) the cosmetics industry and (b) the fashion industry might be concerned with the social and ethical values of their customers.

data interpretation
UK fair trade product sales soar

Sales of fair trade products grew by more than 50 per cent in the UK in 2004, according to figures released by the Fairtrade Foundation. UK shoppers spent £140 million on goods bearing the Fairtrade logo last year. The foundation said UK consumers now supported the concept of fair trade more than in any other country. The scheme promises consumers that farmers in the developing world are paid a fair price for their goods – even when world prices are low.

Harriet Lamb, executive director of the Fairtrade Foundation, welcomed the findings. She said: "When the British public learn about Fairtrade and the positive benefits for farmers in the developing world, the response is dramatic." She added that millions of shoppers now choose to buy products with the Fairtrade mark to "make sure the farmers gain guaranteed benefits".

According to Fairtrade figures, coffee is the best seller, with Fairtrade beans ground at many high street cafes, including Starbucks, Costa Coffee and Pret A Manger. Bananas, chocolate and tea also saw increased sales, followed by newer Fairtrade products including flowers, wine and cooking oils.

Source: news.bbc.co.uk, 28 February 2005

A Explain how businesses selling products branded with the Fairtrade logo have benefited from a change in the social and ethical values of customers.

B Carry out research into the awareness of customers in your local supermarket of fair trade products. The research should establish:
- how many customers recognise the Fairtrade logo and know what it stands for
- whether customers have changed their purchasing habits because of the Fairtrade logo
- the number of fair trade products stocked in the supermarket
- which types of fair trade products customers would like to see on the supermarket's shelves.

C Using the results of your research, recommend whether the supermarket should increase or reduce its range of fair trade products.

Setting the scene: market-oriented and product-oriented businesses

Product-oriented businesses focus on product quality. Essentially they create products and then try to sell them. They assume that consumers will want the product that they are producing. This is a fallacy. Consumers want products that meet their needs as fully as possible, and the highest quality product may not be what they want.

Concorde, the supersonic airliner, is a classic example of the weakness of the product-oriented approach. Launched in the 1970s, Concorde was hailed as the future of air travel. It was very advanced in technological terms, offering luxury and high-speed travel, but failed to be a commercial success. Airlines preferred to use subsonic planes in an era when many consumers were seeking low-cost air travel. Concorde was taken out of service in 2003. Perhaps you can

think of any other high technology products that have not proved popular with consumers?

Any business that develops its production and marketing activities with the needs and ultimate satisfaction of the consumer firmly in mind is market oriented. A market-oriented business attempts to discover the wants and needs of consumers and then designs products to meet these needs and wants. A truly market-oriented business places the needs of consumers at the heart of all its decisions, not just those relating to marketing. The car manufacturer Ford researches its new markets thoroughly and uses the information it gains to help in designing the styling of the company's new models. This may be one of the reasons why the Ford Focus was the best-selling car in the UK in 2003.

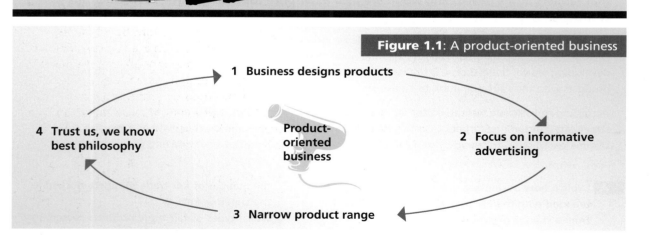

Figure 1.1: A product-oriented business

1 **Business designs products**

4 **Trust us, we know best philosophy**

Product-oriented business

2 **Focus on informative advertising**

3 **Narrow product range**

KEY TERMS

Market research is the systematic collection and analysis of data to enable a business to make better marketing decisions.

Target markets are particular parts of a market at which a business aims its products.

Market-oriented businesses attempt to discover the wants and needs of consumers, and then design products to meet these needs and wants.

Market size is the total sales achieved by all firms in a market. This can be measured by monetary value or by the number of sales.

Market share is the percentage of total sales in a market achieved by a particular business.

A **mass market** is a large market with many consumers buying similar products.

A **niche market** is a small but separate part of a larger market.

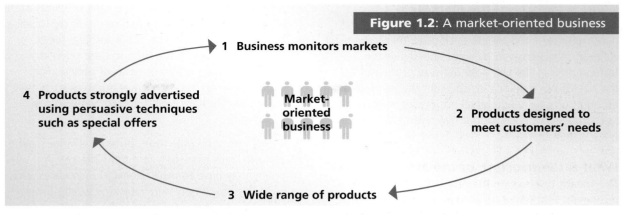

Figure 1.2: A market-oriented business

1 **Business monitors markets**

4 **Products strongly advertised using persuasive techniques such as special offers**

Market-oriented business

2 **Products designed to meet customers' needs**

3 **Wide range of products**

s t o p a n d t h i n k

Some fashion designers such as Gucci might be considered to be product oriented. Do you agree with this view? Does it mean that businesses such as Gucci do not meet the needs of their customers?

The purpose of market research

Market research is the systematic collection and analysis of data to enable a business to take better quality marketing decisions. In simple terms, market research allows businesses to find out what customers want. There are a number of reasons why businesses invest in market research.

1 To identify target markets

Most products are only likely to be purchased by particular groups of customers: the market of young working-class males, for example, is very different to that of middle-aged, wealthy couples. Market research can assist a firm in identifying which parts of the market are most likely to buy its products.

It is vital for a business to know who its customers are. This allows the business to:

■ design products to best meet the needs of these customers

■ target advertising, promotions and special offers at these groups

■ conduct further in-depth research with specific groups of customers to uncover their needs as fully as possible.

In 2001, Bratz fashion dolls were released in the UK. Designed by Isaac Larian, an Iranian who has settled in the USA, Bratz dolls are aimed at a target market of girls aged between seven and 12. Having such a clear target market makes it easy in some ways to research the market for the dolls. MGA Entertainment, which owns the Bratz brand, researches this target market carefully. The company finds out the views of more than 900 girls across the USA before launching new products.

Bratz is a marketing success story. By 2004, Bratz dolls had recorded over 80 million sales globally. In the same year, Bratz overtook Barbie as the best-selling doll in the UK, achieving a 130 per cent increase in sales compared with the previous year. The dolls sell for an average price of £22.

s t o p a n d t h i n k

Many Bratz dolls are bought by adults for children, yet the children are the consumers of the product. How might MGA Entertainment advertise its Bratz dolls when they are purchased and used by different target groups? What problems do you think the company might experience in attempting to discover the views of girls aged between seven and 12?

2 To find out about the market for a product

Businesses need to know what is happening in the market. To be able to plan its product and marketing effectively, any business needs to address three important questions.

What is the size of the market?

In the UK, the fashion doll market is worth approximately £100 million each year. This is the total value of sales achieved by all businesses selling fashion dolls in the UK. Another way of measuring the size of the market is to consider the volume (or number) of sales made by all businesses selling fashion dolls. In 2003, about five million fashion dolls were sold in the UK.

What is the structure of the market?

This means discovering the number and size of businesses that make up a market. Are there, for example, a few large firms, or many small firms, or a mixture of large and small firms? If a business is in competition with large firms, it may decide to avoid competing on price terms as larger firms may be able to produce their products more cheaply. In the UK, there are three major companies selling fashion dolls: MGA Entertainment (Bratz dolls), Mattel (Barbie) and Robert Tonner Dolls.

Is the market growing or shrinking?

Market research can reveal what is happening to sales in a market over time. A business may feel more confident about entering a market which is growing, as it should be easier to win sales when some customers are not yet loyal to particular brands or manufacturers. The market for fashion dolls in the UK has grown recently.

stop and think

Sales of real ales in the UK are declining. How might market research help a brewery trying to adapt to these market conditions?

3 Mass or niche marketing?

It makes sense for some businesses to target a wide range of customers. This is referred to as mass marketing. For other businesses, it makes sense to target small sections of the market. Taken to the limit, this might involve catering for a small select group of customers – a target market that has very specific needs.

In mass marketing, businesses aim their products at most of the available market and normally try to sell a range of similar products to all consumers. Mass marketing is possible if the products are popular and purchased by many different types of people. For example, groceries and consumer durables such as washing machines are well suited to being sold in mass markets.

Businesses must be able to produce on a large scale if they are to sell successfully in a mass market. A company may have to invest heavily in resources such as buildings, machinery and vehicles. Usually, firms also have to be very price competitive to flourish in mass markets.

By contrast, niche marketing involves companies identifying and meeting the needs of relatively small areas of the market. The aim is to cater for the needs of customers that have not been met sufficiently by other businesses, and niche marketing is one way in which small businesses can operate profitably in markets that are dominated by large firms. Examples of businesses that operate in niche markets include Tie Rack and the radio station Classic FM.

Market research helps businesses to identify whether they should adopt a mass or niche marketing strategy. In general, this would depend on:

- whether the needs of customers within all parts of the market are being met

- the extent to which a business can provide specialist products capable of meeting the needs of select groups of customers

- the degree to which competitors are currently meeting the needs of all customers within the market.

stop and think

Do car manufacturers carry out niche or mass marketing? Why might it be difficult for a new company to set up as a car manufacturer and establish itself within the market?

Knowledge summary

- Market research is the systematic collection and analysis of data to enable a business to take better quality marketing decisions.

- Market-oriented businesses design products to meet the needs of their customers. They research these needs carefully.

- Businesses research markets to discover information about the target groups who will purchase their products.

- Market research can also uncover details about the market, such as its size and whether it is growing. It can be a valuable source of information about competitors.

quick questions

1 Club 18–30 and 2wentys (a brand of First Choice) aim to sell holidays to the young adult segment of the market. How does this help them to carry out market research?

2 In 2004, India's first low-cost airline, Air Deccan, began operating a service between Bangalore and Delhi. The company's fares are 30 per cent below those offered by its rivals on the same route. Why would market research have been an essential part of Air Deccan's planning?

3 The Smart car is a tiny two-seater produced by DaimlerChrysler. In 2006, the company is planning to launch the Smart car in the giant US market. What information on the US market would the company want to collect through market research before planning its marketing activities?

data interpretation
The mobile phone handset market

In the second quarter of 2004, sales of mobile telephone handsets throughout the world rose by 35 per cent compared with the same three months in 2003. Total sales reached 156 million handsets, with the increase in sales highest in emerging markets such as South America. By mid-2004, Nokia's market share had fallen to 30 per cent, while the market shares of Motorola and Samsung had risen to 16 per cent and 12 per cent respectively (Figure 1.4 has 2003 figures).

Figure 1.3: Forecast of mobile phone service subscribers, selected countries (figures in millions)

Subscribers	2001	2005	2010
UK	45.7	50.2	50.9
US	125.6	181.7	226.8
Brazil	27.8	53.9	76.7
Poland	9.6	18.6	23.5
China	133.9	326.1	575.1

Source: Baskerville

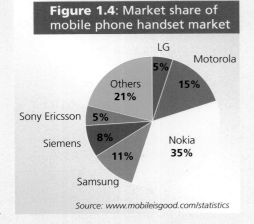

Figure 1.4: Market share of mobile phone handset market

LG 5%
Motorola 15%
Others 21%
Sony Ericsson 5%
Siemens 8%
Samsung 11%
Nokia 35%

Source: www.mobileisgood.com/statistics

Working as a group, use the data in Figures 1.3 and 1.4 and any information you can obtain from the internet (sites such as www.mobileisgood.com) to write a report covering these issues.

A Make the case for why Nokia should spend money on market research.

B Describe the current and expected trends in the global market for mobile phone handsets.

C Explain how the data in Figures 1.3 and 1.4, and the information gained from your own research, might help the management team at Nokia to plan its future marketing activities.

Researching the market

Setting the scene: primary and secondary market research

There are two main ways of carrying out market research.

Primary research **entails direct contact with potential customers within a target market to gather information about their precise needs. It may involve gathering data through interviews or questionnaires, and often businesses use a market research agency to act on their behalf.**

Secondary research, **sometimes called desk research, involves the use of data that already exists in reference books, government reports and, increasingly, from sources on the internet.**

Figure 1.5: The advantages and disadvantages of primary and secondary research

	Primary research	Secondary research
Advantages	■ Provides up-to-date information on the target market ■ Meets the exact information needs of the business ■ Helps businesses to understand customers' behaviour	■ Can be undertaken quickly, allowing earlier decisions ■ Is often a relatively cheap form of market research ■ Can provide information on an entire market including overseas customers
Disadvantages	■ Can be time consuming to collect and analyse data ■ Can be an expensive form of market research ■ May produce biased results if research is not carefully planned with clear objectives	■ The information may be outdated and of limited value ■ Secondary data may not meet the precise needs of the business ■ Some business reports containing secondary data are expensive (£5000 per report).

In 2004, Sainsbury's, one of the UK's leading supermarket chains, conducted market research into demand for organic products. The organic market is growing twice as quickly as that for ordinary groceries and is set to become more important in the future. Sainsbury's wanted to know more about this market. The company chose to use primary market research methods as it wanted in-depth information about the reasons why consumers are increasingly buying organic fruit and vegetables.

Explain why it would not have been appropriate for Sainsbury's to use secondary research to investigate the market for organic foodstuffs.

Types of market research

Before it undertakes market research, a business needs to consider what type of research is likely to provide the most cost-effective means of producing the answers it requires.

1 Primary market research

Primary market research is the gathering of information directly from customers within the target market. This can be carried out in a number of ways.

Surveys

One way of finding out more about customers' wants and needs is to ask them directly through a survey. Surveys may be conducted through face-to-face interviews using a questionnaire, often in the high street or a shop, or carried out by telephone or post. Surveys are a very common form of primary research.

stop and think

Why might a firm decide to use a postal survey to investigate a particular market, rather than relying on street interviews? In what circumstances might a street interview be more appropriate?

Observation

Businesses can learn much by watching consumers in different situations. Observation can provide market researchers with information on how consumers react to in-store displays, prices or the location of products. Supermarkets make considerable use of observation as a research technique.

Consumer panels

Consumer panels consist of a number of people from the target market who meet regularly to provide businesses with market research data. They are used to discover consumers' attitudes to new products, and can provide in-depth information about consumers' habits and attitudes.

Test marketing

An expensive form of market research, test marketing involves trialling a new product on a part of the market to discover consumers' views prior to a full-scale launch. Often products are tested in one television region, supported by advertising, before a decision is taken on a national launch.

2 Secondary market research

Secondary market research relies on information from already published data. This secondary data can be obtained from a variety of sources.

Government statistics

The government and its agencies, such as the Department of Trade and Industry, produce vast amounts of detailed information that can be useful

stop and think

Perween Warsi is managing director of S&A Foods, one of the UK's largest manufacturers of Asian ready-made meals. She had to persuade supermarkets to use consumer panels to confirm the quality of her company's products before they would place orders. Why do you think consumer panels are used extensively by the food manufacturing industry?

for businesses. Key publications include the Annual Abstract of Statistics and Social Trends.

Commercial research reports

Several companies publish research reports that contain information on market size (by volume and value), the market share held by leading businesses, recent trends in the market, forecasts of future sales and market segments. These research reports are very expensive, but some can be found in larger libraries. Mintel and Keynotes are two of the best-known publishers of market intelligence reports.

The business's own data

Most businesses have data on their customers and sales patterns over recent years. Developments in IT have allowed businesses to collect and analyse vast amounts of information using techniques such as customer loyalty cards. Loyalty cards and other methods of capturing sales data can provide businesses with detailed information on customers and the types of products that they buy.

Presenting research findings

Data collected by market research needs to be analysed and presented appropriately. It should be grouped using sensible categories and presented using tables, diagrams and graphs.

1 Grouping data

People new to market research will often present results without grouping the data in some way. This approach produces very little new information.

By focusing on key characteristics, it is possible to group data into sensible categories. For example, the responses to a question on customers' favourite brand of chocolate bar could be grouped by age range. This might reveal a pattern in buyer behaviour and indicate which age group(s) a particular brand should be targeted at.

2 Presenting findings

After grouping market research data, using several different categories, the findings should be presented using tables, diagrams and graphs.

- **Tables** are appropriate when a number of different results need to be displayed alongside each other. A graph or chart would contain too many items and would be difficult to comprehend.

- **Diagrams** are useful for conveying key relationships discovered by market research. They summarise key findings and can be used to convey both qualitative and quantitative information. A diagram can be used to focus on interesting features of market research data and often carries a greater impact than a table of figures.

- **Graphs and charts** are most appropriate when focusing on particular trends or features contained within the market research data. For example, a graph might be used to illustrate the trend in sales of two products over a period of time. Graphs should be used sparingly and should not contain too many different sets of data. In general, 3D charts should be avoided as they are difficult to interpret and convey no additional information.

Figure 1.6: Market research questionnaire

Questions	Your age?	How many times do you visit a cinema each month?	What is your occupation?	How much do you spend on buying movie DVDs each month?
Options	12–14 15–18 19–25 26–35 36–45 46+	Never Once Two to three times More than three times	Student Unemployed Employed – please state	Please state amount to nearest £5

Knowledge summary

■ **Primary market research gathers new data, while secondary market research uses information previously compiled for other purposes.**

■ **Primary data can be more expensive to collect, but is usually more focused and up to date than secondary research data.**

■ **Primary data is collected through direct contact with customers, either through written questionnaires or telephone surveys or by meeting with small groups of consumers.**

■ **Secondary data can be gleaned from government sources, from the press and from reports written by specialist market intelligence businesses.**

■ **The results of market research should be grouped using appropriate categories, such as age, before analysing the data**

quick**questions**

1 Read these scenarios and then identify an appropriate method of market research for each scenario. In each case, you should justify your choice.
   ■ Nestlé is considering launching a new chocolate bar.
   ■ An entrepreneur wants to investigate the market for a new DVD and computer games rental shop in a small town near Norwich.
   ■ Asda wants to research the impact of using new packaging on some of its own-brand products.
   ■ A high street clothing store wants ongoing information about consumers' spending patterns and the types of consumers purchasing its products.
   ■ A UK-based brewer is contemplating supplying beer to the Eastern European market.

2 Adam Lawrence is planning to start a business as a mobile car mechanic in his home town. He does not have much capital to start up his business and has approached his bank for a loan. The bank has asked him to carry out some market research. Explain the methods of market research that would probably be most appropriate given his resources. Suggest how he might present the findings of his market research.

Britain's leading retailer, Tesco, is seeking to expand its activities in the UK. The company has three main options.

■ It can open more stores on similar lines to its current supermarkets, selling groceries, clothing, etc.

■ It can move into new areas of business, possibly selling other types of products.

■ It can move into overseas markets and try and establish the Tesco brand abroad.

Look at the data in Figures 1.7–1.10 and research any terms with which you are unfamiliar. You will need to analyse this data to complete the tasks.

Figure 1.7: Household expenditure, UK

Indices (1971 = 100)

	'71	'81	'91	'01	'02	£ billion (current prices) 2002
Housing, water and fuel	100	117	138	152	154	118.4
Transport	100	128	181	242	251	98.3
Recreation and culture	100	161	283	545	570	79.5
Restaurants and hotels	100	126	167	194	199	76.6
Food and non-alcoholic drink	100	105	117	137	138	60.8
Household goods and services	100	117	160	268	296	43.3
Clothing and footwear	100	120	187	340	371	37.8
Alcohol and tobacco	100	99	92	89	91	26.3
Communication	100	190	306	790	828	15.0
Health	100	125	182	175	179	10.1
Education	100	160	199	250	218	8.4
Miscellaneous	100	119	230	280	290	82.0
Less expenditure by foreign tourists, etc.	100	152	187	210	219	-14.3
Household expenditure abroad	100	193	298	669	715	24.6
All household expenditure	100	122	167	227	235	666.9

Source: Office for National Statistics

Figure 1.8: Projected UK population change, 2002–2011

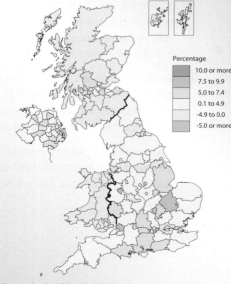

Percentage

- 10.0 or more
- 7.5 to 9.9
- 5.0 to 7.4
- 0.1 to 4.9
- -4.9 to 0.0
- -5.0 or more

Source: Regional Trends 37 2004

A Explain how the data contained in Figures 1.7–1.10 could have been presented using different formats such as tables, diagrams or charts. You should consider two of the figures and explain, in each case, why your chosen format might be an effective way to present the data.

B Advise Tesco's managers on:

■ which regions of the UK might be favoured for new supermarkets

■ what other products Tesco might consider selling

■ which other UK markets Tesco might consider entering.

Figure 1.9: Households by size, Great Britain

	Percentages				
	1971	1981	1991	2001	2003
One person	18	22	27	29	29
Two people	32	32	34	35	35
Three people	19	17	16	16	15
Four people	17	18	16	14	14
Five people	8	7	5	5	5
Six or more people	6	4	2	2	2
All households (=100%) (millions)	18.6	20.2	22.4	24.2	24.5
Average household size (number of people)	2.9	2.7	2.5	2.4	2.4

Source: Census, Labour Force Survey, Office for National Statistics

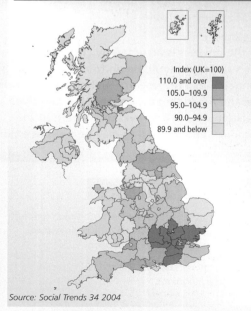

Figure 1.10: Household disposable income per head, by area, 1997–1999

Index (UK=100)
110.0 and over
105.0–109.9
95.0–104.9
90.0–94.9
89.9 and below

Source: Social Trends 34 2004

The marketing mix: product and price

Setting the scene: the product life cycle

All products have a finite life span. Some last for many years: Cadbury's Dairy Milk was launched in 1905 and is still going strong. Other products, especially those in the fashion, entertainment and technology industries, often only have a short life span. The pop group Hear'Say lasted for about two years.

As Figure 1.11 shows, products pass through four stages during their life cycles.

■ **Introduction**
Most new ideas for products never actually reach the market. Marketing plays a key role in determining which ideas actually get turned into products. Market research helps a business to determine the specification, look and packaging of any new product which is introduced to the market. During the introduction stage, the company will be using marketing to raise both consumer and retailer awareness of the product. Unless retailers agree to stock the product, and give it some exposure in their stores, it is unlikely to succeed. Heavy expenditure will be required to promote the product during its introduction stage. For example, Sony has committed considerable resources to launch its new PlayStation Portable (PSP) games console.

■ **Growth**
If the product is accepted by customers, sales and revenue should begin to rise. The results of ongoing market research will guide managers on the marketing actions that are necessary. Customers will become more aware of the product, and marketing may be used to extend product awareness to new target markets. Apple's iPod is a growth product. Apple sold more than two million iPods in a three-month period in 2004, an increase of 150 per cent on the previous quarter. With competitors such as Sony introducing rival products, Apple will have to work hard to maintain this level of sales growth, and it has already responded by launching a new iPod model promising a larger memory and longer battery life.

■ **Maturity**
During this stage, sales level off and the product should be profitable. Marketing activities may concentrate on reminder advertising and producing improved versions of the product to continue attracting new customers. Coca-Cola is a classic mature product which has seen relatively steady sales over a long period of time. Coca-Cola uses a combination of advertising and sponsorship of high-profile events and sports competitions to maintain brand awareness.

■ **Decline**
Eventually sales will decline for a product. Businesses may decide to try and stimulate sales for a little longer by producing revamped versions of the product or by reducing prices. At some point, a business will have to decide to stop selling the product. For example, few businesses now produce pipes and pipe tobacco; this market is in a definite decline. Well-managed businesses introduce new products long before their established ones reach the decline stage of the product life cycle.

KEY TERMS

The **marketing mix** is the four marketing tools (product, price, promotion and place) used by businesses to influence consumers' buying decisions.

Product is a general term for the goods and services supplied by a business.

Price is the amount charged by a business for its goods and services.

Place is another term for distribution. It covers the range of activities necessary to ensure that goods and services are available to customers.

Promotion is a series of marketing activities designed to make consumers aware of products and to persuade them to buy those products.

Market share is the percentage of total sales in a market achieved by one business.

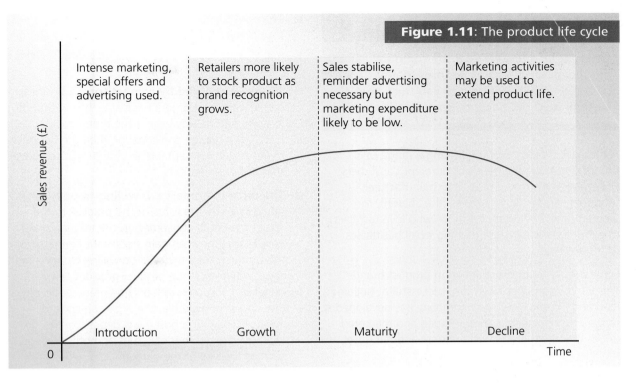

Figure 1.11: The product life cycle

Sales revenue (£)

Intense marketing, special offers and advertising used.

Retailers more likely to stock product as brand recognition grows.

Sales stabilise, reminder advertising necessary but marketing expenditure likely to be low.

Marketing activities may be used to extend product life.

Introduction | Growth | Maturity | Decline

Time

0

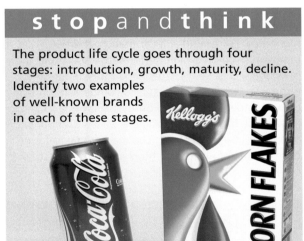

The marketing mix

The marketing mix refers to the main variables that make up a firm's marketing strategy. The four main elements of the mix are:

■ product

■ price

■ promotion

■ place.

These elements are sometimes referred to as the four Ps. Some writers identify more than four Ps, including factors such as packaging and people. However, we shall concentrate on the four main elements of the mix: product, price, promotion and place. In this section, you will consider product and price. The other two Ps, promotion and place, are dealt with in Topic 6.

Product

This term product covers services (car insurance and health care, for example) as well as goods, such as cars and houses. Many marketing managers believe that the product is the most important element of the marketing mix.

A successful product needs a number of features. Its design must include characteristics that appeal to the consumer. For example, mobile phones are capable of performing a variety of functions, but to be successful they need to have the functions that are most valued by the target market. The needs of the customer should have been identified through market research. Businesses look to include features that appeal to customers, offering products that are variously:

■ fashionable

■ safe

■ reliable

■ durable

■ convenient.

s t o p a n d **t h i n k**

Dell is designing a new laptop computer. What are the most important features that a customer might require? Do you think that all customers would have the same requirements?

A business should consider offering a range of products to meet the needs of different consumers. For example, Ford, the global car manufacturer, produces cars for large families (the Sharon), for women drivers (the Ka), for those who love fast cars (the Probe) and for those running small businesses (the Transit van).

Firms should try to develop strong product brands. The Virgin group has been very successful at building its brand. Richard Branson's company has developed a range of products that are packaged and marketed under the Virgin brand, including air and rail travel, mobile phones, soft drinks, music and financial services. Launching a new product under a familiar brand name is less risky: consumers recognise the brand and may identify it with certain qualities such as "reliable" or "fashionable".

Price

Price is the amount charged by a business for its products. The factors determining the price of a product can be summarised as the three Cs: cost, competition and customer value.

- **The cost of producing the product**. If a business is to make a profit, then it clearly needs to charge a price that covers the cost of making and selling the product.

- **The price charged by competitors**. A business might want to charge a price at or below that of its competitors. However, if the product is sufficiently unique and superior, then the business might feel it is acceptable to charge a price above that of its competitors.

- **The price customers are willing to pay**. This is determined by the value of the product to the target market. If consumers in the target market believe that they can gain significant benefits from the product, then they will be willing to pay a high price. However, if the product provides few benefits, consumers will only be prepared to pay a low price. For example, the price someone is willing to pay for a house will depend on its location, the number of rooms and other factors such as the size of the garden.

A business will consider all these factors before deciding on a price for each of its products. In certain situations, it may be appropriate to set a relatively high price. For example, a car manufacturer may set a premium price on a high-performance sports car that is recognised as being superior to other models (produced by the manufacturer's competitors) in its class. In other situations, a business may opt to set relatively low prices. For example, a new company operating in a very competitive market may set low prices relative to its competitors in an attempt to win business and build a customer base.

Apple's iPod made the digital music player a very desirable, even sexy, product. It had an award-winning design, a high price and was launched using a global marketing campaign. Consumers were desperate to buy iPods. Why did Apple use a high price strategy with the iPod? Do you think that the company may eventually have to change the price of the iPod?

Knowledge summary

■ The marketing mix describes the decisions a business takes about the product, its price, how it is promoted and how it will be distributed and sold.

■ All products pass through a life cycle of four stages. Marketing activities are very different in each stage of a product's life cycle.

■ Product is arguably the most important element of the marketing mix. Firms seek to produce well-designed products that meet consumers' needs.

■ Businesses decide on the price of their products by considering three factors: costs, competition and customer value.

quick **questions**

1 Many companies have launched rivals to Apple's hugely successful iPod. What features do you think that a rival product to iPod would need to give it a good chance of being successful?

2 Explain why the prices of flat screen digital televisions were very high when the products were first launched but have fallen over time.

3 Ryanair has very successfully employed a strategy of price penetration. In 2003, the company's profits exceeded £100 million. How can a company that charges very low prices generate such high profits?

data**interpretation**

The games console market

Games are big business. Hit games like Grand Theft Auto sell millions of copies. There are three big players competing to sell games consoles, the platforms on which many games are played. These are Sony, with its PlayStation console, Nintendo and Microsoft, with the Xbox. Figure 1.12 shows the actual and forecast revenue earned by Sony from sales of PlayStation in 2002/7, and Figure 1.13 the actual and forecast shipments of games consoles over the same period.

Figure 1.12: PlayStation revenue forecast ($million)						
	2002	2003	2004	2005	2006	2007
PlayStation 1	350	216	83	0	0	0
PlayStation 2	5642	4236	2982	1609	1103	476
PlayStation 3	0	0	0	2275	4095	5400

Source: In-Stat/MDR

A Estimate the likely sales revenue from the three PlayStation products in 2008. Justify your answer.

B What evidence is there that Sony has managed its product development well?

C PlayStation faces tough competition from Nintendo and Microsoft's Xbox. Using all the evidence available to you, discuss how the three Cs might determine the price Sony charges for its PlayStation 3.

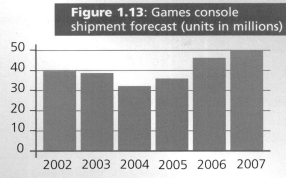

Figure 1.13: Games console shipment forecast (units in millions)

Source: In-Stat/MDR

Topic 5 The marketing mix: product and price

The marketing mix: promotion and place

Setting the scene: Dell's marketing mix

Michael Dell founded the Dell company in 1984 while he was still a student. He built his company by making and supplying computers directly to customers rather than through shops. Dell has been highly successful over recent years. The company's growth has been astonishing, with sales increasing from £700 million in 1992 to more than £30 billion in 2003. The company made profits in excess of £1 billion during the first six months of the 2004/5 financial year. This was 29 per cent higher than in the previous year.

Dell has employed a highly individual marketing mix to achieve higher profits than all of its rivals in the computing industry. The company has adapted this mix to meet the changing demands of the businesses and individuals who buy its products across the globe.

- **Product** – Dell has broadened its product range from computers to include printers, cash registers and a digital music player to rival Apple's iPod.

- **Place** – Dell distributes its products directly to consumers. Customers can order its products from Dell's website or from its call centres.

- **Price** – Since 2003, Dell has pursued a policy of price cutting at every opportunity. In August 2003, the company announced that it was slashing its prices by up to 22 per cent.

- **Promotion** – Because Dell's products are not available in shops, the company invests heavily in placing inserts into magazines and newspapers. These leaflets promote its products and special offers, and they tell

customers how they can order products through Dell's website and customer service call centres.

This combination of the four Ps has been highly successful for Dell. Not only has the company achieved high sales growth, but it has also gained an increased share of the fiercely competitive computer market. You can find out more about Dell by visiting its website (www.dell.com).

One of the reasons for Dell's success has been its policy of selling its computers direct to customers rather than through retail outlets. What do you think are the advantages of this policy for Dell and what are the benefits for customers?

KEY TERMS

The **marketing mix** is the four marketing tools (price, promotion, product and place) used by businesses to influence consumers' buying decisions.

Place is another term for distribution. It covers the range of activities necessary to ensure that goods and services are available to customers.

Promotion is a series of marketing activities designed to make consumers aware of products and to persuade them to buy those products.

Advertising is a means by which businesses pay for communication with actual and potential customers through newspapers, television, radio, the internet and other media.

A **brand** is a name, symbol, sign or design used by a business to differentiate its products from those produced by its competitors.

Promotion

Promotion is a series of marketing activities designed to make consumers aware of products. The ultimate aim, of course, is to persuade them to buy those products. Promotion is an important part of the marketing mix, and businesses can use a variety of different types of promotion.

1 Advertising

Advertising is a means by which businesses pay for communication with actual and potential customers through newspapers, television, radio, the internet and other media. It can be expensive, but advertising is often highly successful in influencing consumers' purchasing decisions.

Advertising can be informative, by setting out to increase consumer awareness of a product. This type of advertising is based on facts rather than images. On the other hand, persuasive advertising attempts to convince consumers to purchase a particular product. Persuasive advertising aims to persuade that the advertised product is better than the competition.

2 Sales promotion

Sales promotion is any activity that provides a financial incentive to purchase a product. Figure 1.14 illustrates the main forms of sales promotion. How many of the sales promotion techniques illustrated in Figure 1.14 have you experienced? Did any of them make you buy the products being promoted?

3 Merchandising

The term merchandising covers a range of tactics used by businesses at the point of sale (the location at which products are actually purchased) to achieve higher sales figures.

For example, a business might offer retailers special display stands or point-of-sale adverts to encourage them to place the business's products in a more favourable and prominent position within stores.

Merchandising can be important when:

- consumers make decisions at the point of sale
- competitors make extensive use of merchandising
- a variety of rival products are on display in stores
- rival products have only minor differences.

4 Public relations

Businesses seek good publicity, and public relations (PR) is designed to improve a business's standing in the eyes of consumers and other interested groups. Most larger organisations have their own PR staff. Businesses engage in a variety of PR activity including:

- making donations to charities
- sponsoring sporting and cultural activities
- allowing the public to visit the business.

Public relations can be a very expensive form of promotion, and it can be difficult for businesses to assess the effect of public relations on sales.

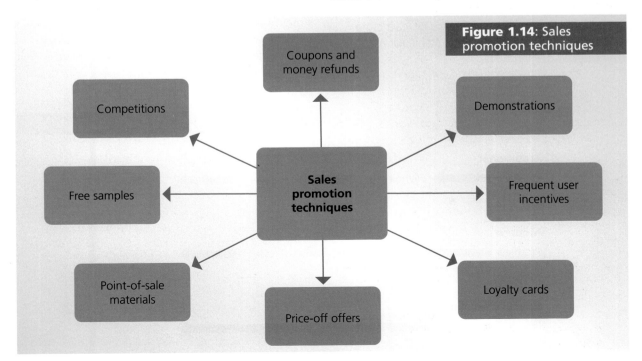

Figure 1.14: Sales promotion techniques

- Coupons and money refunds
- Competitions
- Demonstrations
- Free samples
- Sales promotion techniques
- Frequent user incentives
- Point-of-sale materials
- Price-off offers
- Loyalty cards

Place

Place is another term for distribution. It covers the range of activities necessary to ensure that goods and services are available to customers. Deciding on the right place involves a range of decisions.

1 Selecting a distribution channel

Figure 1.15 summarises the options available to a business. When deciding whether to use the services of a wholesaler and retailers, a business needs to consider the most cost-effective way of getting its products and service to the final customers. It needs to consider whether it has the ability to supply large numbers of retailers or final customers with relatively small quantities of its products. It needs to look at the implications for its profit margins of each means of distribution.

stop and think

A wholesaler buys products in bulk from manufacturers and breaks them up into smaller units to supply retailers. Why does the UK supermarket industry make little or no use of wholesalers?

The growth in use of the internet has encouraged even small businesses to sell products directly to consumers. It allows businesses to use websites to sell their products to what can be a global market. This can be a highly cost-effective means of reaching a wide target audience, but is not suitable for all businesses and all products.

2 Choosing the right outlets

Some manufacturers aim to persuade the maximum number of outlets to stock their products. For example, chocolate manufacturer Nestlé will achieve its desired high levels of sales if its products are stocked in as many supermarkets, garages, cinemas and newsagents as possible. This is an appropriate strategy because Nestlé's products are purchased by large numbers of people and many sales are impulse purchases; it makes sense for Nestlé to ensure that its products are available at any place where people might want something to eat.

Chocolate and other confectionery products are bought by a wide cross-section of the public. In contrast, some products are only purchased by a small minority of the population. These products are only available through limited, and often exclusive, outlets. Gucci, famous for making a range of luxury goods including clothes, handbags and sunglasses, restricts the number of outlets that can sell its goods. This is part of its strategy to position itself as an upmarket luxury brand, enabling the company to charge high prices for its products.

3 Getting the right mix

Place is the final element of the marketing mix. Businesses seek to design marketing mixes that are complementary and work together to benefit the business and to maximise sales. For example, Lidl promotes its supermarket chain to its target audience on the basis that it offers the lowest possible prices. Place is important to Lidl, and the company locates stores in areas where income levels are relatively low and its low-price foodstuffs are attractive to many local residents. Product is relatively unimportant within Lidl's marketing mix.

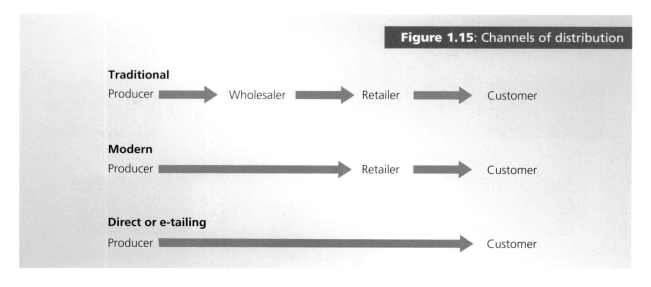

Figure 1.15: Channels of distribution

Traditional
Producer → Wholesaler → Retailer → Customer

Modern
Producer → Retailer → Customer

Direct or e-tailing
Producer → Customer

Knowledge summary

- Promotion is designed to increase consumer awareness of a product as well as to increase sales.

- Methods of promotion include advertising, merchandising, public relations and branding.

- Place is the means by which products are made available to consumers. This part of the marketing mix includes the selection of outlets as well as channels of distribution.

quick **questions**

1 Since 2002 most tobacco advertising has been banned in the UK. How might a tobacco company such as BAT adapt its marketing mix to overcome this development?

2 Explain why merchandising (part of promotion) and place are particularly important elements of the marketing mix for Mars, the confectionery manufacturer.

3 Paula Reeves is a watercolour artist, based in a rural part of Devon. Recently she has started selling her pictures through a website she designed herself. Draw up a list explaining the advantages and disadvantages to Paula of being able to sell her paintings via the internet.

data **interpretation**
Nokia sees mobile market shrink

The world's biggest mobile phone maker, Nokia, has seen its market share shrink in 2004. Its sales were down 5 per cent on 2003 to £4.4 billion. The Finnish firm said it estimated its market share in the May to June 2004 period was 31 per cent, down from 32 per cent in the first quarter of 2004 and 39 per cent a year ago.

Nokia has been cutting prices in order to remain competitive. "During the second quarter, we employed pricing selectively with certain products to stabilise our ... market share," said Jorma Ollila, chairman and CEO. Prices have been cut by up to 25 per cent on some phones.

Nokia also warned that profit margins would remain under pressure. The news came on the same day as rival Sony Ericsson posted a 34 per cent rise in second quarter profits.

Figure 1.16: Mobile phone manufacturers, global market share

Manufacturer	2000	2001	2002	2003	2004
Nokia	33.9	34.8	34.7	36.0	29.0
Motorola	12.7	14.8	15.5	14.1	15.4
Samsung	4.8	6.9	9.6	10.5	14.5

Source: www3.gartner.com

A Explain, with the aid of an example, what is meant by market share.

B Price is an important part of Nokia's marketing mix. Explain possible reasons why the company cut its prices selectively rather than cutting the prices of all its products.

C Nokia competes with other manufacturers in the mobile phone handset market. Discuss how the company might design its marketing mix to compete effectively over the next few years.

Topic 7 Enterprise skills

Setting the scene: are you enterprising?

Before starting up in business it's worth thinking through whether you have the necessary skills and personal characteristics to make your business a success.

One way to do this is to ask yourself some key questions.

- Are you a self-starter? Are you good at planning and meeting deadlines? Can you rely on yourself to get things done?

- Can you sell? Do you enjoy the challenge of finding prospective customers? Could you convert potential customers into actual customers? Could you keep customers?

- Do you enjoy taking on responsibility? Do you like to take charge and see things through?

- Do you enjoy hard work? Can you cope with pressure without it affecting your home life?

- Do you have your family behind you? Is your family supportive and willing to take the same risks as you?

- Are you starting your business for the right reasons? Are you realistic about how much work is involved?

Why do you think these questions are important ones for anyone setting up their own business? Do you think you have the necessary skills and personal characteristics to set up in business?

Qualities and abilities

Enterprise refers to the skills and knowledge possessed by entrepreneurs or owners of a business. Anyone who owns a business needs to acquire and coordinate a range of resources – physical, financial and human – to ensure that the business is successful. They need to make crucial decisions about the types of products the business offers, how these products will be produced and the prices charged to customers.

In the introduction to this topic (see setting the scene, above), we listed some of the questions you might ask yourself before starting your own business – before becoming an entrepreneur. This questionnaire is designed to make you think about whether you have the personal attributes and skills needed by an entrepreneur.

KEY TERMS

Enterprise skills are the skills and personal characteristics possessed by successful business people or entrepreneurs.

Enterprising behaviour occurs when business owners or their employees demonstrate enterprise skills, such as when taking profitable risks or inspiring co-workers to achieve objectives.

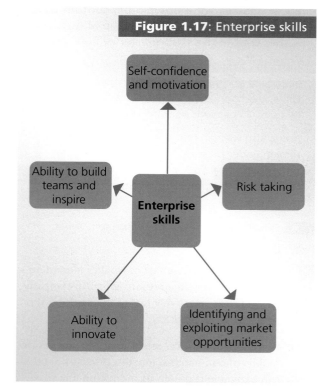

Figure 1.17: Enterprise skills

Figure 1.17 illustrates a range of enterprise skills – qualities and abilities which enterprising people possess. Now let's consider these qualities and abilities in more detail.

1 Self-confidence and motivation

Enterprising people are clear about their goals. They are self-starters – they can push themselves to achieve their goals and don't need other people to make them believe in their own abilities. Their business ideas might have seemed silly at first, but they had sufficient belief in their own abilities and knowledge to ignore negative opinions and continue on their own path.

2 Risk taking

Enterprising people aren't afraid to fail – they recognise that failure is an essential part of future success. Most successful entrepreneurs will happily tell you that they didn't initially succeed, but whenever they failed they learned some valuable lesson that, later on, helped them to achieve success. Entrepreneurs invest both time and money in their businesses and receive, as a reward for the risk of failure, the benefits provided by a successful business.

3 Identifying and exploiting marketing opportunities

Enterprising people can see opportunities to meet customer needs, and have the drive and motivation needed to take advantage of these opportunities. For example, few people thought that mobile phone users would pay for ringtones based on hit tunes, but the entrepreneurs who spotted this market have received large profits in return for their ability to identify and exploit a market opportunity.

This is a difficult skill to develop and is often acquired through working in a particular industry for several years. Alternatively, some entrepreneurs seem to be blessed with an ability to spot future trends in customer needs across a range of markets.

4 Ability to innovate

Enterprising people can think of ways to improve products – they can look beyond traditional perceptions and ask new questions. Innovating isn't the same as inventing. An inventor is often driven by a desire to achieve something new or make a technological breakthrough. However, an innovator sees new ways of using a product, or improves it.

Alexander Graham Bell invented the telephone in 1876, partly as a result of his interest in the education of deaf people. Other entrepreneurs, including those in Bell's own company, developed his invention to enable it to meet customer needs in various ways. This process of innovation continues today with the mobile phone. Mobile phones were originally designed for voice communication, but subsequent innovations have enabled them to send and receive text messages and pictures.

5 Ability to build teams and inspire

Entrepreneurs have often been thought of as driven and talented individuals – people who know what they want and can achieve their goals without the help of others. While this is still often the case, it's increasingly true that good entrepreneurs need good people skills – they must be able to share their vision and enthusiasm with other people. Richard Branson (Virgin) and Anita Roddick (The Body Shop) are just two examples of entrepreneurs who have built successful businesses by developing enthusiastic and committed teams of employees.

stop and think

James Dyson, the man who invented the bagless vacuum cleaner, showed enormous determination in turning his idea into a commercial success. Find out more about James Dyson's struggle to develop a successful product and business at www.dyson.co.uk. Explain why James Dyson possesses a wide range of enterprise skills.

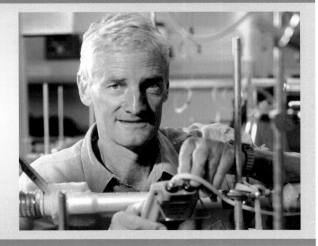

Enterprising behaviour

Business owners are not the only people who demonstrate enterprise skills. Successful businesses recognise the importance of employees and the benefit of recruiting and retaining staff who can demonstrate enterprising behaviour. Many organisations realise the importance of flexibility and quick decision-making within their organisations. Employing enterprising people is one way that a business can improve its ability to respond to competitor actions and to ensure the achievement of its SMART objectives.

Enterprising behaviour can be demonstrated in a wide variety of job roles and positions. For example, sales personnel certainly require self-confidence and motivation when prospecting for sales and closing deals. In addition, they will be required to take risks when identifying new clients and proposing solutions to their requirements. It may require innovation to develop new markets for products – to find new ways in which existing products could be exploited. The ability to identify and exploit marketing opportunities will probably distinguish an outstanding salesperson from an adequate one.

Many businesses have large sales teams rather then a single salesperson. The ability of a sales manager to coordinate the sales team, to build trust and to inspire the staff can often be the difference between a satisfactory sales year and an outstanding one.

stop and think

Identify ways in which enterprising behaviour is demonstrated within your school or college. You might find examples of enterprising behaviour by the staff or by your fellow students. The enterprising behaviour does not have to be profit oriented. For example, it could have been demonstrated when raising funds for a charity.

Knowledge summary

- **Enterprise skills describe the skills and personal characteristics required of successful business owners.**

- **Enterprise skills include self-confidence and motivation, a capacity for risk taking, a talent for identifying and exploiting market opportunities, an ability to innovate, and an ability to build and inspire teams.**

- **Enterprise can be demonstrated by employees of a business as well as its owners.**

- **Enterprising behaviour is an essential ingredient for any successful business and helps businesses to respond quickly to competitor actions.**

quick questions

1 Explain why enterprise skills are important for anyone undertaking these occupations:
  a) manager of an estate agency
  b) surgeon working in a private hospital
  c) aid worker, such as an Oxfam field worker based in a developing country
  d) head teacher (or principal) of a school or college.

2 If an individual possesses self-confidence and motivation, will he or she also be able to build teams and inspire? Explain your answer.

3 Do you think it would be possible to develop enterprise skills in someone with no aptitude for independent work? Justify your answer.

data**interpretation**
Dragons' Den

In the BBC television show, *Dragons' Den*, prospective entrepreneurs are invited to pitch their start-up idea before a panel of five hard-nosed, "been there, done that", successful business people – the dragons.

The entrants have to convince one or more of the dragons to invest in their business in the face of a potentially brutal bombardment of questions and criticism. Two of the successful entrants in the first series were Tracey Graily and Tracie Herrtage.

Ms Graily runs Grails, a tailoring company that makes bespoke ladies suits. Customers pay around £700 for a made-to-measure suit using the materials of their choice. Ms Graily, who has a degree in textiles and clothing, quit a successful career in retail – she had previously worked for Mothercare and Next – to start up the company.

Essex property developer Tracie Herrtage didn't have to quit a top corporate job to start up her business Le Beanock, as she had been her own boss for a number of years. But instead of sticking to property development, her company is based around a piece of furniture that came to her as a brainwave a number of years ago. Fed up with the family's dogs getting their hairs all over the beanbags in their lounge, Ms Herrtage wondered why she didn't raise the bags off the floor using chains drilled into the ceiling. Hey presto, she had invented Le Beanock, a cross between a beanbag and a hammock. Ms Herrtage said her friends and family were all saying she should launch the Le Beanock as a product, and so she did in January 2004, with a retail price of around £750.

A Explain how Tracey Grails and Tracie Herrtage had already demonstrated enterprise skills before entering the *Dragons' Den* challenge.

B Explain why you think the business ideas presented by Tracy Grails and Tracie Herrtage gained financial backing from the dragons.

C Investigate an employee or business owner who you think possesses enterprise skills and who has successfully demonstrated enterprising behaviour. Produce a five-minute presentation that communicates the individual's enterprise skills, illustrating these with specific examples of his or her enterprising behaviour.

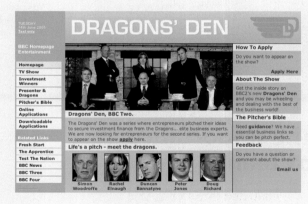

Teams

Setting the scene: the importance of teamwork

The article produced below describes government plans to introduce enterprise activities into schools. Do you think that these types of activities are a good way for students to learn about working together in a team?

Enterprise activities in schools

From 2005, all 15 and 16 year olds will be entitled to five days of "enterprise activity". Announcing the initiative, the then Education Secretary, Charles Clarke, said: "Enterprise education is vital to our future economic success. It equips young people with vital skills that businesses have told us that they want to see more of. This isn't just about growing the next generation of entrepreneurs; enterprise skills will be valuable to all young people."

The challenge for one group of teenagers: create 50 origami ducks

and ship them over to France to sell. The first task for students at Holywells High School in Ipswich was to form companies in groups of 10 and work out who was going to do what. Roles, such as managing director and company chairman, all had to be decided upon before they devoted the day to organising their business venture. In total 180 pupils (aged 13 and 14) took part and the school hall has been a hive of activity, with pupils buying materials from a supply depot, making the ducks, designing a

company logo, costing the shipping expenses to France, and so on.

Chloe, 13, who was accountant for her company, said the day had encouraged her to be creative. "I've been counting up the money, counting up how much the lorries will cost and petrol and how much the ferry will be. It's been really good fun." Business adviser to her group, Danielle, 13, said she learned about teamwork. "You can't work on your own, it's important to work together and in a team. It's really hard otherwise."

Source: news.bbc.co.uk, 17 November 2004

The importance of teams

If you have ever been involved in running a mini-enterprise, organising a school event or been involved in team sport you will appreciate the importance of teams and effective teamwork. You might also appreciate that a team is much more than a group of people. People in a team help, complement and support each other. This doesn't happen automatically – people have to work at being a team.

A group of people can be viewed as a team when it has these features:

- a collective consciousness – people in the group think of themselves as a team

- a shared sense of purpose – the members of the group have the same tasks, goals or interests

- interdependence – the people in the group need each other if they are to achieve their aims and objectives

- interaction – the people in the group communicate with one another, influence one other and react to one other

- collective action – it is a unified collection of people.

From this list you should see that a team has a strong identity, is capable of change, has resilience and, possibly above all else, can learn from its mistakes.

KEY TERMS

Teams are groups with clear objectives. In a team the individual members of the group work together and support each other.

Belbin team roles describe particular styles of working within a team. Meredith Belbin suggested nine different team roles which collectively help to establish an effective team.

Leadership style describes the way in which the leader of a team encourages team members to work towards achieving the team's tasks.

The components of teams

Transforming a loose group of people into an effective team requires planning and good leadership.

The initial construction of the team is very important. If a team is made up of people who don't get on with each other or who have very similar characteristics, then it is difficult to build an effective team.

The team leader plays a vital role in transforming a group into a team. Without a thoughtful but incisive team leader, it is likely that the individuals within the team will pull in different directions.

1 Team membership

Team members usually adopt different roles – that is, people within a team behave according to certain personal characteristics. An effective team is composed of varied team roles that complement and support each other. Figure 1.18 illustrates this process.

Each piece of the jigsaw represents a different team role – the roles are described in Figure 1.19 – and an effective team requires all of the pieces of the jigsaw to be in place.

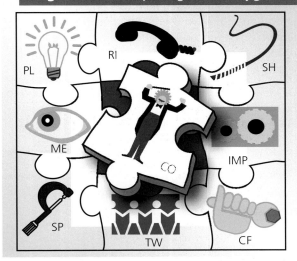

Figure 1.18: Completing the team jigsaw

Figure 1.19: The Belbin team roles

Team role	Contributions	Allowable weaknesses
Plant (PL)	Creative, imaginative, unorthodox. Solves difficult problems.	Ignores incidentals. Too preoccupied to communicate effectively.
Co-ordinator (CO)	Mature, confident, a good chairperson. Clarifies goals, promotes decision-making, delegates well.	Can often be seen as manipulative. Off-loads personal work.
Monitor/evaluator (ME)	Sober, strategic and discerning. Sees all options. Judges accurately.	Lacks drive and ability to inspire others.
Implementer (IMP)	Disciplined, reliable, conservative and efficient. Turns ideas into practical actions.	Somewhat inflexible. Slow to respond to new possibilities.
Completer/finisher (CF)	Painstaking, conscientious, anxious. Searches out errors and omissions. Delivers on time.	Inclined to worry unduly. Reluctant to delegate.
Resource investigator (RI)	Extrovert, enthusiastic, communicative. Explores opportunities. Develops contacts.	Over-optimistic. Loses interest once initial enthusiasm has passed.
Shaper (SH)	Challenging, dynamic, thrives on pressure. Has the drive and courage to overcome obstacles.	Prone to provocation. Offends people's feelings.
Team worker (TW)	Co-operative, mild, perceptive and diplomatic. Listens, builds, averts friction.	Indecisive in crunch situations.
Specialist (SP)	Single-minded, self-starting, dedicated. Provides knowledge and skills in rare supply.	Contributes only on a narrow front. Dwells on technicalities.

An effective team could be built because each member of the team is flexible and willing to adopt a different role as and when required. However, in reality, most people find it difficult, or uncomfortable, to switch their team roles. Identifying the role (or roles) that each team member is likely to adopt is a vital part of constructing an effective team. This knowledge comes in useful if you need to assess why a team is not functioning effectively, because it enables you to identify which piece (or pieces) of the jigsaw are missing.

Dr Meredith Belbin described the team roles found to be essential for effective teamwork. These are shown in Figure 1.19.

stop and think

Why does each Belbin team role represent an important aspect of effective teamwork?

The Belbin team roles can be grouped into three categories:

- active roles – shaper, implementer and completer/finisher

- people roles – co-ordinator, team worker and resources investigator

- thinking roles – plant, monitor/evaluator and specialist.

When building a team, or trying to understand why a team is not functioning, these three general roles help to identify the way forward. Perhaps the team is not balanced and team members are taking on too many of one type of role at the expense of other roles. Perhaps the team is not flexible enough and the team dynamic cannot cope with new situations. The team leader will need to reflect on questions like these when he or she is building an effective team.

stop and think

Identify a time when you were working with a group of people to achieve a task, such as when taking part in a team sport or a mini-enterprise. Using the idea of active, people and thinking team roles, explain why the group did or did not operate as an effective team.

2 Leadership

Team leaders need to be flexible. Building an effective team can sometimes be very difficult – particularly, for example, if team members are not co-operating with each other. At other times, it can be a very simple task, especially if the team contains a good mix of active, people and thinking personality types.

No single style of leadership is appropriate for every situation a team faces. During the lifetime of a team, the leader will need to adopt a number of different styles. This is why team leaders need to be flexible.

Management theorists have produced many theories of leadership. One particularly useful theory, certainly when looking at teams, is Fred Fiedler's theory of leadership effectiveness. This theory identifies two styles of leaders:

- relationship-motivated leaders – these leaders enjoy working with people and they are people oriented

- task-motivated leaders – these leaders enjoy getting the job done and are task oriented.

Neither style is appropriate for every situation, and the choice of style depends on three factors:

- the quality of the relationship between the leader and the team

- how clear and structured the team task is

- how much power and authority the team leader has.

Fiedler found that in extreme situations, where all three factors were very favourable or very unfavourable, a task-oriented leadership style worked best. In intermediate situations a people-oriented style was more effective.

stop and think

Which style of leadership – relationship-motivated- or task-motivated – might be most appropriate for a new team? Explain your answer.

Knowledge summary

- A group of people needs to demonstrate a number of collaborative features before it can be considered to be a team. These include a shared sense of purpose and a degree of interdependence and interaction.

- Belbin's team roles describe the different roles taken on by members of teams and are useful when analysing why a team is or is not effective.

- Team leaders play a crucial role in building and maintaining effective teams. No single style of leadership is appropriate for all situations, and team leaders need to be sensitive to the needs and circumstances of the team.

quick **questions**

1 Would you consider the group of students that are taking the AQA GCE Applied Business course with you as a team? Explain your answer.

2 Which Belbin team role do you think is least important for a school or college mini-enterprise team? Justify your choice.

3 Explain whether a people-oriented or a task-oriented leadership style would be suitable in these situations:

a) a fire-fighting team called out to deal with a fire on the sixth floor of a 10-floor accommodation block

b) a sports team with a 10-point lead at the top of the league with four games left (assume 3 points for a win, 1 point for a draw and no points for a loss)

c) an experienced and successful sales team given the task of launching an existing product in a new foreign market.

data **interpretation**
Aid struggles to reach Indonesia

Search and rescue teams have begun to arrive on the Indonesian island of Nias, which was worst hit by Monday's massive earthquake.

Damaged infrastructure and bad weather are hindering rescue efforts. Nias residents have been scrambling for aid supplies and searching for survivors. The main town, Gunung Sitoli, has been largely destroyed.

The UN has confirmed 518 were killed in the 8.7-magnitude tremor, but it is thought up to 1,000 may have died. Monday's quake caused panic across the Indian Ocean region, which is still reeling from the massive waves that killed some 300,000 people in December 2004.

Source: news.bbc.co.uk, 30 March 2005

A Use the concepts of Belbin's team roles and Fielder's leadership styles to explain how a search and rescue team could deal with the challenges described in the article.

B Research the Belbin team roles that characterise the members of your class. This is a class task, and you should negotiate the best way of collecting and presenting the evidence with other members of your class. The objective of the task is to convince your school or college that your class is capable of working together as an effective team.

Building effective teams

Setting the scene: how to build effective teams

This question and answer is an extract from an article on Entrepreneur.com – an American website (www.entrepreneur.com) that provides guidance for entrepreneurs.

Question

I have a big task to undertake, and I'm not sure if I should do it myself or put a team together to do it for me. What's your advice?

Answer

Today, most business owners use a team approach to solve problems, generate ideas and complete tasks. But before building a team, the entrepreneur needs to resolve these key questions: can I complete the task myself, do I have the time and resources to complete this task, and can some other person or group be even more effective than I can?

If the answers favour getting others involved, it's time to consider the advantages and disadvantages of teams. On the upside, teams combine various employee skills, ideas, knowledge bases and perspectives. Teams usually increase individual productivity and workplace satisfaction.

However, all is not necessarily rosy – there are some disadvantages to using teams as well. For example, teams may take longer to achieve a goal than an individual would, and teams grow through predictable stages that are time consuming, such as member selection, organisation, socialisation and creation of final products or ideas.

The good news is, with effective direction from the right team leader, team-building can be a very productive and cost-effective process. To help ensure success, the team needs to consider five crucial success factors:

- clear identification and ownership of the team goal
- clear definition and acceptance of each person's role and responsibilities
- clear delineation of team processes, such as decision-making, conflict resolution, communication and participation
- clear opportunities to build trust between participants
- clear acceptance of each other's strengths and limitations in a manner that encourages positive working relationships.

Building the team

Effective teams need time to develop confidence in their own abilities. As the Entrepreneur.com article shows (see setting the scene opposite), an effective team is not created in a day. Teams typically need to go through four phases before they become effective.

Forming

The team has just been formed or put together. This is an anxious stage where group members are getting to know each other, worrying about what's expected of them and how they should behave.

Storming

The group has been working on the task. Familiarity sets in and conflict can emerge between sub-groups. The leader may be challenged as individuals react against his or her attempts to direct them.

Norming

The group begins to settle down and harmonise. Group cohesion is evident and norms emerge. Mutual support develops, and it's clear that this is a functioning group – a team.

Performing

The team becomes flexible in the way individuals perform tasks – it is capable of dealing with complex problems and is on the way to achieving its objectives.

When a team is finding it difficult to move from the storming to the norming stage, it is useful to reflect on the behaviour of individual team members. In particular, these types of behaviour are likely to limit the performance of a team:

- aggressor – spoilt child who acts like a bully, defies authority and is envious

- blocker – always look on the negative side and disagrees without reason

- recognition-seeker – tries to manufacture situations to show themselves in a good light

- playboy or playgirl – this team member is far too busy doing something else of much greater importance

- dominator - the "big head" of the group who is always trying to gain control of the team

- help-seeker – seeks attention by continuously claiming an inability to cope when this is obviously not true.

If a group has one or more of these problem types, then the team leader will need to address the issue. Given the authority and the ability to replace team members, this could be solved by removing problematic individuals from the group. However, this is often not an option, and the leader needs to adjust the behaviour of the problem individuals. Sometimes this can be achieved through group pressure, while at other times individual one-to-one performance reviews will be required.

stop and **think**

Think about past group events you have been involved in, including classes at school or college. Did any of these groups ever make it to the performing stage of team behaviour? If not, what factors got in the way of the group developing into a functioning team?

The time it takes to get from the forming to the performing stage depends on several factors including:

- the complexity of the task

- the quality of the leadership

- the power and authority given to the leader by the business

- the personality types and characteristics of the team members

- the resources available to the team.

Perhaps one of the most important factors is the selection of team members. These can be selected in a number of ways, but this often depends on the organisational structure of the business.

Many businesses organise themselves in a hierarchical way with teams structured according to functional areas. So, for example, they have production teams, customer care teams and delivery teams.

These functional teams are likely to be stable and relatively easy to build because:

- the tasks set are probably easier to understand and accept
- team members are familiar with each others' backgrounds and work methods
- a strict hierarchy, with clear responsibilities, is probably in place.

However, building a team around functional areas can have drawbacks. The lack of variety within the team could result in conservative approaches to problems. The task might be completed, but opportunities could be lost. For this reason, some businesses structure teams on a project-by-project basis and select team members from across the organisation. For example, when developing a new product it would make sense to involve people with different backgrounds and expertise such as accounts, design and marketing.

stop and think

What might be the advantages and disadvantages of a team involving people from a number of different backgrounds?

Implementing business plans

Business plans, complete with aims and SMART objectives, are of little use if they are not implemented. While individuals may well be able to get on with simple tasks by themselves, it is likely that teams will needed to tackle more complex tasks.

Knowledge summary

- **Teams move through four stages before becoming effective: forming, storming, norming and performing.**
- **Teams structured by functional area are likely to be easier to establish but are likely to be less creative and will possibly miss opportunities to innovate.**
- **Teams are vital to the implementation of business plans that involve anything other than simple tasks.**

The additional benefit of using a team is that of innovation and creativity. Individuals, left to their own devices, often repeat past working habits and use assumptions that – while valid once – may no longer be appropriate. Teams help to break down these constraining and restrictive working habits.

The article below illustrates the benefits of using a multidisciplinary team in the context of improving elite athlete performance. Given such a complex task – improving the performance of an athlete – it makes sense to construct teams with a variety of specialisms. Faced with complex tasks, businesses also benefit from a multidisciplinary approach.

Can athletes go faster, higher, stronger?

Since the Sydney Games in 2000, there has been a focus within the UK on developing the sports science and medicine infrastructure to improve the support available to elite athletes.

The English Institute of Sport (EIS), a network of experts within the field, teamed up in 2003 with the British Olympic Association's Medical Centre to form the Olympic Medical Institute (OMI).

The result? An integration of performance and rehabilitation programmes for the UK's leading sports stars. This development has delivered a number of advantages, according to the OMI's general manager, Nick Fellows.

"We have a multidisciplinary team on site. We can accelerate [an athlete's] recovery by having everybody around them.

"We assess their fitness as to what they can or cannot do, then put them through appropriate training alongside their rehabilitation and injury management programme."

Source: news.bbc.co.uk, 27 May 2004

quick questions

1 How might these activities help a team to move from storming to the norming stage?

a) a group evening out, paid for by the business
b) a leader adopting a task-oriented leadership style
c) individual performance reviews of group members by the team leader.

2 Explain why multidisciplinary teams might be effective in these situations:

a) a local authority investigating whether to pedestrianise parts of the city centre
b) a car maker attempting to differentiate its products from those of its rivals
c) a supermarket investigating ways to improve the internal layout of its stores.

Effective leadership training

BP employees attend an effective leader course to improve all areas of coaching and team building. The course involves outdoor activities and skills workshops. It starts with an informal meal where the staff, from various different levels within the organisation, meet and chat. After dinner, unknown to the staff, they will have a musical session with a conductor.

Conducting Business is a training company that, in partnership with BP, aims to offer new insights into management and leadership techniques. It does this by demonstrating the parallels between business and music. The class of 15 are taken through the processes of singing a round in four parts. The first two parts are songs that are familiar to the staff: *Swing Low, Sweet Chariot* and *When The Saints Go Marching In*.

But the next two verses are new ones and, as each new verse is added, the challenge is to remember the words, keep the pace and stay in tune. They are taken through the process one step at a time. Starting with stretching and breathing they learn a song that they are familiar with before being slowly introduced to new things.

Out of the 15 staff on the course, many already had considerable experience in managing people. "It's about making people feel that they've done a good job," said Jonathan, one of the course members. "A lot of it is encouraging people to look over the parapet – and be bold."

"You have to encourage communication," added Linda, a fellow participant. "Some staff struggle because you look too busy for them to approach."

So what do they think are key motivators for their teams? They range from being given confidence to having trust in their colleagues. These are the top ten tips according to BP's team leaders.

Source: adapted from news.bbc.co.uk, 30 October 2002

A Explain how the training course might improve the ability of BP team leaders to manage teams.

B Rank BP's motivational top 10 in order of importance. Justify your choices.

C Produce a five-minute presentation on "The best way to motivate a team".

BP's motivational top 10
Giving confidence to speak out and be original
Being able to trust colleagues
Feeling part of a team
Not being criticised
Being listened to
Not bulldozing through things
Having clear objectives
Being able to step back and see the whole picture
Being specific
Knowing what to do before you do it

Business in practice: Tesco's story

Since the takeover of Safeway by William Morrison in 2004, the UK market for groceries has been dominated by four large companies. As Figure 1.20 shows, the four major supermarket chains have over 70 per cent of the market. However, overall the grocery market in the UK is growing slowly. This means that a company like Tesco can only achieve substantial rates of growth in food sales by taking customers from rivals such as Sainsbury.

Figure 1.20: The major players in the UK grocery market

Supermarket	Employees	Number of stores	Market share 2003	Market share 2004
Tesco	200,000	775	26.8%	28.0%
Asda	117,000	258	17.0%	16.9%
Sainsbury	174,000	517	15.9%	15.3%
Morrisons*	138,000	599	14.5%**	13.6%*

* Including Safeway following the takeover   ** Combined Morrisons & Safeway figure.

Sources: Adapted from www.news.bbc.co.uk and www.corporatewatch.org.uk

Working for Tesco

The success of Tesco has partly been due to a number of internal changes carried out in the late 1980s. It took a close look at the performance of its management staff – particularly the company's store and departmental managers – and found that they were performing at a lower level than their competitors. Tesco implemented a development programme for its store and departmental managers which contributed to the present success of the company.

Today Tesco places a strong emphasis on developing effective teams within each store. Every Tesco employee is encouraged to work towards achieving the company's core purpose: "to create value for our customers, to earn their lifetime loyalty."

This purpose is further defined by the five aims:

■ Tesco will be a growth business

■ Tesco will become the business people value more than any other

■ Tesco will have loyal committed staff

■ Tesco will be a global retailer

■ Tesco will be as strong in non-food as it is in food.

In order to achieve these aims and its core mission, Tesco encourages its employees to adopt a set of key values. These are set out in two parts. First, Tesco wants its employees to be part of a company that "tries harder for its customers". Tesco staff should:

■ understand customers better than anyone

■ be energetic, be innovative and be first for customers

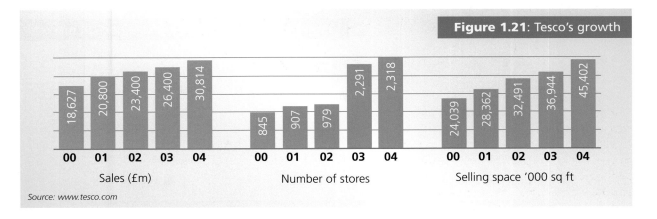

Figure 1.21: Tesco's growth

Sales (£m)
00: 18,627
01: 20,800
02: 23,400
03: 26,400
04: 30,814

Number of stores
00: 845
01: 907
02: 979
03: 2,291
04: 2,318

Selling space '000 sq ft
00: 24,039
01: 28,362
02: 32,491
03: 36,944
04: 45,402

Source: www.tesco.com

- use their strengths to deliver unbeatable value to our customers

- look after our people so they can look after our customers.

Second, Tesco's employees are encouraged to "treat people how we like to be treated":

- there's only one team … the Tesco Team

- trust and respect each other

- strive to do our very best

- give support to each other and praise more than criticise

- ask more than tell, and share knowledge so that it can be used

- enjoy work, celebrate success and learn from experience.

How does this work out in practice? Some evidence of the reality of working for Tesco comes from these quotes taken from the website "Where women want to work" (www.www2wk.com).

- I am raising a family (on my own) and developing a successful career – and working for Tesco makes that a fantastic experience, not the unachievable task that many make it out to be!

- Tesco's culture is very much of one team, and for that to be so well lived, diversity has to be key. The working policies also make it a joy to balance raising a family with developing a successful career.

- The one-team approach of Tesco makes me question whether they value diversity or they want diverse people who all buy into the Tesco team – when you challenge issues, you are perceived as not wanting to be part of the team.

- Tesco is a dynamic company with a wealth of opportunities – whoever you are and wherever you come from – but you have to work hard!

Tesco's current position

Tesco has steadily increased its market share – the percentage of the market that it holds – at the expense of rivals, and this trend shows no sign of stopping.

As a result of this growth, Tesco has become the UK's largest retailer. During 2004, the company's sales rose by 8.3 per cent compared with the previous year. Its profits for the financial year 2004/5 are expected to exceed £2 billion (that is £2,000 million). One pound in every twelve spent in UK shops is spent in a Tesco store.

In 2004, the company opened 64 new stores and expanded the range of retail outlets it operates. But Tesco does not just rely on sales through its stores: it is the world's largest internet retailer and its e-business is operational in a number of countries throughout the world.

The company has performed well in food sales, but recently has begun to enjoy strong sales growth in non-food items such as clothing. The company has also entered new markets by:

- becoming an internet service provider (ISP)

- operating a mobile phone service

- issuing credit cards

- selling online music.

The company carries out all its activities under the Tesco brand. The company believes that this brand is trusted and that consumers recognise that it represents value for money.

Figure 1.21 illustrates the substantial growth achieved by the company in the first years of the twenty-first century, and Figure 1.22 (on page 54) shows the extent to which the company has developed its business outside its traditional UK base.

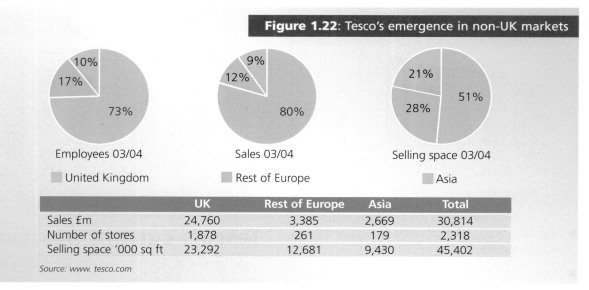

Figure 1.22: Tesco's emergence in non-UK markets

Employees 03/04 — 73%, 17%, 10%

Sales 03/04 — 80%, 12%, 9%

Selling space 03/04 — 51%, 28%, 21%

■ United Kingdom   ■ Rest of Europe   ■ Asia

	UK	Rest of Europe	Asia	Total
Sales £m	24,760	3,385	2,669	30,814
Number of stores	1,878	261	179	2,318
Selling space '000 sq ft	23,292	12,681	9,430	45,402

Source: www. tesco.com

Tesco's marketing activities

Tesco operates in a number of different markets. These can be defined both by geography (the different regions in which it operates) and by product (the different products and services that the company offers). Tesco has developed appropriate marketing activities for each of these markets. All of these activities combine to help the company achieve its corporate objectives.

1 Expand in overseas markets

As well as operating in the UK, by 2004 Tesco had stores in six other countries in Europe: the Republic of Ireland, Hungary, Czech Republic, Slovakia, Turkey and Poland. The company has a total of 261 stores across Europe, and this year it became the leading hypermarket retailer in Central Europe. Its European stores enable it to reach over 175 million people. Tesco plans to open more stores in this region.

In 2002 Tesco opened its first stores in Malaysia. The company plans to increase its operations in the developing markets of Thailand, South Korea, Taiwan and Malaysia, giving it access to a population of approximately 155 million people.

In March 2004 Tesco revealed that the company had bought a 50 per cent stake in Ting Hsin International, a Chinese retail food group. China has a population of 1.3 billion, and in 2004 its economy was growing at 10 per cent a year. Tesco is clearly attracted by the huge scale and potential of the Chinese market, although it faces competition from other global retailers such as Wal-Mart and Carrefour that already have a trading presence in China.

2 Selling new products

Since 1998 Tesco has steadily expanded the range of products that it sells. The company has opened a number of stores with larger floor areas to enable it to stock clothes, household products and electrical goods. This has increased the company's sales significantly and has been one of the factors behind the spectacular increase in turnover.

The company has become a highly successful retailer of clothes, rivalling established businesses such as Marks and Spencer in this market. It has also enjoyed some success in providing financial products to its customers. Tesco offers car and house insurance, loans and credit cards, and has marketed these products relentlessly.

In September 2003 Tesco announced that it was entering the telephone service market. The company will take on British Telecom in providing a range of packages to UK consumers for their landline telephones. Tesco claims that its packages could cut the cost of calls for residential consumers by up to 30 per cent.

In 2004 the company announced that it was branching out into another new market by launching an online music service which it hopes will rival Apple's iTunes. Tesco says its digital music will sell at 79 pence per song, and it intends to offer more than 500,000 tracks and improved sound quality.

3 Opening different types of stores

The UK's major retailers have encountered increasing difficulty in obtaining planning permission for new out-of-town superstores. In response, there has been a move to open smaller stores in traditional high street sites in an attempt to keep increasing sales turnover. Tesco has been at the forefront of this development, opening its Metro and Express stores in high streets across the country.

This move into local stores continues. In 2004 Tesco bought 45 small stores in the London area for

£54 million. The shops were sold by the Adminstore Group, and Tesco plans to convert them into its Express brand by February 2005. This move attracted criticism from several of Tesco's rivals. Iceland, for example, claimed that it may not be in the best long-term interests of consumers.

activities

1 Describe how these external environment factors might have affected the ability of Tesco to achieve its aims:

a) local, national and international levels of economic activity

b) the degree of competition within the markets Tesco operates in.

2 Explain how enterprise skills and effective teams could have contributed to Tesco's success.

3 Explain in detail how Tesco uses marketing activities to help it achieve its aims. (Visiting Tesco's website at www.tesco.com might help you to answer this question.)

4 Evaluate the key factors contributing to Tesco's success.

THIS UNIT EXAMINES THE KEY ROLE THAT PEOPLE play in helping any business organisation achieve its aims and objectives. It looks at the range of job roles and responsibilities within a business organisation and considers important human resource management issues such as performance management, staff motivation and training.

The second half of the unit considers the recruitment and selection process. It sets out the legal and ethical responsibilities of businesses in recruiting staff, the procedures that are commonly followed and the techniques that are used to interview and assess job candidates.

People in business

Intro   Introducing people in business

Setting the scene: Renault plans its new workforce

In 2005 the French car manufacturer Renault confirmed its expansion plans. One of the company's aims is to expand its sales in international (as opposed to French) markets.

Renault had enjoyed a prosperous period in the run-up to this announcement, and sales had risen by 15 per cent in 2004. In part this has been due to the launch of models such as the Renault Mégane, which has been very successful and has helped to revitalise the company's fortunes. But Renault has also benefited from the success of its Japanese partner Nissan, in which it holds a 44 per cent stake.

Renault's plans have significant implications for the company's workforce. In order to implement its ambitious expansion, the company plans to hire 14,000 new employees to increase production capacity.

The company will be seeking to recruit managers, employees with engineering and other technical skills, as well as workers to carry out a range of duties on the company's production lines.

In addition, some 4,000 new employees will work in Renault's chain of car dealers, selling cars and providing after-sales service for customers.

A Renault spokesperson admitted that the success of the plan depended on appointing "talented people". This will be crucial if Renault is to thrive in the face of the tough competition that exists in the car manufacturing industry.

KEY TERMS

Recruitment is the process of finding new employees to join a company.

The **selection process** is the method of choosing a candidate for a job.

Appraisal is the process of reviewing and reporting on how well each member of staff is working.

Motivation examines the factors that influence people to behave in certain ways.

Why are people important to businesses?

When we think of businesses, many things come to mind. Some businesses have world-famous brands. Coca-Cola is thought to be the second most commonly spoken term in the world – the first is OK –

and is of huge value to the company. Other businesses are famous for the physical assets that they own. For example, Eurotunnel, the Anglo-French company, is completely associated with the Channel Tunnel, its prime asset.

Assets – both physical and intangible – are clearly necessary for any business to operate. However, many managers argue that a business's employees are the most important assets that an enterprise possesses.

There are several reasons why business managers hold this view.

- Employees can be creative. The team working for Microsoft has been endlessly ingenious in designing a range of computer software products that have made the company one of the largest and wealthiest in the world. Microsoft announced in 2005 that its quarterly profits had doubled following rising sales of its Windows operating system and its Xbox games console.

- Employees can satisfy consumers' demands and create a reputation for high-quality products. Lotus, the sports car manufacturer, prides itself on designing innovative and unconventional cars for customers whose passion is driving. To achieve this reputation for excellence, Lotus is heavily reliant on the high-quality design, engineering and assembly skills of its employees.

- For many service businesses – such as banking, restaurants and hairdressing – the staff's skills determine the customers' experience to a great extent. There is no point in locating a restaurant in a beautiful building and staffing it with poorly skilled chefs and shoddy waiting staff. Diners are unlikely to enjoy their experience.

- Employees represent a major knowledge base for most organisations. In recent years, many businesses have attempted to cut costs by slimming down workforces and by cutting numbers of middle-ranking managers in particular. One of the consequences of this downsizing has been a reduction in the pool of knowledge and experience shared by the remaining employees, and this has affected the quality of management decision-making in some companies.

- All businesses can only achieve aims and objectives with the help of their employees. The example of Renault (opposite) illustrates the importance of planning the numbers and types of employees required when taking any major strategic decision. This process is known as workforce planning.

What this unit covers

This unit examines the roles that people can play in helping the organisation to achieve its goals, and the means by which businesses recruit, train and motivate their staff.

Roles and responsibilities

You will first study the key roles within an organisation and the duties and responsibilities associated with these roles. The unit considers the skills, qualifications and personal qualities required in order to fulfil different job roles effectively, the degree of decision-making and problem-solving involved in each role, and typical terms and conditions of employment.

Staff development and training

The key issue of staff development is explored by explaining the different methods used by businesses to train and develop employees and their appropriateness for different job roles. This includes both on-the-job training and off-the-job training methods, and the accreditation of training by a business organisation.

Motivating employees

It is important for any enterprise to retain its staff, and businesses use a range of financial and non-financial incentives to influence the behaviour and performance of their employees. This unit looks at the ways in which businesses motivate employees, and the legislation that affects and protects the wellbeing of employees. It covers appraisal and performance review processes, and discipline and grievance policies.

The recruitment process

Businesses need to recruit staff for many reasons. You will look at the elements that make up the recruitment process including the key recruitment documents used by businesses, and review the legal, social and ethical issues that govern and influence the recruitment and selection of employees.

The interview process

Finally, this unit reviews the techniques that businesses use to select potential employees from a small group of people who make it through to the final stages of the recruitment process. This covers the different methods of assessment used in the selection of staff, and evaluates the effectiveness of interviews in recruiting and selecting candidates for vacant posts.

Job roles and responsibilities

Setting the scene: working at McDonald's

Each McDonald's restaurant employs a team of 60 or more people that perform a wide range of job roles.

In a typical McDonald's restaurant there are managers, crew members, customer care specialists, party entertainers, maintenance people and, perhaps, trainee business managers. Each job role makes a different contribution to McDonald's overall business, and each involves a range of responsibilities.

For example, this is how McDonald's describes the role and duties of a general manager at one of its large city centre restaurants:

Managing a business as large and complex as this involves financial, marketing and operational know-how, as well as a talent for team-building.

Running a McDonald's restaurant is commercial management in its fullest sense. As a restaurant manager, you'll set targets, plan budgets, control stock, recruit, train and inspire your team, create and drive marketing campaigns and build bridges with the local community. Put simply, your ideas, initiative and personality will shape your restaurant.

Source: www.mcdonalds.co.uk

KEY TERMS

Managers plan and co-ordinate activities within a business.

Supervisors and **team leaders** take day-to-day responsibility for employees within their work area, ensuring they work effectively and dealing with problems as they arise.

Support staff and other employees have responsibilities defined in their job role. They provide functional support to the business and essential specialist services to enable the business to work effectively.

Authority is the power to act within a business. Managers have the authority to take decisions within their area of responsibility.

Responsibilities are the duties that come with a particular job function or position.

Job roles

Businesses need to have a range of job roles in order to function effectively. Each job role is different. Our jobs are differentiated through:

- the type of job we do
- the level of responsibility we hold
- the level of authority we have
- the extent to which we make decisions
- the type of work we do.

If a business is to perform successfully, it is essential that it creates an appropriate mix of job roles. The roles that people play within the business are critical to its success. Figure 2.1 shows a simplified set of job roles in a limited company, linked by the chain of command.

We will use this categorisation to look at the various job roles that exist in a business and the different responsibilities that are associated with each role.

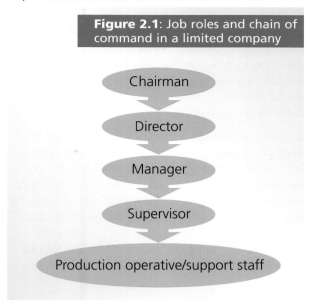

Figure 2.1: Job roles and chain of command in a limited company

Chairman

Director

Manager

Supervisor

Production operative/support staff

1 Directors

Directors are appointed by the shareholders of a business to control and manage the activities and affairs of the business. The role of directors is largely strategic; they have to identify opportunities and set corporate objectives for the business. The board of directors usually appoints one of its members to act as chairman.

2 Managers

A manager has a variety of activities to carry out. As Figure 2.2 shows, these activities can be grouped

under four main functional headings: planning, organising, motivating and controlling. These groupings indicate broadly what managers do in practice. They can be applied to supervisory and junior management positions as well as to middle and senior management roles.

3 Supervisors

A supervisor provides a link between a manager and the operatives and support staff. They are classed as the first line of management, taking on some management functions through delegation of authority.

With the move towards flatter organisational structures, more organisations are passing authority lower down the organisational structure. This process – known as delayering as it involves stripping away layers of middle management – has resulted in many supervisory and junior managers being given more responsibility and authority.

The responsibilities of a supervisor include:

■ controlling the day-to-day work of operational and support staff

■ decision-making in respect of issues that may arise on a day-to-day basis

■ monitoring the work that their staff do to ensure targets are being met

■ advising management of any problems that arise in the work of the business

■ taking corrective action to get back on target if there are any shortcomings.

Figure 2.2: Four key management activities

Planning

A plan is a design for achieving something. Strategic plans – planning for the long term – are usually made at higher levels of management. Tactical plans, such as setting budgets or planning a marketing campaign, have more of a short-term focus and are made at lower levels in the business, such as middle management or supervisor levels.

Organising

In implementing plans, managers need to decide on the activities that need to be undertaken and allocate responsibilities to their staff. This involves allocating staff and resources in order to carry out tasks and achieve the objectives.

Motivating

In order to achieve the goals and objectives of the business, managers have to gain the commitment and co-operation of employees. Managers need to demonstrate leadership to ensure that employees work towards the business's objectives.

Controlling

Managers have to evaluate the effectiveness of work undertaken by employees for whom they are responsible. This requires monitoring performance against required standards and taking corrective action where improvements need to be made.

job profile: Kitchen supervisor

As a kitchen supervisor in a hotel or restaurant, you may be in charge of particular areas of the kitchen. For example, you may be a section chef, an under-chef or sous chef.

Kitchen supervisors are trained chefs or cooks who organise and oversee the work done by their team. They make sure that the food is prepared and produced at the right quality, the right price and the right time. They plan menus, order food and keep control of the budget.

Kitchen supervisors and managers decide which tasks are to be done each day and delegate these to members of their team. They produce duty rotas, making sure that enough staff will be on duty at all times. They also deal with health and safety issues and disciplinary matters.

Source: www.learndirect-advice.co.uk

stopandthink

In what way does the role of the supervisor differ from that of a manager? Think about the degree of decision-making and problem-solving involved in each of these two job roles. To what extent do you think they differ?

4 Operational and support staff

The job role of other employees in a company depends on the type of business in which they are working. For example, operational staff may be working on a production line in a manufacturing plant or as retail assistants within a shop. Operational employees have lower levels of authority than a supervisor, and the type of work they do is usually routine in nature.

Problem-solving tends to be based on everyday situations that may occur in their work; decision-making is at a low level. For example, a retail assistant may have to deal with the return or exchange of goods in a shop. Any significant issues that may arise will be referred up to a supervisor, who has more authority to make decisions.

Support staff provide a specialist service to staff at all levels in a business. Examples of support roles include information technology support, administration and secretarial services. Some support work can be highly specialised and technical. The level of decision-making and responsibility will depending on the extent and nature of the support role. Similarly, pay rates are likely to vary considerably depending on the type of skills required for each support role.

Knowledge summary

- **The roles that people play within the business are critical to its success.**

- **There is a wide variety of job roles in most businesses, each linking to the different levels and parts of the organisation structure.**

- **Directors, managers, supervisors, operational staff and support staff have different responsibilities and job functions.**

- **The level of responsibility in any job role is usually reflected in the terms and conditions of employment, including the pay rate and any associated benefits.**

- **Each job role involves a varying degree of decision-making and problem-solving.**

job profile: Telesales agent, easyJet

Personal qualities

As a telesales agent, you need to be friendly and customer focused, able to remain calm and work efficiently under pressure, be an excellent communicator with people of all ages and of different cultures, and be able to take direction and accept feedback.

Responsibilities

You will be responsible for driving sales for the business, and work with other members of the telesales team to ensure that all calls are responded to in line with policy guidelines.

Skills and qualifications

You are expected to be fluent in written and spoken French (to A-level standard, or to be a native speaker); to be fluent in written and spoken English; to have a good general standard of education to GCSE level or equivalent, to be prepared to work flexible hours including some weekends and evenings, and to have excellent keyboard skills.

Source: www.easyjet.com

job profile: Store manager, B&Q

B&Q offers a "fast track" management development programme, which can lead to new entrants becoming store managers at one of the company's retail stores.

Responsibilities

Managing a group of team leaders who each control their own department in the store, and responsible for achieving sales targets, staff development and appraisals. Managers are accountable for driving sales and exceeding profit targets, developing and implementing business plans, and communicating targets and objectives to their team.

Skills and personal qualities

The ability to handle many tasks at once, and to be able to prioritise effectively and decisively. Mentoring and supporting teams, sound interpersonal skills.

Experience

Applicants should have previous retail management experience.

Terms and conditions

Store managers at B&Q receive £25–£35,000 plus bonus, profit share bonus and a benefits package.

Source: www.diy.com

A Suggest why easyJet insists on these minimum requirements for the telesales agent job.

B Explain how this job role can be classed as a support function.

C Compare the telesales job to that of a store manager of B&Q. What differences are there in the responsibilities of the two roles?

D How might the terms and conditions of employment differ between the two job roles?

Training and development

Setting the scene: reasons for training

Why do many businesses put money into training programmes? Why do they invest in staff development? What methods and approaches do they use?

These are questions that we will consider in this topic. But first note that not all businesses place a high priority on training. As the news clipping shows, many people think that companies do not take enough responsibility for training their staff.

So why does a business train its staff? There are many reasons why a business should train and develop its workforce:

- to ensure staff are fully able to meet the needs of the job role
- to motivate staff to deliver the organisation's objectives
- to adapt and respond to change
- to avoid the costs of lost business opportunities
- to reduce wastage and re-work costs
- to be able to maintain a competitive advantage in the market
- to help staff to meet their potential
- to raise staff morale – people prefer to be creative, innovative, adaptable and productive
- to retain staff.

Source: news.bbc.co.uk, 16 November 2004

Firms 'must train or face fines'

Most people in Britain agree that employers who do not train their workers properly should be fined by the government, a survey suggests.

Some 59 per cent think companies cannot be relied upon to take responsibility for improving skills, the Association of Colleges says. Of the 2,045 people interviewed in England, Wales and Scotland, 74 per cent were in favour of fines.

KEY TERMS

Training is the process of imparting new skills.

Development is the process of consolidating new skills and building them to greater levels.

On-the-job training takes place in the normal work environment.

Off-the-job training takes place away from the normal work environment.

Induction training is given to new employees.

Accreditation is a formal endorsement of training – often overseen by an independent body and marked by awarding a certificate upon successful completion of a course.

Training methods

There are many methods available to develop and train individuals and teams. A business needs to decide which methods best suit its specific purposes, taking into account cost, convenience and the fact that some methods are better suited to particular training needs or circumstances.

In all cases, however, one of the first decisions a business needs to take is whether to provide on-the-job or off-the-job training, or a combination of the two approaches. Figure 2.3 shows the advantages and disadvantages of each approach.

	Advantages	Disadvantages
On-the-job training	■ easy to organise ■ relatively inexpensive ■ job-specific ■ adaptable to meet the needs of the trainee	■ disruptive in the work environment ■ reliant on the trainer having specialist skills and knowledge to pass on to the trainee
Off-the-job training	■ run by a specialist trainer ■ training is intensive and focused ■ no workplace distractions ■ new theories and ideas can be considered ■ trainee exposed to new people	■ possible lack of relevance of the training back at work ■ may be difficult to apply training in the workplace ■ costly ■ disruptive – removes employees from their normal place of work

On-the-job training

On-the-job training, as the name suggests, uses the workplace as the learning tool. Methods like job shadowing, job rotation, sitting with Nellie, coaching, mentoring and computer-based training can be delivered on-the-job. Training tends to be practically focused – centred, for example, on learning a skill or a procedure – and trainees benefit from be able to learn from experienced work colleagues. Figure 2.4 shows the rich variety of ways in which work-based learning can be delivered.

Coaching

Coaching is an on-the-job method of training that involves regular informal meetings between the manager and the employee. Discussion of

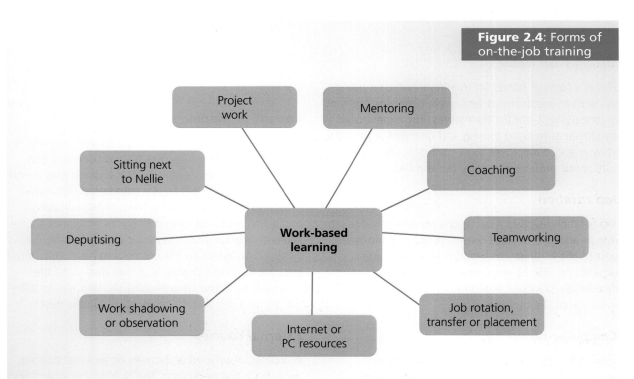

Figure 2.4: Forms of on-the-job training

- Project work
- Mentoring
- Sitting next to Nellie
- Coaching
- Deputising
- **Work-based learning**
- Teamworking
- Work shadowing or observation
- Internet or PC resources
- Job rotation, transfer or placement

performance takes place, allowing the manager to identify any strengths or weaknesses in the employee's performance at work. This will highlight the employee's potential for promotion and any skill gaps that may be met through further training and development opportunities.

Mentoring

Mentoring formalises a method of on-the-job training that has been used in a more informal way for years. The employee is allocated a mentor in the workplace, who acts as adviser to the employee and passes on their own experiences and personal knowledge.

Mentoring can be cost effective and it is less disruptive than off-the-job training as it takes place while the employee is working. However, as a training method it relies on each mentor's knowledge and experience, so it is essential to select mentors carefully. It can be difficult to ensure that mentors provide the right quality of training required by the employee.

Job shadowing

This type of on-the-job training involves trainees observing the work of an experienced member of staff. As trainees observe the experienced worker, they can ask questions and watch how daily situations are handled in that area of work. It enables trainees to see at first hand what the job entails, and to see if the job roles match their expectations. Unlike "sitting with Nellie", this observational approach does not involve any practical, hands-on experience in the job they are being trained to do.

Sitting with Nellie

This is a form of hands-on training in which a trainee sits with an experienced employee, observing the task before trying it out for themselves. The experienced employee is on hand to help and give advice until the inexperienced employee feels confident and sufficiently proficient to carry out the task unaided.

Job rotation

Job rotation involves moving employees from one job role to another, or from one work area to another part of the business, to broaden their skills and experience. This enables employees to become more flexible, as they gain experience in a variety of job roles within the business.

Computer-based training

Many training resources are now available as PC resources (for example, on CD-ROMs) or on the internet. This has the benefit that the training materials can be accessed at convenient times, as and when they are wanted by employees.

Computer-based training is now commonly used to provide employees with details about new products that they need to be familiar with in their workplace, or as part of a programme to develop specific skills such as time management. Computer-based training may also be provided off the job, with more time-consuming packages likely to be studied away from the workplace, perhaps in a separate training room.

Off-the-job training

Off-the-job approaches allow individuals time away from the workplace to undertake development or training. In-house training, such as induction, external courses, placements, bought-in training, simulations and workshops are often delivered in this way.

Off-the-job training can be delivered in-house, by the company's own trainers or by consultants delivering training at a room or centre on the company's premises, or externally, by attending a course run by an external provider such as a local college or a training company.

In-house training

Some companies arrange their own training programmes, often run by someone within the business who has the skills and experience to offer the training to other members of staff. The training may take place in a training room within the workplace or, particularly in larger businesses, there may be a dedicated training centre to which employees may travel in order to take company-run training courses.

Bought-in training

If a business is not able to provide its own training, it may buy in training expertise from a company that specialises in training delivery. This training may be off the shelf: the business buys a standard programme that has been prewritten by the training company, and a trainer is sent in to deliver the programme. Alternatively, the business might choose a bespoke programme, enabling the business to have some input into the design of the training that they want the company to deliver. This enables the business to tailor the training programme to meet its specific needs.

External courses

A business may send employees on external courses away from the workplace. This may be because it isn't practical to deliver off-the-job training on business premises or at a company's training centre, or because the external training provider offers a better course than could be provided in-house.

External courses include study at a college or university to obtain skills and qualifications relevant to job roles within the business. For example, a business may send employees to a college to take NVQ or management qualifications that equip them with the skills and knowledge they need to perform their job role effectively. External courses could also include distance learning programmes requiring attendance at some study days in order to achieve the qualification.

Placements

Placements involve an employee taking time out of their current job role to spend time working in a different business, or a different part of their current business, to learn about a new job role, or to work within a different environment to their own.

Simulations

Simulations may be used to train people in specific situations. For example, a simulation exercise may be used to train people in first-aid techniques. Simulation exercises often form part of a wider training event, to help to develop and reinforce knowledge and skills in a specific area.

Induction training

Induction training is a specific type of off-the-job training. Its purpose is to help a new employee settle down quickly into the job by becoming familiar with the people, the surroundings and the business. Without this training, it has been proved that new recruits tend to leave the business earlier, and overall staff retention rates are lower than in a business that provides an effective induction course.

According to Businessballs, a free on-line development resource for people and organisations:

> Induction training is more than skills training. It's about the basics that seasoned employees all take for granted: what the shifts are; where the noticeboard is; what's the routine for holidays, sickness; where's the canteen; what's the dress code; where are the toilets. New employees also need to understand the organisation's mission, goals and philosophy, personnel practices, health and safety rules, and of course the job they're required to do, with clear methods, timescales and expectations.

(source: www.businessballs.com/traindev.htm).

stop and think

Philip attended an external training course to learn the skills he needed to become a wheelwright. What are the benefits of attending an external training course? What are the disadvantages of this type of training? Consider any on-the-job methods of training that could have been used to train Philip effectively in these skills. What are the potential benefits of training on the job?

Wheel turns on family tradition

Renewed interest in rural crafts could mean the industry overtakes farming as the biggest contributor to the rural economy within 15 years, a study by the government's Countryside Agency suggests.

Philip Gregson, 21, is one person working in rural crafts as he continues a family tradition of wheelwrighting. His great-grandfather, grandfather, father and uncles were all wheelwrights.

He is one of 30,000 rural craftspeople working today. After taking a one-year training course at Herefordshire College of Technology when he was 19, he has set up his own business.

Source: Adapted from news.bbc.co.uk, 17 November 2004

Mixed approaches

Some training, such as apprenticeships and national vocational qualifications (NVQs), can involve an element of both on-the-job and off-the-job training, where work-based learning is supplemented with attendance at a college, say for one day a week.

National vocational qualifications (NVQs)

Employees gain these occupational qualifications by demonstrating that they are competent to carry out a range of tasks connected with their occupation. Assessment is based on evidence that an employee collects from their place of work rather than through test or exercises in a classroom or laboratory.

Ranging from NVQ level 1 through to 5, they are nationally recognised awards and developed to meet the needs of all groups of employees, from operator, through to supervisor and senior manager.

Apprenticeships

Apprenticeships acknowledge the length of time taken to develop sufficient skills, knowledge and experience to be able to work effectively in a trade. Apprenticeships blend on-the-job and off-the-job training activities over a period of typically 2–4 years, providing time for an apprentice to receive a wide range of practical experiences and a vocational qualification.

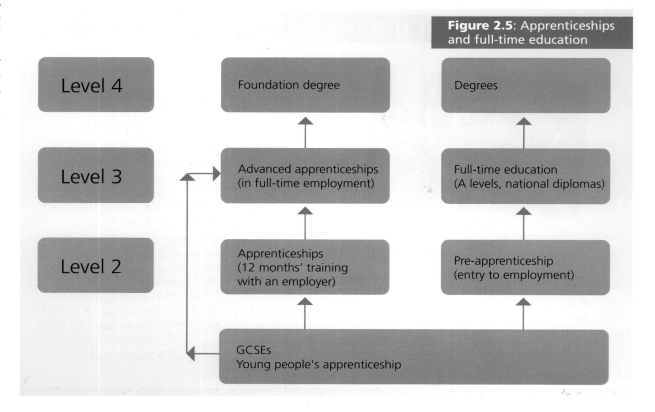

Figure 2.5: Apprenticeships and full-time education

The government backs an apprenticeship scheme (called modern apprenticeships until May 2004) that provides young people with the opportunity to learn on the job while working towards vocational qualifications. Figure 2.5 shows the link between the apprenticeships and full-time education, and the different pathways that can be followed.

There are over 180 different types of apprenticeship on the government-backed programme, available in 80 industry sectors from business administration and customer service to specialist areas such as engineering. Although the scheme is supported by the government, each apprentice is taken on by an individual employer and the relevant training is designed by business. The scheme's website (www.realworkrealpay.info/employer) sets out the business benefits of employers taking on apprentices.

> Apprentices make a contribution to the business from day one; they learn while they work, so their knowledge is up to date. And because their training is on the job, the practical skills they gain are the ones that are right for the business.

> Apprenticeships can help businesses. They are established qualification that can be trusted. Unlike many training courses, apprenticeships ensure that young people have the practical skills to do the job.

stop and think

Over the next five years, 50 per cent of British Gas engineering recruits will be on government-backed apprenticeships. A British Gas spokesperson said: "We are judged by how we treat our customers in the home and that, of course, rests with our 7,000 engineers, many of whom begin as apprentices. The advantage of running our courses in-house is that we can instil our own core values, the most important one being our commitment to customer care."

Source: www.realworkrealpay

Find out the key benefits a business such as British Gas can expect to gain through the apprenticeship scheme.

New Deal

The New Deal comprises a number of training and education schemes for different groups of people who are out of work and claiming benefit.

New Deal: aged 18–24 – All people aged 18–24 who have been claiming jobseeker's allowance (JSA) for six months have to participate in the New Deal. Participants first enter the "gateway" for one to four months. This is a period of intensive help and support in finding work, guided by a personal adviser. Participants are then given a number of options, one of which is to take employment with a New Deal employer who receives a subsidy for six months for taking on a trainee

New Deal: older long-term unemployed people This programme for people aged 25 and over who have been unemployed for 18 months or more involves help in finding work and activities such as work experience, help with motivation, and training in workplace skills.

Accreditation of training

Many training courses are approved and accredited by independent external bodies. Anyone completing an accredited course successfully receives a qualification that should be recognised by other employers as well as colleges and universities. Trainees should receive a certificate of achievement indicating that they have completed the course to the defined standard.

Examples of training courses that have accreditation include a wide range of professional qualifications in, for example, accountancy, personnel, marketing, chartered surveying, many business qualifications such as the Diploma in Management and Master of Business Administration (MBA) awards, and all national vocational qualifications (NVQs).

Knowledge summary

- **There is a rich variety of approaches that businesses may use to train their staff, including both on-the-job and off-the-job methods.**

- **Businesses may decide to use accredited training courses approved by an external body. Examples include all national vocational (NVQ) courses.**

- **The training and development opportunities provided by a business will depend on what it wants to achieve in terms of developing the skills of its workforce. Different types of training may be offered to different job roles within the business.**

case study: Corus

Formed in 1999, through the merger of British Steel and Koninklijke Hoogovens, Corus is a leading international steel producer. It has manufacturing operations in many countries, including the UK, the Netherlands, Germany, France, Norway and the USA, and an international network of sales offices and service centres.

The driving force behind Corus's recruitment policy and the company's investment in training and development is the aim to improve competitiveness. Corus strives to be "a true learning organisation", by inspiring staff to invest in their personal development, recruiting people that have the potential to develop, and offering training to allow them to reach their full potential.

People development

Corus believes in recruiting people that have the potential to deliver success to the company, and it offers development to allow people to reach their full potential.

Corus has its own management training college, using an in-house training team called i2i. This training business unit provides training and development courses for staff at all levels – from new starters to senior managers – across all functions. It uses a variety of methods for training, including experimental role play and activity-based learning.

Corus also offers:

- in-house courses, delivered on site, enabling people to be trained and developed in a familiar work environment and relate their learning back to their everyday job role

- government-approved apprenticeship schemes which lead to vocational and academic qualifications following study at a further education college

- a graduate talent development programme, encouraging all graduates to pursue their areas of interest within their career.

Adapted from: www.apprenticeships.org.uk

case study: Clarkson Evans Ltd

Clarkson Evans is a Gloucestershire-based electrical contracting firm. It has contracts with almost all of the UK's premier house builders. The company employs a workforce of nearly 200 and each year turns over in excess of £7.5 million. Training takes place in-house, using a purpose-built modern training centre at the company's headquarters in Gloucester.

Gerald Crittle, a director of Clarkson Evans, explains why the company has developed its own training centre: "To meet customer demand, we needed to expand our workforce, but as there weren't enough qualified electricians available, we decided to train people ourselves [through the government-backed apprenticeship scheme]." The company has identified several advantages of this approach:

■ training can be tailor-made to meet specific business needs

■ individual progress can be monitored and extra tuition provided where required

■ there are very high staff retention and apprenticeship completion rates.

"Having a highly trained, quality workforce undoubtedly has major business benefits," says Gerald Crittle.

"There are high levels of satisfaction and confidence in both our workmanship and customer service, and increased skills help minimise wastage of electrical materials."

This has enhanced the company's business reputation, making it easier to attract applicants for jobs, allowing the company to be highly selective in its recruitment as well as helping it to win extra business.

A What advantages have Corus and Clarkson Evans found from using on-the-job training?

B Why did these companies set up their own in-house training centres?

C What are the major business benefits from the training programmes offered by the two companies?

D Why do you think that both companies have opted to use the apprenticeship scheme within their businesses?

E How might they benefit through using accredited training schemes in their staff development programmes?

Staff motivation and retention

Setting the scene: Argos

Argos recognises that motivated employees perform better, benefiting not only the individuals concerned but the company as a whole. Argos believes that a well thought-out staff incentive programme can help to reduce staff turnover by making staff feel valued.

Argos's business solutions service offers advice on developing motivational programmes for other businesses. Its business-to-business website (www.argos-b2b.co.uk) claims that "whether your staff are in field sales or call centres, we have flexible and tailored solutions that will enable them to choose their own reward from thousands of top branded products".

Rewards offered range from gift vouchers through to a fully managed online reward management programme called The Hive – an online programme which other businesses can buy into and Argos will manage on their behalf – taking out the time-consuming administration associated with running such a benefits scheme.

Why do you think that businesses would want to buy in services such as The Hive? What benefits do companies hope to gain for their businesses from such schemes?

Adapted from www.argos-b2b.co.uk.

The importance of motivation

Consider what happens if people are unhappy in their work: they are unlikely to perform as well as they might, and they are more likely to want to leave, to join a business that offers them a more satisfactory working environment. In contrast, keeping employees happy in their work can help to retain staff, improve performance levels and create the environment that attracts potential new recruits.

Businesses therefore need to ensure that their employees are motivated and there is good morale,

otherwise they can potentially suffer the twin penalties of poor performance and high staff turnover rates. Poor performance can lose business and high staff turnover is extremely costly – the business loses the money invested in staff training and development, it faces loss of performance and disruption if it is short-staffed or lacks people with the right experience, and it must meet the cost of having to recruit new people to fill vacant posts.

Motivational factors

The challenge for companies, therefore, is to find ways of motivating their staff to stay in the business and to perform to the best of their ability. Motivation of people in work can be affected by many different factors, from the way they are managed to the environment they work in.

How can we improve the chances that people will feel motivated in their jobs? One key factor affecting motivation and staff retention is the way that people are managed: people don't leave their jobs, they leave their managers. To become an employer that people want to work for, begins with the way that the business recruits its staff and continues with the way in which it treats employees once they are working in the business. Employers should look for indications that staff are dissatisfied at work (see Figure 2.6).

KEY TERMS

Motivation is the desire, interest or drive to want to work.

Staff retention measures a business's ability to retain its staff.

Delegation involves giving authority to lower levels of management so they have the power to use the business's resources to produce and deliver goods and services. For example, authority could be delegated to supervisors by their manager enabling them to allocate staff duties or have some control of a budget.

Empowerment is an approach to managing people which permits team members to exercise greater decision-making in day-to-day work matters.

Indicator	Explanation
Turnover of staff	When staff are dissatisfied, they are more likely to leave the business. They may also demonstrate this by withdrawing from the job rather than moving with their feet, putting in minimal work effort before eventually leaving the company.
Attitude and work performance	There is likely to be a negative attitude to work when staff are dissatisfied.
Mental health (general wellbeing)	Dissatisfied staff are more likely to suffer poor health; there may be an increase in sickness absence.
Interpersonal relationships	There may be some friction and ill feeling between staff resulting from their dissatisfaction with work.

Of course, it is important to offer the right incentives, and businesses use a variety of financial and non-financial motivators to create a benefits package. They can offer a variety of financial motivators on top of (or as an alternative to) basic pay:

■ piece rate – payment per item produced that meets a defined standard

■ commission – an additional payment made if a sales target is achieved or exceeded

■ bonuses – flexible performance-related occasional payments aimed at motivating staff to work harder.

Companies can also offer a range of non-financial motivators such as:

■ fringe benefits – company car, cheap travel, holidays, vouchers

■ good conditions of work – hours of work, holidays, flexibility

■ prospects – opportunities for development, promotion and interest in the job.

But, as we suggest above, motivating staff isn't just about incentives, it has much to do with the way employers treat and manage staff. Figure 2.7 suggests methods of treating and managing staff to encourage motivation. Consider how a shop manager, for example, could use the ideas presented in Figure 2.7 to help manage and motivate the shop assistants.

Figure 2.7: Ways of encouraging staff motivation

Give your staff	Purpose
Responsibility	Empower staff to carry out decision-making within the job role. Delegate control and responsibility to your team leaders or supervisors for managing their team.
Goals	Provide your staff with clear goals that are both challenging and achievable.
Resources	Ensure you provide your staff with the resources they need to carry out their work effectively.
Support	Provide support for your staff, including training and guidance with open and frank communication.
Variety	The very spice of life! Give your staff some element of variety to avoid boredom in their work.
Fairness	Always be seen to be fair. You gain a lot more respect that way and staff will feel valued.
Regular talk time	Through talking on a regular basis, you will soon be alerted to any issues that may affect your staff's short-term performance – and it shows you care!
Encouragement	Encourage your staff to give you feedback and put forward their suggestions. Enable your staff to feel that you trust them and value their opinions.

Management and motivation

How do managers such as Sven-Göran Eriksson motivate their staff and players? Eriksson managed to motivate the England team to qualify both for the 2002 World Cup and Euro 2004. How did he manage to motivate his players to play as a team?

If we look at Maslow's hierarchy of needs, we can learn what factors may be contributing to the lack of motivation of any team. Abraham Maslow suggested that people are motivated by a range of needs which he presented as a hierarchy. He assumed that employees will try to move from one level of need to the next, striving to move up the hierarchy until they reach the higher-order needs. Working from the bottom up, Maslow defined the five levels as:

- physiological (basic life) needs such as air, food, drink, shelter, warmth, sleep – key employment factors here are pay, conditions of work
- safety needs, including the need to seek order during times of change – in work this means protection, security, order, limits and job stability
- belonging and social needs – group or team work, relationships at work
- self-esteem – confidence, achievement, status, prestige, recognition, status (job title, job perks such as a plush office), reputation, responsibility
- self-actualisation – job satisfaction, personal development through growth and fulfilment, control over the work, promotion.

Between 1990 and 2001, England's national team had six different managers. No appointment lasted longer than four years. With such inconsistency, it is hardly surprising that the team's lower-order needs of "safety, security and order" were not being met.

Sven-Göran Eriksson began by taking an active interest in his team. He brought in younger talent, tried out new players and encouraged innovative ideas. From the start, Sven set out to get the best from the outstanding individual talents in his team.

By securing the lower-order needs within the team, Sven had effectively ensured that the players were no longer feeling dissatisfied, which is a key cause of demotivation. As the team has grown, players have felt a greater sense of pride and purpose in playing for England, which meets with Maslow's status and esteem needs. By being encouraged to play to their own strengths, they also start to meet the higher-order self-actualisation need.

If we look at Hertzberg's two-factor theory, we see a further range of factors that affect people's attitudes to their work. Frederick Hertzberg, an industrial psychologist identified two sets of factors that he believes influence job satisfaction: motivators and hygiene factors (see Figure 2.8).

The motivators are factors that managers must focus on if they want their employees to experience job satisfaction and be motivated to work. The hygiene factors are not in themselves sufficient to motivate employees, but are necessary factors to be met in order to prevent dissatisfaction of people in work. In other words, true motivation comes from the motivators, providing the hygiene factors have been addressed. The hygiene factors do not motivate us directly, but they will cause dissatisfaction at work if they are not right.

Hertzberg concluded that hygiene factors such as working conditions do not actually motivate people. Taking the England team as an example, their high salaries did not motivate them to perform better as a team. Whether Sven-Göran Eriksson can find the motivators to take the team to another level remains to be seen.

Figure 2.8: Hertzberg's two-factor theory

Motivators	Hygiene (or maintenance) factors
Achievement – completing a challenging project	Status
Recognition – praise for doing a job well	Job security – length and stability of the employment contract
The work – variety, creativity, the chance to do complete tasks	Relationship with subordinates
Responsibility – accountability, responsibility within job role	Personal life/relationship with peers
Advancement – opportunities for development and promotion	Salary – any financial rewards that are offered
Salary – can be a positive feature	Work conditions – and company policy and administration
	Supervision and relationship with supervisor

Source: The Motivation Handbook, Sarah Hollyforde and Steve Whiddett (CIPD, 2002)

stop and think

Kingfisher is a leading home improvement retailer. In the UK it owns the B&Q chain and Screwfix Direct. Kingfisher offers managers and their teams a competitive salary and bonus scheme, pension scheme, BUPA cover, sharesave scheme, five weeks' paid holiday, an in-store discount card and discounts on motor insurance, cars and holidays.

Why does Kingfisher offer this wide range of benefits to staff? To what extent do you feel it is in the company's interest to do so?

Why is it important for businesses to compete on the range of benefits they offer staff? What aspects of Hertzberg's two-factor theory can you identify in the Kingfisher package?

Knowledge summary

- Staff retention rates are a key indicator of whether a business has got the recruitment and selection process right, and whether staff are motivated and satisfied in their work.

- There are several methods that may be used to motivate employees, involving not just financial and non-financial benefits but the way employers treat and manage staff.

- Frederick Hertzberg's two-factor theory and Abraham Maslow's hierarchy of needs provide two frameworks for understanding what motivates people to work.

data interpretation
Unilever

Unilever is proud of its reputation of being among the UK's most admired employers and best places to work. It is committed to enabling its employees to achieve their full potential.

Unilever has developed a comprehensive and highly competitive employee benefits package including an excellent company pension plan, a sharesave scheme and private medical cover. The company's commitment extends outside of the workplace, through its provision of flexible working policies, career break schemes and progressive maternity policies.

Unilever UK is committed to embracing diversity in the workplace, bringing together a rich mix of people with differing perspectives and from different backgrounds, and placing value on those differences.

> People deliver their best when they feel valued, and when their opinions are welcomed, respected and acted upon. This means everyone in Unilever UK knows they can realise their full potential, which in turn helps us to foster an enterprising and diverse culture within which the very best people want to come and work – making us a magnet for talent.

> All of this not only makes people proud to work for an organisation, it also leads directly to higher performance, and the creation of a special buzz which helps everyone to raise their game, deliver exceptional performance – and enjoy doing so.

Source: www.unilever.co.uk/careers

A Describe the ways in which Unilever UK has provided an environment that motivates its staff. (You may need to get information from the company's website www.unilever.co.uk.)

B Using Maslow's hierarchy, explain how Unilever UK is meeting the needs of its employees.

C Using Hertzberg's two-factor theory, identify which key motivators Unilever UK is committed to providing for its staff.

D Evaluate how the provision of motivators might be different in another type of workplace, such as a restaurant chain.

Topic 3 Staff motivation and retention

Managing performance

Businesses rely on their managers and staff to meet company objectives and, ultimately, to prosper. For all except the smallest businesses, it is necessary to put processes into place in order to operate effectively. In terms of performance management, these processes give a direction for staff – guiding their efforts – and provide feedback on their contribution.

Organisations as diverse as the AA, AstraZenica and universities use performance management systems. Why might they introduce these systems? What benefits might they gain? This topic looks at the processes commonly used by businesses to manage performance – including the discipline procedures that might be used when poor performance is an issue – and sets out some of the benefits to be gained from effective performance management.

Performance management

Performance management covers all the processes and procedures relating to the managing and monitoring of an individual's performance. It covers the setting of performance objectives, appraising performance, discipline and grievance procedures, and payment and reward structures.

Payment and reward structures

Many businesses structure their payment and reward systems around the performance of individual employees or work groups. The aim is to provide financial incentives for good performance. There are several ways of structuring a pay and reward system to include performance-based incentives.

Payment by objectives or management by objectives – Here, a proportion of an individual's salary is dependent upon successful delivery of an agreed number of objectives.

Commission-based salaries – Some businesses pay their sales staff a commission based on the number of sales achieved. The idea is that the sales team is motivated to achieve higher levels of sales. Some jobs operate on a commission-only basis, others offer a low base-level salary plus commission.

Bonus payments – Another system to encourage and therefore manage performance is to offer either

KEY TERMS

Appraisal is an assessment of an individual's progress. As part of an appraisal process, a manager will usually meet with subordinates individually to review their work and agree on future objectives.

A **grievance** is a complaint that an individual worker may have with management.

A **disciplinary procedure** is a formal way of warning a worker officially that he or she is breaking rules or not performing to the standards expected.

team and/or individual bonuses. These systems need to be carefully planned to make sure they are seen as fair and equitable.

Performance appraisal

Many businesses have formal performance appraisal processes. The aim is to provide feedback to individual members of staff on their performance – often against any agreed objectives – over the previous period (typically 6–12 months).

The performance appraisal is the most significant means of identifying individual development needs. During the appraisal interview, new performance objectives are set for the coming period, and a training and development plan is agreed. To do this effectively, appraisal usually involves two processes:

- assessing performance of an individual against some expectations or targets

- looking at capability, the strengths and weaknesses that lie behind the performance.

As there are two parts to the process, the documentation used is often split into separate sections to ensure that both of these processes are reviewed – some businesses hold two separate reviews to ensure this happens.

Although performance appraisal is usually conducted between managers and their direct subordinates, it can involve other personnel. For example, some businesses have opted to use completely open feedback in the form of a multi-input or 360-degree appraisal process. This involves collecting feedback from team members, subordinates, colleagues and customers (internal and, sometimes, external), who each provide their personal view of how they see others perform.

It is important that, whatever process the business decides to use, performance appraisal is fair and just. The performance appraisal process can be very motivating for staff (see Topic 3) if it is carried out well. However, as the following case illustrates, it is essential that the process is not abused by staff.

Personal development plans

Businesses may include a further document within the performance appraisal, the personal development plan. This is not an integral part of an appraisal form, but a live and current document used by individuals themselves.

A personal development plan may include:

- training needs – arising as a result of the performance appraisal or highlighted through discussion with team members

- skill needs – arising as a result of changes to the job role, as discussed with the individual's line manager or supervisor

- career aspirations – the training and development needs the individual has in order to enhance skills and work towards achieving specific long-term goals

- personal development needs – any training and development the individual would like to be able to have if opportunity arises.

Managing poor performance

When an individual is working below the level expected, the business needs a process to manage poor performance. It is typically part of the disciplinary process of the business. Performance could be seen as poor for a number of reasons:

- a reduction over time of the work effort and performance in the job

- failure to adapt to a change of role or work practice

- a specific incident that has occurred with significant implications

- an action that is inconsistent with the values of the business.

Disciplinary procedures are often thought of as a means of enforcing rules and regulations within an organisation. However, they should also be followed where there is a fall in the expected standard of performance of an employee.

An effective disciplinary process will have the ethos of natural justice and will, where possible, try to improve the individual's performance. It will usually have a number of steps:

- investigation of the facts and collection of evidence

- communication of the "charge" to the member of staff involved

- a hearing to discuss the case

- a remedy, which could be a verbal warning, a written warning, a final written warning or dismissal.

Look on the Advisory, Conciliation and Arbitration Service's website www.acas.org.uk. Find information on the ACAS code of practice on disciplinary practice and procedures in employment. How might use of a disciplinary procedure help to ensure that an individual improves their work performance? What additional support might a business offer in order to improve an individual's performance?

HELPLINE 08457 47 47 47

acas

Search our site [____] GO

| Home | A-Z of work | Training | Other Services | Policy & Research | Contact Us | About Us |

You are here: Home

Current Features:

> **What's New**
Latest Acas news and websites updates.

> **News Release**
Acas calls for employers to beat skills shortages by making the most of older workers.

> **New Advice Leaflet**
Acas today launched its new advisory leaflet Employing Older Workers.

Acas aims to improve organisations and working life through better employment relations. We provide up-to-date information, independent advice, high quality training and we work with employers and employees to solve problems and improve performance.

Quick Links:

> **Rights at work**
Get the facts before there is an issue.

> **E-learning**
Six new free online learning packages to help organisations on:
- absence in the workplace
- redundancy handling

> **Training sessions**
Acas offers training for businesses of all sizes on key employment issues. Book online for a session near you.

> **Our publications**
Available here to view, print and order online.

> Employment forms

Grievance procedures

If an employee has cause to complain about something that happens at work, he or she needs a means of dealing with the problem. By having a grievance procedure, a business can ensure that employees have a mechanism that they can use to air their problems and sort them out.

A grievance procedure can help to prevent a minor disagreement from sparking off a major conflict and can improve employee retention. Without a procedure, disgruntled employees may feel that they have no option but to vote with their feet and leave the business. A grievance procedure can therefore play an essential part in the motivation and retention of staff.

The grievance procedure should:

- be in writing

- be clear as to whom employees should take any grievances to in the first instance

- give the employee the right to be accompanied by a colleague or trade union representative

- state who the grievance may be referred to should it remain unresolved

- specify time limits in which the complaint should be dealt with

- ensure that all grievance meetings are properly minuted with records sent to all concerned parties.

Find out what a performance management system might look like – either through looking at documentation from a business or from investigating through the internet for examples of performance management systems and documentation. What features do they have? How successful do you think they would be in terms of motivating the staff to perform well?

Knowledge summary

- **Performance management includes the setting of performance objectives, appraising performance, and payment and reward structures.**

- **Appraisal is a formal process during which individuals receive feedback on their performance against work objectives.**

- **Businesses need a process to manage situations in which individuals are working below expected levels. Poor performance is typically handled by a business's disciplinary process.**

- **A grievance procedure is used if an employee has cause to complain about the business. Such a procedure can help to prevent a minor disagreement becoming a major conflict, and can improve employee retention.**

Performance management in practice

These articles explore the importance of performance management within business. They are extracts from Chartered Institute of Personnel and Development (CIPD) press releases.

How to make your people feel they're more than just numbers

A classic story about appraisal is that a boss stopped at a set of traffic lights, wound down his window and shouted at an employee in the car next to him: "It's performance appraisal time – I'll put you down for a '3' . . . OK?" This is obviously the worst kind of performance management – pointless and demotivating. Yet there is clear evidence that people perform best when they know what is expected of them and when they are given support, resources and development.

Effective performance management is all about putting these principles into practice. Unfortunately there are so many different systems and techniques available that even experienced practitioners are often unsure about which are the most appropriate.

In order to develop an effective system, businesses need advice, for example, on how to define performance measures and agree objectives, carry out performance and development reviews, and address performance problems and discipline underperformers. They need to offer motivational training to both appraisers and appraisees and constantly evaluate and improve the whole system.

At its best, performance management can boost team cohesion, increase employee commitment and job satisfaction, and promote a climate of openness while streamlining corporate results. At its worst, it can become just a meaningless box-ticking exercise completed by resentful employees.

Source: www.cipd.co.uk, 28 August 1998

Line managers are key to good performance management

Over 95 per cent of employers see the performance management process as an essential tool in the management of organisational culture. It can make the difference between a good company and a great company. But organisations must ensure line managers have the tools, skills and understanding to manage performance effectively.

Good performance management is about ensuring managers manage their staff well and, in particular, ensuring that people understand how they fit into the organisation, regularly communicate what is expected of them and support their development.

Angela Baron, author of *Performance Management*, says: "Performance management is a powerful tool that can raise the performance of individuals and the organisation as a whole. But success, or failure, depends on the line managers. If they recognise the value of performance management in enabling them to meet their targets and objectives, they are likely to be more positive about it."

Source: www.cipd.co.uk, 27 October 2004

A Explain the importance of performance management to businesses.

B What effect might a poor performance management process have on the staff in a business? How might problems be avoided?

C How does the performance management system link into development of the individual?

D What impact can an effective performance management system have on an organisation? In what way is the line manager involved in the system?

E If an organisation has a performance management system in place, would it still need a discipline and grievance procedure? Explain your answer.

The recruitment process

Setting the scene: Airbus

Airbus is the world's leading aircraft manufacturer, and the company received a total of 370 firm orders in 2004. Two orders for new aircraft came from Eurofly and JetBlue.

Eurofly orders Airbus A319 long-range aircraft

Italian leading charter carrier Eurofly has signed a contract for one A319 long-range aircraft and plans to acquire a second, becoming a new customer for the Airbus Corporate Jetliner (ACJ) family.

JetBlue orders 30 A320s

New York-based low-fare carrier JetBlue Airways has ordered 30 new Airbus A320s. Like the rest of the airline's extensive A320 fleet, they will be powered by International Aero Engines V2500s. Deliveries of the newly contracted aircraft will begin in 2006 and run through 2011. To date, JetBlue orders for Airbus aircraft total 173.

For Airbus, increased demand can mean there is a need to recruit additional staff in order to fulfil new orders. Look at the two press cuttings. What effect will these new order have on the demand for staff in Airbus? Do you think that this is likely to generate a long-term or short-term need? How do you think a company like Airbus can effectively recruit the staff it needs without risking long-term overstaffing?

Reasons for recruiting staff

Why do vacancies occur in businesses? There could be several reasons a business needs to recruit more employees. Certainly demand is one factor, as is the case at Airbus. An increase in orders may be linked to other business activities such as a proactive advertising and promotion campaign.

However, it is vital that a business uses information about any changes in its commercial environment – and internal changes within the business – to accurately project the quantity and quality of human resources that will be required. This assessment of employee demand is part of the process is known as human resource planning.

Businesses have to look particularly closely at any external factors that may affect their demand for staff in the future. There is a range of political, economic, social and technological influences which might increase (or decrease) the need for staff within a business.

At the political level, for example, if new employment laws limit the number of hours employees can work each week – say, an extension of the European Union's working hours directive – then a business might need to recruit more staff. Conversely, if more people expect and want to work past the traditional retirement age, a business might need to recruit fewer staff as its older workers choose to stay on.

KEY TERMS

Recruitment involves looking in the right places to find the best staff for the business.

Selection is the process of choosing the best staff from those who apply.

The government is committed to removing age discrimination at work. Find out more about the government's campaign by visiting www.agepositive.gov.uk. What are the aims of the campaign?

In what ways might age discrimination affect young people in the workplace? What do you think will be impact be of anti-age discrimination legislation on (a) a small business employing fewer than 20 staff and (b) a large, private-sector business in the transport sector.

Age on the agenda

Marks and Spencer, Sainsbury and Tesco along with B&Q are actively employing people in their 50s. There's a hard-edged business case for companies to employ older workers. We are actually moving towards full employment as a social trend in the UK and staff involved in recruitment will have to look at stopping discriminating on any grounds, because the pool of available people is getting smaller and smaller.

People Management, 17 June 2004

Wider societal trends in both employment and age demographics can have a wider impact on recruitment policy. Issues such as age, welfare and diversity may affect the number, and quality, of potential employees that a business is seeking to reach.

Changes in the economic environment may generate an increase (or a decrease) in demand for a business's products, and therefore have staffing implications. For example, an increase in income tax rates would lower consumers' disposable income and dampen demand for certain goods and services. Conversely, a cut in interest rates could raise consumer confidence, boost the housing market and lead to increased demand.

New technology can have a considerable impact on staffing levels. If the implementation of new technology into a business leads to efficiency gains, a company might be able to reduce staff. Conversely, the new technology may enable the company to produce better-quality goods, generating an increase in demand which may require additional staff. Advancing technology – and changing consumer demands – also create a need for new skills. A business may try to meet this need on a temporary basis – hiring consultants or freelance subcontractors to fill skill gaps – or it may need to recruit new staff or retrain a substantial part of the workforce.

In order to meet changes in demand for employees, businesses try to achieve flexibility in the workforce. This can be achieved through various measures:

- new contractual arrangements – short-term rather than permanent contracts

- flexible hours contracts – employees agree to a specified number of "floating" hours which they can be called upon to work at the request of the business

- annual hours contracts – employees are contracted to work a given number of hours over a 12-month period, enabling the business to meet fluctuations in consumer demand by varying staff hours from week to week

- flexitime arrangements – employees can choose the start and finish times of their working day provided a specified number of hours are worked and core times are covered

- shift work – enabling a business to operate longer production hours

- teleworking – employees are contracted to work from home, enabling the business to reduce some of the costs associated with hiring office space.

In April 2005, MG Rover went into receivership, halting production at the company's Longbridge plant. The move followed the breakdown of talks between MG Rover and the Chinese car manufacturer SIAC. Over 6,000 Rover employees faced redundancy.

What external factors might have contributed to the problems at MG Rover? What effect will the closure of Longbridge and the loss of thousands of skilled jobs have on recruitment within the UK car industry as a whole?

These changes enable businesses to be able to react quickly to changes in customer demand, and to match their staffing levels more closely to peaks and troughs in customer demand. They can improve productivity and reduce costs, enabling them to be more competitive.

Apart from external factors, vacancies may occur within a business for many reasons. These include:

- a member of staff promoted within the business

- a member of staff resigning

- a member of staff retiring, or a death in service

- new posts or new job roles being created

- business expansion or diversity into new markets.

In each case the business has the opportunity to reassess the requirements of the post. Can the job duties be reallocated to other posts, saving the need for recruitment? Other questions that should be asked prior to recruiting to fill the vacancy include:

- has the function of the post changed in any way?

- does it need to be a full-time or part-time post?

- are there any changes in the post's skill needs?

- do the duties and responsibilities of the post need to be amended to reflect changing business needs?

- does the post need filling at all?

The recruitment and selection process

The aim of every recruitment and selection process should be to ensure that the right person is chosen for the job. Failing to do so can have huge adverse implications in terms of organisational effectiveness, staff and individual morale, and staff turnover. Add this to the cost of the recruitment process itself and getting recruitment wrong represents a huge drain on a business's finances. Getting recruitment right represents a worthwhile investment.

A robust, systematic recruitment and selection process is vital to ensure that the right person is found for the job, and unsuccessful applicants are left with a good image of the business and feeling that they have been dealt with fairly throughout. The aim is to:

- recruit staff with appropriate skills and experience

- appoint on an appropriate employment contract

- ensure fairness, and respect equal opportunities

- make recruiters follow structured guidelines

- monitor and review the process regularly

- ensure the process is efficient and cost-effective.

Although each business will have its own procedures, Figure 2.9 shows the stages that make up a robust and fair recruitment and selection process.

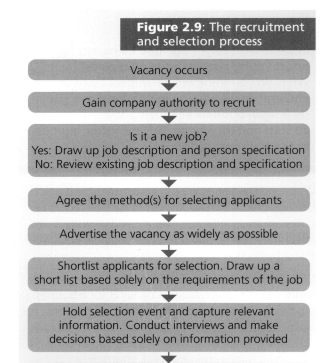

Figure 2.9: The recruitment and selection process

Vacancy occurs

Gain company authority to recruit

Is it a new job?
Yes: Draw up job description and person specification
No: Review existing job description and specification

Agree the method(s) for selecting applicants

Advertise the vacancy as widely as possible

Shortlist applicants for selection. Draw up a short list based solely on the requirements of the job

Hold selection event and capture relevant information. Conduct interviews and make decisions based solely on information provided

Review candidate information against role requirements and person specification to make selection decision

In the rest of this unit, we look at aspects of this process in more detail. Topic 6 reviews the legal, ethical and social issues, while Topic 7 looks at recruitment documentation. Topics 8 and 9 explore the selection event and interviewing techniques.

Knowledge summary

- **Demand for staff is driven by a range of political, economic, social and technological issues.**

- **Businesses have to consider demographic issues such as age, welfare and diversity to ensure they attract a suitable pool of candidates.**

- **It is vital that a robust and fair process is used to ensure that the right person is found for the job.**

These articles provide two contrasting examples of good news on the job front. Both raise a number of recruitment issues.

Rail link to deliver jobs boost

Plans for a £140 million rail link for Glasgow Airport could create more than 600 jobs in the area over the next 10 years, a report has claimed. Economists also believe it would help to lure an extra 52,500 visitors and would contribute towards extra tourism spending worth £10 million per year.

According to Alistair Watson of Strathclyde Passenger Transport "the rail link will help to contribute to the continued growth of Glasgow Airport, which is a major employer".

If the plans are given the green light by MSPs, trains could be running by the end of 2008. Passenger numbers at Glasgow Airport, according to the authorities, are set virtually to double from 8.2 million by 2030.

Source: news.bbc.co.uk, 28 February 2005

Avon calling to sell insurance

Cosmetics firm Avon is recruiting 20,000 sales agents, who may help it sell financial services door to door. As well as the usual lip gloss and perfume, consumers may be offered life and car insurance and credit cards.

The Financial Times reported that Avon was negotiating with potential partners for a marketing push in 2006. However, an Avon spokeswoman later told BBC News that no negotiations had taken place but that it "may go down that route in future".

The firm, which made profits of £18.6 million last year, plans to add to its 160,000 agents over the next five years.

Jerry McDonald, president of Avon UK, said that selling financial services to the firm's large number of female customers could prove profitable. Women often enjoy lower life insurance and car insurance premiums than men, because they are safer behind the wheel and live longer, yet many financial service providers find it difficult to tap into this market.

Source: news.bbc.co.uk, 16 February 2005

A What external factors have caused the potential boost in jobs in and around Glasgow?

B Where would these additional jobs be? Which organisations would need to plan for additional recruitment in these circumstances?

C Explain the reasons that might lie behind the potential boost in jobs for Avon.

D What recruitment and selection process might Avon use to recruit these new agents?

Legal, ethical and social obligations

Setting the scene: drive to recruit ethnic officers

New efforts are being made to increase the percentage of black and ethnic minority officers in Leicestershire's police force.

The county is currently top of the national league table with 5 per cent of the force coming from black and ethnic minority communities, but the Home Office target is 15 per cent.

Chief Constable Matt Baggott officially launched the Breaking Through campaign. He said that the Constabulary "was committed to achieving a workforce that fully reflects the ethnicity and cultural mix of Leicester, Leicestershire and Rutland".

The poster campaign will feature serving Leicestershire police officers. The police force has also planned a number of recruitment events across the county.

Source: adapted from news.bbc.co.uk, 11 October 2004

The legal framework

There is a wide range of legislation that exists to protect employees. This is designed to ensure that employers observe their responsibilities – relating particularly to avoiding discrimination and respecting equal opportunities – both to existing staff and to applicants during recruitment.

There is legislation covering sex discrimination, employment equality (religion or belief, sexual orientation) regulations, disability discrimination and employment protection. There is also a further range of legislation designed to protect the wellbeing of employees, such as restricting the number of hours they work in a week, setting the minimum wage that can be paid to employees, and regulations with regard to leave arrangements. In this topic, we explore some of the legal framework surrounding the employment of people in businesses.

A business must ensure that it follows its legal and ethical responsibilities relating to discrimination and equal opportunities when recruiting staff. This includes job advertisements. Once appointed, the business must continue to abide by the legislation.

In short, this means that employers have legal as well as ethical responsibilities both to prevent discrimination in the work place as well as to apply equal opportunities policies in the recruitment and selection process. This does not mean that

Source: timesonline.co.uk, 27 Feb 2005

Move to give women parity

Companies are likely to be forced to carry out equal pay reviews for female staff. A woman's right to earn the same as a man may be enforced by "equality police" in the office with firms being forced to carry out equal pay reviews.

A draft copy of the Women and Work Commission's paper says companies could be made to carry out compulsory pay reviews to force them to narrow the pay gap between men and women.

It argues that radical measures are needed to plug this pay differential, more than 40 per cent for part-time workers and 18 per cent for full-time employees.

stop and think

Cherie Blair, the employment lawyer, has privately argued in favour of "naming and shaming" firms that fail to respect equal pay law. What might be the impact of this policy? How is it likely to change a firm's behaviour?

organisations are unable to apply some positive discrimination measures in certain circumstances. For example, the recruitment campaign by Leicestershire police (featured opposite) is, perhaps not surprisingly, lawful. Organisations can run positive recruitment campaigns where there is a low proportion of a particular group employed by the business.

Figure 2.10 shows the range of anti-discrimination legislation now in place in the UK. If businesses fail to comply with this legislation, they face both the legal consequences – fines and compensation to the victim – as well as possible claims for civil damages. In addition, they can receive extremely negative press coverage, which can damage their public image and have a negative impact on their trade.

Though most businesses' first response may be that they need to uphold the law to avoid the financial and other negative consequences of noncompliance, they should realise that equal opportunities good practice also brings benefits, including a positive impact on the motivation, retention and recruitment of staff.

Businesses need to be aware that the law is frequently being updated and changed. For example, the UK government has pledged to bring in legislation to tackle age discrimination in employment by 2006, and in 2004 new regulations came into effect to strengthen the law preventing discrimination against disabled people.

From October 2004, it has been unlawful for any employer to discriminate against a disabled person when choosing someone for a job, considering people for promotion, transfer, training, dismissal or redundancy. A disabled person should not be treated less fairly than other workers, or subjected to harassment.

stop and think

A small newsagent is concerned about complying with the new disability legislation. Would the newsagent be expected to adapt the interior of the shop completely so that the business was able to employ a wheelchair user as a counter assistant?

In fact, the disability legislation expects businesses to make changes as far as is reasonably practicable to do so. In this instance, it may be possible for the shop owner to be able to adapt the premises for wheelchair usage at a reasonable cost, therefore the owner would be expected to do so.

Figure 2.10: Key anti-discrimination legislation

Legislation	Purpose
Sex Discrimination Act 1975 (amended)	Sex discrimination covers all aspects of employment, from recruitment to pay, and from training to contract termination. Employers should not discriminate on the grounds of sex, marriage or because someone intends to undergo, is undergoing or has undergone gender reassignment.
Employment Equality (Religion or Belief) Regulations 2003	Designed to protect employees from discrimination on the grounds of all religions and beliefs. All businesses must treat everyone fairly regardless of their religion or belief.
Employment Equality (Sexual Orientation) Regulations 2003	Designed to protect employees on grounds connected with sexual orientation. All businesses must treat everyone fairly regardless of their sexual orientation.
Race Relations Act 1976	Makes it unlawful to discriminate in employment against men or women on the grounds of race, colour or ethnic background.
Equal Pay Act 1970	All businesses must treat employees of both sexes equally; a woman doing the same or comparable job as a man must receive the same pay and have similar working conditions.
Disability Discrimination Act 1995	Makes it illegal for an employer to treat a disabled person less favourably than other staff. Employers are required to make reasonable adjustments to the working environment so that disabled people can be employed or access training opportunities.

The Disability Discrimination Act makes it unlawful for an employer to discriminate against the disabled when applying for a job as well as in employment. This includes avoiding discrimination in application forms, interview arrangements, proficiency tests, job offers and terms of employment. Businesses must consider, therefore, any reasonable adjustments that can be made in the arrangements and location for the interview, testing arrangements, and terms and conditions of employment being offered. Some adjustments are practical, simple and effective: for example, by printing application forms and job descriptions on pastel-coloured instead of white paper makes reading easier for anyone who has dyslexia.

Many small employers find changes in the law difficult. But disability is more common than many think, and it is important that small businesses such as the newsagent realise that disability does not automatically mean a wheelchair user. For example, there are many people who are hearing impaired, and with an induction loop they would easily be able to work in a shop. There are many types of disability: you cannot always tell just by looking at someone whether they are disabled.

Job advertising

In every aspect of recruitment, a business needs to be fully aware of the rights and responsibilities both from the employer's perspective and the employee's. The business needs to ensure that it does not discriminate against the candidate, either through its advertisement, its selection techniques or through the interview itself.

Job advertisements need particular care. The Race Relations Act 1976 makes it unlawful to publish advertisements that discriminate on racial grounds, or to make arrangements for such advertisements. The law recognises two types of discrimination.

Direct discrimination occurs when someone is treated less favourably on racial grounds. Racial grounds include not only grounds of race but also those of colour, nationality, citizenship and ethnic or national origin.

Indirect discrimination occurs when rules, requirements or conditions that appear to be fair — because they apply equally to everyone — can be shown to put people from a particular racial group at a far greater disadvantage than others, and the rules cannot be objectively justified. A racial group may be defined by race, colour, nationality (including citizenship), or national or ethnic origin.

Consider these examples. Are they discriminatory? If so, why?

A job advert asks for ability to speak Bengali

This requirement discriminates indirectly against people who do not speak Bengali, and will be unlawful unless it can be justified by the nature of the job. For example, it would be justifiable to ask for a Bengali speaker if the job involves working with people who can only communicate well in Bengali.

A job advert invites applicants who speak English as their mother tongue

This requirement, too, discriminates indirectly against people who speak English fluently, but not as their mother tongue. This kind of requirement is rarely justifiable. If a high standard of English is needed for a particular job, it would be better to just ask for "a very high standard of written and spoken English" or "fluent English".

Throughout the recruitment process, both the employing organisation and applicants have an ethical obligation, above all, to be honest and objective. The job advert and job description must give a true and accurate picture of the job and the organisation without misleading potential applicants. There is little point in painting an over-attractive picture in order to attract candidates, because if the job does not measure up to what they expect they will soon leave.

Resentment will occur if an applicant who is subsequently appointed to a post discovers that claims and promises made by a business are not actually fulfilled upon appointment. A business has to recognise that such actions might also deter other applicants from applying for future posts.

Fairness and confidentiality are also essential in the recruitment process. It is important that a business follows an objective procedure in order to be fair to every applicant. This should also ensure that the business selects the best candidate for the job, and that no subjective criteria such as personal prejudice have an influence on the selection.

The employer needs to leave candidates in no doubt that they have been dealt with fairly, keeping them informed at all times about what is happening in the recruitment procedure, and providing objective and fair feedback on their applications if they should not be selected to the post. Applicants need to be able to trust that any information provided to the business in their applications is kept confidential.

Knowledge summary

- All employers have to comply with legislation protecting employees at work. There is also legislation covering the recruitment and selection of staff, particularly in relation to discrimination and equal opportunities issues.

- By conducting a systematic, fair and robust recruitment and selection process, a business both ensures that it complies with all relevant legislation and projects a positive image.

data interpretation
Disability rights

The Disability Rights Commission provides guidance on how businesses can comply with the law and take steps to attract more disabled people. Here are some extracts.

Job descriptions/person specifications: These should only include requirements that are clearly related to the duties for that post, otherwise a disabled applicant may be deterred from applying or be inadvertently discriminated against in the selection process. It is essential not to be too specific about "how" the task or duty can be achieved. A good approach is to focus on what the job can accomplish. Including unnecessary – or marginal – requirements in a job specification can lead to discrimination.

Job advertisements: Adverts for jobs should actively encourage disabled people to apply. They should be available in a wide range of formats, such as large print, tape, disk or e-mail. Job details on websites should be accessible to disabled people who use screen-reading technology. Adverts should also be placed where disabled people are more likely to see them including, for example, with the disability employment advisers at jobcentres and in specialist disability magazines.

Applications: Businesses need to take special care that they do not discriminate against disabled people in the way they deal with applications. Adjustments may need to be made such as providing an application form in a different format. It is good practice to give applicants – through standard questions in the job application – the opportunity to say whether any special provisions or facilities are required at interview. It is possible to ask applicants if they are disabled, and whether they will need adjustments to be made in the selection process, or in the job itself.

Selection: Businesses need to ensure that their selection procedures do not disadvantage disabled people at the interview or when completing assessment and selection tests. The job requirements and person specifications need to be justified in relation to the job.

A An employer prefers all employees to have a certain level of educational qualification. A woman with a learning disability which has prevented her from getting the preferred qualification is turned down for a job because she does not have that qualification. Has she been unlawfully discriminated against?

B An employer sets candidates a short oral test. An applicant has a bad stammer, but only under stress. What reasonable adjustment could be made by the employer? In what circumstances would it be right to insist on the oral test?

C Would it be reasonable for an employer to allow a candidate to submit an application in a different format (perhaps by telephone, on tape or typed rather than handwritten) from that specified for candidates in general?

D A business requires that an employee visit customers in their own homes within a local area, and decides to limit recruitment to people who can drive. Would this requirement be considered a reasonable criterion on a person specification for a job? Suggest an alternative criterion that the business might use.

Recruitment documentation

Setting the scene: compiling a CV

Some job advertisements asks you to apply in writing. In these cases, you will need to send both a curriculum vitae (CV) and a covering letter.

Your CV should give any potential employer a profile about you. It should include your qualifications, where you were educated, any work experience you may have had and any interests you may have as well as, in time, details of your working career to date.

There are many resources that provide advice on writing a CV. For example, if you visit the BBC onelife website (www.bbc.co.uk/radio1/onelife), you can find comprehensive advice about CVs by first clicking on "work" and then on "CVs". This site gives you hints and tips on how to complete your CV.

Use the aims and content section of the onelife CV pages to prepare your own CV ready to use in future job applications. Look at the sample job description page of this site. This will advise you on how to pick out key details about the job for which you are applying that you can focus on when preparing your CV and writing a covering application letter.

Key recruitment documents

Businesses use several standard documents in the recruitment and selection process. In this topic, we will consider some of the key documentation used by businesses during recruitment.

1 Authority to recruit

Once it is established that there is a need to fill a vacant post, managers need to know whether there is sufficient budget to cover the cost of the vacancy. Usually decisions on giving budgetary approval for new staff are taken at senior management level, and authority to fill the post must be given before the recruitment process is started.

2 Job descriptions

A job description should be created for every job role. This document should set out the overall purpose of the job and the key tasks and responsibilities of the post. Figure 2.11 shows the five main components of a job description.

Figure 2.11: Structure and components of a job description

Component	Function
Job title	This should be a short descriptive title that explains the nature of the job, such as customer service assistant or senior team leader.
Purpose	Usually a one-sentence summary of why the role exists: for example, to provide customer service support to the retail sales team.
Key tasks	These should be specific activities and described clearly using action words: for example, to co-ordinate, calculate and produce sales reports.
Scope of the role	Gives the boundary of responsibility: that is, who the job holder is responsible to (who they are managed by) and who they are responsible for (who they manage). This section should also list any budgetary responsibilities.
Special requirements	Specific requirements such as shift or flexible work patterns, travelling requirements, essential languages and professional qualifications.

3 Person specifications

An accurate person specification is an essential part of an effective recruitment process. It sets out the criteria needed for effective performance in the job role. It allows selectors to make accurate comparisons between candidates against the specific requirements of the person needed to fill the job role.

There are three essential components to a person specification:

■ essential requirements – requirements without which an applicant could not be considered for the job

■ desirable requirements – it would be good if candidates had these attributes, though they are not required in order to start the job (and they could be subsequently developed through training)

■ contra-indicators – criteria or features which would make any applicant immediately unsuitable for the job: for example, unspent criminal convictions for theft or fraud are contra-indicators for any post that involves handling cash.

It is important to establish how each criterion will be evaluated – for example, by CV, application form, test

or interview. At shortlisting, all applicants who do not meet the essential criteria should be rejected, irrespective of whether or not they meet some or all of the desirable attributes.

4 Job advertisements

All job advertisements should be consistent with the job description and the person specification, which should be prepared well in advance before any position is advertised. All advertisements should be worded to attract suitable candidates who match the essential job and person criteria, and should provide a positive public image of the business.

A business needs to make sure it attracts a sufficient number of suitably qualified applicants to apply for the job. So it needs to advertise in the right places. One of the key decisions a business needs to make is whether to restrict the job to internal candidates or to invite applications from people outside the company. There are benefits in keeping recruitment in-house: it is cheaper, it can be good for staff morale, and all applicants will already be familiar with the business. However, by looking for external applicants, companies will be able to draw from a much wider pool of talent and, obviously, all businesses need fresh blood at some stage. Figure 2.12 shows the options for advertising vacancies.

Figure 2.12: Means of advertising job vacancies

Internal advertisements	External advertisements
On company noticeboards	Newspapers – local or national
In a company newsletter	Contact with schools, colleges and universities
In an internal vacancy bulletin	Specialist magazines
On the premises in the form of a poster	Job centres
E-mail to all (or selected) staff	Internet – company websites Recruitment agencies Recruitment or job fairs Radio and television advertisements

Jobs that require specific skills need to be advertised to ensure they reach the right audience. Much thought has to be given to ensure that an advert is correctly placed to attract the right applicants.

An advertisement should include:

■ job title and job description

■ title and description of the organisation

- location of the work and any travel involved

- type of person required (qualifications/experience)

- pay, conditions, benefits (to be competitive and make the post appealing)

- how to apply (such as complete application form, send in CV and letter of application)

- timescale (closing date for receipt of applications).

The advert could also include other material that might attract a wider net of suitable candidates. For example, it might briefly outline the philosophy of the organisation, its positive attitude to disabled people, or its commitment to family-friendly policies.

In general, the advert should be presented so that it captures readers' attention, arouses interest in the company, creates desire and incites readers to action. A good advertisement will attract prospective candidates but deter those who would be unsuitable to meet the specifications of the job. It is also essential that the job advert conforms with equal opportunities legislation (see Topic 6).

stopandthink

Use the job description and person specification for the office manager in Figures 2.13 and 2.14 to draw up a suitable job advertisement for the post. Suggest three suitable places where the post might be advertised, giving reasons why you have suggested each one.

5 Shortlisting candidates

There are many different methods used by businesses to compile a short list of candidates. Most typically, applicants are asked to return either a curriculum vitae (CV), a competed application form or a letter of application. Sometimes they are asked to supply two, and occasionally all three, of these different means of job application.

These applications are then used to assess the strengths and weaknesses of applicants, which allows the business to draw up a short list to go through to the final stage of the selection process.

At this point, there is a further piece of recruitment documentation used within the interview process – a form for recording and assessing the strengths and weaknesses of each candidate during the interview. This is considered as part of an in-depth look at interview techniques in Topic 8.

Figure 2.13: Job description for office manager post

Position
Office Manager
Salary £18,000

Job role
Responsible for the day-to-day running of the office, and management of one secretary. Will report to the managing director.

Main duties and responsibilities

Manage and deal with supply of office furniture, equipment and stationery

Manage budgets, and record and report on expenditure to the managing director

Carry out administrative tasks in order of priority

Supervise and oversee the work of the secretary

Deal with customer enquiries

Ensure compliance with office lease, office security and health and safety requirements

Oversee the supply of IT and other communication equipment, and ensure that any problems are resolved

Source: Racial equality and the smaller business (www.cre.gov.uk)

Figure 2.14: Person specification for office manager post

Applicants are expected to demonstrate:

- Experience of managing budgets

- The ability to supervise staff and delegate tasks, and to ensure work is completed to the required standard

- Experience of meeting strict and conflicting deadlines, under pressure

- The ability to communicate accurately and persuasively with colleagues, customers and suppliers

- Knowledge of suppliers of office IT equipment, and experience of drawing up contracts

- Experience of managing office facilities, including health and safety requirements

Source: Racial equality and the smaller business (www.cre.gov.uk)

Unit 2 People in business

Knowledge summary

- Key documents used in the recruitment and selection process include the job description, person specification, job advertisement and a form for assessing the strengths and weaknesses of candidates.

- Job advertisement should be accurately based on the key requirements set out in the job description and the person specification. The advert should be posted in the most effective manner to attract the right applicants to apply.

- During shortlisting, the organisation screens each application against the key requirements of the post set out in the job description and person specification. Shortlisted applicants will then be invited to the selection event, which will usually include an interview.

data interpretation
Royal Mail

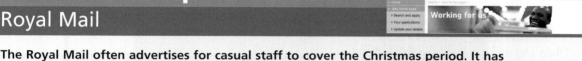

The Royal Mail often advertises for casual staff to cover the Christmas period. It has sent a mailshot to individual homes in the form of a Christmas card offering "season's greetings" with a job advertisement on the reverse of the card. It has also placed this advert on its website (www.royalmail.co.uk).

Want to earn extra cash this Christmas?

Our job of delivering millions of letters and packages becomes even bigger at Christmas. At the height of the season, we handle over 130 million mail items a day.

To make sure we deliver all this mail, and all our customer promises, at this busy time of year, we need teams of seasonal workers to help out in our mail centres from the end of November through to Christmas. We are looking for people who will be enthusiastic about working as postmen and postwomen, sorters, customer advisers and drivers.

You could be out delivering mail, working indoors in a mail centre or driving a van. And your tasks could include:

- sorting mail to correct address order ready for delivery
- carrying bags of mail for delivery on foot or by bike
- collecting mail from post boxes and businesses
- transporting mail by road between mail centres, stations and airports
- advising and talking to customers.

You do not need any experience. You just need to be 16 or over, conscientious, reliable, a team player and flexible enough to work a variety of shifts.

A Why does the Royal Mail need additional staff during the Christmas period?

B Look at the job advert that appeared on its website. What would you expect to see in the job description for this role?

C Give three reasons why the Royal Mail might use a mailshot as well as advertising on its internet site.

D How might the mailshot increase the effectiveness of the staff recruitment process for the Christmas period?

E Suggest other ways in which the Royal Mail might advertise for these posts. You may wish to consider where you have seen other businesses advertise for Christmas staff. Would any of these be appropriate for the Royal Mail to use?

Interview techniques

Setting the scene: the funnel technique

Selection interviews are commonly used to assess job applicants that make it to a short list stage. Questions should be prepared from the person specification criteria to gather specific information that can be used to make final decisions about the suitability of the candidates for the vacant position.

The funnel technique is a most effective tool to use for this purpose. It uses different types of questions to obtain the required information from the interviewees.

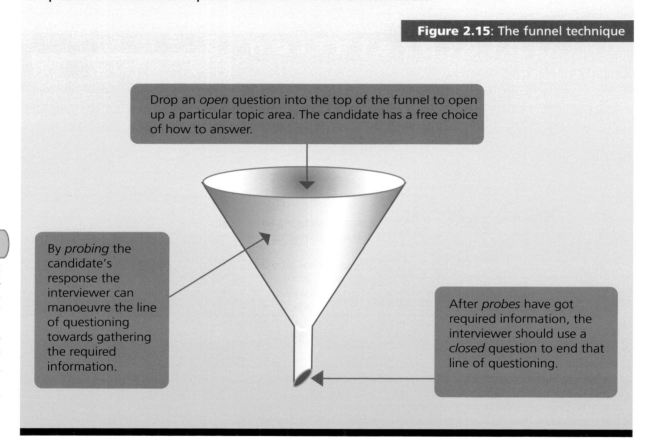

Figure 2.15: The funnel technique

Drop an *open* question into the top of the funnel to open up a particular topic area. The candidate has a free choice of how to answer.

By *probing* the candidate's response the interviewer can manoeuvre the line of questioning towards gathering the required information.

After *probes* have got required information, the interviewer should use a *closed* question to end that line of questioning.

The selection interview

Interviewing is the most common method of gathering evidence from candidates. (Other methods of assessing and selecting candidates are reviewed in Topic 9.) Good preparation, effective questioning, active listening and summarising accurately are the key skills in interviewing.

1 Preparation

It is essential that the interview process is structured. This ensures that interviewers concentrate on gathering information which has previously been identified as important for effective job performance and which helps to identify if candidates meet the criteria in the job description and person specification for the post.

Questions should be prepared in advance. Interviewers should plan the format of the interview – the introduction, the rapport-building process, testing, giving information about the job and the organisation, allowing time for questions. If there is to be more than one interviewer, members of the interview panel should be allocated roles setting out who will undertake what part of the interview.

The interview may be held on a one-to-one basis, and conducted either by a member of the human resource team or by the manager in charge of the job post. Alternatively, a panel of interviewers may conduct the interview. A panel interview consists of a range of individuals from the business with responsibility for recruitment and selection. This panel often includes a member of the human resource team, who can ensure that the interviews are conducted fairly and efficiently and can act as a point of reference to clarify any contractual issues relating to the terms and conditions of the appointment.

stopand**think**

Consider the advantages and disadvantages of having a panel interview compared to a one-to-one interview.

There are also several administrative tasks which need to be undertaken in advance of the interview:

- organise an appropriate time and place for the interviews to be held and make sure that there will not be any unwanted interruptions

- inform applicants about the time and date of the interview well in advance and ask them to bring any necessary documentation such as proof of their qualifications

- provide applicants with directions – details of public transport, where to park, etc. – and tell them who to report to and what expenses (if any) will be reimbursed

- if the selection process also includes some form of testing, arrange that testing facilities are available and properly equipped

- collate all relevant documentation, including the job description, person specification, interview form and company literature

- provide the interview panel with details on each interviewee, including any completed application form, CV and references.

2 Building a rapport

The interview is a two-way process – to find out information from the candidate, and enable them to find out more about the job and the organisation. It is therefore essential that the candidate is encouraged to talk and feel at ease. Establishing a rapport with the candidate will encourage them to open up and respond to questions asked during the interview.

To ensure fairness to each candidate, the interview should follow the same pattern. The interviewer should maintain control and direction of the interview. It is useful to have planned a line of questioning in advance. In this way, the interviewer is in a better position to drive the interview process in an efficient and objective manner.

Opening the interview with some general enquiry or small talk, such as whether the candidate had an easy journey or whether documentation about the business has been received, will help to build rapport at the beginning of the interview.

3 Questioning

Figure 2.16 (see page 94) shows the different types of questions that can be used by interviewers. In general, open questions invite the candidate to provide extended answers, probe questions seek specific information, while closed questions invite short (often yes/no) answers.

You need to be clear about the purpose of your questions before you ask them. The best predictor of future behaviour is past performance, and a structured interview can be used effectively to assess a candidate against the criteria required for the post. For example, if the person specification states that it is essential that the candidate is able to manage a disciplinary situation, the interviewer could ask "tell me about a time when you were faced with a difficult disciplinary situation; how did you manage it?" – and, by probing further, the interviewer can determine the behaviour pattern followed in the past by the candidate.

One of the objectives of the selection interview is to give candidates a fair hearing, so they must be allowed to do plenty of talking. Open questions should get the interviewee talking, and the answers can be used to probe more deeply into the relevant areas of the applicant's background. The suggested balance of communication between interviewer and candidate is between 70:30 and 80:20 in favour of the candidate. This means that the interviewer must adopt ways of allowing the candidate to continue while, at the same time, keeping control of the interview direction.

Use link questions to make the transition smoothly from one type of question to another, or to move to another topic of enquiry. For example, use questions such as "you mentioned just now that ... how did this affect your work?" or "you were saying earlier on that ... what happened after that?"

Remember not to ask too many closed questions unless the situation really calls for it. If the candidate is talking too much, you may wish to change the pace of the interview by using more closed or specific questions for a while. You may break eye contact, or summarise the main points and move on. Using closed questions is also appropriate when you are bringing the interview to a close.

The aim is to get the interviewee to talk, not to suggest right answers or to embarrass, confuse, discourage or mislead the interviewee. Avoid questions that prompt a desired answer – "I take it you believe that ..." – or that indicate bias or could be discriminatory – such as "when do you intend to start a family". Also don't confuse or mislead by asking trick questions, by asking several questions at once, or by being too long-winded.

So how do you put this into practice? Here is an interview checklist:

- keep your objectives firmly in mind and establish a pattern of questioning which can be followed

- within this pattern ask open questions and then follow up with probe questions

- restrict the use of closed questions and don't ask counter-productive or misleading questions

- use plain language

- allow the candidate thinking time to make a response

- analyse responses, noting the way the interviewee communicates and the words that are being used

Figure 2.16: Types of questioning

Type	Purpose	Question form	Examples
Open	To establish rapport	Contact	Introductory questions to put interviewee at ease, perhaps reference to mutually shared experiences, unusual leisure activities as indicated on the application form, etc.
Open	To explore background information	General	"Please tell me about ...."
Open	To explore opinions and attitudes	Opinion-seeking	"How do you feel about ..." "What do you think about ..."
		Trailer	Making a broad comment on a subject and then pausing in anticipation of a response
Probe	To show interest or encouragement	Non-verbal noises	Non-verbal prompts – Umm? Er? Ah? Oh? Hmm? – together with appropriate facial expression (smiles, raised eyebrows, etc.)
		Supportive statements	"I see?"; "And then?"; "That's interesting" (i.e. tell me more)
		Key word repetition	Repetition of one or two words to encourage further response
		Mirror	Repetition of a short reply as a query
Probe	To seek further information	The pause	Allied to various non-verbal signals
		Simple interrogative	"Why?"; "Why not?"
		Comparative	"How do your responsibilities now compare with those in your last job?"
		Extension	"How do you mean?" "What makes you say that?"
		Hypothetical	"What would you do if ...?" "How would you feel if ...?"
Probe	To explore in detail particular opinions or attitudes	Opinion-investigation	"To what extent do you feel ...?" "Just how far do you think ...?"
		The reflection	"You think that ...?"; "It seems to you that ...?" "You feel that ...?"
Probe	To demonstrate understanding, clarify information already given or to regain control	Summary	"As I understand it ...?" "If I've got it right ...?" "So what you're saying is ...?"
Closed	To establish specific facts/information	Yes/No response	"Are you ...?"; "Do you ...?"; "Have you ...?"
		Identification of person, time, location, number	"How many people report to you?" "How long did you have that job?"

- observe and interpret the details of the respondent's non-verbal signals
- maintain an atmosphere of friendly neutrality
- and don't talk too much.

To give you an example, the extract below is from an interview for an administrator post. The interviewer is trying to establish evidence against a criterion in the person specification that the applicant should be "able to make decisions on priorities".

4 Active listening

When interviewing a candidate the aim should be to establish and maintain a smooth flow of information. Careful or active listening is essential here in order to probe behind what the candidate is actually saying to establish or clarify the information required.

Far too many interviewers are busy thinking about asking the next question instead of concentrating on the information coming forth, and miss many potential leads. Certainly careful questioning will be of no use if the interviewer(s) does not listen to the answers given by the candidate.

Active listening is an important skill – this involves not just listening carefully but demonstrating to candidates that the interviewer has taken in their answers by:

Interviewer: "Tell me about a time when you had to decide which task to do first. What happened?"

Candidate: "My director asked me for some material to be prepared for the next day's conference. My immediate boss had asked for some minutes to be typed up for his approval as a priority since they needed to be sent off urgently. I had to establish how much time I had to complete both tasks, and then decide which I could do first – I decided to do the minutes – still having time to complete the preparation material that afternoon."

Int: "How successful was your decision?"

Can: "Being fairly quick at typing, I was able to complete the minutes in a short time, have them checked, and send them out. I had the afternoon to prepare for the conference and put my ideas forward to the director. She was happy to receive these before I finished work that day, and read over them that evening, getting them back to me the following morning with her updates".

Int: "How often would you have this type of decision to make?"

Can: "Regularly."

Int: [Pause]

Can: "The type of work involved meant constantly looking to meet deadlines, all of which were important tasks and had to be prioritised."

Int: "You mentioned preparation for a conference, what did this involve?"

- maintaining eye contact

- nodding

- gesturing

- keeping an open posture

- linking questions to previous answers

- accurately summarising the interviewee's replies.

Remember that even with your mouth firmly shut, you will still be communicating, whether you like it or not. The expression on your face, together with your head movements and the way you are sitting, are positive signals for the interviewee just as much as the questions you ask and the way in which you ask them. Figure 2.17 shows some of the attitudes you can communicate – consciously or unconsciously – through non-verbal signals.

Figure 2.17: Non-verbal signals

Warmth	Hostility
Sympathetic gestures	Aggressive posture
Proximity	Harsh tone of voice
Relaxed tone of voice	"Set" mouth
Smiles	Distance
"Crinkled" eyes	Staring eyes
Expansive gestures	

Control	Submissive
Speaking loudly/quickly all the time	Speaking quietly/saying little
Ignoring responses	Allowing interruptions
Interrupting	Meek tone of voice
Controlling tone of voice	Downcast eyes
Stabbing fingers	Hand wringing
Other forceful gestures	Nervous gestures

5 Making judgements

Interviewers should take notes and not rely on memory. A specific form for assessing the strengths and weaknesses of each candidate may be used. For example, the form may be based on the key requirements of the post, and could list a number of set opening questions that are asked of every candidate. There may be a rating system on this form, allowing interviews to mark candidates on how closely they match the criteria for the post.

Some businesses now use competency-based or criterion-based interviewing, in which the key criteria for the post are written on the form with a structured series of questions aimed at eliciting behavioural information against the specific job-related competencies or criteria. Using a structured interview

assessment form helps to ensure that each interview has a consistent and objective structure, avoiding subjective opinions and "chats" which do not follow any pattern. It will also help to avoid any discriminatory issues.

Be aware that the introductory stages of the interview will serve to form impressions on both sides. First impressions can have a disproportionate impact, and the interviewer needs to be aware of the "halo and horns" effect. If a candidate has an interest, background or point of view that matches your own, there is a tendency to elevate that person in your esteem. This is the halo effect. Conversely someone with an interest, background or point of view strongly opposing your own may appear lower in your esteem. This is the horns effect.

You should be aware of – and correct – any halo or horn influences prior to the selection decision being made. One way of overcoming the halo and horns effect is to ask contra questions, to allow the candidate the opportunity of redressing the balance. For example, if during the interview it is perceived the candidate is overly decisive (a horns effect), then questions such as "tell me about a time when you had difficulties making a decision; what did you do?" will provide the opportunity for the candidate to redress the balance, ensuring fairness in the interview.

Further pitfalls and problems associated with interviews are covered in more depth in Topic 9.

Knowledge summary

- **A structured interview is essential in helping to select the most suitable candidate for the post. Interviewers need to plan and structure the interview carefully.**

- **Questions should be based on establishing how closely the candidate matches the key requirements of the post as stated in the job description and person specification.**

- **A key interview skill is the ability to listen actively to what is being said and to let candidates do most of the talking.**

- **Interviewers need to be aware of subjectivity, discrimination issues and the impact and influence of non-verbal communication.**

This exercise is designed to develop your practical skills in interviewing through a role-play interview for a vacant post. The vacant position is a crew member at McDonald's.

McDonald's Restaurants Ltd

Due to continued growth we are currently recruiting high quality staff members for a variety of positions. Do you fit the bill?

Age: secondary school leaving age upwards
Appearance: clean, neat and well groomed
Personality: cheerful and pleasant
Other qualities: able to work at a fast pace both supervised and unsupervised; a good communicator and able to keep cool and courteous under hectic conditions; excellent timekeeping.

The main function of a crew member is to work under the direction of all managers and to maintain and improve McDonald's high levels of quality, service and cleanliness, achieving the company's goal of 100% total customer satisfaction.

Duties include operating a till, assembling orders, working in the kitchen area, preparing and cooking all menu items, carrying out extensive cleaning projects and other various duties involved in the running of a busy McDonald's restaurant.

Starting rate up to £5.25 per hour (dependent on age)

We offer all employees the following benefits (some after a qualifying period):

■ Competitive rates of pay
■ Performance-related pay
■ Free meals (when working) and uniform
■ Four weeks paid holiday
■ Excellent training
■ Good promotion prospects that could lead to management career
■ Employee discount card that can be used at various retailers

Source: advert appeared in Flintshire Leader, *3 June 2004, copyright McDonald's Corporation 2004.*

A Prepare a form for assessing the strengths and weaknesses of candidates applying for this post.

B Prepare suitable interview questions including at least one open question, probe question and closed question

C With your fellow students take part in an interview for the post. Take turns as the interviewer and the job applicant. After you have taken part, answer the remaining questions.

D Explain what is meant by a counter-productive question and give an example.

E What is meant by the halo and horns effect? Explain one way in which this effect can be redressed during the interview.

F Why are non-verbal gestures important during the interview?

G What is meant by active listening? How would you demonstrate to someone that you were actively listening to what they had to say?

Setting the scene: aptitude tests

Employers are increasingly incorporating aptitude tests into assessment procedures – both for selection of personnel and for development or counselling purposes.

There is good evidence that aptitude tests which are professionally used and evaluated can provide objective, reliable and relevant information concerning the likelihood of job success and satisfaction.

Tests can help candidates:

- **to be fairly assessed in a competitive situation**
- **to find out more about their own strengths and weaknesses**
- **to be comprehensively assessed for selection, development or counselling purposes.**

Tests can enable the employer:

- **to select people best suited to the demands of the job**

- **to identify areas of weakness for staff development**
- **to counsel staff appropriately**
- **to place personnel appropriately within an organisation.**

Aptitude tests measure skills relevant to the job, position or responsibilities for which the candidate is being considered. While different jobs make different demands on individuals, extensive analyses of many managerial and professional jobs have shown that competence in verbal and numerical critical reasoning is a common requirement.

Source: adapted from a leaflet by SHL, a leading company in the science of psychometrics in the workplace.

The assessment process

Businesses use a range of methods for assessing the suitability of a candidate for a post. This includes different types of testing of candidates. However, the most common way of choosing the person to fill a vacancy is still to invite the candidates on the short list to an interview (or a series of interviews).

So, before we look at some of the tests that businesses use to assess candidates, let's focus on some of the issues involved in using interviews as the sole method of assessing job candidates.

Interviews

Topic 8 set out a range of good practice that organisations should follow when conducting job interviews. However, many businesses do not follow these guidelines, and interviews can be a poor method of selection for many reasons. One of the main reasons is that many people who conduct job interviews are not trained. They are therefore unaware of the many pitfalls that can occur in interviewing, and can lack the skills to avoid making mistakes.

There is considerable information generated within an interview. An essential part of the interview assessment process is to judge the importance of each piece of information. It is important that personal views and judgements do not bias this process.

In selecting the right candidate for the job, it is essential to decide in a systematic way which applicant has the required skills, experience and qualities. Interviewers often decide to accept or reject a candidate far too early in the interview, long before they have collected and considered all the evidence. Many interviewers tend to place more importance on negative information than on any positive evidence they encounter during the interview – almost as if they are looking for a reason to reject candidates. Even before they get to meet candidates, an interviewer will have formed an impression about them by looking at their CVs, application forms and covering letters.

To ensure the interview process is effective, all interviewers must be aware of these pitfalls, learn how to avoid them and look objectively at each candidate based on the criteria for the job. Everybody involved in the selection process must understand the legal requirements so that discrimination is avoided from the first stages of the recruitment process onwards.

It is because of the problems associated with reliance on the interview alone that many businesses opt to use additional methods for assessment of candidates, including different types of tests.

Psychometric tests

Now becoming used more often during the recruitment process – particularly by larger organisations – psychometric tests offer an increased level of objectivity than interviews. A psychometric test can assess ability, personality and interest types.

As Figure 2.18 (see page 100) shows, the personality "test" is often constructed as a questionnaire. The personality questionnaire does not contain any right or wrong answers. It is aimed at presenting a picture of a how a person will behave, given particular circumstances.

Businesses may use these tests as they believe they help them to shortlist – and remove applicants who do not match the criteria for the post – and select, providing them with a more accurate picture of the applicant.

Work study tests

Work study tests are usually constructed by a business itself to test a specific skill. For example, they might be used to test word processing skills. Another common type of test is an in-tray exercises – a test of prioritising and problem-solving based on a number of activities found in the test in-tray.

Some candidates are asked to take part in trial presentations and simulations which are observed by the selectors. For example teachers applying for jobs normally have to teach a trial lesson which is observed by a teacher or governor in the school looking to fill a vacancy.

Assessment centres

An assessment centre utilises a wide range of methods in order to assess candidates. They were once used for the appointment of senior management posts, but they are growing in popularity and are used to assess candidates for a wider range of positions. The combination of tests that can be carried out at one selection event enables a business to recruit and select with objectivity. However, assessment centres can be costly to run.

Evaluating recruitment and selection

One indicator of good recruitment and selection practice in a business is low labour turnover: if you select the right staff, they are likely to stay with the company; if there is high staff turnover, the business may be appointing the wrong people, and it should try to gather information on the impact of the recruitment and selection process from exit interviews.

Key issues to address when evaluating the effectiveness of the recruitment and selection process are:

- cost and efficiency
- legal compliance
- employee performance.

Cost

Recruitment isn't a cheap process. The cost includes advertising expenses and the cost of accompanying documentation, staff time taken to administrate the process, and the time and expense of interviewing and testing applicants.

Legal compliance

Employers should ensure that their recruitment and selection procedures meet legal requirements. They should monitor the number of complaints or grievances that are received as a result of the recruitment and selection process, review the number and type of any formal discrimination claims against the company, and check that all documentation and criteria used in the selection process conform with equal opportunities good practice.

Employee performance

Monitoring how well an employee performs once appointed is perhaps the best way of determining how successful the process has been. Looking at how well the new member of staff is performing will show whether the right person for the post has been selected.

This can be done through looking at reports from the employee's line manager, appraisals, feedback received from customers, the level of support the new employee has needed, and the training and development needs of the new employee.

Figure 2.18: Extract from a psychometric test

Employers may feel I am ...

☐ much more competitive than others

☐ a bit more competitive than others

☐ about as competitive as others

☐ a bit less competitive than others

☐ much less competitive than others

What is your attitude toward praising others?

☐ it is largely overrated – praise may hinder their performance

☐ it should be used sparingly – there is a risk it may slow down performance

☐ praise should be given whenever it is appropriate – it typically improves performance

☐ one should always praise others – even when there are no obvious reasons for it

When you've achieved an important goal, such as graduation, what is your reaction?

☐ I often think it a measly step toward my ultimate goal – it would be pathetic to make a big deal out of it

☐ I enjoy the feeling of satisfaction for a while before I work towards another goal

☐ I reap the fruits of my labour for as long as I can

When conversing with someone who has a less extensive vocabulary or has a lower education level ...

☐ I feel superior and I get a confidence boost out of it

☐ I brush them off – I have no patience for "slow" people

☐ I get impatient and try to find an excuse to end our conversation

☐ I pretend that I don't notice

☐ I try to adjust my speech to put the person at ease and to facilitate understanding

When I am very frustrated ...

☐ people shouldn't provoke me (for their own sake)

☐ I can be provoked but try to control my temper

☐ I try to calm down before I do or say anything.

☐ I step back from the situation and put things in perspective.

☐ I withdraw – I cover up my frustration.

I take part in recreational activities (walks, working out, reading, chess, etc.) ...

☐ less than once a week

☐ once or twice a week

☐ several times a week

☐ every day

☐ most of my time consists of recreational activities

☐ I engage in nothing but recreational activities

My glass is...

☐ always half empty

☐ usually half empty

☐ usually half full

☐ always half full

If I am ready to go but have to wait for someone else ...

☐ I get very impatient and let it show

☐ I get very impatient but don't let on

☐ I may get slightly impatient and let it show

☐ I may get slightly impatient but don't let on

☐ I don't mind – I enjoy the moment

Your existing job is satisfactory and the salary is perfectly adequate but you've been offered a higher paying job. If you take the new job, you must move across the country. Your long-term partner cannot make the move. What do you do?

☐ I give my partner an ultimatum – go with me or lose me

☐ I discuss the options with my partner

☐ I refuse the job

In general, I feel ...

☐ very discontented – there is something wrong with everything and everybody

☐ discontented – there are many things that bother me

☐ contented – generally I am satisfied with my life, but things can always be better

☐ completely fulfilled – I've everything I've ever wished for

Knowledge summary

- Businesses use different methods to draw up a short list of candidates for final selection, including asking for completed application form, curriculum vitae (CV) and letter of application.

- Interviewing is the most common method used in the final selection process. Other methods of selection include personality and aptitude tests, sometimes in combination with a job interview.

quick **questions**

1 When interviewing for jobs it is important that personal views and prejudices do not interfere with the process of objective and fair selection. How do you establish which information can be used as part of the selection decision?

2 Explain how each of the three key issues of cost, legislation and monitoring performance can be used to evaluate the effectiveness of the recruitment and selection process.

data **interpretation**
Recruitment for Disneyland Resort Paris

Disneyland Resort Paris employs over 10,000 cast members. It wants people that can bring dynamism to the company and who are able "to use their professional skills and enthusiasm to work magic". This is an extract from the jobs section of the Disneyland Paris website.

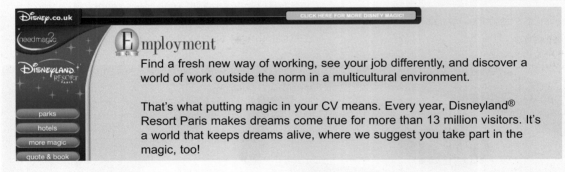

Disney.co.uk — CLICK HERE FOR MORE DISNEY MAGIC!
needmagic?
DISNEYLAND RESORT PARIS
parks
hotels
more magic
quote & book

Employment

Find a fresh new way of working, see your job differently, and discover a world of work outside the norm in a multicultural environment.

That's what putting magic in your CV means. Every year, Disneyland® Resort Paris makes dreams come true for more than 13 million visitors. It's a world that keeps dreams alive, where we suggest you take part in the magic, too!

A How much information is provided about the job vacancies on the Disneyland Paris website?

B What do the company mean by "putting magic in your CV"?

C What are the benefits to the company of allowing people to make either online or postal applications?

D How would Disneyland Paris measure the effectiveness of its recruitment and selection procedures?

Business in practice: Boots Group plc

Boots is one of the best-known retail names in the UK, selling health and beauty products and employing around 75,000 people. Its products are sold in 130 countries worldwide. In addition to retailing, it has international sales and marketing operations, and it also develops and manufactures its own products.

The company offers a wide variety of careers and career paths. It claims that it is "keen to support people's development and growth, and will work closely with you to help you achieve your career ambitions".

Boots is organised so that staff have many options in developing their careers, particularly by moving across and through the stores, group, area and regional structure. Figure 2.19 (see page 104) shows some of the career paths open to managers across the company's stores, groups, areas and regions.

Staff motivation

Boots believes it is essential to gain the commitment of its employees:

"A business will only thrive when it builds on the skills and retains the commitment of the people who work within it. It's a key part of our corporate responsibility to achieve this by the way we reward our employees, develop and train them, and earn their trust. Our focus on wellbeing should be reflected in our management style as well as our customer offer."

Benefits offered within the Boots Group plc include:

- discounts for staff purchases
- family friendly practices, flexible working
- employee share scheme
- pension plan
- bonus.

The company encourages and supports employee participation through training programmes. It offers training in new skills, with investment in training to meet the changes taking place in the business, and commitment to ongoing staff development.

Figure 2.20: Job description for store manager, Boots

Company	Boots Stores
Ref.	02 139
Position of	Group Store Manager Kettering
Start date	Immediate
Closing date for applications	18 April 2005
Department	Talent Management
Location	Northamptonshire

Job description

People
Lead and develop group and store teams to deliver the Boots customer experience. Deliver pipeline plans to grow and develop talent within the store/group, area and region.

Customer
Deliver a great customer experience in every shop within the store and group every time, ensuring we are always "Ready for Customers". Understand and identify current and future customer trends across the store/group.

Sales
Lead the store/group team to drive a culture of "Licence to Trade" and "Driving Pharmacy" in the store/group where everyone aims to beat sales and item targets. Identify and exploit opportunities to drive maximum profitable sales growth. Ensure compliance with all relevant legal and professional requirements.

Operational and professional standards
Lead the delivery of a sustainable and efficient operating platform, and support the delivery of a professional service across the store/group to maximise stock and legal requirements.

Partnerships
Provide local insights and expertise to identify trends and growth opportunities across the store/group and area. Drive the sharing and delivery of best practice and act as external ambassador for the Boots Company across the group and area in key local forums.

Time horizon
Think a year ahead and balance short- and medium-term priorities and the balance scorecard targets and tolerances.

Experience
Customer focused/senior management experience
Previous store management experience
Deep understanding of retail market and an awareness of competitors

Remuneration Excellent

Benefits Competitive benefits package including 30 days holiday, 22.5% in-store discount on all Boots products, profit-related bonus scheme, annual allocation of shares and a share purchase scheme, Stakeholder Pension Plan, relocation expenses and a company car or car allowance.

Travel required 20%
Travel extent Local
Contract Full-time

The company seeks to maintain an environment where every member of staff feels respected and valued. It encourages staff to be involved in Boots community investment programme, offering a certificate of recognition as a community associate to add to the CV of those who volunteer.

Store managers

According to the Boots website, the aim of store managers is to create a winning team that will grow sales through creating a customer-focused environment. Store managers should have a deep understanding of what customers want so that sales targets are constantly beaten.

Boots seeks natural leaders, with a passion for people, who can identify, coach and develop talent throughout the store. "You'll get broad responsibility to lead the whole business, pulling everything together to get great results that are clearly down to you. It's a good job you like a challenge."

Source for case study material: www.boots.com.

Figure 2.19: Boots management career paths

Customers

Stores		Store Manager	
Groups	Group Pharmacy Manager	Premier/ Group Store Manager	Group Operations Manager
Areas	Area Pharmacy Manager	Area Manager & Deputy Directors	Area Operations Manager	Area Loss Detection Manager
Regions	Regional Pharmacy Manager	Regional Sales Manager	Regional Director	Regional Operations Manager

Great Leadership

activities

1 Explain the recruitment and interview process that Boots might use, including the structure and purpose of documentation used in the process and the interview itself. Describe the relevant legal, social and ethical issues that Boots must consider in the recruitment process.

2 Look through the material on the store manager position at Boots and then:
   a) describe the role and responsibilities of the management post
   b) explain the qualities that the manager should have
   c) find out what training and development opportunities are offered to managers of Boots stores
   d) give examples of how Boots motivates its staff in order to ensure a high retention rate
   e) give examples of any relevant political, economic, social or technological factors that Boots may need to consider in the recruitment process.

3 Using the information given in the job description, compile a person specification for the store manager position. Think carefully about the essential and desirable characteristics. How might you test for each of these attributes in the selection process?

4 Now draft a job advertisement for the store manager role using the supplied job description and the person specification you produced in Task 3. What should be included in your advert? What benefits will you offer to attract staff?

5 Use this documentation along with an interview assessment form to role play job interviews for the post with fellow students. How will you make this an effective interview (dos and don'ts)? Detail your interview plan. Evaluate the interview when you have been through the selection stage.

6 Describe how you could evaluate the effectiveness of the selection process. Apart from the selection interview, what other forms of testing can you use to add to the effectiveness of the process?

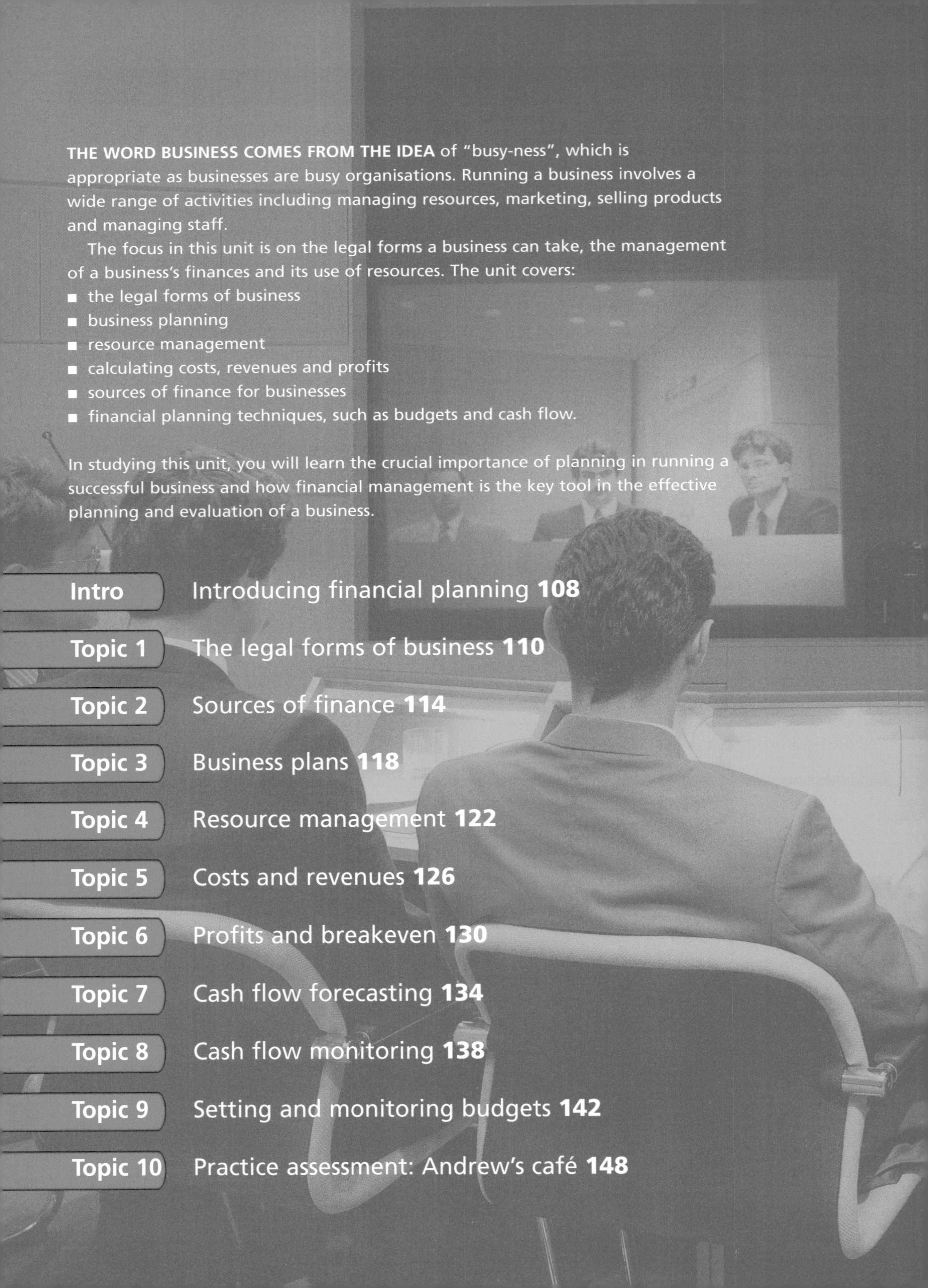

THE WORD BUSINESS COMES FROM THE IDEA of "busy-ness", which is appropriate as businesses are busy organisations. Running a business involves a wide range of activities including managing resources, marketing, selling products and managing staff.

The focus in this unit is on the legal forms a business can take, the management of a business's finances and its use of resources. The unit covers:

■ the legal forms of business
■ business planning
■ resource management
■ calculating costs, revenues and profits
■ sources of finance for businesses
■ financial planning techniques, such as budgets and cash flow.

In studying this unit, you will learn the crucial importance of planning in running a successful business and how financial management is the key tool in the effective planning and evaluation of a business.

Financial planning and monitoring

Introducing financial planning

Setting the scene: financial planning at Fiat

Fiat, the Italian car manufacturer, is facing troubled times. In 2005 the company ended its partnership with the huge American car maker General Motors (GM). This relationship had existed since 2000 and had seen the companies involved in a number of joint ventures. Although Fiat will continue to manufacture GM's diesel engines, it will no longer work with GM on other projects.

The end of the partnership with GM has highlighted Fiat's financial problems. Fiat's debts are reported to be in the region of £5,600 million and it must make regular heavy interest payments. In the short term these have been eased by a payment of £1,100 million from GM to buy itself out of the partnership deal. However, the payment from GM is not enough to resolve Fiat's serious underlying financial problems.

Further difficulties for the company are that its sales of cars are declining and it is losing market share in its home market; once the company had a 60 per cent share of the Italian car market, latterly it has fallen to 25 per cent. Fiat's overall sales fell by 9 per cent in 2004.

The challenge facing the company's managers is to find ways of ensuring that the company is able to survive in financial terms in the medium term. GM's money will help in the short term, but unless Fiat can increase sales and revenues, its bankers may become nervous about the company's ability to pay its debts as they become due.

A key element of the company's financial planning will be to consider ways in which the company can reduce its costs over the next few years. The company's managers are reported to be seeking a new partnership with another car manufacturer as a means of cutting costs. The other important issue for Fiat will be to manage its cash effectively. The company is facing falling sales, and it will need to invest in new models to improve its market standing. This may stretch the company's limited reserves of cash.

KEY TERMS

Financial management is the process of producing and interpreting accounts that record a business's expected or actual costs, revenues and profits. This helps managers to take good decisions.

Costs are the expenses paid by a business, such as its employees' wages.

Revenue is the income received by a business from selling goods and services.

A **budget** is a financial plan for the future operations of the business. Budgets are used to set targets to monitor performance and control operations.

A **business plan** is a detailed statement setting out the proposals for a new business or describing the ways in which an existing business will be developed.

Cash flow is a measure of the amount of money moving into and out of a business over some time period.

What is financial planning?

Financial planning is the drawing up of forecasts or estimates of future costs, revenues and profits (or losses) to help managers to make decisions. Financial plans come in a number of different forms.

Businesses estimate their likely sales and the revenue or income they expect to earn from these sales. In 2004 Fujitsu, the Japanese electronics firm, reported that its sales were significantly below forecasts, mainly because consumers were purchasing fewer technological products.

Businesses also estimate costs of production. These are not always easy to forecast. For example, in 2004 many airlines faced unexpected rises in their operating costs because of a sharp increase in fuel prices.

By putting together expected or budgeted costs and revenues, businesses are able to estimate future profits or losses. In 2005 Barclays Bank reported profits of £9,400 million, roughly in line with its forecasts.

Businesses also forecast cash flows. This is an important part of financial management because if a business runs out of cash, it may be unable to pay its bills. Drawing up a forecast of cash outflows and inflows for the year ahead is an important part of financial planning. Cash flow problems are a very common cause of business failure.

Banks pull the plug on Courts

Courts, the furniture retailer, disappeared from UK high streets in 2005 because of cash flow problems. The company was forced to cease trading and go into administration because it had insufficient cash to pay the interest due on its loans.

What this unit covers

This unit examines how businesses manage and review their finances and other resources. You will investigate a number of issues relating to the management of resources.

The legal forms of business and sources of finance

Entrepreneurs can set up businesses using various legal forms. The best known form of business is the company, but this unit considers all four main legal forms that a business can take and reviews the advantages and disadvantages of each form. It also examines the sources of finance that are available to businesses, and the benefits and drawbacks of using each source.

Business planning

All businesses should engage in planning. It is vital for a new business as a means of assessing the viability of the venture, but planning is equally important for an existing firm intending to engage in a major new project. The section on business planning considers sources of finance available to businesses, the value to be gained from business plans, as well as the key elements that a business should include in its plans.

Resource management

To make their enterprise as efficient as possible, business managers should aim to use the minimum amount of resources necessary to achieve their aims and objectives. This unit identifies the types of resources commonly used and how they vary between different businesses.

Costs and revenues

What are the different types of costs that businesses have to pay? How can costs be best classified? What is revenue and how does a change in product price affect the amount of revenue received by a business? This unit looks at and answers these questions.

Financial planning

This is a major element of this unit. You will investigate important techniques such as breakeven analysis, cash flow forecasting and the setting of budgets. You will see how each of these techniques operates and make some assessment of their value.

Financial monitoring

This part of the unit compares financial plans (cash flow forecasts and budgets, for example) with outcomes – what actually happened in practice. This is important information for managers in making decisions.

Setting the scene: off-the-shelf private limited companies

One way to start a private limited company is to buy a ready-made company. These are companies that are established by businesses specialising in this particular service. Using this method it is possible to start a private company for less than £100.

The businesses supplying the "off-the-shelf" service will prepare all the necessary documentation, help with a choice of a company name, and many provide a free website for those choosing to trade online. This extract describes some of the services offered by @UK PLC.

@uk PLC **Company Formations** *online* FROM JUST £24.99 | FREE COMPANY NAME CHECK SERVICE! [ ] CHECK AVAILABILITY ▶

You can now form a new company online, usually within three hours. It takes just minutes to check the availability of your company name, enter your details, and submit a registration.

@UK PLC are much more than just the leading company formation agent, we have a network of @Advisors that can help you get your company up and trading online with an effective e-commerce website that earns you money. We provide the complete personal service, company formation, domain names, website, e-commerce, accountancy, phones at great prices so that you can focus on making your business profitable.

Your company formation includes a website and a listing in the @UK PLC Business Directory. Our directory is used by over 1000 portals and is a great way of getting your newly formed company in front of as many customers as possible, with @UK PLC company formation is just the start of your journey.

With the Premier package, costing £89.50, we supply:

Electronic Mem and Arts of Association
Electronic certificate of incorporation
Printed certificate of incorporation
Company Seal and Register
Six bound copies of Mem and Arts
Free website worth £24+ VAT
Note: Price includes UK delivery only.

Source: www.uk-plc.net/companyformation/index.htm

KEY TERMS

A **sole trader** is a business owned and operated by a single person.

A **partnership** is a group of between 2 and 20 people who contribute capital and expertise to an enterprise.

A **company** is any incorporated business.

Shareholders are the owners of a company.

Limited liability provides protection for the owners of a company (normally the shareholders). They only risk the amount they have invested in the business in the event of its failure.

Limited liability

Before looking at different legal forms businesses can take, it is useful to begin with the important concept of limited liability. Limited liability is regarded as a privilege and was first provided in 1855 through the Limited Liability Act. Limited liability means that the owners of the business (normally shareholders) only risk the amount they have invested in the business in the event of its failure. It is a major element in the legal structure of public and private companies; however, most partnerships and all sole traders do not benefit from limited liability.

With the protection of limited liability, a shareholder's financial liability is limited to the amount of capital invested in the business. If a shareholder invests £20,000 in either a public or a private limited company and the company fails, the maximum the shareholder can lose is that £20,000 investment. The shareholders are not responsible for meeting the debts incurred by the company.

In direct contrast, all sole traders and most partnerships do not have limited liability. If a sole trader's business runs into trouble, the sole trader is personally liable for meeting all the business's debts. This means that sole traders can be forced to sell their houses and other personal possessions to meet their business's debts and, in the worse cases, they face not only losing their businesses but also bankruptcy.

Types of business

1 Sole traders

A sole trader (or sole proprietor) is a form of business organisation in which an individual owns and operates a business. It is a very common form of organisation in the UK and one which has grown in number over recent years. The number of sole traders within the EU is growing by about 2.5 per cent each year.

The essential feature of this type of business is that each sole trader has full responsibility for the financial control of their business, for meeting capital requirements and running costs, and full personal liability in the case of debt. Sole traders do not have the protection of limited liability, but their activities are not heavily regulated. (Any individual could set up their business as a company, but complying with the additional legal requirements involves more time and cost although it does grant limited liability.)

Typically, sole traders are small shopkeepers and market traders or have self-employed occupations such as plumbers, electricians, hairdressers and consultants. They are likely to trade in local or, at most, regional markets. Most trade under their own names. However if the business is to be run under a name different to the proprietor's, then registration is required under the Business Names Act 1985.

Although many sole traders work on their own, this need not always be the case. In theory, a sole trader could employ hundreds of staff and own several factories but in practice it is unlikely that a single person could raise the amount of capital needed for such a large business.

2 Partnerships

A partnership is a group of between 2 and 20 people who contribute capital and expertise to an enterprise. Every partner is entitled to participate in the management of the business. Some may choose not to do so, in which case they are termed sleeping partners. Partnerships are common in the professions. It is a typical form of business organisation for lawyers, accountants and doctors, and although most partnerships are only permitted to have a maximum of 20 partners, the Companies Act 1985 permits more for practices of accountants and solicitors.

A partnership dissolves on the death, resignation or bankruptcy of a partner, or on the agreed termination of the business. In order to avoid disruption to the business, it is usual to draw up a deed of partnership. A deed might cover arrangements for sharing of profits, liabilities in case of debt, continuation after death or resignation of a member, and so on.

Most partnerships do not have the benefit of limited liability. However, the Limited Liability Partnerships Act 2000 offered a means by which partnerships could obtain limited liability. By setting up as a limited liability partnership (LLP), a partnership can provide limited liability for its members while retaining the flexibility of organising its internal structure as a traditional partnership. The LLP is a separate legal entity and, while the LLP itself is liable to pay debts using all its assets, the liability of the members or partners is limited. Limited liability partnerships were introduced in 2001.

3 Companies

A company is formed through the process of incorporation. This creates a separate legal identity for the business. Legally the business (or company) and its owners are two separate entities. The business has a legal life of its own. For example, it can enter into contracts and sue people or other businesses. Each owner of an incorporated business has the protection of limited liability.

The creating of a company requires the completion of two major documents: the memorandum of association and the articles of association.

The memorandum of association states:

- the company's name, and the address of its registered office (in England, Wales or Scotland)
- its objectives – the object may simply be to carry on business as a general commercial company
- the company's share capital.

The articles of association set the rules for the running of the company's internal affairs. These cover:

- the rights of shareholders
- the names and powers of directors
- the rules governing company meetings.

In the UK, two main types of company exist: public limited companies and private limited companies. Public limited companies are expensive to create. They are usually much larger than private limited companies. They can sell their shares on the stock exchange and are distinguished by the letters plc after the company name. Private limited companies are smaller, subject to less regulation and have the term Ltd after their name.

Private limited companies

This type of company is suitable for small and medium-sized operations. It is particularly suitable for family firms and for small enterprises involving just a handful of people. In some cases, a private limited company may just have a single director.

By forming as a limited company, it is easier for a business to attract capital because investors have the benefit of limited liability and, by being able to get capital in this way, it is easier for the firm to grow.

In some circumstances, private limited companies may trade internationally. For example, some major and well-known businesses are operated as private companies, including Richard Branson's Virgin Group and Dyson. However, it is usual for this type of business to trade regionally and perhaps nationally.

Private limited companies cannot advertise their shares for sale and, as such, they do not have their share prices quoted on the stock exchange. However, they can convert into public limited companies through a process known as flotation.

Public limited companies

The letters plc at the end of its name distinguishes a public company from a private limited company. Most of Britain's most famous businesses are public limited companies. Examples include Tesco, Vodafone, BP and Manchester United.

All companies with share prices quoted on the London Stock Exchange are public limited companies, but not all public limited companies are listed on the stock market. Some smaller public companies, that

Figure 3.1: The advantages and disadvantages of the main legal forms of businesses

Legal form	Advantages	Disadvantages
Sole trader	Simple to establish and operate The business owner receives all the profits	The business owner takes all the responsibility There is no protection from limited liability
Partnership	Partners are able to share responsibility for the business A partnership has greater ability to raise capital than a sole trader	There is no protection from limited liability Partners can argue or fall out leading to the termination of the business
Private limited company	The company benefits from limited liability Relatively easy and cheap to establish The business is able to raise finance by selling shares	The company cannot sell additional shares without approval from existing shareholders The company is obliged to publish some financial information
Public limited company	The company benefits from limited liability It is able to raise large sums of money (such as by selling shares on the stock exchange) The company is likely to be in the media frequently	The company has to publish detailed financial information, perhaps benefiting rivals The company is vulnerable to takeover by any organisation with sufficient funds

are unable to obtain a full listing on the stock exchange, trade their shares on the AIM – the Alternative Investment Market.

To become a public limited company, a business must have an issued share capital of at least £50,000. Other requirements include that:

- it is a company limited by shares

- its memorandum of association has a separate clause stating that it is a public company

- it publishes an annual report and balance sheet

- its shares are freely transferable – that is, they can be bought and sold (through stockbrokers, banks and share shops).

Quoted companies can be tracked each day by reference to the stock exchange listings in financial pages of newspapers.

Public limited companies benefit greatly from their wide access to funds. Being able to sell shares on the stock exchange allows public limited companies to experience fewer difficulties in raising capital than most other types of business. Not only can they sell additional shares to raise capital, their high public profile also makes it easier to arrange loans from financial institutions. Because of this ability to raise large sums of money, public limited companies can compete in tough international markets.

quick questions

1 Why might an entrepreneur decide to start up a business as a sole trader without the protection of limited liability?

2 Why should a business trade as a partnership when it is easy and cheap to establish a private limited company?

3 What are the financial drawbacks of operating as a public limited company?

data interpretation
Home car care

Alan Williams is just about to start a new business repairing and servicing cars. He plans to offer a call-out service, carrying out the work at his customers' homes or business premises.

His brother has offered to put up £3,000 towards the business, but Alan needs to raise another £5,000 to purchase the van and the tools he will need to carry out his work. He intends to work on his own at first, and will only employ other people if he manages to expand the business. His market research has suggested that there might be sufficient local trade to generate a profitable business initially with the hope of expansion later on.

Alan has little experience of running a business, although he is a qualified and skilled car mechanic. He has approached a local business adviser for help and has been told he will have to decide on a legal form for the business. He could, the adviser said, operate as a sole trader, form a partnership with his brother, or establish a private limited company.

A Explain the key features of sole traders, partnerships and private limited companies.

B Analyse the benefits that Alan might receive from the protection of limited liability.

C What legal form of business should Alan adopt? Justify your answer.

Topic 2 Sources of finance

Setting the scene: Fiat's finances improve

As we saw in the introduction to this topic (see page 108), the Italian car manufacturer Fiat saw some improvement in its financial position following the end of an agreement with the giant American motor manufacturer, General Motors. The US company paid Fiat £1,100 million in compensation for ending the joint venture agreement between the two companies.

The ending of the deal has proved to be a blessing in disguise for Fiat as the company was in desperate need of finance to cover losses and to invest in developing new models. However, analysts have pointed out that the money from General Motors will only provide a breathing space for the underperforming company to reorganise itself and return to profitability. If a quick improvement is not achieved, then the management team at Fiat may be looking for other sources of finance.

The company had already considered a number of sources from which to raise the much-needed capital. Because of its weak financial position, many of these sources were external (that is, from outside the company). The Italian prime minister, Silvio Berlusconi, had indicated that his government was happy to offer a loan to the car manufacturer, so long as it met strict European Union rules on loans by governments to businesses. The Agnelli family, which owns Fiat, also considered injecting capital into the business. However, the most likely source of finance for Fiat appeared to be raising cash by selling company assets such as property and shares.

Why do businesses raise finance?

Businesses require finance for various reasons. A large public limited company such as Tesco might want to raise millions of pounds to invest in superstores in new markets such as China. At the other end of the scale, a farmer running a sheep farm in Cumbria might need £35,000 to purchase a new tractor.

Both businesses – Tesco and the Cumbrian sheep farmer – face the same challenge: how to raise money to finance business improvements. However, they are likely to look for funding from very different sources. This topic will consider the diverse sources from which businesses may raise finance.

Internal sources of finance

An internal source of finance is one that exists within the business. The major internal sources of finance are reinvesting profit, working capital and the sale of assets.

1 Reinvesting profits

Profits are perhaps the major source of long-term finance, particularly for smaller businesses. A business can use its profits in two ways: by distributing them to shareholders in the form of dividends, or by retaining them for investment in the business. By using profits for investment a business avoids interest

KEY TERMS

An **internal source of finance** is one that exists within the business.

An **external source of finance** is an injection of capital into a business from individuals, other businesses or financial institutions.

A **share** is a document representing part ownership of a company.

Assets are anything owned by a business from which it can benefit. Assets include land, vehicles, stocks and brand names.

Trade credit is a period of grace offered by suppliers before payment for goods and services is due.

Collateral is the security offered to back up a request for a loan. Usually this is in the form of property, as this is unlikely to lose value.

charges but it risks upsetting shareholders, who may receive a lower dividend as a consequence. Furthermore, it is a method of finance only open to firms during profitable trading periods, and even then it may not provide sufficient funds to purchase more expensive capital assets such as property.

stop and think

Reinvested profits are the most commonly used source of finance for businesses. Despite lower dividends, why might some shareholders approve of reinvesting profits?

2 Working capital

Working capital is the day-to-day finance required by a business to pay its bills as they arise. Working capital is needed to pay for fuel, raw materials, wages and other expenses. By reducing stock levels, chasing up debtors (organisations that owe the business money) more urgently and delaying payment to suppliers, a business can reduce demands on its working capital and free up cash that can be invested elsewhere.

One way to reduce demands on working capital is to improve the trade credit terms that the business is offered by its suppliers. Many suppliers grant their customers an interest-free period of grace in which to pay for goods and services they have received. From the customers' point of view this is a useful form of finance that helps fund working capital at the expense of the seller's cash flow. The typical credit period offered to business customers is 30 days. If a business can extend this period to, say, 60 days, it is equivalent to a month's free loan.

3 Sale of assets

Firms can raise cash by selling assets that they no longer require. For example, a business might have land or buildings that are surplus, and the business owners may decide to sell these assets to raise capital for expansion.

A popular technique of raising funds in recent years has been sale and leaseback. Under this arrangement firms sell valuable assets and lease them back again. This means that they have the capital from the sale as well as the continuing use of the assets, so that their business is not disrupted. In 2005 Boots, the high street chemists, announced it was selling 300 of its stores and then leasing them back again. This action is expected to raise £250 million for the company and strengthen its financial position.

stop and think

What is the case for and against Boots plc raising money through selling its stores and then leasing them back? What alternatives might have been open to the company?

External sources of finance

When individuals, other businesses or financial institutions provide capital to a business, this is termed an external source of finance.

1 Loan capital

Bank loans are relatively straightforward to arrange if the business which is seeking the credit is solvent and has a satisfactory financial history. The financial institution advances the business a set figure, and the business makes repayments over an agreed period of time. Normally banks charge about 2 per cent over their base rate of interest for loans. Interest rates can be fixed or variable.

If the bank lending the capital considers the loan in any way risky, then it is likely to charge a higher rate of interest. Small businesses, in particular, suffer here because banks tend to regard them as more uncertain prospects than large, more established enterprises.

Banks often require security for their loans and this will usually be in the form of property. If the business defaults on the loan, the bank would sell the property and recoup the money that was loaned. In this way the bank lowers the degree of risk it incurs in making loans to businesses.

2 Share or equity capital

This is a very common form of finance, providing both start-up capital and also additional capital at later stages of a business's life.

Firms raise capital in this way by selling, quite literally, a share in their business to investors. A share is simply a certificate giving the holder ownership of part (or a share) of a company. By selling large numbers of shares, companies raise significant sums of capital. Of course, the company needs to convince prospective shareholders that the business has good prospects – in other words, that the shares represent a good investment.

Issuing shares can be very expensive, which means it is only appropriate for raising very large sums of capital. Selling shares is much more feasible for public limited companies which are quoted on the London Stock Exchange or other stock markets. Private limited companies are restricted in the ways in which they can sell their shares, and this makes raising finance more problematic for them.

There are a number of benefits from selling shares or equity as a source of finance. Although the companies will be expected to pay an annual return to shareholders (dividends), the level of this payment is not fixed, and in an unprofitable year it may be possible for the company to avoid making any payment.

3 Government grants

Businesses in designated areas of the UK can benefit from a number of schemes offered by the government or by agencies on its behalf.

Selective Finance for Investment in England (SFI)

SFI normally takes the form of a grant or occasionally a loan. In each case the amount of finance offered will be the minimum necessary for the proposed project to go ahead. There is a minimum threshold for applications of £10,000 grant. Scotland, Northern Ireland and Wales have slightly different systems.

Consultancy initiative

Firms with fewer than 500 employees that operate in less prosperous areas of the UK can claim 66 per cent of the cost of hiring consultants.

Small Firms Loan Guarantee

The Small Firms Loan Guarantee (SFLG) underwrites (that is, guarantees) loans from the banks and other financial institutions for small firms that have viable business proposals but which have failed to get a loan

Figure 3.2: Sources of finance

Type of business	Possible sources of finance	Key issues for consideration
Sole trader	Owner's savings, banks, suppliers, government grants and loans	Security for those lending funds Loss of control by owner Evidence that business has growth potential Financial history of business/owner
Partnership	Partners' savings, banks, suppliers, government grants and loans, hire purchase and leasing companies	Problems of introducing new partner Lack of collateral Expense of raising large sums of money Should partners form a limited company?
Private limited company	Depending upon the size of the company: suppliers, banks, factoring, leasing and hire purchase companies, government grants and loans, venture capital institutions, private share issues	Getting agreement of existing shareholders Difficulty finding suitable new shareholders Loss of control by existing shareholders Lack of collateral and security for lenders Element of risk in the loan
Public limited company	Suppliers, banks, factoring, leasing and hire purchase companies, government grants and loans, venture capital institutions, public share issues via the stock exchange	State of economy and stock market Move to area receiving government aid? Recent financial performance Reputation of company and senior managers

from a bank. These loans are available for periods of between two and ten years on sums ranging from £5,000 to £250,000. SFLG guarantees 75 per cent of the loan. In return for the guarantee, the borrower pays the Department of Trade and Industry (the sponsoring government agency) a premium of 2 per cent a year on the outstanding amount of the loan.

Business start-up scheme

This scheme provides financial assistance to people who were previously unemployed and who wish to start businesses. Schemes vary from area to area, but applicants are usually expected to make a substantial capital investment and, in return, receive a weekly wage and appropriate training and support.

Knowledge summary

- **Businesses can raise finance from internal and external sources.**

- **The most common source of finance is reinvested profits. This also has the advantage that the business incurs no additional costs in obtaining the finance.**

- **The major external sources of finance are bank loans, the sale of shares, and government grants.**

quick**questions**

1 Outline the disadvantages of using internal sources of finance to fund major investment programmes.

2 Why might a business try to avoid borrowing large sums of money for long periods of time?

3 What criteria might a small business have to meet to attract financial support form the government?

data**interpretation**
Reinvesting profits or paying dividends?

All companies face tough decisions in deciding on the proportion of profits to be held back for reinvestment in the business and the amount to be distributed to shareholders in the form of dividends.

For a growing company the priority might be to reinvest heavily to ensure continued growth and the financial benefits of operating on a large scale. Shareholders may be prepared to accept low dividends in these circumstances (for a limited period at least) because they hope to benefit from increasing share values and higher dividends in the future. However, this policy might not be acceptable to shareholders in an established company.

Microsoft, the US software giant, took the step from being a typical growth company using its profits for reinvestment to one which pays substantial dividends to its shareholders. In autumn 2003 the company announced that it was doubling its dividend to shareholders. The company had been under pressure to increase dividends as it had cash reserves of approximately $50 billion (£31.25 billion) and shareholders argued that they were not getting a fair deal. Microsoft is proving to be a market leader in paying large dividends to its shareholders, as most technology firms in the United States have never paid dividends.

Source: adapted news.bbc.co.uk, 12 September 2003

A What are dividends?

B Explain two ways in which Microsoft may have benefited from holding back a large proportion of its profits for reinvestment.

C Vodafone has achieved high rates of growth through the sale of shares. Consider which source of finance might be most suitable for a large multinational company planning to expand. You should justify your decision.

Setting the scene: business advice websites

The internet has transformed the market for business advice, making it much easier for budding entrepreneurs to find help and support.

In the past anyone wanting advice on starting or expanding a business would have to make an appointment with an adviser from a bank or the local council, or arrange to meet their accountant or solicitor. Today, they just need to turn on their computer to find a range of online resources.

BizHelp24 is one of these new resources. Its website (www.bizhelp24.com) offers individuals and small businesses information, news, help and services. As well as informing and educating on many key areas of business, BizHelp24 also recommends quality UK business and finance service providers.

BizHelp24 provides information and services on a variety of business and financial issues, ranging from credit policy, cash flow control and business loans to bankruptcy, home working and business accounting.

BizHelp24 promotes itself as the UK's premier small business advice website. However, if you conduct a search on the internet you will find many other websites offering business advice.

What are the possible advantages of getting business advice from a website? Can you think of any disadvantages? Visit www.bizhelp24.com to help you reflect on these questions.

What is a business plan?

A business plan is a detailed statement setting out the proposals for a new business or explaining the ways in which an existing business might be developed. Business planning involves researching and collecting information, and analysing and presenting this information in such a way as to aid decision-making.

A good business plan contains background information and comprehensive details on the proposals. It should include:

■ a summary outlining the proposal's key features

■ a statement of the business's aims and objectives

■ a description of the business to be started or the nature of the development of an existing business

■ market research data, which can be used to make and support sales forecasts

■ details on any operational requirements, including premises, IT, machinery and production facilities

■ details of all other resources required (finance, staff, etc.) to carry out the proposal

■ some information about the manager or management team of the business

■ financial forecasts showing the expected profit or loss for the first year or two, as well as estimated inflows and outflows of cash.

Business planning is not a static, one-off process. A plan should be updated to allow for new information or any unexpected changes that may occur. For example, plans may need to be revised if a new competitor enters the market; financial forecasts would need to change if the price of energy rises sharply, thereby increasing the business's costs. The aim is to set out clear plans supported by accurate forecasts.

KEY TERMS

A **business plan** is a detailed statement setting out the proposals for a new business or describing the ways in which an existing business will be developed.

Marketing is the management process that identifies, anticipates and supplies customer requirements efficiently and profitably.

Business objectives are the targets or goals of the entire organisation.

Profit measures the amount by which revenues received from selling a product exceed the total costs involved in supplying it over some time period.

Cash flow is a measure of the amount of money moving into and out of a business over some time period.

Every year about 500,000 businesses are started up. Only around 300,000 (or 60 per cent) will survive their first three years of trading. A major reason for failure of newly established businesses is poor initial planning. Even established businesses still need to plan very carefully when expanding or implementing a new strategy for the company.

Financial planning

Arguably, the financial forecasts and statements are the most important elements of a business plan. The financial plans normally contain three elements.

1 Statement of sources of finance

Most new businesses require capital. Some businesses – or new business ventures – may require vehicles, machinery and buildings. Others may simply need the working capital to meet their running and living costs before they start to receive income from sales. A vital part of financial planning is to detail how the business will pay for its capital expenses. The plan will state whether the money is to be borrowed, raised by selling shares (in the case of companies) or obtained from other sources such as retained profits, redundancy pay or savings.

2 Forecasting cash flows

Cash flow is a measure of the amount of money moving into and out of a business over time. Businesses often experience cash flow problems when expanding or starting trading. This means that cash (from sales) does not flow into the business in time to allow expenses to be paid promptly. If suppliers are not paid, they might become anxious – especially if they are dealing with a new business – and they can force the business to close down. Any potential lenders will want to see a cash flow plan or forecast to show that major cash problems are not expected or, if they are, plans are in hand to deal with them.

3 Forecasting profits

Potential lenders will also be interested to see when the project is expected to make a profit. This aspect of financial planning will be of particular interest to anyone buying shares in the business, as shareholders will expect to receive a return on their investment in the form of dividends financed out of profits.

Business planning

Planning is important because it helps the business's stakeholders to make decisions. A business plan will help managers decide whether to proceed with a proposal, and it will help potential investors decide whether to invest money in the venture. It can also be used to monitor the business's actual performance.

1 The business's owners

Planning helps entrepreneurs to think in depth about their business proposals in an analytical way. Without proper planning, the reasons for starting or expanding a business may remain unclear. Producing a business plan concentrates the mind, especially where financial matters are concerned. The plan might indicate that the project, although apparently a good idea, would not be profitable. On the other hand, planning may suggest the project will be extremely profitable.

The planning process is useful for anyone starting their own business in that it makes them consider whether they have the skills necessary to run an enterprise successfully. Many of the UK's banks produce materials to assist entrepreneurs plan a new business.

Business plans are also vital management documents. The plan can be used to monitor progress and to see whether the business is performing as expected. If something is going wrong – if, say, sales are lower than forecast – managers receive an early warning. By monitoring progress against the business plan in this way, they get a chance to take corrective action.

2 Banks and other investors

One of the most important reasons for any business to prepare a business plan is to raise money. Most businesses, even prosperous ones, are likely to need external finance when implementing important new proposals. It is imperative that they provide banks and other potential lenders with detailed information.

Lenders are likely to be especially interested in the market for the product and in sales forecasts, the cash flow associated with the product – will the business receive a steady inflow of cash, for example – and the profitability of the plan over the first year or two.

Banks and other lenders are taking a risk by investing money into a new enterprise. They will expect to see a thorough and well-prepared business plan. For example, they are more likely to respond positively to any request for finance if they can see that careful financial forecasts have been made and that the business is likely to be able to repay loans over time.

3 Suppliers

A business's suppliers will be reassured if a new or expanding business has drawn up a financial plan. This plan entails forecasting cash outlays, and it helps a business identify and find remedies for any periods of potential cash shortage. This makes it more likely that suppliers will be paid on time, assisting them in managing their own cash flow.

Business advice

There are a number of organisations that can help an entrepreneur when starting a new business or offer advice and support to established organisations.

Professional advisers

Accountants are experts in providing financial advice, particularly in respect of matters such as financial record-keeping and business taxation. Solicitors can advise on a range of legal issues relating to setting up and operating a business. Banks can also provide a range of advice for entrepreneurs and experienced managers. For example, banks can offer support with business planning, and they may be able to advise on whether a business is entitled to financial support from the UK government or the European Union.

Business Links

Business Links offer a variety of help to small and medium-sized businesses. This includes seminars and workshops on business issues, advice on UK government and EU grants, and fact sheets on key business management issues. They also offer tailored advice, support and information services.

Most areas of the UK have a local Business Link. Visit www.businesslink4london.com to find out more about one of the UK's largest Business Links, or search for your local Business Link on www.businesslink.gov.uk.

Chambers of commerce

Chambers of commerce support businesses as well as trying to influence governments to implement business-friendly policies. You can find out more about chambers of commerce at www.chambersonline.co.uk.

Trade associations

Trade organisations provide a service to specific industries and, as such, they are able to give highly specialised advice to businesses trading in that industry. For example, the Association of British Travel Agents (ABTA) and the Booksellers Association are the trade associations in the travel retail sector and the bookshops business respectively.

stop and think

Figure 3.3 shows the results of a survey on the sources of advice most used by business. Why do you think that accountants and banks are the most popular sources of advice?

Figure 3.3: Sources of advice used by small and medium-sized businesses

Source of advice used	Nov 2002 (%)
Accountant	42
Bank	32
Business Link	8
Trade association	6
Chamber of commerce	4
Solicitor or lawyer	3
Colleagues or other business people	4
Local business adviser or consultant	3
Financial adviser	2
Local council or government	2

Source: Adapted from www.euro.gov.uk/surveys

Knowledge summary

- Businesses normally draw up business plans before they first start trading, when they are expanding or when they are implementing a new strategy.

- Financial planning is particularly important. Financial plans should detail sources of finance and forecast cash flow and profits.

- Business plans can be used by managers as an early warning system (by monitoring progress against planned targets) and have a vital role to play in raising finance.

- There are numerous sources of help for drawing up business plans, including accountants, chambers of commerce and Business Link.

quick**questions**

1 Imagine you are planning to start a café in a town near to you. You have identified some premises in the high street which are empty and should be suitable. You now need to write a business plan.
- What headings would you put in your plan?
- Which parts of the plan would be of most interest to your bank manager?

2 What benefits might you gain from drawing up a business plan for your café?

3 Your café has been open for one year. Explain how you would use your business plan to judge whether your café had been a success.

data**interpretation**
Innovation in car design

121

A Outline the planning Toyota would have to carry out prior to starting the project to manufacture and sell robotic pods.

B How might business planning have helped Toyota to reduce the risk of this project? Explain your answer fully.

C Some people argue that a large company such as Toyota does not need to engage in business planning for ventures such as the robotic pod project. Discuss the case for and against this view.

Toyota's robotic pods challenge traditional car design

A new breed of wearable robotic vehicles that envelop drivers are being developed by Japanese car giant Toyota.

The company's vision for the single passenger in the twenty-first century involves the driver cruising by in a four-wheeled leaf-like device or strolling along encased in an egg-shaped cocoon that walks upright on two feet.

The models are being positioned as so-called personal mobility devices, which have few limits.

Both these prototypes will be demonstrated, along with other concept vehicles and helper robots, at the Toyota stand at Expo 2005 in Aichi, Japan.

Also on display at the show will be the egg-shaped "i-foot". This is a two-legged mountable robot-like device that can be controlled with a joystick.

Standing at a height of well over seven feet (2.1 metres), the unit can walk along at a speed of about 1.35km/h (0.83mph) and navigate staircases into the bargain.

Source: adapted from news.bbc.co.uk, 10 December 2004

Topic3 Business plans

Setting the scene: all doesn't go to plan at Cadbury

In autumn 2003 Cadbury Schweppes, the confectionery products and soft drinks manufacturers, announced that it was planning to cut 10 per cent of its 55,000 workforce.

As a part of this rationalisation programme, the company planned to shut 20 per cent of its factories around the world. Already, Cadbury Schweppes has revealed that it will close two UK factories (in Manchester and Chesterfield), with 550 jobs being lost as a consequence.

The rationalisation programme is designed to cut the company's costs by an estimated £400 million each year. Cadbury Schweppes intends to use some of the savings to market its products more effectively. For example, it hopes to sell more chewing gum in the UK, a market in which it has not been successful in the past.

And why has the company decided upon this drastic action? Because the company has not been performing to expectations. In the six months prior to the announcement, the company made a £294 million profit, one-third less than in the same period in the previous year and well below the forecast (or budgeted) figure. Cadbury Schweppes's managers decided that the company's costs were too high and took action to reduce its cost base.

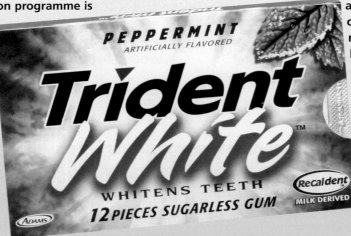

Making effective use of resources

1 Human resources

A business's human resources are all the people that work for the organisation, including office staff, operational and shop floor employees, supervisors and managers. A well-managed business seeks to employ the minimum number of employees necessary to provide goods and services at an appropriate level of quality. This helps to control costs and boost profits.

Some managers will try to control labour costs by paying low wages. They may be prepared to accept that some staff may leave the business after a short period of employment to get better paid jobs elsewhere. Some companies even move operations to regions or countries with lower labour costs. For example, Norwich Union has opted to transfer some

KEY TERMS

Human resources are the people who work within an organisation, including office staff, operational and shop floor employees, and managers

Physical resources are an organisation's fixed assets such as premises and vehicles, as well as tangible items such as stocks of raw materials, components and finished goods.

Financial resources are a business's cash and capital resources. An assessment of a business's financial resources involves examining profits and profitability as well as cash flows, working capital requirements and company financing (that is, loans, share capital and reserves).

Allocative efficiency is the process of distributing resources effectively so that the minimum number of resources are in the right place at the right time.

jobs abroad to countries such as India where wages are much lower than in the UK.

Other firms seek to manage their human resources effectively by developing a long-term relationship with their staff. These companies aim to develop the skills of their staff. This entails investment in training, but companies hope to see benefits both in terms of improved output as well as in producing motivated and highly skilled staff who can produce better quality products and deliver enhanced customer satisfaction. Businesses that adopt this approach aim to recruit staff with the potential to perform to a high standard.

2 Physical resources

All businesses, even internet-based firms, require some physical resources, including a space to work and the equipment needed to produce and deliver goods and services. Many companies will have substantial physical assets such as equipment, buildings, vehicles and stocks of raw materials and components. It is important to manage these resources as efficiently as possible to minimise costs. Keeping costs to a minimum allows managers to reduce prices or to make higher profits. For example, manufacturers want to utilise their factories as fully as possible, so that the costs of running the building are spread over as many units of output as possible.

3 Financial resources

Most businesses aim to make a profit. For this reason, it is vital that a business's finances are carefully managed. Costs should be minimised; revenues and income should be increased as much as possible. To help manage a business's finances, managers draw up budgets – financial plans setting out expected costs and revenues. If costs are higher than expected – or revenues lower than anticipated – it is important that remedial action is taken. Failure to meet its financial targets is what prompted Cadbury Schweppes to embark on a cost-cutting exercise (as we highlighted at the start of this topic). Budgets are discussed more fully in Topic 9 (see page 142).

Businesses must also manage their working capital and cash flow effectively to make sure that they have the financial resources available to meet day-to-day expenditure. For example, they need working capital to purchase new stocks, pay employee wages and meet utility bills as they fall due. An inability to make payments to suppliers, employees and other creditors can signify the start of major financial problems for many organisations. This area is so important that cash flow forecasting and management are covered in depth in Topics 7 and 8.

4 Information resources

Accurate information is the key to effective decision-making. If managers are to allocate and use their resources to maximise efficiency, they need reliable information on which to base informed decisions. Much of the information used by a business will come from its own internal historical data. With good records and information management, a business should be able to access information on:

- sales – value and volume, trends, best and worst selling lines, and profit margins

- employee details, plus pay rates and absence rates

- production data such as productivity, capacity utilisation, quality records and waste

- supplier records incorporating product ranges, prices, reliability and delivery times

- financial information, including cash flows, current available finance, and debtor and creditor records

- customer details – names, addresses, credit records, frequency and type of purchases

- records of costs, expenditure, budgets and targets.

stop and think

EasyJet is one of the UK's best-known budget price airlines. It offers an average fare of below £50 for travel on its European flights. It also manages to keep the capacity utilisation of its planes at around 88 per cent. This means that, on average, 88 out of very 100 seats on each easyJet flight are occupied by paying passengers. What benefits does easyJet gain from this effective management of its physical resources?

Benefits of resource management

Not all businesses will employ the same type and mix of resources. Some businesses, for example, are labour-intensive, others are capital intensive. Service organisations are likely to place great emphasis on human resource management; a manufacturer will need to manage significant physical resources. International businesses are likely to have greater and more sophisticated information needs than companies that operate on a national or local basis.

However, although the challenge might vary from business to business, all enterprises will benefit from managing their resources properly. By managing resources effectively, they can achieve what is known as allocative efficiency. This is the ability to ensure that the right resources (human, physical and financial) are available in the right place at the right time.

By doing this, the business prevents duplication by having too many resources, avoids idle time and minimises waste, maximises capacity utilisation, reduces costs and cash outflows, and increases profits.

Business software

Obviously, achieving allocative efficiency relies heavily on having accurate information on which to base resource decisions. To obtain accurate and up-to-date information, many businesses rely on software applications such as databases and spreadsheets.

Databases

Databases consist of collections of related information that can be manipulated to produce reports on various aspects of the business's operations. Typically, databases are used by organisations to gather and store large amounts of information on activities that need to be regularly monitored. Most businesses use databases to provide information on:

- employee details – age, name, address, pay rate, taxation rate and service record

- stock records – type, number, size, colour, minimum re-order level and supplier

- fixed asset schedule – type, age, number, location and maintenance record

- customer records – contact and account details, payment record, purchases made

- supplier records – name, address, products, prices and supplier rating.

Spreadsheets

Spreadsheets are software applications specifically designed to store and manipulate numerical information. They are therefore ideal for keeping records and monitoring financial transactions.

Records of sales and expenditure

Spreadsheets can be organised into categories detailing specific sales of individual products, departments and geographical locations, and can be recorded in terms of both sales value (£s) and volume (units). They can be used to provide reports on:

- sales per day, week, month or in total

- sales per area

- best selling and worst selling products

- trends over time

- changes in price and volume sold relationships.

Similarly the business can get reports on expenditure itemised into specific categories so that spending levels can be compared and monitored over time.

Budgets

Spreadsheets are particularly useful when setting and monitoring budgets. They can be used to set up the original budgets and, by entering the actual figures as they occur, can be set up to calculate variances (see Topic 9, page 145). This allows managers to see which areas are performing above or below expectations and to take actions to improve efficiency before problems become too great. By linking budget worksheets together, a business can also create a master budget (a forecast profit and loss account), which enables managers to assess quickly the overall effect of any transaction or change in circumstance.

Cash flow forecasts

One of the main uses of spreadsheets in business is in cash flow forecasting (see Topic 7). By setting up a cash flow forecast on a spreadsheet, a business is able to monitor its cash position constantly. Spreadsheets also enable a business to easily assess the impact of any changes in cash inflows and outflows, or any planned spending decisions on its bank balance. Managers can model alternative courses of action, and use the results to choose the option that minimises the risk to the company's cash position. This helps prevent the business from incurring cash flow problems. The advantage is that once a spreadsheet is set up in this way, a business can model any "what if" scenario immediately and automatically.

Year-end accounts

By linking various spreadsheet worksheets together – those holding records of sales and expenditure – a business can set up another worksheet to automatically follow the format and layout of a profit and loss account. This will automatically update every time a new record is made in any of the sales or expenditure categories, thus enabling the business to obtain information on its level of profitability at any point in time.

quick **questions**

1. Give two advantages a company could gain from managing its human resources effectively.

2. Outline three ways a business can employ databases to help manage information.

Knowledge summary

- **Effective human resource management can motivate staff, but its main benefit is in ensuring that the right number and type of staff are employed.**

- **Physical resources need to be managed to ensure that employees have the right equipment and appropriate premises to enable them to work effectively.**

- **Management of financial resources should help reduce costs, maximise profits and avoid cash flow problems.**

- **Attaining allocative efficiency relies heavily on good decision-making. By using business software, managers can access accurate, up-to-date information to help guide and inform their decisions**

data **interpretation**
Loyalty cards

Many organisations have introduced customer loyalty card schemes, such as the popular Nectar scheme and Tesco's clubcard. Not only do the customers gain benefits, such as rewards, money-back vouchers and discounts, but the companies themselves also gain by learning more about their customers.

By analysing the information gathered from customers when they use their clubcards, Tesco can learn:

- what day that customer usually shops

- what time they usually shop

- what products they usually purchase and how frequently

- how much that customer spends on average each visit

- the type of household

- the customer's geographical location

- their usual method of payment.

All this information can vastly help Tesco to manage its business and allocate resources more effectively. However, to do this, Tesco must first manage the information it collects efficiently.

A Explain what type of software applications would help Tesco manage the information it collects on customers.

B Visit Tesco's website, www.tesco.co.uk, and analyse the ways Tesco encourages customers to use its clubcard. Why does the company do this?

C Using the information you obtained for Task B and any ideas of your own, write a report outlining how Tesco's clubcard scheme could help the company allocate its resources more efficiently.

Costs and revenues

Setting the scene: British Airways faces higher costs

British Airways announced in 2005 its intention to increase the prices of its tickets to cover the increasing cost of fuel for its aircraft. Fuel is a major cost for airlines such as British Airways and an important influence on the prices that they charge. The current high price of aviation fuel has been caused by record crude oil prices.

British Airways said it was raising the fuel surcharge on long-haul tickets to £16 per journey, from £10 at present. For short-haul passengers, the fuel surcharge would rise to £6 from £4 per trip. The surcharge will be levied on each leg of a return flight – this means a long-haul passenger would pay £32 more for a return trip. British Airways' price increase follows a similar decision by rival Virgin Atlantic.

"Our fuel bill next year is expected to be an extra £300 million," said BA commercial director

Martin George. "With prices continuing to rise, a surcharge increase is regrettably unavoidable."

British Airways blamed high fuel prices for a 40 per cent drop in its profits during the final three months of 2004. During this time the company's fuel costs rose by 47 per cent or £106 million. British Airways' total fuel bill was approximately £1,100 million in the 2004/5 financial year and it expects it to rise to £1,400 million during 2005/6.

Source: news.bbc.co.uk, 22 March 2005

Business costs

For any business that aims to make a profit, this formula is of prime importance:

profit = revenue – total costs

Using this formula, managers can calculate the profits the business makes on its activities or, if costs exceed revenues, the losses it incurs. Clearly, it is important that any business manages and controls its costs. A cost is expenditure a firm incurs while trading, and if costs get too large, the business risks incurring a loss.

Let's look at business costs in more detail by considering an example. Bagley's is a well–established

manufacturer of chocolate. The company's best-known brand is Cream Dream. As a normal part of manufacturing Cream Dream, Bagley's might have to pay:

- the costs of buying milk, cocoa beans and sugar to make Cream Dream
- wages for staff who work in the factory
- rent for the factory
- the costs of buying lorries to deliver Cream Dream to retailers
- insurance against fire and accidents in the factory.

Many businesses divide their costs into two categories: fixed costs and variable costs. This division helps managers to calculate the impact of a change in output on the costs of producing goods and services. We'll see later how the managers at Bagley's can calculate the costs of producing Cream Dream at various levels of production.

KEY TERMS

Fixed costs are costs that do not vary with the level of output. Fixed costs exist even if a business is not producing any goods or services.

Variable costs vary directly with output. They include labour, fuel and raw materials.

Total cost is the sum of fixed and variable costs.

Semi-variable costs are expenses incurred by a business that have fixed and variable elements.

Revenue is the income a business earns from selling its goods and services.

1 Fixed costs

Fixed costs do not change when a business alters its level of output, at least in the short term. As an example, Bagley's rent and business rates do not vary if there is a short-term increase or decrease in sales of chocolate.

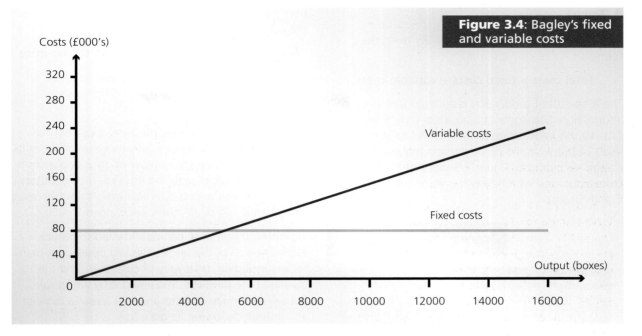

Figure 3.4: Bagley's fixed and variable costs

Figure 3.4 illustrates how fixed costs do not change as the production of Cream Dream rises or falls. When production levels are high, the factory and other resources are used more intensively. At other times the factory may not even be used; however, rent still has to be paid. Other fixed costs that Bagley's might have to pay include marketing costs, business rates and interest on loans. These will also be unaltered if production levels of Cream Dream change.

2 Variable costs

Variable costs vary directly with output. They include labour, fuel and raw materials. If Bagley's doubles its output of Cream Dream, then these costs would rise in proportion – that is, the variable costs would double. If Bagley's reduced its output, it could expect variable costs to fall.

Figure 3.4 also shows variable costs. Bagley's spends £15 in variable costs for each box of Cream Dream it manufactures. These variable costs are expenses such as ingredients (milk, cocoa and sugar) as well as wages for production line workers. The total variable costs of producing 10,000 boxes of Cream Dream each week is £150,000.

It is usual to illustrate variable costs as a straight line as in Figure 3.4. This suggests that expenditure on items such as fuel, labour, cocoa and milk rise steadily along with output of Cream Dream. Variable costs are drawn this way for simplicity. In the real world, the line may gradually flatten out. Bagley's may, for example, be able to negotiate lower prices with farmers if it buys larger quantities of milk.

3 Semi-variable costs

Semi-variable costs are those expenses incurred by a business that have fixed and variable elements. An example is the expenses associated with Bagley's delivery lorries. The insurance and road tax for the lorries are a fixed cost as they are unchanged no matter what levels of production the business achieves. Other aspects of the costs of operating a lorry depend on the level of production within Bagley's and the amount the lorry is used. Fuel would be an example of a variable cost associated with operating a lorry. In practice, many of the costs faced by businesses are semi-variable, as many have fixed and variable elements.

4 Total costs

Total costs can be calculated simply by using the formula:

total costs = fixed costs + variable costs

The total cost of production is an important piece of information. Managers of a business such as Bagley's can use this information to take decisions on the levels of output to be produced and the prices to charge for products. Figure 3.5 shows the production costs associated with Bagley's most popular brand Cream Dream.

Figure 3.5: Total cost of producing Cream Dream

Monthly production of Cream Dream	Monthly fixed costs	Variable costs	Total costs
0	£80,000	0	£80,000
2,000	£80,000	£30,000	£110,000
4,000	£80,000	£60,000	£140,000
6,000	£80,000	£90,000	£170,000
8,000	£80,000	£120,000	£200,000
10,000	£80,000	£150,000	£230,000
12,000	£80,000	£180,000	£260,000
14,000	£80,000	£210,000	£290,000
16,000	£80,000	£240,000	£320,000

Fixed costs do not change as output alters – they remain at £80,000. Variable costs are £15 per box of Cream Dream and rise directly with production. Total costs are simply the fixed and variable costs added together.

stop and think

What would be the variable and total costs of production if Bagley's produces 20,000 boxes of Cream Dream in a month?

Business revenues

A business's revenue is its income or earnings over a period of time. You may also encounter the term sales revenue which has the same meaning. Businesses calculate revenue from the sales of a single product or from sales of their entire product range. In either case, the calculation is the same:

revenue = quantity sold x average selling price

In most circumstances, a firm can exercise some control over the quantity it sells and hence its revenue.

If a business reduces its selling price, it can normally expect to sell more product. Whether this increases its revenue depends on the number of additional sales it makes as a result of reducing its price. If competitors also reduce their prices, then few extra sales will result and revenue will be relatively unchanged.

Similarly a rise in price can be expected to reduce sales. The size of the fall in sales will depend on many factors including the loyalty of customers and the quality of the products. The amount by which sales fall will determine whether the firm receives more or less revenue following its price rise.

Figure 3.6 shows how the levels of sales (or demand) determine the effects of price changes on revenue.

Figure 3.6: Impact of price changes

Price per box of Cream Dream	Sales per month	Revenue
£30	22,000	£660,000
£40	12,000	£480,000
£50	8,000	£400,000

As Bagley's raises its prices from £30 per box to £50 per box, the level of sales declines significantly. Demand is sensitive to price, perhaps because Cream Dream faces a lot of competition. In this case, because of the large fall in sales, revenue actually falls as a result of the price rise. If demand had been less sensitive to price, the price rise might have increased revenue.

Some businesses attempt to maximise their revenues by setting a low price and selling as much as possible. This makes sense in markets where consumers are looking for the lowest possible price and are not loyal to any particular products. For example, the market for basic foodstuffs is very price competitive, and some supermarkets have adopted a price-cutting approach to increase their sales and revenues.

On the other hand, some businesses sell products which are unique or regarded as highly desirable, perhaps because they are fashionable. Some clothes producers, such as Dior, can charge high prices and generate higher revenues than they might achieve with lower prices (even though their overall sales might be lower).

Finally, let's look at what impact this has on profits. As you saw at the beginning of this topic, a business makes a profit when over a period of time its revenue exceeds its total costs of production. So, for example, if Bagley's decides to sell Cream Dream for £40 per box, Figure 3.6 shows it would achieve monthly sales of 12,000 boxes and generate £480,000 in revenue. Figure 3.5 shows that its total costs at this level of production are £240,000, so it would make a profit of £220,000 (that is, £480,000 – £260,000).

stop and think

How much profit would Bagley's have made on sales of Cream Dream if it had set the price at £30 per box? Which price should it set – £30, £40 or £50 – if it wants to maximise profit?

Knowledge summary

- **Fixed costs are those such as rent which remain unchanged when output alters. Variable costs alter directly with the level of output or production.**

- **Although costs are classified as either fixed or variable, many are considered to be semi-variable.**

- **Revenue is determined by price charged and the level of sales (which is affected by consumers' reaction to price levels).**

- **Profits are calculated by deducting total costs (fixed costs and variable costs) from revenue.**

quick questions

1 Explain the difference between variable and semi-variable costs with the aid of examples.

2 A business sells 10,000 chairs a year for an average price of £45. Its variable costs are £20 per chair, and its annual fixed costs are £12,000. What is the total cost of producing 10,000 chairs and what profit would it make from selling this number of chairs?

3 An entrepreneur decides to increase the price of his product from £10 to £12. As a result he expects weekly sales to fall from 350 to 310. What is the change in his weekly revenue? Is this a good decision?

data interpretation
The T-shirt manufacturer

A T-shirt manufacturer produces and sells 1,000 T-shirts every month for £20 each. The company's production costs are:

Expenditure	£
Monthly rent	1,450
Cloth and cotton per T-shirt	8
Wage cost per T-shirt	4
Marketing costs per month	600
Heating and lighting per month	350

A Calculate the manufacturer's monthly profits or losses.

B Suppose that the manufacturer's buyers request 500 additional T-shirts per month and are willing to pay £22 per T-shirt. To fulfil this order, wage costs rise to £10 per T-shirt because of overtime. Calculate the effect on profits.

C Why might the T-shirt manufacturer find that profits do not rise as a result of accepting the extra order? Explain your answer fully.

Profit is one of the most important business goals. It is the profit motive that drives many people towards starting out in business in the first place.

Business owners want to know how successful they've been, and profit is one of the main ways a business monitors its success or failure. One of the key factors in determining how much profit a business makes is how much it has managed to produce (and at what cost) and sell (and at what price).

Imagine you are setting up a business or launching a product. It is important you know how much your product costs. This information will help you decide:

- how much to charge
- how many you need to sell to make an acceptable profit
- how much you could afford to drop prices, or let costs rise, before you start losing money
- how many products you have to sell to cover costs and avoid losing money.

Breakeven analysis is a simple and valuable forecasting technique. Businesses can use breakeven analysis to:

- estimate the levels of output they need to produce and sell
- assess the impact of price changes on profit and the output needed to break even
- assess how changes in costs impact on profits and breakeven output
- determine their margin of safety and what changes in levels of demand they can survive.

Costs and revenue

In working through this topic, we are going to consider breakeven in relation to a manufacturer of trainers. Suppose the fixed costs of the factory that manufactures trainers is, say, £20,000 a month – this cost has to be paid regardless of the level of production or sales.

stop and think

Suppose you are about to open a nightclub and you are currently looking for suitable premises. You have written a business plan and conducted market research. By using breakeven analysis, you can model how many customers paying entrance fees and how much drink sales are needed each night before you make any profit. Why might it be valuable to know this information before setting up the business?

KEY TERMS

Profit arises when a firm's revenue is greater than its total costs. A loss occurs when revenue is less than a firm's total costs.

Revenue is the income a business earns from selling its goods and services.

Fixed costs are costs that do not vary with the level of output. Fixed costs exist even if a business is not producing any goods or services.

Variable costs vary directly with output. They include labour, fuel and raw materials.

Breakeven is the point at which a business sells exactly the right number of products so that its revenue equals its costs. In other words, at breakeven the business makes no profit but also incurs no loss.

Margin of safety is the amount current output exceeds the amount necessary to break even.

Variable costs are costs that are dependent on the production level. If production increases, then costs like wages and raw materials also increase. The variable cost per unit is the cost of producing one unit of a good or service. So, if the cost of producing 1,000 pairs of trainers is £7,500, the variable cost is £7.50 per pair.

Total costs are the sum of the fixed and variable costs. So, in the case of our example of the trainer manufacturer, if the factory produces 1,000 pairs of trainers a month, its total monthly cost is £27,500 (that is, £7,500 + £20,000). The total cost or producing each pair is £27,500/1,000, that is £27.50 each.

Revenue is the income that a business receives from selling goods or services. If each pair of trainers sells at £32.50, the total revenue received each month by the manufacturer is £32,500 (assuming all 1,000 pairs of the monthly output are sold).

stopandthink

Suppose the trainer manufacturer manages to double output while holding its fixed costs constant. What happens to the total cost of each unit?

Calculating breakeven

Breakeven is calculated by using the formula:

$$\text{breakeven point} = \frac{\text{total fixed costs}}{\text{selling price} - \text{variable cost per unit}}$$

Applying the formula to our trainer manufacturer:

$$\text{breakeven point} = \frac{20,000}{(32.50 - 7.50)} = 800 \text{ units}$$

So, in order to break even, the factory must make and sell 800 pairs of trainers each month. Obviously by making 1,000 pairs a month, factory output is currently above the breakeven point. There is a simple relationship between breakeven and profit

■ if total output and sales are greater than breakeven, then revenue is greater than cost – the business makes a profit

■ if total output and sales are equal to breakeven, then revenue equals total costs – the business breaks even

■ if total output and sales are less than breakeven, then revenue is less than total cost – the business makes a loss.

Construction of breakeven charts

The breakeven point can also be represented by a chart. This is useful, as diagrammatic representation makes it easier for non-mathematical people to understand. A breakeven chart is compiled from plotting costs and revenue information on a graph.

Step 1: fixed costs

These remain the same no matter how much output is produced, so fixed constants are represented by a horizontal line.

Step 2: variable costs

These rise in direct relationship to production. If there is no output, variable costs are zero, but as output is produced, variable costs increase in direct proportion to output. So the variable cost line is shown sloping upwards from left to right, with the slope of the graph representing the corresponding rise in cost as output rises.

Step 3: total costs

This is plotted by adding the fixed cost and variable cost lines together. At zero output there are no variable costs, but still fixed costs. So the total costs line starts at the fixed cost level and rises, with output, in the same relationship as variable costs.

Step 4: revenue

Revenue is the income from sales. If there are no sales, revenue is also nil. But as sales rise, so does revenue. So the revenue line is shown sloping upwards from left to right, with the slope of the graph representing the corresponding rise in revenue as sales increase.

Figure 3.7 (see page 132) shows the breakeven chart for our trainer manufacturer. It shows the profit (or loss) made at each level of production. The amount of profit or loss at any level of production is shown by the vertical distance between the total cost and revenue lines. If actual production and sales levels are below breakeven output, the business will be making a loss; if production and sales levels are above breakeven, the business will be in profit. The margin of safety is the difference between breakeven output and the current level of output. It represents the number of units by which production and sales can fall before the business starts to make a loss.

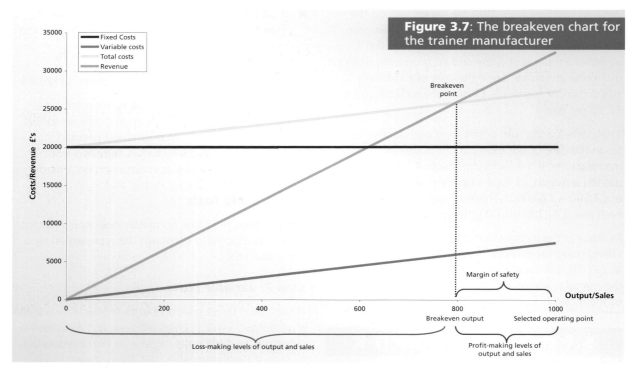

Figure 3.7: The breakeven chart for the trainer manufacturer

Strengths and weaknesses

The key strength of breakeven analysis is that it allows managers to model "what if" situations. Few business situations remain constant. Changes in the economy, markets and fashions affect costs and revenues. The breakeven point will change if a business's costs or prices change. Figure 3.8 summarises the effect that some price and cost changes will have on a company's breakeven position.

Breakeven is a simple method to examine the effect of any changes in the business cost or price structure on overall profits. It is a quick exercise to perform and, as results can be displayed in chart format, it is easy to see the impact any changes have. However, it is important to note that any information gained from breakeven analysis is only as accurate as the information it was based upon. Collecting accurate information can be expensive and time-consuming.

Although a simple and easy tool, breakeven analysis has drawbacks:

- fixed costs are unlikely to stay constant in the long run, and are likely to change as productive capacity changes

- variable costs and sales revenue are also unlikely to be straight lines – factors like discounts, bulk buying and overtime cause constant fluctuations

- breakeven analysis makes the assumption that a business sells its entire output – in reality, businesses are rarely able to sell all they produce

Figure 3.8: Factors affecting breakeven

Change	Impact on breakeven
Fixed or variable costs rise	Total costs also rise, so more units have to be sold to cover costs. The number of units needed to break even increases.
Fixed or variable costs fall	Total costs also fall, so fewer units have to be sold to cover costs. The number of units needed to break even falls.
Sales price rises	Each unit produces more revenue, so costs are covered more quickly. The breakeven number of units decreases.
Sales price falls	Each unit sold earns less revenue, so it takes more units to cover costs. The breakeven output point increases.

- breakeven is a static model of dynamic business forces, and the model must be recalculated each time a single factor changes.

Breakeven analysis should not be used as the only management tool when making decisions as it can sometimes be misleading. For example, business relationships are rarely straightforward. If a manufacturer of chocolate bars is struggling to break even and make a profit, it may decide to raise the selling price of each bar from 35p to 40p. In theory, this should help it to break even (or even make a profit). In practice, the business needs to consider the impact of any price rise on its sales.

Knowledge summary

- Breakeven is an easy way to measure the impact on profits (or losses) as levels of business activity change.

- Breakeven can be used to examine "what if" situations. It allows a business to analyse different scenarios.

- Increases in costs make it more difficult to break even; falling costs mean fewer sales are needed to break even.

quick**questions**

1 Explain the term breakeven. Why is the determination of the breakeven point important?

2 Explain two ways in which breakeven charts can help managers make decisions.

3 Why might calculating breakeven be more useful than drawing breakeven charts? Conversely, when might drawing a chart prove helpful?

data**interpretation**

Beasty Burgers

Beasty Burgers was set up by John and Nick Amis following a trip to the United States. They decided that the burgers in the UK were poor in comparison to US versions. Although slightly more expensive than many competitors, Beasty Burgers' reputation for quality and size has helped John and Nick establish a successful business. Figure 3.9 has data on Beasty Burgers' average costs and prices for its last financial year.

Figure 3.9: Beasty Burgers costs and prices

Annual sales/ output of burgers	Total variable cost (at £2.00 each)	Annual fixed cost	Total cost	Total revenue (selling price of £3.00)
0	0	£40,000		0
16,000	£32,000			£48,000
32,000	£64,000			
48,000				
64,000				
80,000				

A Complete Figure 3.9 by calculating total cost and sales revenue at each level of production.

B Using your findings construct a breakeven chart and calculate the profit or loss made at 30,000, 50,000 and 70,000 units of output.

C Beasty Burgers expects its variable costs to rise by 10 per cent next year and its rent to go up by £1,000 per month. John is totally unconcerned; he says they can just raise prices by 10 per cent. Work out Beasty Burgers' new breakeven point should these changes take place. Draft a memo advising John and Nick of any other factors they should take into account when considering a price rise.

Once a company has determined and agreed its aims and objectives, the business needs to ensure that it actually has the finances in place to execute its plans. Without sufficient cash to realise its plans, it may not even be in a position to start to trade.

For example, the major mobile phone companies like Vodafone, Orange and mm0$_2$ have had to spend large sums to secure licences for the right to operate 3G services and to set up the necessary mobile networks. They had to meet these upfront costs before they could supply 3G services to any customers – in other words, these businesses faced large cash outflows before any cash inflows would be forthcoming from customers.

If these companies were to meet their objectives to establish a successful 3G mobile phone business, they had to be able to finance their 3G networks. The companies needed substantial finance to meet the costs of each stage of implementation. If any company failed to have sufficient cash to pay for costs, contractors, licences, advertising and marketing, it risked falling behind its competitors or, at worst, being unable to complete the launch of its 3G service.

Preparing cash flow forecasts is a form of proactive management. All businesses are aware that the delay between the outlay on materials, stock and wages and the receipt of income from sales can cause difficulties. So rather than waiting for cash flow problems to arise and then trying desperately to solve them (reactive management), a skilled manager tries to anticipate problems in advance using cash flow forecasting, and actively plans ways of maintaining a good cash position.

A cash flow forecast is a detailed examination of a company's expected future cash inflows and outflows over a future period (such as one year ahead). They are usually calculated on a monthly basis and, by keeping a running total of the business's anticipated bank balance, managers can highlight times when cash difficulties may arise.

Banks encourage their business account holders to draw up cash flow forecasts. Most high street banks produce a range of information and material to help their customers with forecasting; some, for example, provide templates that allow firms to compile cash flow forecasts online.

The purpose of cash flow forecasts

Monitoring cash flows helps a business maintain its position so that sufficient funds are available to finance its day-to-day operations. More small businesses in the UK fail as a result of poor cash flow than for any other reason (such as lack of profits).

stop and think

Why is it important that managers can identify periods of poor cash flow? For example, what might be the consequences for a retail business like Matalan if it finds that it has insufficient cash to pay its employees' wages or its utility bills? If a cash flow forecast suggests that a business might have some difficulty with its cash position in the future, what help could it arrange with the bank to prevent the problems occurring?

KEY TERMS

Cash flow is the money that enters and leaves a business as it makes and receives payments.

Cash flow forecasts are detailed estimates of when and how cash is expected to flow into and out of a business.

Cash inflows are money received by a business from sales, investments or loans.

Cash outflows are money that leaves a business through paying for wages, materials, marketing, fixed assets, etc.

Constructing forecasts

Cash flow forecasts are constructed using historical information (past company data) and the forecasts contained in the budgets. They have sections:

- cash inflows
- cash outflows
- the running balance.

Cash inflows

Cash inflows – money received by a business – can come from a variety of sources. The main source is usually sales revenue – payments from customers for goods bought. In cash flow forecasting, it is important to understand the distinction between cash and credit sales. Goods sold on cash terms generate income that the business can use immediately. With credit sales, however, customers are given a set amount of time to pay for the goods or services after purchase. Credit terms typically range from 30 days from the date of purchase to longer-term deals like the "buy now, pay in 12 months" offers available from some furniture retailers. Businesses that make credit sales need to be aware that they won't receive the cash from sales for perhaps a considerable period of time.

Other sources of cash inflows include:

- loans – although loans eventually have to be paid back to the lender, a loan initially results in a cash inflow into the business's account

- grants – these are often awarded by government agencies or through EU programmes to help firms create jobs or promote environmental protection

- capital – money paid into a business by its owners, including the funds received by a company when it sells more shares.

Cash outflows

Cash outflows – money paid out by the business and leaving its bank account – arise through payments for:

- purchases, including raw materials
- wages and salaries
- heat, light and water bills
- rent and rates on business premises
- interest on loans
- capital expenditure
- taxation.

Figure 3.10: An example cash flow forecast

	April	May	June	July
Cash inflows				
Sales	126,300	126,700	127,300	127,200
Loans	30,000	nil	nil	nil
Capital introduced	nil	10,000	nil	nil
(1) Total cash inflow	156,300	136,700	117,300	117,200
Cash outflows				
Purchases	20,136	20,144	20,176	20,700
Wages and salaries	42,080	42.720	43,680	43,520
Heat and light	800	800	800	800
Water	500	500	500	500
Telephone	1,120	1,120	1,120	1,120
Advertising	28,700	5,000	3,000	3,000
Administration expenses	19,240	19,870	20,100	20,000
Distribution expenses	6,400	6,550	6,720	6,680
Capital expenditure	nil	60,000	nil	16,200
(2) Total cash outflow	118,976	155,606	94,998	112,520
(3) Opening bank balance	(14,300)	23,024	4,118	26,420
(4) Net cash flow (1 – 2)	37,234	(18,906)	22,302	4,680
(5) Closing bank balance (3 + 4)	23,024	4,118	26,420	31,100

This is not a complete list. Many businesses will incur other types of expenditure, such as distribution expenses, administration, advertising, cleaning, maintenance and repair costs. The actual categories for each business will vary depending on the type of industry in which it operates. Note also that just as businesses can make sales on cash and credit terms, so they will often purchase items on credit terms.

stop and think

What items would need to be included as major items of cash outflow if you were constructing a cash flow forecast for your school or college?

The running balance

This running balance is a calculation of the net effect of the cash inflows and outflows on the business's bank balance on a monthly basis. It shows how much money the company anticipates it has (or hasn't) got in its bank account at the end of each month.

Figure 3.10 shows a simple cash flow forecast. In practice, many actual cash flow forecasts will contain more detail – with more categories of expenditure, for example – due to their key importance in assessing a business's financial health. In appearance, however, a cash flow forecast will look like Figure 3.10, with a layout similar to a business's other budgets.

A cash flow forecast like Figure 3.10 would be compiled by taking information and forecasts from budgets and by using historical data. The calculations are made in the lines numbered 1–5. Lines 1 and 2 are simply the respective totals of the cash inflows and outflows. The running balance is calculated and displayed in lines 3–5: the business's closing bank balance at the end of each month is forecast by adding the net cash flow (which might be a negative number of course) to its starting bank balance.

Benefits of cash flow forecasts

A major benefit of cash flow forecasting is that it enables managers to anticipate periods when cash flows may be high or low, thereby indicating periods when cash might be available for spending and investment or, more importantly, periods when cash is likely to be tight.

Cash flow forecasting is not just a defensive activity. It brings a number of positive benefits for a business:

- ensuring liquid assets are available to meet payments and maintain working capital

- identifying periods of cash shortfall so remedial action like overdrafts can be arranged

- identifying periods of cash surplus so high-cost items can be purchased at little risk

- highlighting periods when large expenditure is not possible, so businesses may have to spread payments for fixed assets over monthly instalments

- limiting borrowing and minimising interest payments, as a cash flow forecast should enable a business to only borrow the sum that it needs

- highlighting cash surpluses that can be more profitably invested elsewhere

- supporting applications to lenders by demonstrating that funds would be available to meet interest and capital repayments on loans.

Knowledge summary

- **Cash flow forecasts provide a prediction of how much money a firm will have available at the end of each month.**

- **Cash flow forecasts provide a method that allows managers to anticipate periods of cash shortages or surpluses.**

- **There is often a considerable delay between companies having to expend money (cash outflows) and receiving payments from customers (cash inflows)**

- **By being proactive, a business can avoid a poor cash flow position and benefit from increased business stability and performance.**

quick questions

1 Why do banks encourage businesses to use cash flow forecasts?

2 Explain the difference between cash and credit payments.

3 What is the significance of the running balance on a cash flow forecast?

Brian Harvey runs his own catering business out of small shop outlet in London's East End. Business has been growing and he has decided to approach the bank for a loan to help him purchase a new delivery vehicle. Although the bank's small business manager is satisfied that Brian's company is successful (making satisfactory profits for the last two years), she is not convinced the business can afford to spend £22,000 on a new van with integral heated and refrigerated units.

Brian is determined that the business needs the new vehicle to be able to provide a reliable and high-quality service to clients. Although the emphasis (and recent expansion) of Brian's business is based on the quality of food that he prepares, he is convinced that by being able to deliver the product in perfect condition he will attract bigger clients and contracts. He will not be restricted to delivering only to venues with facilities to serve his hot and cold buffet selections. Brian has decided to produce a cash flow forecast for the next six months to persuade the bank to accept his plan.

Figure 3.11 shows some initial figures that Brian has produced, setting out his forecasts for sales revenue and expenditure on purchases over the next six months. Brian's other expenses and cash inflows are detailed below.

Brian intends to purchase the van in March by borrowing £22,000 from the bank. The bank charges 8 per cent interest, and this would mean monthly repayments (including interest) of £780 per month. He wants the funds to enter his account during the first week of March and he intends to purchase the van in the following week.

Figure 3.11: Forecast sales revenue and purchases

	Sales revenue	Purchases
January	£6,000	£1,600
February	£6,000	£1,600
March	£9,000	£2,400
April	£9,000	£2,400
May	£9,000	£2,400
June	£10,000	£2,800

In order to help boost his sales immediately Brian is going to start advertising in the local press. This will cost £700 in January and February, but will decrease to £500 per month for the rest of the six-month period. He will also start to offer 30-day credit terms. He anticipates that from March, £2,000 of sales each month will be on credit.

Brian has a business mortgage on his shop that costs £1,450 per month, but he is able to offset part of this cost by renting out the flat above the shop to students for £580 per month.

Currently Brian pays himself £1,750 per month and employs one kitchen hand at a cost of a further £800 per month. Brian's wage bill is expected to rise in March to £1,600 a month as he expects that he will need an extra employee to meet increased demand.

Utility costs to cover all the business bills are currently £850 per month and Brian expects these to stay the same during the period. Running costs for the new van are difficult to estimate but Brian reckons that insurance and fuel will only amount to £360 per month. Other business costs, miscellaneous and sundry items, usually come to about £150 each month.

Brian will have an opening bank balance of £840 at the beginning of January.

A Compile a cash flow forecast for Harvey Catering from the information given.

B What difficulties does offering credit terms cause Brian?

C Using the information given, and any ideas of your own, draft a letter to the bank from Brian outlining why he should be given the loan he requires.

Cash flow monitoring

Setting the scene: Pro Game Retail

Pro Game Retail was set up in 2002 by a group of business graduates to sell games consoles, games and peripherals. The company was successful and profitable, but in late 2004 it began to run out of cash and was in danger of closure.

Cash flow problems arise because in the usual course of business activity companies have to spend money on buying stock and machinery and paying employees before they are in a position to sell products to customers. In other words, companies must meet the costs of bringing products to the market before they can receive income through sales.

Pro Game's problems happened for exactly this reason. As the company expanded by opening more stores, it had to order more stock, buy fixtures and employ extra staff. Each new shop incurs costs, but it takes time for customers to become aware of the new outlet and start using it, especially in such a competitive marketplace.

How would a company like Pro Game Retail try to encourage custom and generate sales from the new store? What implications would this have for its cash flow before its sees the sales benefit from any increase in customers?

Interpreting cash flow statements

Simple analysis of a business's cash position can be undertaken by using a cash flow forecast to examine the closing balances at the end of each month. This will determine whether any cash flow problems are likely, by showing if a low or negative cash balance is forecast. A more in-depth examination would involve:

■ determining whether the cash problem is likely to deepen or improve over time – that is, is it a short-term or long-term problem?

■ finding the cause of the cash flow problem – is it a temporary one-off problem or the result of several cumulative underlying difficulties?

■ looking at the timings of receipts and payments – can the situation be resolved by spreading any large payments into several smaller ones over time?

KEY TERMS

Trade credit is an arrangement in which suppliers allow customers a period of time (usually one or two months) to pay their bills.

Overtrading occurs when a firm expands too rapidly without having the cash resources in place to adequately finance the expansion and meet its day-to-day commitments as well.

Working capital is the excess of current assets over current liabilities.

■ assessing the accuracy of the forecast – when applying for loans many businesses tend to be overly optimistic, assuming, for example, that extra advertising will automatically produce greater sales

■ identifying periods when the business has relatively large amounts of available cash – this is the ideal time to make expensive purchases or investments without putting the company at risk.

Cash flow problems

Cash flow problems can arise for all sorts of reasons. Many small businesses simply suffer from the fact that their owners assume that their enterprises are inherently profitable and pay themselves too high a wage (drawings). Some owners fail to reduce their wages in times of decreased sales as they have personal financial commitments to meet such as mortgages and household bills. Identifying the reason why the cash flow problem has arisen can in many cases go a long way to providing the answer for how to remedy it. Here are some of the common causes of cash flow problems.

Excessive borrowing

To be competitive in many markets requires expensive equipment, substantial marketing or a prime business location. Many companies take out substantial loans and mortgages to meet these high-cost expenses. However, all loans and mortgages need repaying with interest. Some businesses find out that having the right resources and locations does not automatically generate quality products, good customer service and high sales: they must also be well managed, and they struggle to meet the monthly repayments on outstanding loans and mortgages.

Excessive trade credit

Many companies offer credit terms to attract customers and increase sales. However, this can mean that cash inflows from sales are not realised quickly enough to meet outflows. The business is faced with bills and wages before it receives the income from sales.

s t o p a n d **t h i n k**

Although supermarkets do not sell goods to customers on credit, it is still possible for them to suffer cash flow problems. Think of two reasons why this situation could occur.

Excessive stocks

Buying in bulk is cheaper per unit than buying stock in small orders – it therefore helps reduce costs and increase profits. However, a business needs the cash to buy in bulk, and having too much stock represents a large outflow of cash that is not generating income. Stock has to be stored while waiting to be sold, causing more outflows with no inflows.

Overtrading

Overtrading results when a business tries to expand too quickly. This was the situation faced by Pro Game Retail (see setting the scene opposite). Expansion and growth can cause a business to encounter substantial financial outflow before generating a compensating inflow from sales. Payment commitments from existing areas of the business can become difficult to meet as working capital becomes overextended, and a profitable, successful business can face serious financial difficulty including liquidation.

External factors

External factors that impact on a business are more difficult to anticipate and remedy as, in many cases, they are out of the control of the company itself. External factors include:

- the actions of competitors causing loss of sales

- changes in interest rates causing increased loan payments

- changes in exchange rates leading to greater competition from cheaper imports and fewer export sales

- innovation leading to product obsolescence (how many people now own a typewriter?)

- changes in legislation, for example tougher pollution laws or an increase in the minimum wage, requiring increased business expenditure.

Poor planning

Poor financial planning is a frequent cause of cash flow difficulty. Many businesses do not forecast cash flow at all. Others do so, but forget to include or anticipate areas of expenditure like tax payments, or are over-optimistic – they assume that revenue will increase disproportionately to expenditure or they fail to recognise the full impact of seasonal or cyclical factors that can cause cash inflow to slow dramatically.

s t o p a n d **t h i n k**

Yaoh manufactures sun cream and skincare products suitable for vegans. This type of niche business may suffer from seasonal fluctuations in sales that can cause cash flow problems. What steps could Yaoh take to try and prevent cash flow problems from occurring?

Improving cash flow

The key reason for drawing up a cash flow forecast is to prevent a business from running out of cash and being unable to meet its day-to-day running costs. This raises the obvious question of how can businesses improve their situation when in difficulties.

One solution is to arrange an overdraft in advance as soon as difficulties are anticipated, although this may not address the underlying reasons for the situation. However, although an overdraft, like any other loan arrangement, may improve the short-term cash position, it will require making regular interest payments so it does have implications for cash outflows. Alternatively a company can try improving inflows by trying to boost sales, although most forms of promotion will involve an initial cash outflow.

There are other solutions to improve a firm's cash position that do not necessarily add to cash outflows (in the short or long term). These include:

- buying and holding fewer stocks, perhaps adopting a just-in-time approach

- improving credit control, by allowing less time for customers to settle their bills (though this may have an impact on the number of customers the company has)

- rescheduling payments so that large payments are spread over a period of several smaller payments or so that large outflows take place only at times of cash surpluses

- selling fixed assets, such as machinery and vehicles, to gain a cash injection – although the company will no longer have productive use of those assets

- extending trade credit from suppliers, allowing the company more time to garner cash inflows – ideally a company should negotiate a longer payment period with suppliers than it offers to customers.

Finally, if a company is forced to operate its sales on credit terms, it can opt to factor its income. This involves selling the debts owed by customers to a factoring service which will give the company an immediate cash advance on its credit sales. The factoring service collects the debt from the customer as it falls due for payment, taking a percentage commission for its services. This method does improve a company's cash position – it no longer has to wait weeks or months to realise the benefit from credit sales – but it has a detrimental effect on profits as a percentage of all credit sales goes to the factoring service.

stop and think

All the ideas for improving a business's cash position have potential drawbacks. Consider the reaction of (potential) customers of electrical goods retailers like Comet and Curry's if credit terms are restricted or removed entirely.

Knowledge summary

- **Cash flow analysis is not simply designed to identify cash problems. It also involves identifying periods when a company may be cash rich.**

- **Cash flow problems are encountered by many businesses; finding the underlying cause of the problem often provides pointers toward its solution.**

- **Several methods of boosting cash inflows actually also require cash outflows. These solutions are often not appropriate or feasible for some companies to adopt.**

- **Prevention is better than cure. Effective cash flow planning and management is preferable to reacting to cash flow problems once they have happened.**

quick questions

1 Give three reasons for analysing a company's cash flow statement.

2 Explain two changes to external factors that could cause a business to face cash flow problems.

3 Outline three actions a business could take to tackle short-term cash flow problems.

Willcox Web Design

Robbie Willcox runs a website design company. Until recently he has had a team of designers working for him, but now he is left with only one apprenticeship trainee. The problem seems to be that although Robbie's company is receiving more and more orders, he doesn't have the resources to be able to pay his workforce on time, despite taking out a loan in May to help him meet his commitments and buy new equipment and software applications. Figure 3.12 shows data from Robbie's actual cash flow for the last four months.

Figure 3.12: Willcox Web Design cash flow

	April	May	June	July
Cash inflows				
Sales	21,300	11,700	7,300	7,200
Loans received		10,000		
(1) Total cash inflow				
Cash outflows				
Wages and salaries	11,000	6,140	4,700	3,890
Purchases	5,200	4,200	2,400	2,400
Heat and light	90	90	90	90
Water	110	110	110	110
Office rent	3,000	nil	nil	3,000
Rates (for the year)	1,200	n/a	n/a	n/a
Telephone	200	230	190	185
Advertising	150	150	150	150
Loan payments	nil	nil	345	345
Insurance	300	300	300	300
Motor expenses	570	480	390	410
Capital expenditure (new equipment)		8,000		
(2) Total cash outflow				
(3) Opening bank balance	1,427			
(4) Net cash flow (1 – 2)				
(5) Closing bank balance **(3 + 4)**				

A Complete the cash flow forecast.

B Undertake an analysis of your completed cash flow statement. What difficulties has Robbie encountered over the last few months?

C Using the information given, and any ideas of your own, write a report to Robbie advising him of what steps you would recommend he take to try and improve his situation.

Setting and monitoring budgets

Setting the scene: the purpose of budgets and forecasts

Most businesses have an aim or mission statement. The mission statement can be used to underpin a business's goals, objectives and targets.

A good example of a mission statement is Coca-Cola's aim to "get people to drink more Coca-Cola than water". Coca-Cola's objectives and targets must be co-ordinated so that the whole company is working in the same direction at the same time to achieve this mission.

A business as large as Coca-Cola needs to ensure that it has the available resources and finances needed to achieve its planned objectives. This is where businesses use budgets: they provide a plan of future activity and the finances available to fund that activity, and set targets to be achieved – in short, they help staff stay focused on achieving the company's objectives.

The financial proposals and targets contained within budgets are often challenging. Given unlimited funds, most people could organise a successful marketing campaign to raise sales and therefore achieve the target. However, can they do the same within a specified budget and time period?

Think of the launch of a new games console like the PlayStation 2: the marketing and advertising budget has to be sufficient to raise awareness of the product with potential consumers and stimulate them to make a purchase, but small enough that the company still makes a profit. Advertising, production and distribution must all be co-ordinated and financed. Budgets are essential in this planning process.

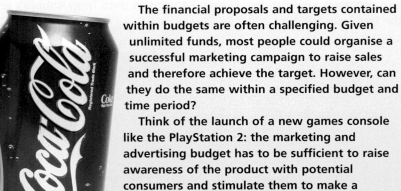

KEY TERMS

A **budget** is a financial plan for the future operations of the business. Budgets are used to set targets to monitor performance and control operations.

Variance analysis is one of the methods used to monitor company performance. It is the comparison of what actually happened with what the business budgeted (planned to happen).

An **adverse variance** occurs when the business's actual results are worse than those anticipated and planned for in the budget.

A **favourable variance** occurs when the actual results are better than those anticipated and planned for in the budget.

The budgetary process

As budgets are so valuable, they can actually be drawn up for any individual person, project or department. However, the main budgets and forecasts focus on key areas of business activity such as sales and expenditure. The budgetary process usually starts with forecasting sales.

Sales budgets

This is the key budget, as the amount a business sells determines the amount it needs to produce or supply, which in turn has implications for the number and type of staff that are employed and how much activity will be taking place throughout major parts of the organisation. Sales are also the main area of

Figure 3.13: An example of a sales budget

	Actual sales			Forecast sales			
	Jan	Feb	Mar	Apr	May	June	July
Sales value (£)	125,000	125,400	126,000	126,300	126,700	127,300	127,200
Sales (units)	5,000	5,080	5,200	5,260	5,340	5,460	5,440

generating cash inflows, so it is also a key indicator of how much money a business expects to receive.

Sales budgets are difficult to forecast, as the amount a company will sell in future is affected by consumer tastes and fashions as well by the actions of competitors. To forecast sales, companies therefore use combinations of:

- historical data

- trend analysis

- market research

- plus their own experience and knowledge of the market and their customers.

One problem for multi-product companies is that the forecast sales may be different for each product, so they may need to draw up a separate forecast and budget for each product they sell.

Notice that the example sales budget in Figure 3.13 shows forecasted sales value and units; this is so there is an estimate both of how much income will be received from sales and how many units the company needs to produce to satisfy demand.

Expenditure budgets

Once it has decided how much it is likely to sell, a company then calculates how much it needs to supply. For a manufacturing business, this would involve producing a production budget setting out how many units need to be made. For a retail outlet, an expenditure budget would be based on a calculation of the amount of stock it needed. This is important because if too few goods are available, a company could lose customers, sales and profits. However if it has too many goods, then it risks either purchasing goods that cannot be sold – this is especially a problem for perishable items like food products – or incurring potentially high storage costs. This budget is important, as invariably the amount a company needs to supply is the major determinant of how much it needs to spend.

First a company needs to ensure that it has enough supplies to be able to satisfy its forecast sales. The expenditure budget sets out the material or stock requirements that will be needed for any department, project or individual product. It is possible that an expenditure budget could be constructed forecasting

143

stop and think

If a business overestimates its future sales, this would impact on other areas of activity. How would a firework manufacturer's profits be affected if it overestimated its future sales? Similarly, what problems might occur if it underestimated its future sales?

each area of expenditure separately and in detail. This budget should ensure that resources are bought and ready at the right place and time.

Next, managers need to decide how many, and what type of, employees they need. Managers need to know if they currently have too many employees or, more importantly, too few. This aspect of planning is crucial so that a business can make sure it has sufficient employees but not so many that some stand around idle.

If a company gets this aspect of budgeting right, it will be optimising potential profits by not losing sales (by not having products or staff available) or wasting money on unproductive staff.

Finally, a company will then forecast any other areas of regular and expected costs in line with its expected level of activity. This would include such items as:

- rent and rates
- distribution
- repairs
- utility bills
- stationery
- miscellaneous or sundry items.

Figure 3.14 shows an example of an expenditure budget.

stopand**think**

What costs may also be incurred by a chain of fashion outlets such as New Look besides those already given in headings in the expenditure budget in Figure 3.14?

Master budgets

Businesses often create a master budget (a forecasted profit and loss account) compiled from the individual budgets. This allows owners and managers to get an idea of how the cumulative affect of the budget decisions is likely to impact on profitability.

stopand**think**

It is likely that at some point a company's employees will want a pay rise. How will the calculation and drawing up of budgets help managers make decisions on pay? In particular, how would the compilation of a master budget help to inform the level of any pay rise offered?

Figure 3.14: An example expenditure budget

	Actual expenditure			Forecast expenditure		
	Jan	Feb	Mar	Apr	May	June
Purchases	52,730	53,100	53,120	53,200	54,120	53,850
Wages	19,700	19,700	21,850	21,850	21,850	22,300
Rates	4,000	4,000	4,000	4,000	4,000	4,000
Utilities	8,200	8,200	8,300	8,300	8,300	8,300
Distribution	7,250	7,300	7,450	7,600	7,750	7,900
Stationery & sundries	1,110	1,110	1,110	1,110	1,110	1,110
Repairs	800	800	800	800	800	800
Total	93,790	94,210	96,630	96,860	97,930	98,260

Benefits of budgeting

As well as a being vitally important in business planning, budgets are also useful:

- to aid communication throughout a business

- to aid co-ordination of activities

- to make managers consider expenditure decisions in advance (proactivity)

- to motivate staff (through communication, delegation and target-setting)

- to help persuade potential lenders to invest money.

All businesses can benefit from budgets. But do you think it is as important for a small local business like a newsagent to budget as it is for a multinational public limited company like Cadbury Schweppes? Would each type of business receive the same level of benefit from budgetary activities?

One of the main benefits to be gained from budgetary exercises is in the monitoring of business performance. Did the business perform as expected? Did some areas perform better or worse than planned? Were costs and/or revenues higher or lower than anticipated? And, most importantly, why did variations occur? This monitoring activity is done using a process termed variance analysis.

Variance analysis

Variance analysis compares actual performance with forecast performance. The purpose of this exercise is to pinpoint and highlight areas of good and poor performance. This allows managers to build on areas of strength and remedy or remove areas of weakness.

A favourable variance occurs when results are better than expected, and an adverse variance occurs when results are worse than budgeted. Figure 3.15 shows an example of variance analysis.

Managers use variance analysis to ask why differences between actual performance and forecast budget occurred. Don't assume an adverse variance is necessarily bad or a favourable variance is necessarily good. In the example in Figure 3.15, wages are lower than expected, mainly because employees have not produced as much output as forecast. Here, the company may have spent less on labour costs (a favourable variance), but at the cost of failing to meet production targets.

Even an adverse variance doesn't mean things have gone wrong: a business may get an adverse variance for the cost of labour, but this may mean it hired more skilled employees who did a better quality job.

In simple terms, all variance analysis involves is placing the forecast budgeted figure side by side with the actual figure incurred, working out the difference between the two (budgeted minus actual) and trying to determine why the variance occurred. By doing this, managers can easily identify any areas that performed below expectations and hopefully determine why this poor performance occurred, in turn allowing them to take steps to prevent the same factors causing poor performance in future.

Similarly, they could identify aspects of the company that achieved better results than forecast, again allowing managers to find out why, and hopefully repeat this in future. In this way, the examination of variances should allow the business to become more efficient and profitable in the future.

stop and think

Using Figure 3.15 try to give one reason why the company appears to have made fewer units than expected, used less labour than expected, but at the same time used more materials?

Figure 3.15: An example of variance analysis

	Budgeted amount	Actual amount	Variance
Wages	£42,000	£37,200	£4,800 favourable
Materials	£27,000	£29,400	£2,400 adverse
Output	14,000 units	12,900 units	1,100 units adverse

Knowledge summary

- Budget forecasts provide a method by which managers can plan and co-ordinate business activities. They make managers think about how to achieve goals.

- Budget forecasts provide managers and employees with targets. They allow managers to monitor the performance of the business against the plan, and thereby identify possible areas of strength and weakness.

- Through planning, a business can ensure it has the right resources in place at the right time. The aim is to prevent the waste of resources without missing out on potential sales.

- Variance analysis allows an assessment of budget accuracy and identification of problem areas. It enables informed decisions to be taken to improve business performance.

quick**questions**

1 Why is it so important for businesses to accurately predict future sales levels?

2 Forecasts and budgets are an important method of financial planning. How might the drawing up of budgets also act as a motivational tool?

3 Basenthwaites makes traditional hardwood kitchen units. The production manager has identified an adverse variance for the amount of time it took his workforce to produce a set of custom-built units. Explain to the production manager why this adverse variance may not necessarily be a bad result.

Muncaster Conservatories produces a range of UPVC conservatories for retail through large DIY superstores. The company prides itself on having a highly skilled workforce that produces conservatories of the highest standard.

Although Muncaster's approach is more expensive than other forms of production, the company believes that customers will pay extra for the guarantee that they are getting a high-quality conservatory. Customers can then choose either to erect the conservatory themselves, to contact Muncaster and hire its team of skilled specialised fitters, or to hire a local firm of builders to fit it for them.

Recently Muncaster's sales have been falling, and it appears that the company faces rising costs to produce each conservatory: profits are starting to decline. Muncaster uses a series of budgets to determine how much it should cost to produce each of its standard conservatory models. Managers have conducted a variance analysis exercise for the Edwardian model. The findings are given in Figure 3.16. During the exercise, there have been no changes in wage rates paid to employees, nor have there been any price rises for supplies of raw materials.

Figure 3.16: Production budget for Muncaster's Edwardian conservatories

	Budget (£)	Actual (£)	Variance
Labour			
Skilled	700	610	
Semi-skilled	420	530	
Manual	200	270	
Materials			
UPVC	2,300	2,475	
Glass	1,300	1,420	
Fittings	120	124	
Total			

A Complete Figure 3.16 by calculating the variances for each item, and calculate the total variance for the whole job.

B Using your findings, draft a short report for the management of Muncaster Conservatories suggesting where you believe the major problems have occurred.

C Include, as a final section in your report, some recommendations explaining how Muncaster could solve its problems. Describe the positive impact your recommendations may hopefully have on the company's falling sales, and why.

Guidance

This assessment has been written to mirror the style of assessment used by AQA in the examination for this unit. It is in two parts. Part A should be completed first and the research carried out before you tackle the questions in Part B. The exam in Part B should be completed within one hour.

Part A: Dunsmore Stores

Andrew looked at his accountant in despair. "The shop's income has fallen again I suppose." It was a statement and not a question; he could predict the answer and he knew he had to diversify if the village shop at Dunsmore was to survive as a business. The accountant did not pull any punches. She explained that his farm's income was down by 23 per cent on the previous year and that he had barely made a profit. Andrew left her office with her final comment ringing in his ears. "You cannot carry on as you are – Dunsmore Stores is not profitable. You must find some new sources of income or the bank may refuse to honour your overdraft. In any event, you won't be making any sort of living."

Three months later Andrew was in the latter stages of planning a new venture. His idea was to open a café alongside the shop utilising some unused rooms. He was lucky that the village was just off a busy main road between Aylesbury and Amersham, and Andrew thought it would be easy to put up signs on the main road publicising his new venture. Andrew's café would sell tea, coffee, sandwiches and cakes for customers to eat in or to take away. He also intended to sell products supplied by other local businesses including curries, pies and pizzas.

Andrew needed a bank loan to finance alterations to the buildings to meet hygiene regulations and to pay for a marketing campaign to publicise the opening of the café. The bank manager asked Andrew for evidence that he had planned the finances of the new

business carefully. This was an essential element of granting the loan. Andrew estimated that he would need £7,500 to give enough capital to open the café and also to provide some cash to help Andrew through the difficult first few months.

Andrew was not concerned, as he intended to draw up a detailed business plan relating to his new venture. However, before he did so and before he definitely decided to open the farm shop he wanted some advice on business planning. He wasn't sure of the best source of information on business planning.

Now complete the research tasks below.

Part B: Further planning

Andrew's plans were progressing, although his business plan was not complete. However, he had made some real progress. He had completed his financial planning including cash flow forecast and budgets for the first six months of trading. Some of his plans are shown in Figures 3.17 and 3.18.

The cash flow forecast (Figure 3.18) suggested that Andrew's business might experience problems for the first few months, but Andrew did not consider these to be serious. He thought that recognising there might be a temporary problem was the main issue.

Market research – conducted through interviews with 60 local people, many of whom Andrew knew personally – suggested that he might attract 200 customers per week during the summer months. The

pre-examination research tasks

A Investigate possible sources of information that Andrew could use to help him to draw up a detailed business plan for the proposed farm shop.

B Investigate the possible sources of finance available to Andrew to fund the opening of the shop.

research suggested that the average amount spent by a customer would be £7.50. Andrew calculated that the variable costs associated with a £7.50 transaction would be £5. He estimated that the fixed costs of operating the shop each week would be £400.

Andrew was unsure whether a bank loan might be the best option for raising finance. The bank manager was asking for considerable information, evidence of detailed financial planning, and also some collateral for the loan. Andrew wondered whether he could use another source of finance. One supplier was keen to operate the business as a joint venture and was willing to put up some capital necessary to open the café. He wanted to run the venture as a partnership, though Andrew had doubts about this proposal.

Andrew was at a point where he needed to take a number of decisions. What source of finance should he use to raise the £7,500 he needed? Would the business be profitable and avoid cash flow problems? Finally, and most importantly, should he go ahead with the new venture?

Figure 3.17: Forecast financial data for the first year of trading Andrew's Farm Shop

Expected revenue during first year of trading	**£66,000**
Variable costs as a percentage of revenue	**67%**
Annual fixed costs	**£20,800**

Figure 3.18: Cash flow forecast for Andrew's café

Cash inflows & outflows	June	July	August	September
Cash sales	5,000	5,400	5,850	6,500
Credit sales	–	–	800	1,250
Capital introduced	2,000	–	–	–
Total inflow	**7,000**	**5,400**	**6,650**	**7,750**
Marketing	1,100	750	500	350
Stock	5,450	4,210	?	4,750
Electricity, gas, etc.	175	180	210	190
Wages and salaries	945	990	1,050	950
Other costs	230	385	240	150
Total outflow	**7,900**	**?**	**8,415**	**6,390**
Net cash flow	**(900)**	**(1,115)**	**(1,765)**	**1,360**
Opening balance	**0**	**(900)**	**(2,015)**	**(3,780)**
Closing balance	**(900)**	**(2,015)**	**(3,780)**	**(2,420)**

activities

1 Drawing on your research (in Part A), outline two sources of information that Andrew might use to gain assistance in drawing up his business plan. In each case suggest the advantages and disadvantages of this source of information.

2 Calculate the profits that Andrew will earn from the café if it attracts 175 customers weekly

3 Give why one reason why Andrew's profits may not increase if he charges higher prices.

4 Describe three different types of resources that Andrew would need to run his café.

5 Analyse two reasons why Andrew might be reluctant to run the café as a partnership.

6 Identify and explain two sources of finance that Andrew might use to raise the £7,500 he needs to open the café. Which source Andrew should use? Justify your decision.

7 Using all the information available to you, examine the case for and against Andrew opening the café. State whether he should open the café and justify your decision.

THE SUCCESS OF ANY BUSINESS PARTLY DEPENDS on its ability to meet customer needs. By offering customers a better deal than that of its competitors, a business is more likely to achieve its aims and objectives. This requires the business to understand who its customers are, what they want and the best way to satisfy their needs.

In this unit you will investigate how businesses identify customers and their needs. This is often achieved by splitting, or segmenting, customers into distinct groups, perhaps according to age or lifestyle. After segmenting customers and identifying the most suitable segments to target, a business needs to understand the motivations behind the target market's purchasing decisions.

In order to understand the needs and motivations of their target markets, businesses should carry out customer research. This requires careful planning and, increasingly, the use of ICT to collect and process data.

Once a business has a good understanding of its target market, and the extent to which it is meeting the needs of this market, it can alter its marketing activities. You will investigate how businesses use product development and customer service to meets the needs of its customers.

Meeting customer needs

Setting the scene: who are a school's customers?

A school or college has several different types of customers. Meeting their varied needs is often difficult. Figure 4.1 shows a school's external customers.

However an educational institution doesn't just have "external" customers. Inside each school or college you will also find "internal" customers. Teachers and lecturers can be regarded as internal customers. They have various resource needs that must be met if they are going to be able to function effectively. For example, classrooms need to be cleaned, science labs need to be kept safe and sports fields need to be maintained.

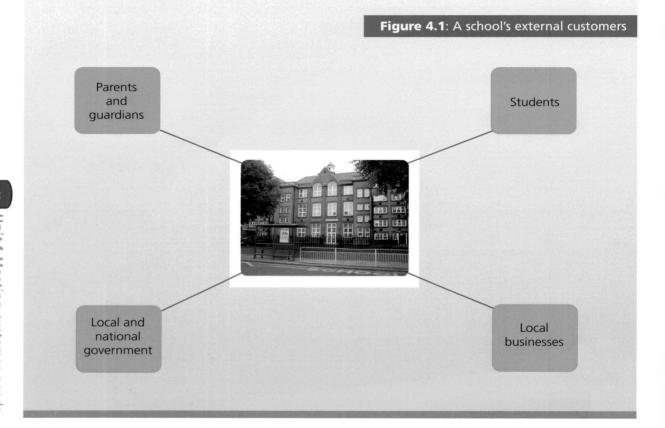

Figure 4.1: A school's external customers

- Parents and guardians
- Students
- Local and national government
- Local businesses

KEY TERMS

A business's **internal customers** are its staff. Employees are internal customers in the sense that they need products and services from other staff within the business or from the business's suppliers to carry out their tasks.

External customers are the people or organisations that buy goods and services from a business. Some businesses' external customers are exclusively other businesses, some businesses trade exclusively with the general public and some have a mix of business and individual customers.

Internal and external customers

The phrase "the customer is always right" might be a little simplistic, but it does illustrate the task any business faces when attempting to meet customer needs. A school or college has many different types of customers, and they are often difficult to please.

One way that a business can begin to identify its customers is to make a distinction between its internal and external customers.

- An internal customer is an employee or functional area inside an organisation that relies on other employees to provide them with products – for example, teachers (internal customers) rely on reprographic services to supply them with printed copies of worksheets.

- An external customer is a an individual outside an organisation who purchases a product from the organisation – for example, a school's reprographics department (the external customer) will purchase materials from a printing supplies business.

As a student, you are often an external customer. You purchase products from a range of businesses and expect those businesses to meet your needs. However, you may also have a part-time job – in which case, you will be an internal customer and might also have to deal with external and internal customers.

Internal customers are important. Businesses that focus solely on the needs of their external customers are likely to find it difficult to deliver products capable of meeting these needs. The employees of a business are its most valuable resource, and ignoring their needs is not sensible. By ignoring internal customers, a business is at risk of becoming inefficient and slow to respond to changing market conditions.

Conversely, by focusing on the needs of internal customers, a business will identify better ways of producing and delivering its products. Employees will, hopefully, feel recognised and take on more responsibility for their activities. This idea is at the heart of an "enterprising organisation", which encourages individual employees to innovate, take risks and find new ways of meeting internal and external customer needs.

Meeting customer needs

This unit investigates the steps a business needs to take when attempting to meet the needs of its customers:

step 1 identify the business's internal and external customers, describing their possible needs

step 2 research the actual needs of the business's customers and how competitors are attempting to meet their needs

step 3 adjust the marketing activities of the business to improve the way it meets the needs of its current and potential customers.

It is not possible to cover all aspects of these steps within the space of this unit. In particular, when investigating step 3 you will focus on how businesses alter their product and customer service marketing activities.

To help your studies, you should whenever possible collect examples of how businesses in your local area attempt to meet the needs of their customers. As an externally assessed unit, you need to develop the ability to explain and review the activities of a variety of businesses. The written paper will use a number of different business scenarios, and you will be expected to make sense of these under timed conditions.

Setting the scene: information technology and segmentation

Most businesses aim their products at particular groups of consumers. Some are very obviously targeting particular groups of people. Club 18–30 organises lively holidays for adults aged 30 or under. Waitrose, one of the UK's leading supermarket chains, targets better-off consumers. Virago is a publisher that produces books for women.

Businesses often want to target particular groups of consumers, and they increasingly use information technology to help them in this task. For example, most supermarkets now issue loyalty cards. These cards encourage customers to spend more with the issuing supermarket, as they receive points for each purchase which can be exchanged for products or gifts at a later date. However, by issuing loyalty cards, supermarkets find out about their customers' spending patterns. This makes it easier to identify the tastes and attitudes of groups of customers and to target them using special offers and direct mail.

Sainsbury's operates its Nectar Card scheme as a joint venture with a number of other businesses including BP and Vodafone. The scheme was launched in 2002 and within a year some 13 million UK consumers had signed up for a card. The company running the Nectar scheme on behalf of the participating companies admits that by having some personal information about cardholders, such as age, marital status and family size, and by knowing what products customers purchase, it is much easier to segment markets and to target specific groups of consumers with offers.

Why do most of the UK's leading supermarkets operate loyalty card schemes? How might this help them to meet the needs of their customers?

Unit 4 Meeting customer needs

KEY TERMS

A **market** is where buyers and sellers come together to trade products and information. It might be a specific location such as a street market, or a means of communication such as the eBay website on the internet.

Market segmentation is the division of potential consumers into groups with similar characteristics.

The **population structure** of a country is described by the proportion of the population that falls within different age groups such 0–5 years, 21–35 years and 45–55 years old.

Social grade	Description of occupation	Example
A	Higher managerial and professional	Company director
B	Lower managerial and supervisory	Middle manager
C1	Non-manual	Bank clerk
C2	Skilled manual	Electrician
D	Semi-skilled and unskilled manual	Labourer
E	Those receiving no income from employment	Unemployed

How markets are segmented

Market segmentation is the division of potential consumers into groups with similar characteristics. Businesses can segment markets in a number of ways.

1 By age

The demand for some products is clearly linked to age, and so it is important for some businesses to segment their market in this way. The holiday industry is a classic example of a sector which segments part of its market by the age of the customers. As its name suggests, Club 18–30 aims its holidays at young people; Saga sells its holidays (and other products) exclusively to customers aged over 50.

2 By sex

Some businesses aim their products specifically at one gender, producing a range of products for women and a separate range for men. This type of segmentation is common in the clothing, cosmetics and magazine industries. Some businesses that have traditionally only produced products for either men or women are attempting to increase sales by developing products that are targeted at the other sex. For example, many cosmetics companies – which traditionally have focused on the female market – now have ranges of products designed for men.

3 By socioeconomic factors

Another way of segmenting the market is by social class and income. This is usually done by considering the occupation of the head of each household and ignoring second or subsequent wage earners. For example, the UK market research industry uses the socioeconomic scale described in Figure 4.2 to provide standardised social groupings. Figure 4.2 illustrates just one method of segmentation according to social class. There are many other classifications, some of which are much more complex with many more subdivisions.

stop and **think**

How might a segmentation of the population by social class and income help a travel company to decide on the types of holidays it might provide?

4 By lifestyle

This method of segmentation attempts to classify consumers according to their individual patterns of expenditure. For example, businesses might classify a family's lifestyle according to how they make their purchases: do they buy products on the internet, make purchases using credit or debit cards, or shop in discount stores? By segmenting the market in this way, businesses can target particular groups with offers that may be appealing. For example, a supermarket like Tesco may want to offer busy and internet-connected people the chance to purchase goods and services online and take advantage of its home delivery service. Tesco does not want to waste resources by trying to sell this service to customers who don't have internet access or who prefer to do their shopping in the stores.

Some products are segmented according to more than one classification. This is not unusual as it allows more accurate targeting of consumers. The market for Loaded magazine, for example, is segmented by age and sex: the magazine is targeted at young men.

When next in your local newsagents, identify magazines with target markets defined by each of the methods of segmentation we have considered here: age, social class, sex and lifestyle. Can you find some magazines that are segmented by more than one of these classifications?

5 Geodemographic segmentation

Geodemographic segmentation groups consumers by using a combination of several geographic and economic factors, such as where a customer lives, the size of their family, the type of house in which they live, and so on. This way of segmenting the market is particularly relevant for businesses planning the location and development of hospitality and tourism operations such as pubs, restaurants and leisure facilities.

One way of applying geodemographic segmentation is to use the ACORN (A Classification Of Residential Neighbourhoods) categorisation. Based on geographic, cultural, socioeconomic and other factors, ACORN identifies 38 different types of residential neighbourhood according to the most common type of housing within that neighbourhood. It allows the country to be divided up into a series of neighbourhoods, each consisting of about 150 homes and defined using postcodes.

Businesses in many industries use this system, including banks and other financial institutions, gas and electricity companies and credit card operators. Businesses using ACORN believe that they can make judgements about consumers and their spending habits from the types of houses in which they live.

UK population structure

The population structure of a country is described by the proportion of the total population that falls within different age groups, such as 0–5, 12–16 and 50–65 years of age. The UK is said to have an ageing population structure as more and more people live to an older age – in other words, an increasing proportion of the population falls within the older age bands. In addition, the birth rate is declining. Both of these changes can be attributed to rising income levels:

- people with higher incomes can afford to look after their health through better nutrition, less stressful lifestyle, etc.

- greater national wealth makes it easier for the government to raise money through taxation to pay for improved health care

- more economic opportunities means that many couples place a greater emphasis on their careers and are less willing to start a family in their twenties.

Changes in population structure affect the size and relative importance of markets segmented by age group. As the retired age group increases in size and proportion (65 years and over for men, 60 years and over for women), businesses will find new opportunities to meet the needs of this age group. Any business should ensure that it does not make false assumptions about the needs of the retired age group – to assume, for example, that all retired people have traditional views and are generally inactive. The market for leisure has particularly benefited from targeting services and products at the UK's older population, as many people within this age group have the time and income to consume leisure products.

Knowledge summary

- Market segmentation is the division of potential consumers into groups with similar characteristics.

- Segmenting a market enables businesses to reach their customers more easily and cost effectively.

- Businesses can segment markets by customers' age, social class, sex and lifestyle.

- Many businesses also segment their markets using geodemographic classifications which take a number of geographic, cultural and socioeconomic factors into account.

- The demographic structure of a country is described by the proportion of the population within different age groups. Changes in demographics are significant for business, creating new potential with, perhaps, particular needs.

quick questions

1 Consider each of these industries in turn: (a) motor car manufacture, (b) sporting and leisure activities, (c) chart music, (d) DIY products and (e) children's toys.

For each industry, identify one or more methods of market segmentation that businesses might employ. In each case, justify your choice or choices.

2 In 2003, Matalan moved from selling in the discount clothing market (a niche market) to compete with retailers such as BHS and Marks & Spencer in the mass market. The company has upgraded its stores and has advertised its new position in the market. Imagine you are responsible for marketing at Matalan. Would you approve this change of strategy or not? Explain your decision.

3 Global Ltd imports exotic plants from around the world for UK citizens to grow in their greenhouses and conservatories. How might this company segment its market to make its marketing more effective?

data interpretation
Northern Ireland

Northern Ireland's population structure is changing, as Figure 4.3 and the article below illustrate.

A Use the article and Figure 4.3 to describe the forecast changes in Northern Ireland's population structure.

B Explain the possible impact of these changes on the needs of customers of (a) schools and colleges, (b) supermarkets and (c) health services.

C Discuss how the changes in population structure might effect Northern Ireland's ACORN classification data. Visit the ACORN website (www.caci.co.uk) to investigate this issue further by downloading the new ACORN brochure.

Source: news.bbc.co.uk, 25 November 2004

Northern Ireland "grows old fast"

There are more young people in Northern Ireland than any other part of the UK, but the population is ageing fast.

Government statisticians have predicted that by about 2017 there will be more pensioners than children, causing major changes to the structure of the economy.

The good news is that fewer people died in Northern Ireland last year than ever before. However, the birth rate is also close to an all-time low.

Figure 4.3: Projected Northern Ireland population structure

	2004	2009	2014
Children	22.4%	20.7%	19.6%
Working age	61.6%	62.1%	62.9%
Pension age	16.1%	17.2%	17.5%

Source: Northern Ireland Statistics Research Agency

Setting the scene: failed expectations

Products do not always live up to expectations. Here are two stories of holidays in Greece that went horribly wrong.

We were on a family holiday in a "family" hotel in mainland Greece. I was pregnant, and unwell, so bowed out of an excursion. The toilets were blocked – again – and while I was resting on the beach, the plumber arrived. He tapped the short wall bordering the beach, grunted and picked up a large sledgehammer. He then smashed a hole through the wall and the main sewer, thus relieving the obstruction. Six weeks of guests' excrement, now in a state of lively fermentation, poured on to the beach, where it remained for the rest of our stay. An unforgettable fragrance.

On honeymoon in Greece ... we went to investigate what sounded like a festival, complete with fireworks. It turned out to be a full-scale anti-capitalism riot from which we eventually escaped, coughing and spluttering from tear gas. Next morning we discovered there was a general strike, which accounted for the mountains of rubbish everywhere and the accompanying rats. We decided to explore some islands, but there were no boats running, nor were there any buses or trains out of Athens. The tourist office wasn't much use, having been fire-bombed in the riot. After two dismal days, we booked an early – and expensive – flight home. We're still married, though.

Stories from: BBC online magazine, news.bbc.co.uk, 29 July 2004

Were any of these events avoidable? How could the hotels or travel companies involved have ensured that the needs of these customers were met?

KEY TERMS

A **basic product** provides for a limited number of needs – for example, a packet of crisps meets the need to snack between meals.

A **complex product** provides for a wide range of needs – for example, a car meets transport, entertainment and status needs.

After-sales services are provided to meet ongoing needs of customers, and include features such as guarantees and information on using the product.

Essential products are seen as being vital to the wellbeing of customers, such as food and health care.

Non-essential products are not vital to customers' wellbeing. Products such as magazines and visits to the cinema are purchased in addition to essential products.

The range of customer needs

People have high expectations of the benefits they will gain from holidays. These include psychological benefits such as excitement, fun, relaxation and comfort. Given these needs, it does not take much for an individual to return from holiday a little disappointed.

Customers have a range of needs, both during and after the purchase of the product. This includes:

- understanding the value and suitability of the product – for example, customers would want to know what a holiday has to offer and whether it fits their personality type, will it be fun and exciting or a calmer, more relaxing experience?

- information about the product and its functions – for example, what facilities does the hotel have, what comforts are available during the flight and what events are included in the holiday package?

- reassurance about after-sales services including guarantees – for example, if a flight is cancelled, will a suitable replacement be offered and what assistance will customers be offered if the hotel fails to live up to expectations?

1 Value and suitability

Customers should feel certain that a product is suitable for their purposes. As these purposes can be complex, businesses might have to provide detailed information about their products.

Some products meet basic needs and do not require much by way of explanation – retailers do not need to provide much information to explain the purpose of a packet of crisps. However, when selling complex products, such as a car, a business will need to take into account the various factors that motivate the customer.

Customer motivations can vary considerably and this is one reason why many businesses choose to segment the market as we discussed in Topic 1. For example, by using geodemographic segmentation, a car manufacturer might have decided to target one of its models at people living in the countryside who require a vehicle capable of dealing with rough roads but also of carrying family and friends in safety and comfort.

2 Product information

After establishing the suitability of the product, customers will often require more specific and detailed information on the functions of the product. They will want to know if – and how – the product can meet a range of needs. This can be achieved very easily for basic products by simply putting information on the product's packaging. When considering buying complex products, such as a mobile phone, customers will require detailed product specifications that explain exactly what the product can do. Attempting to fool the customer at this stage might achieve a sale but will inevitably reduce the reputation of the business in the long term – in this case, honesty really is the best policy.

The product information provided will depend on the buyer behaviour of the targeted market – and businesses might produce a range of literature aimed at different segments of the market. With mobile phones, for example, young consumers might be interested in the graphics features of a phone (pictures, animated wallpaper, etc.) while older consumers might be interested in the calendar and appointment facilities.

stop and think

Visit the Land Rover website (www.landrover.com) and view some of the general information provided about Range Rover. Is the information easy to find and understand? Do you think this information would help the target market to understand the value and suitability of the product?

3 After-sales service

Before confirming a purchase, customers will often enquire about after-sales services. They may want to know what help and support they can expect to receive when using the product and if the product fails to function. In the case of basic products, such as petrol for a car, customers do not expect to receive additional reassurances before they make a purchase and they will rely on consumer law to deal with any problems. However, customers will expect to receive after-sales service for expensive or complex products. For example, when purchasing a £1,500 computer system, a customer might expect to receive:

- free delivery of the computer to the customer's home

- basic instructions on using the product

- a free product guarantee – for, say, one, two or three years – that perhaps covers repairing the computer at the customer's home

- a telephone number or e-mail address to get assistance when using the system.

Failure to offer after-sales service could result in a business losing a sale to a competitor. Failure to live up to after-sales service commitments will invariably result in the customer using a competitor's product in the future and could even result in legal action. The quality and reliability of a business's after-sales service is often the main factor affecting customer loyalty.

Essential and non-essential products

The concept of essential and non-essential products helps a business to consider the amount of information and support it should provide customers.

Essential products are vital to the wellbeing of a customer. For example, it is difficult for anyone to go without food, health care, energy, telephone and transport services: these can be considered as essential products. Customers will expect reliable provision of these essential products, and any supply shortages will cause upset and inconvenience. Any variations in the quality of the product will also disturb customers, and they will often expect a high level of customer service and after-sales support.

Non-essential products are not vital to the wellbeing of the customer. They are purchased in addition to essential products. For example, reading magazines and visiting the cinema might be enjoyable activities but they are not essential. While customer service and after-sales support is still important with non-essential products, customers' levels of expectation are likely to be lower. Customers can do without the product, and the absence of acceptable levels of support is less likely to disturb them. However, in a competitive market, product features and after-sales service may well be the deciding factor when customers are selecting which non-essential product to buy.

Knowledge summary

■ Customer needs for product information and after-sales support depend on the complexity of the product and the factors influencing the customer's purchase decisions.

■ A business should ensure that it delivers the promised product functions and after-sales services if it is to develop and maintain customer loyalty.

■ Customers expect higher levels of customer service and after-sales support for essential products than for non-essential products.

quick**questions**

1 What questions might a customer ask when purchasing:

a) a wide-screen television set
b) an expensive item of clothing manufactured from an artificial material
c) a hair colouring product
d) luxury hotel accommodation?

2 A leisure company is planning to launch a new product aimed at 10–14 year old children. It plans to open a number of rural centres offering sports events and other activities, along with accommodation. Explain how it might convince parents of the product's suitability and what after-sales services it might offer.

data**interpretation**
Buying a complex product

Miller Homes builds houses in England and Scotland. Its website (www.homes.miller.co.uk) contains a wide range of information designed to meet the needs of customers before, during and after they purchase a house from Miller Homes.

Houses are very complex products. Choosing a home that you and, perhaps, your partner feel comfortable and satisfied with takes time and careful consideration. With Miller Homes' prices (as at April 2005) ranging from £90,000 for a one-bedroom flat to over £500,000 for a six-bedroom detached house, customers expect clear information and genuine after-sales services.

A What specific needs might a customer have during and after the purchase of a one-bed flat from Miller Homes?

B Visit Miller Homes' website (www.homes.miller.co.uk) and investigate the extent to which you think the company provides clear information on the functions of its products and offers reassurance about after-sales services.

C Interview a home owner to identify what their needs were during and after the purchase of their current home. Report your findings on one side of A4 paper using diagrams, charts and tables when appropriate.

161

Topic 2 Customer needs

Setting the scene: buying a car

Apart from buying a house or a flat, buying a car is possibly the most important (and largest single) purchase decision made by a customer. This advice on buying a car is taken from the Office of Fair Trading's website.

Test drives

Take advantage of free test drives (some dealers let you test-drive a car over 48 hours). Key points to look out for include:

- **comfort of the seating position**
- **all-round visibility**
- **road handling and braking**
- **seat belts working.**

Agreeing the deal

Don't be afraid to bargain. Discounts are often available, particularly on the less popular models, but it is up to you to get the price down as much as you can.

If you are trading in your old car, make sure you know what it is worth. And make sure you are being quoted the on-the-road price, which includes VAT, number plates, delivery charges and road tax.

Source: www.oft.gov.uk

Features and characteristics

Some products are basic – they have few features and meet limited needs. For example, a ballpoint pen is a basic product – its main function is to transfer ink onto paper, enabling you to write and draw. Few people spend time deciding which ballpoint pen they will purchase. If a particular ballpoint pen feels right in your hand and produces the thickness of line you prefer, then you will continue to buy this make of ballpoint pen. It isn't something you are likely to stay awake at night worrying about!

Other products have several features and meet several needs. Purchasing a car is a difficult decision. Cars meet a variety of needs and they have several features beyond the simple "four wheels and an engine". As a product, a car is both complex and interesting.

These various product characteristics mean that businesses adopt different approaches when attempting to meet the needs of customers.

Products can be classified according to two characteristics: the complexity of the product and the level of involvement customers have in the product.

The complexity of the product is a measure of the range of features it can have and the variety of needs it can meet. The higher the complexity of a product, the more likely it is that businesses can produce different varieties of the product, each meeting different needs.

The level of involvement customers have in the product is a measure of the level of interest in the product and the degree to which the product meets emotional needs such as status, security and happiness. If customers have high levels of

Conway Stewart produces luxury pens. The pen shown here costs £450 (as at April 2005). So what do you get for £450 – according to the Conway Stewart website:

Each pen is hand-crafted from solid sterling silver, complemented with a hand-applied, delicately translucent resin veneer, creating a unique celebration of colour and design. Each pen is hallmarked and fitted with a rhodium-plated 18ct gold nib.

Is a Conway Stewart pen a complex or a basic product? Why might Conway Stewart's customers have a high level of interest in the company's pens?

involvement, they seek further information about the product and are actively involved in the decision to purchase the product. For example, customers might have high levels of involvement in purchasing a new mobile telephone but they might have relatively low levels of involvement in purchasing electricity.

Figure 4.4 classifies products according to their complexity and customer involvement. The table shows that the complexity of a product and the degree of involvement a customer has in that product will affect the customer's need for information and support when purchasing a product.

Given a high level of involvement in a complex product, a customer will require considerable help and support before making a decision to buy a particular business's product. To meet the needs of customers in this situation, a successful business will pay attention to the availability and quality of its product information and after-sales communications. A relationship needs to be developed between the business and the customer that clearly demonstrates the ability of the business to meet the customer's complex needs. A business might use a range of direct mail, product magazines and informative advertising to develop this

Figure 4.4: Product characteristics

Complexity of the product		Level of involvement customers have in the product	
		High	**Low**
High		**Example:** Package holiday **Customer needs:** This is a significant purchase and the customer needs to be provided with a range of information about the product. The business needs to convince the customer that it is providing the best version of the product for the customer's needs.	**Example:** Breakfast cereal Customer needs: Due to the relatively low involvement in the product, customers have no loyalty. Each business will need to provide incentives for current customers to stay with their product and for potential customers to switch from a competing product. For example, a business will ensure product availability and may offer free samples or price reductions.
Low		**Example:** Broadband internet **Customer needs:** Although the customer is involved with the product and perceives it as a significant purchase, each business is producing a similar product. Customers need to be convinced or reminded that they have chosen the best provider, and this could be in terms of price, after-sales service, product reviews in the media or product reliability.	**Example:** Toilet paper **Customer needs:** One version of the product is much the same as another version. The customer has a low level of interest in the product and will purchase the same version of the product out of habit. A business will need to increase the availability and prominence of its product if it is to gain customers. TV advertising might be required to increase familiarity with the product. Financial incentives could also be used.

relationship. Each business's website is likely to contain detailed product information and stress the unique features of its products.

At the other extreme, with low involvement and a basic undifferentiated product, a successful business will initially have to follow an aggressive communication campaign that raises the awareness of its product above that of its competitors. As customers are not really interested in which version of the product they use, the business that "shouts the loudest" – for example, by using plenty of advertising, prominent displays in retail outlets and price discounts – is likely to be the one that gains the largest share of the market.

stop and think

Which breakfast cereals are consumed in your household? Does each member of the household have a favourite type or do they switch? What makes you want to try a different breakfast cereal?

Explain why breakfast cereal manufacturers frequently develop new products and modify existing products.

Knowledge summary

- **Products can be classified according to their complexity and the involvement customers have in them.**

- **Customers purchasing complex products, with which they have a high level of involvement, require considerable information and support during and after their purchasing decisions. Businesses that provide this information and support are more likely to gain and maintain their market share.**

- **Customers purchasing basic products, with which they have little involvement, do not seek information and support – they purchase these products through habit. In these markets, a business should ensure wide availability of the product and advertise on a regular basis to limit the possibility of the customer ignoring its product.**

quick questions

1 Using Figure 4.4, characterise these products and services:

a) chewing gum
b) music on CD
c) a chocolate bar
d) renting a film on DVD or videotape
e) takeaway food such as pizzas and fish and chips
f) a wide-screen television.

2 What information and support might a customer expect when purchasing each of the products listed in question 1?

data**interpretation**
T-mobile

The mobile phone service provided by T-mobile is not significantly different from the services provided by competitors, such as Orange and Vodafone, and T-mobile has to work hard at making its service stand out. Whether you pay as you go or buy into a monthly plan, you are simply paying for the ability to connect to the UK's mobile phone network.

T-mobile offers a wide range of mobile phones to accompany its monthly and pay-as-you-go service plans (see www.t-mobile.co.uk below). To assist customers in their choice of mobile phone, T-mobile's website offers a facility which allows customers to compare the features of up to three products.

Even then the choice is a difficult one to make. Mobile telephone manufacturers such as Nokia and Motorola are constantly developing new products. The range of features offered by each new model increases as competing businesses attempt to attract the millions of customers who now consider a mobile phone to be an essential product.

A Using Figure 4.4 and the information available on the T-mobile website, describe the product characteristics of (i) mobile phones such as the Motorola V3 and (ii) a mobile telephone service – the service that connects the mobile to the phone network.

B Explain why mobile phone service providers such as T-mobile offer a variety of mobile phones to accompany their service plans.

C Research the type of information and support customers expect when purchasing a mobile phone service or a mobile phone. Base your research on your own age group (that is, 16–18 year olds). Produce a five-minute presentation that communicates your main findings.

Setting the scene: customer feedback questionnaires

Joe Ibrahim is director of the painting and decorating division of Axis Europe plc, a London-based construction company. Joe wanted to find a way of measuring how effectively the business was performing.

> We were looking for a proven way to measure our business performance, and customer satisfaction seemed a good place to start. So we devised a customer feedback questionnaire and kept it tightly focused on the areas we wanted to measure. One question, for example, was "did the painters tidy up to your satisfaction?" The possible answers we offered clients were simple – either "yes" or "no" or a satisfaction rating which ranged from one to ten and used faces going from scowls to smiles.
>
> The results haven't always been what we've expected. For example, at first a lot of our clients – around 30 per cent – were saying that the contractors were not tidying up enough after themselves. That figure should be almost zero so we really attacked that problem.
>
> Don't expect all clients to understand the importance of feedback. We're learning as we go along. For the first three months we sent questionnaires out to clients by post with a stamped addressed envelope and the return levels were about 30 per cent. We then tried hand-delivering them for the next three months and we found we had 30 per cent returns again, so we've gone back to the post. Hand-delivering takes a lot of time and 30 per cent is not a bad result.

Source: adapted from www.businesslink.gov.uk

Why do you think it was important for Axis Europe to keep its customer feedback questionnaires "tightly focused on the areas we wanted to measure"?

Unit 4 Meeting customer needs

KEY TERMS

A **closed question** limits responses to a set number of options, such as "yes" and "no". Sometimes a scale can be used – for example, a four-point scale with 4 meaning the person completing the questionnaire strongly agrees with a statement, while 1 means strongly disagree.

An **open-ended question** requires the person being questioned to provide a response in their own words. For example, the question might ask "what could we do to improve your holiday experience?"

Fast-moving consumer goods are products such as baked beans and washing powder that have high unit sales levels. They often have low customer involvement and are relatively basic, with the products offered by businesses in the market being very similar.

Researching customer needs

In Topics 1, 2 and 3 you looked at the meaning of a customer and the range of needs they might have. It is not enough to understand this as a concept – if a business is to actually meet the needs of its customers, then it must research those needs. For example, Joe Ibrahim (see setting the scene opposite) recognised the importance of receiving and analysing customer feedback. He used a simple questionnaire to collect information and then processed the results.

Research methods

In this topic – and Topics 5 and 6 – you will investigate how businesses research the needs of their target markets. We start by looking at methods that businesses use to collect customer data.

1 Customer questionnaires

In Unit 1 (see page 27) you looked at the ways in which businesses could carry out primary research. One way was through the use of surveys. A customer feedback questionnaire is a focused survey. Using a limited number of closed questions, customers are asked to briefly comment on their attitudes towards the provision and content of the product.

Hotels will often leave customer feedback questionnaires in each room, inviting the guest to report on their overall experience of staying at the hotel. Figure 4.5 illustrates an example of the layout and content of a customer feedback questionnaire for a hotel.

2 Consumer panels

A consumer panel consists of a selection of people who represent the target market for the business's products. Several consumer panels could be used to reflect geographic variations or to reflect socioeconomic differences (see Topic 1). Each consumer panel meets on a regular basis and provides detailed feedback on the attitudes and purchasing decisions of the target market.

Increasingly, these consumer panels are "virtual" in that modern information and communications technology allows individual customers to record their purchases and comment on their attitudes from the comfort of their own homes. This technique is useful for receiving feedback on fast-moving consumer goods where customer involvement is low and, perhaps, each business is producing similar products.

stop and think

Design a customer feedback questionnaire to be filled in by students using your school or college cafeteria. Limit it to four questions, but you can choose how many options are provided. The purpose of the questionnaire is to collect feedback on the quality of the cafeteria's "dining experience".

Figure 4.5: Customer feedback questionnaire for a hotel

Please tick one box for each question

	Excellent	Good	Average	Poor
The quality of your room was …	☐	☐	☐	☐
The public areas in the hotel were …	☐	☐	☐	☐
The standard of service you received was …	☐	☐	☐	☐
Your breakfast was …	☐	☐	☐	☐
Your overall opinion of the hotel is …	☐	☐	☐	☐

ACNeilsen Homescan

At this very moment, consumers across the country are deciding whether to buy your product or brand, or to opt for that of a competitor. Others are deciding when to shop and where. ACNielsen Homescan provides insights into buying behaviour across all fast-moving consumer goods outlets including supermarkets, convenience stores and home shopping. Using state-of-the-art in-home scanning technology, ACNielsen Homescan products and services provide clients with valuable insight into consumer shopping behaviour.

Source: www.acnielsen.co.uk

stop and think

ACNielsen provides market research, information and analysis to the consumer products and services industries. Visit ACNielsen's UK website (www.acnielsen.co.uk) to investigate the company's range of customer research services. How might these services help a food manufacturing business such as Heinz to meet the needs of its customers?

3 Test marketing

Test marketing can be expensive. The idea is to trial a product in a limited geographic area and collect quantitative and qualitative feedback on customer attitudes to the product. For example, a breakfast cereal manufacturer might decide that it needs to introduce a new product, perhaps as a response to innovations by competitors. Consumer panels and customer feedback questionnaires might suggest the type of product that should be introduced. Test marketing would help to confirm the correct choice of product features – flavours, texture, etc. – before the manufacturer starts large-scale production. In addition, the test marketing could provide valuable feedback – it might, for example, show that consumers are likely to reject particular texture and flavour combinations.

4 Personal interviews

Personal interviews are used to collect detailed information. This technique is especially useful when considering complex and high-involvement products such as cars (see Figure 4.4, page 163). Personal interviews will tend to involve more open-ended questions designed to gain qualitative rather than quantitative information. This technique is particularly useful for collecting information on customers' attitudes towards products. It will help to identify the factors motivating the target market to purchase a particular business's product.

stop and think

What open-ended questions might be used for a personal interview designed to collect information on customers' attitudes to a new home entertainment system that combines the features of a computer, a television, a video recorder and a hi-fi system? For an example of this type of product, visit www.elonex.co.uk and search for the Lumina 32 or similar media centre.

quick questions

1 Design customer feedback questionnaires – each comprising either three or four questions – for use when:

a) a cinema wants feedback on the quality of service provided by its staff
b) a department store wants feedback on the store layout within its cosmetics department
c) a fitness centre is concerned about its declining membership.

2 Explain whether customer feedback questionnaires, consumer panels, test marketing and personal interviews could be appropriate when:

a) a supermarket is concerned that, as internal customers, the needs of its checkout operators are not being met – operator turnover is high and the operators rarely smile
b) the manager of a BMW car dealership has received several customer complaints about the time it takes for cars to be serviced or repaired.

Knowledge summary

- Businesses need to collect information on customer attitudes towards their products in order to meet customer needs.

- Methods used to collect information on customer attitudes include customer feedback questionnaires, consumer panels, test marketing and personal interviews.

- Customer questionnaires use closed questions and seek specific information on customer satisfaction with the product.

- Test marketing enables businesses to collect information on customer attitudes towards new or modified products.

- Personal interviews are designed to collect qualitative information using open-ended questions, and are useful for complex products with high customer involvement.

data**interpretation**
The UK leisure and recreation market

This information on the UK leisure and recreation market has been adapted from a Keynote Insight Report. The report – available as a free download on www.keynote.co.uk – illustrates the kind of market intelligence produced by Keynote.

It is difficult to summarise any universal trends across UK leisure and recreation, but it is worth highlighting these events and underlying social trends.

Consumers are steadily devoting more of their disposable income to leisure, reaching 27 per cent for the first time in 2000. The "having-it-all" approach to lifestyles means that people tend to take part in more activities than ever before, even if it is only for a few minutes a day.

The options for in-home leisure continue to expand, with some social trends discouraging going out, such as traffic and parking problems, long hours spent working and commuting, fears of street crime, etc. In contrast, homes and gardens have been invested in (against a background of rising house values) to provide a pleasant place for entertaining friends and relatives.

Venues for entertainment and culture are having to work harder than ever to persuade people to come out. Consumers are often content to have a meal out as their main leisure experience outside the home rather than go to the cinema (which is youth-dominated) or to the theatre (which is perceived as expensive).

Physical recreation has shifted away from time-consuming sports and games, and towards keep-fit regimes involving less time (such as going to the gym or jogging), although the largest, modern health clubs and sports clubs also provide a venue for socialising which is seen to be healthier than the pub or restaurant.

A Identify four important trends in the UK leisure and recreation market. In each case, explain why you think the trend is important.

B Explain how secondary market research such as Keynote reports could help businesses in the leisure and recreation industry to meet the needs of its customers.

C Discuss how a leisure centre could use customer feedback questionnaires, consumer panels, test marketing and personal interviews to help it to meet the needs of its customers.

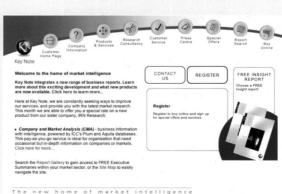

Setting the scene: planning primary research

Business Link, the government-sponsored business support network, publishes advice about conducting research on its website. Here is an extract of its advice on planning primary research.

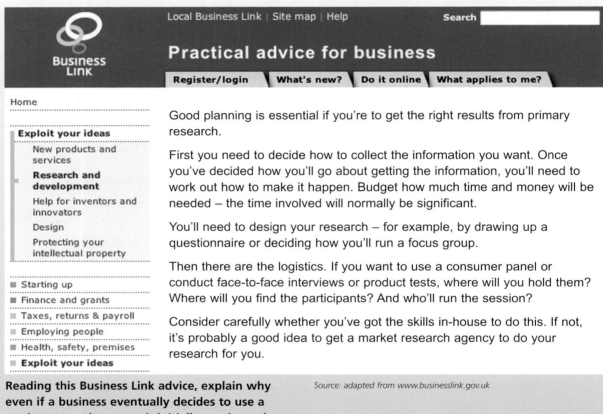

Local Business Link | Site map | Help   Search

Practical advice for business

Register/login | What's new? | Do it online | What applies to me?

Home

Exploit your ideas

New products and services

Research and development

Help for inventors and innovators

Design

Protecting your intellectual property

■ Starting up
■ Finance and grants
■ Taxes, returns & payroll
■ Employing people
■ Health, safety, premises
■ **Exploit your ideas**

Good planning is essential if you're to get the right results from primary research.

First you need to decide how to collect the information you want. Once you've decided how you'll go about getting the information, you'll need to work out how to make it happen. Budget how much time and money will be needed – the time involved will normally be significant.

You'll need to design your research – for example, by drawing up a questionnaire or deciding how you'll run a focus group.

Then there are the logistics. If you want to use a consumer panel or conduct face-to-face interviews or product tests, where will you hold them? Where will you find the participants? And who'll run the session?

Consider carefully whether you've got the skills in-house to do this. If not, it's probably a good idea to get a market research agency to do your research for you.

Source: adapted from www.businesslink.gov.uk

Reading this Business Link advice, explain why even if a business eventually decides to use a market research agency, it initially needs to plan its customer research.

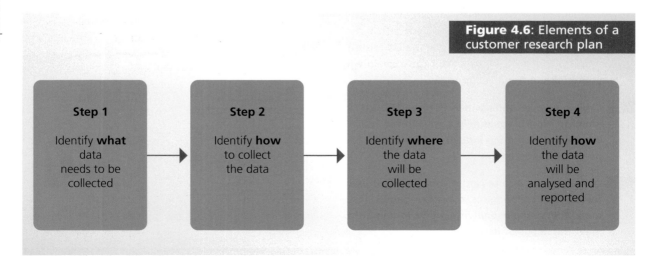

Figure 4.6: Elements of a customer research plan

Step 1	Step 2	Step 3	Step 4
Identify **what** data needs to be collected	Identify **how** to collect the data	Identify **where** the data will be collected	Identify **how** the data will be analysed and reported

Constructing a customer research plan

In this topic, you will consider the steps a business needs to take to collect accurate and relevant data on customer attitudes towards its products. These steps are illustrated in Figure 4.6.

Step 1: What data to collect

The advice provided by Business Link (above) assumes that a business already knows what data it needs to collect. This isn't always obvious and, in many ways, this first step is the most important part of the research process and it is where many businesses go wrong. It is important to take the time to consider exactly what the research is meant to achieve – to be clear about its overall aim.

Once a business has a clear aim, then managers can set a series of research objectives describing the information that needs to be generated if research aims are to be achieved. Identifying the research objectives for customer research helps to define the data that need to be collected.

For example, the governors of a school might want to find out what subjects and courses it should offer in Year 12. From this aim, the research objectives might be to generate information about:

- the attitudes of teachers, parents and students to the current curriculum offered by the school

- the new courses that teachers feel capable of and interested in delivering

- the skills and knowledge that parents and students feel are important

- the aspirations and vision that parents, students and teachers have for the school's post-16 education

- the views of the local education authority, employers and further education institutions.

Given these research objectives, the data that needs to be collected can be identified. For example, the governors might want to collect information on what teachers feel they are capable of teaching and would like to teach, what each Year 12 and 13 student thinks about the relevance of their current courses and what they might like to have been offered, what each parent thinks are the three main purposes of post-16 education, and so on. The identified data should be specific and clearly related to the research objectives.

Step 2: How to collect data

Once the specific data requirements have been listed, identifying how the data will be collected can be relatively straightforward. If the data is quantitative – for example, how often a customer purchases a product – then questionnaire-based methods can be used or a business might be able to generate this data by analysing the use of loyalty cards. However, if the data is qualitative – for example, how customers use the product – then interviews, consumer panels and, perhaps, observations might be required.

At this stage, financial considerations play a role. If the budget for the research is limited, then mass research techniques such as customer feedback questionnaires might have to provide most of the information. However if the budget allows, then in-depth surveys and interviews could be used to generate the required data.

Once the research methods have been identified, the detailed research tools can be designed. For example, the research team can write the questionnaire's closed questions and the interview's open-ended questions, and they can lay out the questionnaire and provide instructions for the interviewer.

Step 3: Timing and location

Having designed the research instruments – such as a questionnaire and interview questions – researchers need to decide on the timing and location of the research.

In relation to where the data will be collected, researchers need to consider whether the research is

to be conducted face to face, by post, by telephone or online (using a web page or via e-mail). The size of the budget and the nature of the questions being asked will partly dictate where the research should be carried out. However, if test marketing or observations are required, then the research will have to carried out at the product's point of sale such as a supermarket or at the point of consumption such as a cinema or restaurant.

At this stage, the timing of the research should also be considered. Researchers need to determine the order in which the various research methods and tasks should be undertaken, and allocate a timescale for carrying out each activity. This could be done using a calendar to mark off the start and end times of each research method.

Step 4: Data analysis

Once the data has been collected, it will need to be analysed. This means sorting and summarising the data, looking for patterns and finding answers to the questions asked by the research objectives. The particular method used to analyse the data will depend on the research objectives and whether the data is quantitative or qualitative. Topic 6 looks at this step. However, when planning the customer research, this step should not be overlooked. In particular,

researchers should take care to ensure that the data collected is capable of being analysed to produce the answers asked by the research objectives. Saying "we're not sure we can answer this question because we didn't collect the right data" is not likely to impress anyone.

Using ICT

Information and communication technology can help to increase the efficiency and accuracy of customer research in various ways.

Some large organisations use their call centres to carry out and process telephone surveys. Smaller businesses can also use their ICT communications to conduct customer research, perhaps by inviting visitors to their websites to complete a short customer questionnaire or by including a link to an online feedback questionnaire in e-mails that they send to customers.

Market research agencies such as ACNielsen use ICT to collect and store consumer panel and other market trend data. Retailers use loyalty cards and the data collected from checkout tills to track customer purchases.

In each case ICT allows researchers to collect data from a wider range of customers than could be obtained cost effectively by relying solely on face-to-face and postal methods. ICT also provides a much more efficient means of storing and analysing research data. Researchers can use ICT to build and maintain large databases capable of storing millions of records, which can be analysed in a fraction of the time that it would take using manual methods.

Knowledge summary

■ Customer research needs to be planned if the aims of the research are to be achieved.

■ Research objectives describe the information that needs to be generated in order to achieve the aims of the customer research.

■ Research objectives help to define the data that should be collected from customers.

■ An important part of planning customer research is to decide how and where data should be collected.

■ ICT can be used to assist with the collection and storage of customer research data, enabling research to be carried out efficiently.

quick **questions**

1 Consider these three research objectives:

a) a fast food restaurant wants to identify whether its customers are satisfied with service times

b) the manager of a fashion retail outlet wants to identify the training that staff feel they need

c) a newsagent wants to establish whether customers are satisfied with the newspaper home delivery service.

In each case, identify two pieces of relevant data that could be collected to meet the research objective.

2 Describe how and where the customer research data you identified in question 1 might be collected. In each case, explain your choices.

data **interpretation**
Planning customer research for EMI

Rather than buy CDs from a music retailer, more customers are choosing to pay for the right to download music tracks online and play them on their computer or a portable music player such as Apple's iPod. EMI for example, as the article below shows, has reported growing music download sales. You can investigate EMI's target market by visiting its website at www.emigroup.com.

Download sales soar

EMI has seen download music sales rise by almost 600 per cent in the six months to the end of September 2004, and says they are becoming a major part of its business.

Analysts said that by 2009 digital music and publishing should account for about a quarter of total turnover. CDs, however, still account for most of EMI's turnover, and overall sales fell at EMI by 11.4 per cent during the half year.

EMI's half-year profits were £36.9 million, down from £39.8 million. Overall sales in the period were £851 million compared with £960 million in 2003.

Source: news.bbc.co.uk, 19 November 2004

A Describe two main trends in the sale of music recorded and distributed by EMI.

B Set out three research objectives that EMI might adopt if it carries out customer research into how people want to listen to music. Note that EMI's target market covers a wide age range, but assume any research will focus on UK customers.

C Identify the data that would need to be collected to meet the three research objectives that you drew up in task B.

D Discuss how and where the data you identified in C might be collected, making reference to the appropriate use of ICT.

Analysing customer research

Setting the scene: so what's the point of 3G?

All the UK's mobile operators have launched 3G services and they are working hard to persuade existing customers to trade up and make efforts to gain customers from rivals.

However, research by mobile phone firm Mobeon could come as something of a shock for 3G operators. The company surveyed 16–19 year olds to find out what they wanted from their phones, and it found that most were utterly turned off by the perceived complexity of getting at data services.

"Almost all of them want very simple services," said Robert Vangstad, Mobeon spokesman. Few were likely to wade through pages of menus to seek out the things that the mobile operators want them to spend their money on, he said.

For this young group, the most important thing about 3G services was the handset. "It was important for them to identify themselves with their telephone," said Mr Vangstad. "Everything about their telephone was helping to create their identity."

The research revealed that there was little loyalty to the operator or affection for any particular service.

What might make a difference was avatars – animated characters – that can tell a phone's owner about things that might interest them.

Without such an interface 3G operators might struggle to get people using all the extras they need them to use, said Mr Vangstad.

Source: adapted from news.bbc.co.uk, 21 March 2005

Making sense of data

In order to produce findings from customer research data, a business will analyse the data. This means making sense of the responses to questionnaires and interviews. It might also mean sifting through data produced by test marketing and consumer panels. So, for example, the research company Mobeon would have analysed its survey data to produce the findings on the 3G mobile phone market reported in the article above.

Businesses can analyse customer research data by:

- grouping the data to discover patterns in it
- looking at how particular data changes over time to discover trends.

1 Grouping data

By grouping data according to customer characteristics – for example, by age group – patterns can be identified.

The first step is to identify the characteristic by which you want to group the data. For example, you might group the responses to a questionnaire on "how I use

KEY TERMS

Extrapolation is the process of using past data to predict future data. For example, by plotting past sales figures against time, you can generate a trend to estimate next year's sales.

Simple trend analysis is a method of extrapolation that assumes a simple linear pattern in the data – that is, a straight line is drawn through the time-series data.

Time-series data is data plotted against months or years. For example, you could produce a time series by recording the number of customer complaints made each month.

A **database** is a collection of records, often stored on a computer. A customer database is a collection of records holding the details of each customer such as their name, address and age.

Data mining is a technique used to analyse large databases in order to uncover previously hidden patterns in the data.

Figure 4.7: Percentage of each age group answering "how many text messages I send on average each week"

Age group	Text messages			
	Less than 5	5 to 10	10 to 15	More than 15
Under 12	50%	42%	8%	0%
12–15	42%	38%	12%	8%
16–19	33%	32%	21%	14%
20–29	26%	25%	29%	20%
30–39	39%	25%	20%	16%
40–49	48%	30%	12%	10%
50–59	62%	28%	9%	1%
60 and over	72%	22%	6%	0%

Note: based on summary data from 1,600 questionnaires grouped by age

my mobile telephone" by these age groups: under 12, 12–15, 16–19, 20–29, 30–39 and so on. Then the individual customer responses should be sorted according to this characteristic.

The next step is to look at the responses to particular questions within each group. For example, Figure 4.7 collates responses to the question "how many text messages I send on average each week" by age group, expressing the results in terms of the percentage of people in each group making a particular response.

After grouping the responses to the question by age group, researchers can then look for any particular patterns to establish a link between age and frequency of text messaging. To assist with this analysis, they might present the data as a stacked bar chart (see Figure 4.8). The use of charts and graphs can help to make patterns in data a little clearer. In this case, a clear pattern does seem to exist.

By systematically grouping customer responses to questions according to different characteristics, researchers can begin to identify patterns in the data which enable them to publish findings.

stop and think

What patterns are shown by the table and the stacked bar chart in Figures 4.7 and 4.8? what is the relationship between age group and frequency of text messaging? What might be the reasons behind this relationship?

As a class activity, you could carry out a survey within your school or college to see if you can establish a relationship between year group and frequency of text messaging.

Figure 4.8: Stacked bar chart showing frequency of text messaging by age group

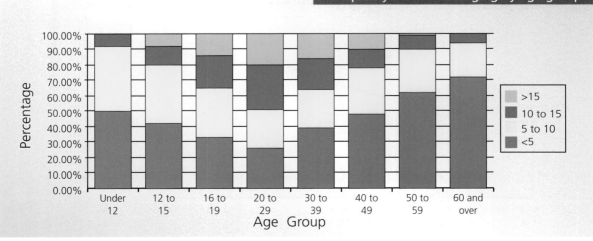

2 Forecasting trends

As well as collecting external data – say from customer questionnaires and interviews – businesses also generate a large volume of internal data over time. Nearly all businesses collect sales data for example, and internal data is a useful source of information. This source becomes even more useful if it can be grouped by customer characteristics such as location, sex and age.

By plotting a graph of sales figures against time, researchers can extrapolate the sales figures. This means that they use trends and patterns in the historical data to look ahead and predict what the sales figures might be next month or next year. This can help a business to forecast future customer needs.

This analysis is even more useful if several graphs can be produced – one for each customer characteristic – so that, for example, a supermarket might be able to predict how many tubs of ice cream might be sold in a particular store next month and which income groups are most likely to purchase the ice cream. This would help the supermarket chain ensure that it stocks sufficient ice cream in each store, and it might also help it take decisions about which particular brands of ice cream to stock.

Various techniques exist for extrapolating data but simple trend analysis is often sufficient to identify basic patterns. Trend analysis looks at data over time – time-series data – and identifies patterns in that data. Simple trend analysis will look for a linear pattern: it will try to fit a straight line through the time-series data that best represents the pattern in the data.

Figure 4.9 shows a simple trend analysis. Sales have been plotted against time (years) and a straight line has been drawn through the data ensuring that as many points as possible are on the line, while trying to keep the number of points above the line equal to those below the line. This graph can then be used to forecast (extrapolate) the sales for 2006 and 2007.

stop and think

Figure 4.10 shows the reported group turnover (sales) figures for Vodafone, the mobile telephone service provider. Using simple trend analysis, extrapolate Vodafone's group turnover in 2005 and 2006. How accurate do you think this forecast is likely to be? Explain your answer.

Figure 4.10: Vodafone's sales figures

Year	2000	2001	2002	2003	2004
Group turnover £m	7,873	15,004	21,767	28,547	33,559

Using ICT

Many businesses store customer data using computer databases. These are often sophisticated, and consist of several linked, or related, stores of data. These relational databases allow businesses to carry out analysis of seemingly unconnected facts and figures.

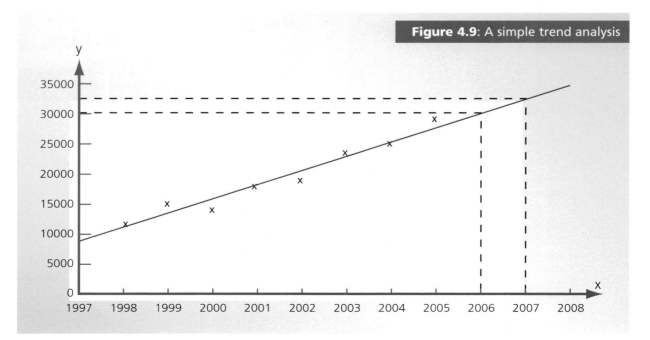

Figure 4.9: A simple trend analysis

This analysis is called data mining and requires specially written computer software that sifts through the data contained in the databases looking for patterns. The software reports any apparent pattern, and then it is up to analysts to determine whether this is a useful discovery from the data mine.

For large retailing businesses such as mail order firms, data mining allows the business to uncover previously unrecognised purchasing behaviours. Using reports from a data-mining session, businesses can improve the way they meet the needs of customers, perhaps anticipating needs the customer has yet to recognise.

Knowledge summary

- **Customer research data can be analysed by grouping data to discover patterns and trends.**

- **Internal sales data can be analysed using simple trend analysis to see how sales change over time.**

- **Simple trend analysis helps businesses produce forecasts from time-series data. It assumes a linear pattern in the data.**

- **Data mining uses software to discover hidden patterns in business information such as customer databases.**

quick **questions**

1 Why might it be important in a customer research questionnaire to collect data on the respondent's age, sex, occupation, house size and type of ownership, and hobbies and leisure activities?

2 When analysing customer research, why is it useful to group results and present findings using tables, charts and graphs?

3 Why might simple trend analysis provide misleading forecasts?

4 Why is it necessary for analysts to assess the significance of findings produced by computerised data-mining techniques?

data**interpretation**
Data mining

SPSS specialises in software, including data-mining products, that help businesses to retrieve new information from their databases. This article, which was published in the SPSS website, shows one application of data mining from the USA.

A Describe how data mining helped the Richmond Police Department to meet the needs of (a) its external customers and (b) its internal customers.

B Explain how large retail organisations such as Tesco and Dixons might use their customer and sales databases to improve the way they meet customer needs during the Christmas sales period.

C Discuss how your school or college could use the data it collects on student progress and examinations results to improve the way it meets the needs of its internal and external customers.

Using data mining to predict and prevent violent crimes

The Richmond Police Department's use of data mining has resulted in increased public safety, increased employee morale and substantial savings. Here's just a snippet of their data mining success story:

Frequent random gunfire on New Year's Eve presents a challenge to many law enforcement agencies. The ability to anticipate violent crime using data mining permits the proactive, or risk-based, deployment of police resources, which promises to increase public safety. Through the use of data mining, the Richmond Police Department identified and targeted locations associated with increased random gunfire during the previous New Year's Eve holiday with additional police resources.

The results demonstrated a 49 per cent reduction in the number of random gunfire complaints, with an increase in confiscated weapons of 246 per cent. Using data mining to target resources, the Richmond Police Department required fewer police personnel than originally anticipated, which enabled the release of approximately 50 employees. Data mining yielded a cost savings of approximately $15,000 during the eight-hour initiative.

Topic 7 How businesses differentiate their products

Setting the scene: Cadbury's product range

Cadbury Schweppes produces a range of chocolate and confectionery products. The company's product range includes many well-known brands such as Dairy Milk, Boost, Snaps, Creme Egg, Crunchie, Easter Egg Delight, Double Decker, Flake, Heroes and Picnic .

All these products provide a similar "core benefit" for customers – a chocolate and sugar snack in a convenient package. However, each product has a distinct way of delivering this benefit.

Cadbury Schweppes makes each product different by using:

- additional ingredients such as nuts and fondant fillings

- different packaging, creating a distinctive shape and wrapper for each product

- new combinations of ingredients, producing different chocolate textures.

Why do you think Cadbury Schweppes produces a range of different chocolate products? How do competing businesses, such as Nestlé, try to make their products different?

KEY TERMS

Core product describes the basic function of a product. For example, a car transports people, allowing the driver to choose the route.

Actual product is the additional features provided by a product. For example, a car might have anti-lock brakes, a turbocharger and a satellite navigation system.

Augmented product is the support aspects of a product. For example, a new car might come with three years' free service and a five-year warranty on parts and labour.

Differentiating the product

In order to meet changing customer needs, businesses are continually developing their product range by introducing new products and/or modifying current ones.

Product differentiation occurs when businesses make distinctive products, providing customers with benefits that cannot be matched by competitors' products. Products can be differentiated by altering particular aspects or features of a product. As Figure 4.11 illustrates, any product can be considered in terms of its core, actual and augmented aspects:

- core product is the basic product function – for example, the core product of a television is its function of displaying moving pictures

- actual product is the additional features of the product on top of its basic function – for example, the television may have a wide screen with a Dolby surround-sound speaker system

- augmented product is the support aspects of the product – for example, the television may be sold with free delivery and installation and come with a five-year guarantee.

1 Core product

The core product describes the main benefits received by consuming or using the product. It is the primary reason an individual purchases the product. If an inventor is asked "what's the purpose of this invention?", the first answer should be to describe the core product. A car's core product is its ability to transport people, allowing the driver to choose the route. A pizza's core product is its ability to provide nutrition with a pleasant flavour and texture combination.

A business can differentiate a product by altering an aspect of the core product. If it can demonstrate that

its product provides greater core benefits, this can be exploited when marketing the product. For example, a manufacturer of a household vacuum cleaner might try to differentiate its model by demonstrating that it does the basic job of cleaning floors, carpets and furniture more efficiently than competing products.

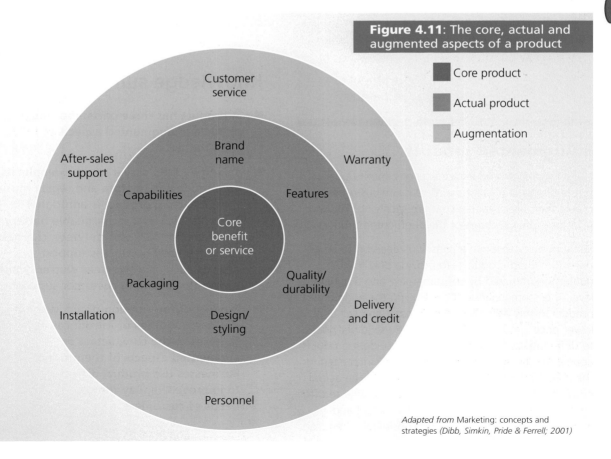

Figure 4.11: The core, actual and augmented aspects of a product

- Core product
- Actual product
- Augmentation

Adapted from Marketing: concepts and strategies *(Dibb, Simkin, Pride & Ferrell; 2001)*

2 Actual product

The core product delivers the essential benefits. The actual product delivers additional benefits on top of these essential benefits. If you asked someone to describe their new car, they would list features of the actual product such as the car's engine size, its safety features, its top speed, how many gears it has, how many gadgets it has, its colour and the materials used in the interior. They might also mention the brand name – for example, a Saab or Audi. All of these features of a product make up its actual product.

Given this additional dimension to a product, it is obvious that businesses have many opportunities to differentiate their products by modifying the actual products. The range of products produced by Cadbury Schweppes, it could be argued, is really a result of altering the actual rather than the core product. Its new Fuse bar still uses chocolate and sugar as the core product, but Cadburys add elements to this basic template to create a distinctly different actual product.

stop and think

Education is a product. The service provided has core and actual products. Using the ideas in Figure 4.11:

■ describe education's core product

■ identify the additional benefits that make up education's actual product

■ explain three ways in which a school or college could differentiate its product.

3 Augmented product

The augmented product consists of benefits external to the product. These benefits reassure customers and makes their user experience more satisfying. Figure 4.11 lists some features of the augmented product.

Some businesses make a conscious decision to limit the augmented product – to provide only the basic guarantees required by consumer law and a minimum level of customer service. By reducing the augmented product in this way, they can cut costs and sell at a lower price – indeed, they can use these lower prices to differentiate their products. These budget products appeal to customers who are really only interested in the core product and, perhaps, aspects of the actual product. For example, budget airlines are able to offer flights at very low prices because the actual and augmented products have been considerably reduced.

However, as their success shows, budget airlines provide what (at least some) airline customers want.

Alternatively, some businesses pride themselves on providing augmented products, and typically offer excellent customer service, lengthy guarantees and first-class after-sales service. Targeting a different market segment, these businesses feel justified in charging higher prices because of the augmented and actual products.

stop and think

Fashion retailers, such as French Connection UK and local independent stores, provide a service. They stock a range of fashion goods and allow you to browse in-store before selecting suitable items. This is the core product.

Using Figure 4.11, explain how fashion stores differentiate the service they provide, targeting different market segments by altering the actual and augmented aspects of their service.

Knowledge summary

■ A product has three parts: the core, actual and augmented aspects of the product.

■ Taking an MP3 player as an example: its core product is to store and replay music files; its actual product is additional features such as a rechargeable battery that lasts for 48 hours between charges; its augmented product is support aspects such as a five-year warranty and a website providing customer support.

■ Product differentiation occurs when a business modifies or introduces new features to the core, actual or augmented aspects of the product. Businesses use product differentiation to improve the way they meet the needs of customers.

1 Explain how each of these businesses could differentiate its products by changing the core, actual and augmented product:

a) a taxi service
b) a window cleaning service
c) a fish and chip shop.

2 Describe the core service offered by supermarkets such as Tesco. Explain how supermarkets attempt to differentiate their service.

data**interpretation**
Go Ballistic

Paintballing is a leisure activity where opposing teams battle against each other. Each team member is armed with a paintball gun and wears protective clothing.

Go Ballistic provides paintballing activities at over 30 locations throughout the UK. A brochure, describing the service can be downloaded from the Go Ballistic website (www.goballistic.co.uk).

As well as offering outdoor paintballing events, the business also has indoor arenas offering "...close-up combat that takes wit, skill and no small amount of guts to come out unscathed and victorious".

Prices for each session vary according to how many paintballs are purchased. Figure 4.12 shows some of the company's "special occasion upgrades", which give an indication of some of its target markets.

Figure 4.12: Go Ballistic special occasion upgrades

Upgrade	Additional price per person	Description
Birthday Bash	£24.99	Includes 300 paintballs per player, a celebratory cap for each member of the group and a birthday cake to help celebrate in style. Make it a birthday to remember and shoot your friends to bits!
Stag Hunt	£29.99	Includes 400 paintballs per player, a stag hunt baseball cap for each member of your group and a special stag hat for the man of the moment! Remember to ask your marshals for a stag hunt at the end of the day.
Hen Fight	£29.99	A special for hen parties includes 400 paintballs per player, bridal veil for the hen and commemorative hats for your group. Come on girls – what better start to the last weekend of freedom ...... than getting down and dirty in the woods!
Office Wars	£24.99	Perfect for a works do or team-building event, includes 300 paintballs per player, luminous shoot-the-boss vest for the man in charge and commemorative caps for all your group. What better way to build team spirit in the workplace than to shoot one another to bits!

Source: www.goballistic.co.uk

A Describe the core and actual products provided by Go Ballistic.

B Explain how Go Ballistic differentiates its paintballing activities. You should refer to the concepts of core, actual and augmented products when relevant.

Topic 8 The role of research and development

Setting the scene: why Fuse?

Fuse is part of the Cadbury Schweppes' product range. Here the company outlines the background to the development of the Fuse chocolate bar.

The Fuse concept was developed after market research identified a growth in snacking and a definite gap in the market for a more chocolaty snack. A number of ingredients were devised and tested following a survey which questioned consumers about their snacking habits and preferences. A research and development team was then asked to develop product recipes which addressed the needs expressed by consumers.

Not all products successfully emerge from the product development phase. Research and development involves combining various ingredients to develop potential new products. Considerable development time was spent on Fuse, carefully engineering the ingredients in order to deliver the right balance of chocolate, food elements and texture. Researchers tried and

tested more than 250 ingredients in various combinations before the recipe was finalised.

Any new product in the snacking sector must establish points of difference from existing products within the market. Unlike other confectionery snacking products that focus primarily upon ingredients and use chocolate only to coat the bar, the product developers decided to use Cadbury chocolate to fuse together a number of popular snacking ingredients such as raisins, peanuts, crisp cereal and fudge pieces.

Do you think that Cadbury has achieved its aims with Fuse? Explain why Cadbury developed Fuse and give some reasons why the product has been successful.

Source: www.cadbury.com

Research and development

Research and development, or R&D, is an essential process for any business if it is to meet the needs of its customers. R&D adopts a systematic approach to

KEY TERMS

Research and development is a systematic approach to product development that draws on research into materials and production technology to develop new products.

A **product range** is the different products offered by a business. For example, a typical car manufacturer produces several different models, and a hairdresser offers different services such as colouring and styling.

product development and is equally applicable to developing goods and services.

Cadbury Schweppes (see above) devoted considerable resources to the development of the Fuse product. This illustrates the importance of R&D – without an understanding of what customers need, the Fuse product may well have been unsuccessful. However, the R&D process also ensured that the finished product was capable of delivering these needs. It played a key role in ensuring that the core and actual aspects of the product delivered the benefits that customers required.

Research

This stage of the R&D process considers very general ideas and investigates what might be possible. For

Cadbury Schweppes, this stage might involve new ways to mix the chocolate ingredients. It might also involve considering a number of different combinations of ingredients.

A fashion manufacturer considering using a range of new fabrics would first carry out research into the qualities of these materials. For example, the manufacturer would want to know the ability of the fabric to hold colour dyes. Research might be undertaken to learn more about the fabric's durability of the fabric, its usability – how easy it is to cut and stitch – and the way in which it hangs.

The research stage of R&D is vital. If the research focuses on the wrong issues, then although a business might think it is making progress, in reality it would be wasting time and resources. The costs associated with the research stage can be very high – if a business does not keep a tight control on the research process, it could jeopardise its financial viability.

For these reasons, many businesses do not undertake the research stage of the R&D process. Instead, they rely on specialist research organisations. These organisations take on the risks associated with research. If their research is successful, they can sell their findings to the highest bidder and make significant profits.

stop and think

TechniTex (www.technitex.org) focuses on research, design and development of new technologies and applications for the textile industry. The partnership works with some 350 companies to bring innovation through to the marketplace.

The board comprises academics from several university research teams together with key industrialists who epitomise the best in scientific research, training and technology.

Visit the TechniTex website to learn more about technology transfer and how individual textile businesses can potentially benefit from the collaboration between academic and industrial research teams.

Development

The development phase of the R&D process uses the findings from the research phase. Figure 4.13 shows the steps businesses need to consider when developing new products.

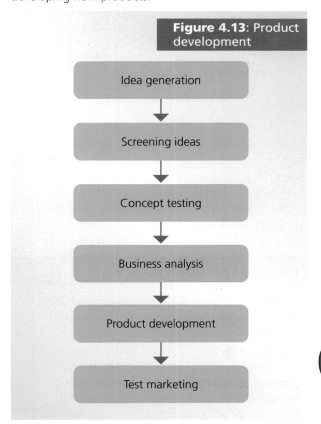

Figure 4.13: Product development

Idea generation → Screening ideas → Concept testing → Business analysis → Product development → Test marketing

Idea generation

Following closely on from the research phase, the R&D team lists a wide range of product ideas that have the potential to meet customer needs. Many of these ideas may be impracticable, but that is not the issue during this stage of the product development process. More enterprising organisations – ones that embrace an enterprise culture – encourage their employees to generate product ideas.

For example, the idea for 3M's Post-It note product came from an employee. He used to mark pages in books using slips of paper. As these slips of paper would invariably fall out, he suggested that sticky backed notes would be useful, especially if they could be reused. 3M had developed adhesive paper that would remain sticky for a long period of time but had yet to find a use for the product.

Screening ideas

While many people have imaginative ideas, practical ideas tend to be rarer. The screening stage takes a cold look at the resources available to the business and the specific needs of the target market. Cadbury Schweppes will have considered a number of chocolate snack ideas before narrowing these options down to two or three achievable products.

At this stage it might be sensible to use a consumer panel to comment on some of the general ideas; however this is usually left to the concept testing stage.

Concept testing

Each of the selected ideas are developed as concepts. This means communicating the core and actual benefits of the products using images and words. Consumer panels, or focus groups, are essential here. The business will try out the product concepts on the consumer panel, recording its responses to each concept's core and actual products. This is a relatively inexpensive way of assessing the viability of a product concept.

stop and think

A electronics business is developing a new mobile telephone aimed at 8–13 year olds. It is establishing a consumer panel for the concept testing stage but is unsure about the composition of this panel. Should it select children or adults? What socioeconomic profile should it focus on? How many people should be in each consumer panel?

Business analysis

During this stage of the product development process a business will assess the likely profitability of the successful product concept. The issue here is whether the business can turn the concept into a real product and make a profit. In addition, the business will need to think about how this new product will fit into the business's existing product range. Will the new product add to overall sales or will it simply take sales from one of the business's current products?

Product development

Having successfully passed the previous stages, the product concept should be acceptable to the target market and the business. This stage takes a potentially successful product concept and turns it into a working model or prototype. For example, a motor car manufacturer might produce a "concept car" to demonstrate the final product's tangible core and

actual benefits. At this stage the product can be tried out and the views of users recorded. If these are negative, then modifications could be made or, in extreme cases, the product abandoned.

This stage of the product development process can be very expensive, and few product concepts get this far. A business has to be genuinely convinced of a product's commercial viability before committing time and resources to producing a prototype.

Test marketing

Testing the final product in specific geographic areas of the target market allows the business to make any required final adjustments to the core, actual and augmented aspects of the product. However, carrying out test marketing with a new product can be very risky. Competitors are able to see the product and, if feasible, might quickly introduce a copy. They might also attempt to disrupt the test marketing process by distracting the selected target market through the use of special offers, increased advertising and other promotional activities. Nevertheless, test marketing represents the final opportunity for a business to reconsider its new product before committing substantial resources to its full-scale production.

stop and think

The Sinclair C5 electronic buggy was an innovative product which seemed to meet the need for a low-cost, environmentally friendly motorised vehicle. However. it was a commercial failure and, as such, an R&D failure.

Explain some possible reasons for the rejection of the product by consumers. Suggest which stage, or stages, of the product development process might have failed to identify the C5's commercial problems. Justify your answer.

Knowledge summary

■ Research and development is essential if a business is to meet the needs of its customers.

■ Research can be both expensive and risky. As such, it is often carried out by organisations funded by the businesses in an industry or by specialist research institutions.

■ Product development adopts a systematic approach to selecting and launching new products – from idea generation and screening to concept testing, business analysis, product development and test marketing.

1 Describe the type of research that might be carried out in:

a) the pre-cooked food industry – ready meals sold in supermarkets

b) the mobile telephone manufacturing industry – Motorola, Nokia, etc.

c) the television industry – media businesses producing reality shows such as Big Brother

d) the motor vehicle manufacturing industry – Ford, General Motors, etc.

2 Explain how each of these small businesses might implement the product development steps illustrated in Figure 4.13:

a) a restaurant

b) a pet shop

c) an estate agent

d) a local builder.

data**interpretation**
BSkyB's remote control handset

In 1996 BSkyB, the satellite broadcasting business, commissioned Frazer Designers to develop a design for a remote control handset. This article, adapted from a study on the Design Council's website (www.designcouncil.org.uk), illustrates the design process.

The design process began with an exploratory study of how people use TV remote controls, with each element of the object analysed in turn. Then, to test for the most comfortable shape, more than 30 full-size foam models were tested by a cross-section of users. These tests were carried out blindfold to ensure that the focus groups were not influenced by the colour or form of the models. After analysis, six shapes were modelled in Frazer's workshop for further blindfold user trials.

Great attention was paid to the design of the battery compartment as research had shown that there is a tendency for lids to become lost or broken. Buttons and graphics were designed to strike a balance between the tiny dots and bumps often found on remotes and the oversized "fumble phone" controls that veer the other way. Button colours were kept to a minimum.

The final design for the first remote, which took nine months development and testing, is a robust unit shaped like a sycamore seed. Frazer claims that the flat, balanced shape and the configuration of the buttons make the Sky product the most ergonomic remote handset ever created.

A Use Figure 4.13 to describe the steps taken by Frazer Designers when developing the remote control handset for BSkyB.

B Explain why BSkyB spent time and money perfecting the design of the remote control handset.

C Choose a product with which you are familiar and use the internet to investigate any new core and augmented products that have been introduced over the past five years. Using your findings, produce a five-minute presentation communicating what you believe to be the significant developments in the product.

Using customer service to meet customer needs

Setting the scene: delivering service improvements

Good customer service gets noticed: first and foremost by customers but also by rival businesses and by industry bodies. Here is an extract from a press release announcing an award for improvements to a bus service in the West Midlands.

What kind of service do you expect when you travel by public transport? How could your local public transport providers improve the level of service they offer their customers?

Arriva wins bus award

Telford and Wrekin Borough Council, Staffordshire County Council and Arriva Midlands have been named winners in the national marketing award for local authority and joint initiatives category at the Bus Industry Awards 2004.

The partnership was nominated for its work on Ruraline 481 – recently named the fastest growing bus route in the UK with an increase in patronage of 68 per cent year on year.

The significant increase in the numbers using the service was achieved by efforts to make the route more attractive to customers, improvements to bus priority measures and infrastructure, and complemented with marketing initiatives ensuring that more potential customers were made aware of the benefits of choosing the bus.

Keith Myatt, communications and publicity manager of Arriva Midlands, said: "This award recognises that local authorities and bus operators working together can achieve great improvements to services.

"We are delighted that this partnership's work in making real, measurable differences to our customers' travelling experiences has been recognised by such a prestigious award – as well as increasing the number of people choosing to travel by Ruraline 481."

KEY TERMS

Added value is the difference between the costs of the materials to make a product or provide a service and the price for which it is sold. In other words, it is the value added by the business.

A product's **unique selling point** is a characteristic that makes it distinct or different from other similar products.

stop and think

What kind of service would you expect if you are:

■ buying an expensive outfit from a small exclusive shop

■ buying vegetables from a market trader

■ using a cash machine in the high street

■ ordering a CD or DVD player from a catalogue.

What do customers expect?

There are limits to what a business can do in relation to how well it can respond to the needs and expectations of customers, just as there are limits as to the level of service an individual customer can expect from the business. A garage offering fuel on a self-service basis expects the majority of customers to serve themselves. It would be reasonable for a customer with a disability to ask for help; it would be unreasonable for a perfectly able-bodied person to ask for help simply because he or she was too lazy to get out of the car.

Businesses recognise that customers can make a choice between different levels of service, and they pitch services to meet different needs and expectations. For example, the quality of the whole package offered by Ryanair and other budget airlines does not necessarily match the quality we might associate with a flight on, say, British Airways.

Although budget airlines don't compromise on service features that relate directly to the health and safety of passengers and crew, they have found a ready market for a no-frills airline service.

The question that all airlines must ask themselves is what is the acceptable level of service that will ensure that customers will keep coming back. Ryanair's flights are cheap but its in-flight service is basic. Ryanair makes its money by filling its planes and packing as many flights into the day as possible. If you prefer a more luxurious flying experience, it is available, but at a cost. British Airways aims to add value in order to attract customers who want to travel in a more stylish fashion.

Figure 4.14: Airline punctuality

Airline	Punctuality (%)
Ryanair	92.4
Air France	86.5
SAS	86.0
easyJet	83.5
Lufthansa	82.3
Alitalia	80.6
Austrian	76.7
British Airways	72.0

Note: Punctuality measured by percentage of flights arriving within 15 minutes of schedule

Source: Ryanair.com

Managing customer expectations

Businesses do not just have contact with customers at the point of sale. If they are to manage and meet customer expectations fully, they must pay attention to the impression that they make on customers before, during and after the sale.

1 Before the sale

In all markets, customers have a wide choice of businesses that are competing for their trade. In exercising that choice, customers are very influenced by the way that businesses market themselves in order to attract their custom. In this pre-transactional phase, it is important that a business sends out the right signals to attract customers.

Customers have very different needs, and their expectations and demands will vary just as much. Both new and existing customers will require information about products to help them decide what to purchase. Customers also need information about opening hours, car parking, disabled access, payment methods and credit terms.

Ideally a business needs to have some unique selling points (USP) that will offer the customer something more than its competitors. This could be a faster service, a cheaper deal, a luxurious experience, more space, or some unique product features such as longer-lasting, disposable and durable.

2 During the sale

Once a customer has chosen to make a transaction, the service the business offers is critical. First impressions count, and if anything goes wrong, a bad impression will linger for a very long time. Read this next case study and ask yourself how the store could have avoided losing Tom's business.

Case study: Getting it wrong – Tom's story

Tom went into a leading computer sales store. He had won £1,000 in a competition and he wanted to buy a laptop to take to university. He looked at different machines. They varied in price from £700 to £1,500, and Tom wanted help to work out the best buy. He stood around trying to look as if he needed help and hoping that someone would approach. Finally, he went to the customer services desk. The assistant at the desk was on the phone. He waited again for several minutes. The assistant eventually put the phone down and apologised for keeping Tom waiting. He explained that he needed help and Tom was directed to another assistant at the far end of the store. By the time Tom had walked to where he had been directed, there was no one there. Exasperated, he walked out of the store and went round the corner to a competitor.

Effective transactional customer service requires staff:

- to be able to listen and respond to the customer efficiently and effectively

- to know about the business's products and be able to answer queries and questions

- to be able to smooth over any problems that might arise and offer reassurances

- to be polite and happy to help.

The customer needs to be able to:

- see the items for sale and that they are in good condition

- feel safe and be able to move around freely

- seek help and advice quickly and efficiently

- know whether they can take purchases away on the day or have to order them

- pay for items quickly using a choice of payment methods.

stop and think

Discuss the kind of expectations you might have when you make a transaction in these different situations:

- you are visiting the cinema to see a very popular film

- you want to buy a desk and chair for your bedroom

- you are buying a new pair of trainers

- you are booking some tickets for a concert on the internet.

3 After the sale

Post-transactional service is also important. What happens if something goes wrong? Can customers get their money back, replace a faulty item, or is there an adequate repair service?

The right or appropriate level of post-transactional service will depend on the product. It is unlikely that customers would expect (or receive) the same after-care service when buying second-hand washing machines as when buying brand new models. If you buy a cheap watch, radio or calculator, you could probably expect little by way of an after-sales service. If you buy similar but expensive products, they would probably come with a guarantee and would be worth mending, at least for a while.

Some products are not returnable. Customers who get "treated" to the holiday from hell cannot return the product: all they can do is try to get some apology and financial compensation from the holiday company. Some experiences are subjective: a customer might think a meal is disappointing, the owner of the restaurant might take a different view. The only redress the customer has is to tell others of his or her misfortune and never go to the restaurant again.

stop and think

What would you expect to receive in terms of after-sales care if you have bought a new car. Visit the Renault website at www.renault.co.uk to find out about its after-sales care?

Knowledge summary

■ The level of customer service is often determined by the nature and quality of the product being offered.

■ Businesses operate in competitive marketplaces and often look for a unique selling point to raise expectations and attract customers.

■ Customer expectations need to be met and managed before any sale takes place, during the selling process, and after the sale.

189

quick**questions**

1 Give two examples of how the behaviour of a member of staff working in a supermarket might help it to meet the expectations of a customer.

2 Explain why it is so important for a business to understand the needs and expectations of its customers.

3 Crazy Horse is a new restaurant selling fast food. The business wants to open in your town. What kind of services would you like to see it offer?

data**interpretation**
Online supermarkets

More and more businesses are selling their goods and services online. Some of the large supermarkets offer this service. Most of the high street supermarkets have online stores at which you can buy groceries.

You can see the type of services many supermarkets now provide for online customers by visiting these sites:

■ www.asda.com

■ www.sainsburys.co.uk

■ www.safeway.co.uk

■ www.tesco.co.uk.

Not all supermarkets have gone down this route. In November 2004, Morrisons' managing director John Dowd said: "Morrisons believes the majority of shoppers are not interested in buying groceries online, despite rival supermarket chains ploughing millions into e-commerce. The group will stick to a tried-and-tested formula to boost its market share."

A Discuss whether you think Morrisons is right to stick to its tried-and-tested formula of customer service?

B Visit the websites of the major supermarkets that offer an online service and assess their strengths and weaknesses.

C Examine the possible pitfalls for a business in trying to create a positive customer service experience on an online service. How might the supermarkets avoid these pitfalls?

Topic 9 Using customer service to meet customer needs

Royal Mail Group is a public limited company wholly owned by the government. Annual sales exceed £8 billion and the business employs more than 200,000 employees.

- Royal Mail Group has three main brands.

- Royal Mail serves both individual and business customers. It collects, sorts and delivers mail to the UK's 27 million addresses, and provides business mail services to help companies communicate with their customers and market their businesses.

- Parcelforce Worldwide collects, sorts and delivers parcels, mainly for business customers.

- Post Office Ltd – operating under the Post Office brand – has a network of 15,000 Post Office branches and offers around 170 products and services. Customers can buy stamps, send mail, collect benefits, pay bills, make cash withdrawals and buy from a range of financial and commercial services such as foreign currency, home, car and travel insurance, unsecured loans, and a home telephone service. Some 94 per cent of people in the UK live within a mile of a Post Office.

The Royal Mail business saw a turnaround in fortunes in the early part of the 2000s. In 2002, the Royal Mail – then known as Consignia – was losing £1 million a day. Two years later, operational and service improvements turned this loss into a profit of around £1 million per day. In the first half of the 2004/5 financial year Royal Mail made £217 million profit.

External customers

Everyone is a customer of the Royal Mail Group. Everyone receives or posts letters and packages from time to time. It is probably a service we take for granted.

Post Office branches are the point of call to post letters, parcels and cards, to obtain a passport form or tax a car. Post Office staff can give information about government initiatives and will change sterling into foreign currency without making a commission charge.

Businesses are also customers, with nearly 90 per cent of the mail posted being from businesses. Many businesses use direct mail as part of their marketing strategies, and Royal Mail has a service to give help and advice on how to make the best of this form of advertising. Many business and financial documents have to be sent using the post. Business customers also take advantage of the Parcelforce Worldwide express delivery service.

	Quarter 2 2004/5	target	Quarter 1 2004/5	3 month change	Quarter 2 2001/2	3 year change
First class	92.1%	92.5%	88.3%	up 3.8%	90.7%	up 1.4%
Second class	98.6%	98.5%	98.0%	up 0.6%	98.5%	up 0.1%

Figure 4.15: Service improvements in postal services

Internal customers

Royal Mail Group employs over 200,000 people. The group has introduced changes in working practices in recent years, but has made significant increases in pay and offered better conditions. The new improved Royal Mail – a business in which targets are being met and the reputation and integrity of the service is growing – has produced a more motivated and happier workforce.

Customer service expectations

Customers expect letters and parcels to arrive on time and undamaged. When people need to use the post office to tax their car or collect child benefit, they do not want to queue for too long. If customers are wheelchair-bound or otherwise disabled, they need to know they can still use the post office. If customers want information about a postcode, or the cost of sending a letter to Africa, or the best way to send a parcel, they want to know that the information is accurate.

The Royal Mail knows that customer expectations are changing. By introducing online services, guaranteed delivery times and computerised systems to make waiting times shorter, Royal Mail is trying to maintain and improve the quality of service to its customers.

Service improvements

Royal Mail has had to reinvent its business to meet the changing needs of customers and to offset increasing competition. Its goal is "to be the world's leading postal service". The government has set targets, but the Royal Mail's initiatives to improve performance have meant that in many cases targets have been met and exceeded.

Modernisation is the key to operational change and to improving customer service. There have been worries that some changes might impact on the most vulnerable members of society.

For example, the Department of Work and Pensions has asked people who collect benefits from Post Office branches to opt to have their money paid directly into a bank account. This impacts on the Post Office because fewer people are visiting branches to collect benefits. Post Office Ltd is seeking this business and generates revenue by offering new services to its customers such as banking facilities, foreign exchange and financial services.

Another important change was the introduction of a single postal delivery to every household in the UK. This replaced a system in which most parts of the UK had two deliveries a day. This change has enabled the Royal Mail Group to improve the wages and hours of its postmen and postwomen.

Improvements have also been made to ensure the integrity of the service. All new recruits are now vetted to ensure that any who attempt to conceal past convictions are prevented from joining the company.

Parcelforce Worldwide is also responding to the needs of its customers. It now focuses on express services guaranteeing delivery within a timeframe. It has restructured and cut its losses, and is on target to break even at the end of the 2004/5 financial year.

People issues

Royal Mail believes that increasing profitability is about improving service and efficiency, and that this is linked to the dedication and commitment of the staff in the business. Increasing quality of service to customers is the number one priority for Royal Mail, and investing in people was seen by directors of Royal Mail as essential if they were to provide an improved service for customers.

In 2002, pay for postal workers was low, and they worked a six-day week. Royal Mail had one of the worst strike records in the country. Customers were suffering the loss of nearly 30 million letters a year and the first-class letter delivery performance was poor.

Postmen and postwomen now work a five-day week, with basic pay of around £300 a week. A new ground-breaking pay deal increased pay by 14.5 per cent. The amount of lost mail has been halved, with 99.92 per cent arriving safely at its destination. In 2005, the Royal Mail announced record annual profits of £537 million and said that postal workers would receive a "share in success" payment of £1,074.

The company has openly tackled bullying and harassment issues that had caused some problems.

Harmony within the workforce will hopefully be reflected in the service to customers.

In the spring of 2004 there were 20,000 temporary employees. This has now been reduced to 2,500. A pool of experienced, trained temps has been established to ensure people are available when there is a short-term need for extra workers. Training has also been improved, and new recruits are assigned a mentor to help them pick up the job more quickly.

Monitoring customer satisfaction

Postwatch (www.postwatch.co.uk) is the consumer watchdog and Postcomm (www.postcomm.gov.uk) is the postal services regulator. Both bodies monitor the performance of the Royal Mail. They carry out regular surveys to record the satisfaction levels of customers.

Postwatch and Postcomm conducted a survey of customer experiences at Post Office branches in October 2004. The survey used mystery shoppers to sample services at 302 urban branches. The survey looked at:

■ exterior and interior presentation of offices

■ information available on products and services

■ staff performance when dealing with customers

■ accuracy, quality and completeness of information.

The main conclusions of this Postwatch survey were that:

■ staff were seen to be polite, calm and efficient, but they were not always well informed and sometimes did not give the correct advice

■ wheelchair access was not universal

■ one in five mystery shoppers had to wait in queues of more than five minutes before being served – Post Office Ltd serves 29 million customers a week, with the large majority being served within 5 minutes

■ of a sample survey of packages sent first class, 71 per cent arrived the next day but 22 per cent of packages were left unattended at recipients' houses.

Royal Mail and the law

The Royal Mail is highly regulated. The government sets targets, and these are reviewed on a regular basis. Service standards are carefully monitored and regulated by Postwatch and Postcomm. Prices for services are also carefully controlled. Royal Mail would like to have more autonomy in the way it sets prices for its products so that it can compete more vigorously with its rivals.

The business has to adhere to consumer legislation and must not make claims about its services if these cannot be met. Customers must be safe, and there should be access for those with disabilities.

The challenge

In 2004 Adam Crozier, chief executive of Royal Mail, said: "The progress we have made in improving both our service and profitability supports our vision to be demonstrably the best and most trusted mail company in the world.

"We are determined to consistently provide the highest quality, dependable mail services, and that includes innovative products for all our customers as well as the one-price-goes-anywhere universal service to the UK's 27 million addresses.

"The challenge now is to make a commercial return that's acceptable to our shareholders and, above all, allows us to make the investments we need both in our people and in improving quality further."

Websites

www.royalmailgroup.com

www.royalmail.com

www.parcelforce.com

www.postoffice.com

activities

1 Describe the range of needs that external customers might have during and after purchasing Royal Mail products.

2 Describe the actions taken by Royal Mail's management to improve the ways in which it meets the needs of its internal customers.

3 Explain how the Royal Mail might use ICT to collect and process customer data in order to generate useful information.

4 Discuss how the Royal Mail has used these concepts to meet the needs of its external customers:

(a) core, actual and augmented products
(b) research and development
(c) customer service.

You will need to research the websites listed on this page (see above) to answer this question fully.

COMMUNICATION IS AN INTEGRAL PART OF running a business. Good communications prevent poor decision-making, duplication of effort, misallocation of resources and poor customer relations.

This unit looks at the communication methods used by business. It considers the ways in which a business can improve its communication systems, reviewing in particular the use of ICT and software applications to help the communication process.

Businesses also rely on up-to-date and accurate information. Business information systems increasingly use IT applications to improve cost efficiency and gain competitive advantage. However, as the unit shows, using IT has implications for the way a business must store, manage and protect the information it holds.

Business communication and information systems

Setting the scene: effective communication

Good communication is a key element of business operations. A business must be able to communicate clearly with its customers and other stakeholders.

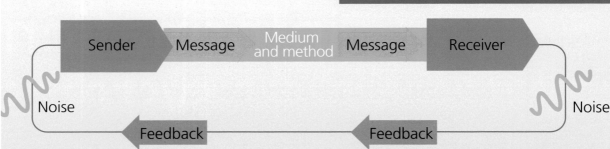

Figure 5.1: The communication process

It is also necessary for a business to communicate effectively with internal audiences. Businesses need to ensure that employees are aware of company aims, objectives and targets and that these are achieved (on time).

A large part of good communication revolves around having accurate information resources and good data management. Figure 5.1 illustrates the key components of the communication process.

Sender – the individual, group or organisation wanting to communicate.

Message – the use of text, images and sounds, to convey ideas and information.

Method – the format of the communication, whether verbal or written, formal or informal.

Medium – the platform used to deliver the message, such as post, e-mail, internet or intranet.

Receiver – the individual, group or organisation the message is intended for. The receiver interprets the message and attempts to understand its meaning.

Feedback – the receiver's response to the message.

Noise – anything that gets in the way of the receiver understanding the sender's true message.

What is communication?

Business communications take place for a variety of reasons, but most communications have one of these definite goals as their intention:

- provide information

- give instructions

- keep people up to date

- make checks

- receive feedback

- negotiation

- confirmation.

A key aspect of good communications is to consider the objective of the communication message. This should determine the method of communication. If the correct communication methods and mediums are not used – or if the correct systems are not in place to monitor communications – communication problems can arise. Breaks can occur between the intended message and the action taken by the receiver, and these breakdowns can be costly in terms of operational efficiency and have can financial consequences.

Core to the success of any organisation is clear, efficient and accurate channelling of information, data and communications. To be a good communicator takes practice and experience. The five main communication skills are speaking, listening, reading and writing, use of information technology, and non-verbal communication.

Speaking

This need not necessarily be face to face, but could include telephone conversations or presentations.

Listening

Communication is a two-way process: the recipient must actually actively listen to a verbal message to be able to interpret it correctly.

Reading and writing

Written messages can be formal communications such as letters and reports, or more informal notes and e-mails. In all cases, however, the language used must be clear, unambiguous and suit the intended audience. The presentation of information and data needs to be well thought out before the communication takes place to ensure the reader interprets the message correctly.

Information technology

Advances in information technology have transformed many traditional ways of communicating. Data can now be transformed and manipulated easily as well as distributed quickly and reasonably cost effectively. However, the use of IT as an effective communication tool relies on having properly trained employees.

Non-verbal communication

Not all communication relies on written or verbal skills. Many messages can be enhanced by the use of body language, expression and images.

What this unit covers

How businesses communicate

There are many methods available to a business to convey a message from the sender to the receiver. Ideally communications should reach the intended receivers in time, cost effectively and avoiding noise. The first requirement for cost-effective communication is selecting an appropriate method. For example, Boots wouldn't inform its shareholders of the company's financial performance through face-to-face

individual meetings – it would cost too much and take too long. Having chosen an appropriate method, a business next needs to decide the medium for the exchange. We consider different communication mediums – the ways of sending messages to their intended recipients – in Topic 4.

How businesses use information systems

Accurate communications depend heavily on accurate and up-to-date information. All information and data held by a company needs to be efficiently stored and correctly processed, so that when it is accessed by employees or customers it is in a form that they can understand. Some information held by business organisations will be sensitive – containing either financial and commercial data that could benefit rival businesses, or personal information on employees and customers. This data should remain confidential, and it should be stored securely.

Use of software applications

Spreadsheets, word processors, databases, graphics packages, presentation software, as well as e-mail, intranets and the internet can all help to store, organise, process and communicate information. However, these packages are not suitable for every purpose; each possesses individual specialist functions. The unit considers the purpose and use of different software applications.

Legal considerations of using software

Business organisations can hold sensitive and confidential information on both their employees and customers. All organisations that store data on private individuals have a legal duty to use the information responsibly. The unit looks at how the Data Protection Act and the Computer Misuse Act regulate and influence the use of information.

Prioritising and planning work

A key aspect of storing, processing and communicating information is to achieve company aims and objectives. Jobs, tasks and activities need to be prioritised, planned and monitored to ensure that they are completed in time. A plan of activities can act as a form of communication in itself, by allowing employees to know what they are meant to be doing. This unit concludes by looking at different methods of planning and communicating activities.

Setting the scene: walkout after false rumours

More than 600 contractors at one of the biggest oil refineries in Europe staged a walkout, claiming it was unsafe to work at the sprawling Pembroke site.

It was the second walkout caused by false rumours about safety. A similar incident occurred in June, when a bomb scare caused 900 workers to leave the site.

But oil giant Texaco and union leaders at the refinery joined forces to appeal to them to return. Both sides claim that safety issues at the site have been fully dealt with, and are calling for the men to return to work.

Danny Fellows, regional manager with the T&G union, said part of the problem stemmed from unfounded rumours about safety at the site. These had been circulated on the plant's own internal communications system, but it was not known who had started the false suggestions.

"We had one report that someone had broadcast an alert saying workers are 'dropping like flies' because of a gas leak," he said. "Another said that a contractor had broken his back in an accident. Neither report was true."

He added: "The plant itself is huge with almost 3,000 people working here, and there are some who have never worked here before who are overawed. It can be a frightening and alien place. There are huge cranes and steam and loud bangs – it doesn't help when people spread rumours."

Source: news.bbc.co.uk, 16 September 2003

KEY TERMS

Formal communications take place using the approved channels of communication.

Informal communications take place outside the recognised communication channels.

Internal communications are the systems and methods used to ensure accurate information flow between departments, projects or employees in an organisation.

External communications are the systems and methods used to ensure accurate information flow between an organisation and its customers and other external stakeholders.

Types of communication

Communication – and the clear and effective channelling of information – is key to the success of any business. Poor communications can lead to costly mistakes, poor decision-making and tasks not being undertaken. In contrast, good communication enables:

- effective messages to be sent to customers
- correct orders to be sent to suppliers
- employees to know what they are meant to be doing.

- proper co-ordination of business activities

- good allocation of resources and
  time management

- accurate gathering of information

- good decision-making

- improved motivation and industrial relations.

A good business organisation will expend time and effort analysing and managing its communication system. In doing so, it needs to consider both formal and informal communications, and communications with customers and external stakeholders as well as those within the organisation.

1 Formal communications

Formal communications are interactions or exchanges that take place using an organisation's approved channels of communication. The communication is documented, traceable and follows an ordered structure. It may be written (such as a letter) or verbal (such as a face-to-face interview) but the communication will have a defined role and purpose. A business meeting, for example, is a combination of formal communications, with agendas, minutes and verbal exchanges designed to meet a specific communication need.

2 Informal communications

Informal communications take place outside an organisation's recognised communication channels and methods. These include communications that have no specific order, structure or traceability, although they may still impart useful information. Examples of informal communications include conversations, telephone calls, messages on notice boards and unofficial meetings, such as when a manager calls subordinates together for a verbal progress report.

Informal forms of communication are just as necessary as formal methods to the smooth and efficient running of a business. However, by their nature, they can also be responsible for spreading gossip and rumours, or transmitting confidential information to the wrong parties.

3 Internal communications

Communications must be made in such a way that information flows freely through an organisation and reaches the people who need to act on it. In a small business, this is fairly easy to achieve – it is relatively straightforward to ensure that all staff have an idea of what is happening and know who to go to if they need to find out something specific. In a large organisation, this is not always as easy to organise. Communications need to reach their destination, but in a format that allows the receiver to understand and act upon the messages.

Obviously a large amount of internal communications takes place through face-to-face or telephone conversations, but frequently a written record is required. Formal internal communications include memorandums, agendas, minutes and reports. These are all covered in depth in Topic 2. In this section, we consider some other forms of internal communication.

Internal letters, papers and briefs

Letters, papers and briefs are more formal than a memorandum, but usually less specific than a report. These documents take the format of asking for or providing additional information to assist in the decision-making process. They may include details of arguments for and against a particular decision, or requests for and responses to clarifications of particular points. In simple terms, they are more expanded documents than memorandums but less specific than a report. They are, though, a *formal* mode of communications.

Notice boards and newsletters

Businesses use mass internal communicators – such as notice boards and newsletters – to pass on information to large numbers of employees at the same time. These can be formal or informal in type. They are used to convey open non-confidential information such as policy changes affecting all staff, company closure dates for Christmas holidays, or upcoming social activities.

stop and think

Why might staff notice boards not be the most effective method of communicating a change in company policy toward customer complaints for a major supermarket chain like Asda?

Bespoke documents

Many organisations design and use their own documentation for specific purposes such as stock or purchase requisitions, making holiday requests, recording complaints, and reporting faults or damage. These forms are designed to streamline and regulate standard procedures so that managers are not bombarded with memos and notes and they can deal with problems, requests and complaints efficiently. This type of bespoke document is often colour-coded for easy recognition, so employees know what to use for what purpose, and so they can easily be routed to the appropriate person or department.

Electronic communications

Many businesses now use e-mail or a company intranet for much of their internal communications. These communication mediums are considered in detail in Topic 6. Businesses also increasingly produce common document templates, such as house style memos, in electronic format.

An organisation might organise its internal booking schedules electronically, producing forms that show the availability of particular resources such as conference rooms or company pool cars. This not only communicates to staff the availability of resources on any given day, but also allows them to book the resources they need. Figure 5.2 shows an electronic booking sheet used in a college that allows staff to reserve places in the IT suites and learning centres.

External communications

Communications with customers, suppliers and other external bodies such as accountancy firms and government agencies are just as important as internal communications. Many communications, such as responding to a customer enquiry, may take place informally, but others will require formal records. The public image and perception of a business is greatly influenced by the way in which it presents and manages its external communications. This can affect:

- corporate image and reputation
- customer perceptions and sales figures
- the ability to attract potential employees
- the organisation's ability to attract potential investors or to secure finance.

It is important that businesses choose the correct form of communication to reach the target audience. Formal external communications include advertising, press releases and annual reports, as well as more individualised communications such as letters.

stop and think

Many companies such as easyJet insist that staff wear distinctive uniforms. Think of four ways this aids communications for easyJet.

Figure 5.2: An electronic booking form

Week: 18-Apr-05					SIC 24 pcs max Staff initials		No of pcs	Total pcs booked	NETWORK W1 16 pcs max Staff	Number	LEARNING SHOP 24 pcs max Staff	Number	S2 13 pcs Staff	Number	S16 12 pcs Staff	Number
Mon	18-Apr-05	8:55	10:15	A				0	ECDL	ECDL	N/A	N/A	sb	11	RS	12
		10:15	11:25	B	smo		17	17	ECDL	ECDL	N/A	N/A	CP	13		
		11:45	1:00	C	awh		4	4	ECDL	ECDL	N/A	N/A	CP	13		
		2:00	2:40	Tutor				0			N/A	N/A				
		2:40	3:55	D	sb		22	22					pma	11	sm	12
Tue	19-Apr-05	8:55	10:15	B	pc		20	20	ECDL	ECDL	N/A	N/A	CP	13		
		10:15	11:25	C	awh	cs	4 6	10	ECDL	ECDL	N/A	N/A	CP	13		
		11:45	1:00	D	smo		20	20	ECDL	ECDL	N/A	N/A				
		2:00	2:40	Tutor				0			N/A	N/A	CP	3		
		2:40	3:55	E	cs		10	10								
Wed	20-Apr-05	8:55	9:55	D				0	ECDL	ECDL	N/A	N/A				
		9:55	10:55	E	awh		16	16	ECDL	ECDL	N/A	N/A	lt	13		
		11:15	12:15	A	sb		11	11	ECDL	ECDL	N/A	N/A	Sm	13	RS	12
		12:15	1:15	B				0	ECDL	ECDL	N/A	N/A				
		2:15	3:55	Enrich				0					CP	13		
Thur	21-Apr-05	8:55	10:15	C	cs		6	6	ECDL	ECDL	N/A	N/A	sb	11		
		10:15	11:25	D	awh		16	16	ECDL	ECDL	N/A	N/A				
		11:45	1:00	E				0	ECDL	ECDL	N/A	N/A				
		2:00	2:40	Sub C				0			N/A	N/A	CP	7		
		2:40	3:55	A	cs		8	8								
Fri	22-Apr-05	8:55	10:15	E	cs		10	10								
		10:15	11:25	A	cs		8	8	ECDL	ECDL	N/A	N/A				
		11:45	1:00	B				0	ECDL	ECDL	N/A	N/A				
		2:00	2:40	One to one C				0			N/A	N/A	CP	5		
		2:40	3:55	C				0					sb	11		

Staff booking any of the areas above are required to supervise their students in the sessions booked.
The highest demand from individuals is during periods 2 & 3 so try to prioritise your booking of the afternoon session especially in the Learning Shop

Letters

Any letters sent outside to individuals or organisations must be accurate, professional and presentable. Most firms have headed paper displaying their logo, contact details, company registration and VAT numbers. This stationery forms part of the corporate image. Many businesses insist that letters are presented in house styles – rules about how a letter should be laid out.

Forms

It is often useful to use standard forms to assist communications with external agencies. A standard form ensures that the organisation always collects the information it wants and needs. Standard formats are also quicker and easier for employees to process.

Forms are usually used for purposes such as customer orders, job applications or complaints. Although they may have standard formats, forms can also be used with a degree of flexibility, allowing the business to communicate additional information – a customer order form might have a panel displaying the current special offers – or to request additional information.

Other formats

Many other types of external communication methods are used to convey particular messages or information to external bodies as well as customers. These include adverts and promotional displays but also items like press releases, direct mail, brochures, websites, vehicle liveries, and signage in and around premises.

The way these "messages" are presented – and the easy with which they can be understood – will help to form a business's corporate image and will have an impact on its ability to achieve its objectives.

Knowledge summary

- **Effective communications help a business achieve its objectives.**

- **Standard forms can aid the flow, speed and accuracy of communications.**

- **External communications influence the way customers and other stakeholders perceive the business.**

quick**questions**

1 Distinguish between formal and informal communications.

2 Give two reasons why a firm might want to design its own bespoke documentation.

data**interpretation**
Online headache troubles marketers

Long derided as a purveyor of junk mail, direct marketing is repositioning itself through better targeting and the use of digital media. But it can still be an uphill struggle as legitimate companies find themselves tarred with the spam e-mail brush.

Every year the Royal Mail handles five billion direct mail items, a number expected to grow as competition in the postal sector drives prices down. But the direct mail industry plays down consumer fears that people could be swamped by similar numbers of e-mails and text messages.

The E-mail Marketing Association has been set up to bring best practice into digital marketing. But there are clearly still many operating outside its parameters – one-third of the 300 million e-mails sent in the UK each day are reckoned to be spam. Consumers can now be targeted by anything from income and driving habits to postcode and nationality. While firms will be able to pinpoint the consumers they want, it might mean less unwanted mail for those outside target groups.

Source: adapted from news.bbc.co.uk, 23 October 2002

A Describe three ways a business uses IT to communicate either internally or externally.

B Explain why the presentation and perception of external communications is important to a business.

C Discuss the difficulties a legitimate business may face by finding itself "tarred with the spam e-mail brush".

Setting the scene: warning over Microsoft Word files

Writing a Microsoft Word document can be a dangerous business, according to document security firm Workshare.

A survey by the firm revealed that up to 75 per cent of all business documents contained sensitive information most firms would not want exposed. To make matters worse 90 per cent of those companies questioned had no idea that confidential information was leaking.

Andrew Pearson, European boss of Workshare, said: "The efficiencies the internet has brought in, such as instant access to information, have also created security and control issues."

Sensitive information inadvertently leaked in documents published on the internet includes confidential contractual terms, competitive information that rivals would be keen to see, and special deals for key customers. The problem is particularly acute with documents prepared using Microsoft Word because of the way it maintains hidden records about editing changes. As

documents get passed around, worked on and amended by different staff members, the sensitive information finds its way into documents.

Workshare surveyed firms around the world and found that, on average, 31 per cent of documents contained legally sensitive information, but in many firms up to three-quarters fell into the high risk category. The discovery of this hidden information could prove embarrassing or advantageous for companies if, for instance, those tendering for contracts found out about their competitors' terms for a deal being negotiated. Problems with documents could also mean legal trouble for firms as regulatory bodies step up scrutiny and compliance laws start to bite, said Mr Pearson.

Source: adapted news.bbc.co.uk, 28 January 2005

Confidentiality

All businesses need to be aware that they hold potentially sensitive information that needs to be kept confidential. In practice, this means that they must distinguish between two types of communication:

■ confidential communications – exchanges of information that need to be kept private or restricted

■ non-confidential communications – open communications where anybody is allowed access to the information.

Most businesses possess information about employees and customers that should be kept confidential. However, much detailed knowledge about a business's

own operations should also be restricted to selected individuals who have a need to know and act on the information. This could include:

■ financial information such as bank details

■ confidential material about products or new product development

■ job application forms

■ market research data

■ information on structural change in the business.

Access to sensitive information needs to be restricted to those employees who need to know it for operational reasons. Confidentiality can be maintained by password protecting files or documents, having restricted access filing areas, or by using sealed and marked envelopes. Other policies to protect the privacy of information include ensuring that computer monitors are not left switched on displaying information, or locking workstations when employees are away from their post.

Failure to take proper steps to keep sensitive information confidential can be costly. For example, businesses could incur financial penalties for breaking the Data Protection Act (see Topic 7, page 224) or loss of competitive position if competitors are able to exploit the business's new product ideas.

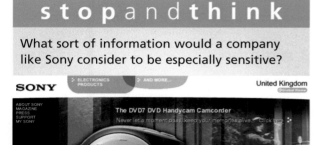

stop and think

What sort of information would a company like Sony consider to be especially sensitive?

Not all business information is confidential. Many aspects about a business – information about the availability of its products, for example – need to be widely known to anybody within the organisation. This sort of communication can take place using open access methods like notice boards, newsletters, company-wide intranets or public internet sites. Open communication channels should be used for any communication that needs to reach as wide an audience as possible.

Methods of communication

In order for communications to be effective – for the recipient to understand the communication sent – it is important that the communication is expressed and presented in the proper way. The method of communication can be as important as the actual message or information itself. For example, if someone sends you a request to do something scribbled on a note, would you respond in the same you way as you would to a formal letter making the same request?

Some methods of communication are formal, others more informal (see Topic 1). The important point to realise is that different methods are appropriate for different types of communication. In the remainder of this topic, we focus on written communications. In Topic 3, we consider other forms of communication.

Written communications have some advantages over other forms of communication. It's easy for writers to keep copies of the communication for their own reference. Recipients can also keep hard copies to refer back to when necessary. This means that written communications are particularly useful for giving detailed messages or instructions.

1 Letters

Letters are a formal mode of communication, and are usually considered to be more formal than e-mails or memos. Letters are most often used for external communications and so must convey a good impression of the business.

Styles of writing business letters vary. Many business have their own house style, including letterhead, company logo and layout. The most common layout format is the fully blocked style. In this style, all the lines and paragraphs begin against the left-hand margin, only the date is usually put on the right-hand side for filing reasons. This layout is fairly modern and it is influenced by the use of word processors that usually operate on an align left page setup.

In general, a business letter should include:

- company name and address

- telephone, fax numbers and website

- company registration number

- name of the head of the organisation – such as the managing director or principal

- date of writing

- the name and details of the person for whom the letter is intended

- the signature of the writer.

Letters should be clearly written and be neatly presented. A good style is to keep sentences short. You should be polite, set out any facts clearly and only include relevant information. Try to avoid using clichés, slang words, abbreviations (unless they are defined) and unnecessary symbols – for example, use "and" rather than "&" (ampersand). Great care should be taken to spell the names of people and companies correctly and to avoid spelling and grammar mistakes.

2 Memorandums

Memorandums (or memos) are mainly used for communications within a business between different functional areas or departments. They are relatively short communications usually dealing with individual issues or queries. If communicating more than one issue, it is usual to bullet or number each point.

Memos have the advantage of being relatively quick and easy to write and clear to understand. A memo usually has a set structure, saying exactly who it's from, who it's to, when it was sent, what it is about and whether a reply is expected or not. Memos are often copied to more than one recipient at a time (useful when lots of people need to know the same thing such as a meeting time or agenda).

Figure 5.3: Memorandum template

Memo templates can often be found in template wizards on word processing applications. Figure 5.3 shows a memorandum template adapted from Microsoft Office.

3 Agendas

Agendas set out the topics to be covered at a meeting. They are usually sent out in advance of a meeting to all people who are due to attend. An agenda usually clearly states the time, date and venue of the meeting, and has a circulation list so that recipients know who is due to attend. The substance of a meeting might be organised as follows:

- apologies for absence
- minutes of the last meeting
- matters arising from the last meeting
- new reports or areas to be discussed
- any other business.

By preparing an agenda in advance, a business can ensure that people know who is to attend the meeting, where and when it is, and what they need to bring or be prepared to discuss so that the time is used efficiently.

4 Minutes

Minutes are the record of what actually took place at a meeting. They would usually include who was present, what was discussed and a copy of any reports received. Importantly, they would also record what decisions were made, what tasks were allocated to individuals or areas, deadline dates for any follow-up actions, areas for future action or discussion, and the time and date of the next meeting.

Minutes ensure that an accurate record has been kept of a business meeting and that individuals and areas know what they have to do in response to the decisions that were made. Minutes are often distributed with the agenda for the next meeting and are checked as part of that meeting.

5 Reports

Reports usually contain information, research and analysis on a specific aspect of a business. For example, reports may be written to present project progress, market research findings or budget figures.

Reports help provide detailed background and figures to assist decision-making. They usually include a brief summary of any findings, and make recommendations about what action the business should take in response to the findings. A report should follow this format:

- terms of reference – a statement about what the writer of the report was asked to do

- procedure – how the information contained in the report was obtained

- findings – statements regarding what facts and information were discovered

- conclusion – an overall summary drawing together the findings

- recommendations – an outline of possible courses of action and activities that should be undertaken as a result of the report's findings.

Reports should be signed and dated.

6 Notices

Notices are displays – boards or pieces of paper – giving general information or instructions such as fire procedures and the location of fire exits. Notices include signs, announcements, posters and adverts.

Notices are an open form of communication. When producing a notice, make sure that:

- it is clear and easy to read

- it contains sufficient information to convey its meaning but not too much so as to confuse

- it is placed in locations where it will be seen (and be likely to be read) by the intended audience.

7 Itineraries

Itineraries are detailed plans of events or journeys. They are similar to timetables in that they show when activities are due to take place, the duration of the activity and often the location. Typically an itinerary would be issued to someone who is about to undertake a journey: it would show times of trains and/or flights, and departure and arrival locations. An itinerary might also be issued in advanced to participants at a conference, showing travel arrangements but also times and locations of conference events.

8 Schedules

Schedules are lists of planned activities or tasks that need to be done. They show the dates when activities are planned to happen and the date by which tasks should be completed. Schedules can be as simple as a timetable, planning list (such as a work plan) or perhaps a wall planner. However, a range of more specialist tools exists for planning business activities, such as Gantt charts and critical path analysis, and these are covered in some depth in Topic 9.

Knowledge summary

- **Much information held by a company is confidential, and access should be restricted to those personnel who need to know and use the information.**

- **Open communications are a good way of distributing non-confidential messages to large numbers of people.**

- **Written communications tend to be formal in nature with agreed uses and structures.**

- **The choice of communication method affects the way recipients receive and respond to the communication.**

quick questions

1 Why might sending a written communication have a better communications impact than a verbal request?

2 What is the purpose of an agenda for a meeting?

3 When would it be preferable to use open channels of communication?

By the very nature of the industrial espionage it is impossible to quantify, but experts are in agreement that the issue is real and growing. And the galloping pace of technology is making espionage, such as eavesdropping or theft, ever more of a potential problem for companies today.

Mobile phones and the internet simply provide the bad guys with a number of additional ways to get at a company's information, helped on by an ever more sophisticated and easily obtainable array of gadgets and tools with which to do their dirty work.

The Institute of Directors (IoD) confirms that, from talking to its members, the potential for becoming a victim of industrial espionage now seems to be bigger than ever. Some 60 per cent of members have suffered from theft – be it electronic or of the more traditional form – while 14 per cent have reported internet crime in one form or another, explains IoD head of business policy Richard Wilson.

"It is certain that the increased use of mobile phones and the internet means the potential to suffer from industrial espionage is bigger than ever ... every cloud has a silver lining though, so to speak, and it does provide a lot of opportunities for security companies to offer protection," Mr Wilson said.

Bugging devices are found at 4–5 per cent of UK companies that ask for checks, according to C2i International, one firm which helps businesses prevent and counter industrial espionage. "In some cases the bugs could have been in place for months or years. People are just utterly horrified when they find out, just devastated," Justin King, managing director of C2i said.

Mr King says the extent of the problem is evident when you realise that, according to industry estimates, more than £10 million of bugging devices have now been sold in the UK. Considering some bugs cost as little as £40 each, that could be an awful lot of bugs.

And Mr King is in no doubt about the motivating factor behind the bugging trend: money. "Information is vital when the markets are tight and people want to get an advantage. This is especially vital in cases of mergers or hostile takeovers."

Some well-known companies have been caught spying on competitors. In 2001 Procter and Gamble admitted spying on rival Unilever for information on its shampoos. Boeing was punished by the US Air Force in 2003 for resorting to espionage in order to better its defence rival Lockheed Martin.

Source: news.bbc.co.uk, 4 July 2004

A Explain three types of information a business would like to keep confidential.

B Analyse the reasons why a multinational company like Proctor and Gamble might undertake industrial espionage.

C Discuss the problems a company could encounter from leaks or theft of confidential information.

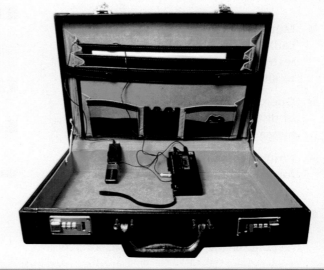

Topic 3 · More communication methods

Setting the scene: enhancing communication skills

There are many non-verbal and diagrammatic ways of enhancing the way a communication is presented to help it convey its meaning.

There are many software applications to help businesses communicate more effectively and efficiently. Packages such as SmartDraw or Microsoft Visio help produce clear and attractive technical drawings or flowcharts.

Training is another option. A quick internet search will show many companies that offer courses in improving both verbal and non-verbal communications to boost a person's selling or presentation techniques.

You don't even have to attend a course: some companies offer training through teach-yourself learning packages. Win Squared, for example, advertises itself as persuasion, sales and negotiation software – a tool to improve an individual's communications abilities.

The important idea behind all these training packages and audiovisual techniques is that the success of a communication depends on the receiver hearing (or reading) the message accurately and responding accordingly. This can only happen if the receiver has been able to understand it and interpret its meaning and tone.

Verbal communication

Most communication in any business setting is verbal. This communication ranges from face-to-face discussions, meetings and interviews to telephone calls and video conferences.

Verbal communications have some advantages over written communications. They are quick and cost effective, and a considerable amount of information can be exchanged rapidly. Verbal communication also has the advantage of being almost instantaneous – there is very little delay between exchanges of information. The recipient can respond immediately and seek clarification if anything is not understood.

1 One-to-one discussions

A typical purpose of one-to-one conversations in organisations – particularly those between managers and subordinates – is to check on progress or update individuals on activities that are taking place. Of course, formal checks can be made by asking for progress reports; however, these take time to prepare, and a manager can get an immediate update through a quick conversation.

One-to-one conversations are a good way of providing basic information, although they are not so good for communicating complicated issues such as instructions that need to be followed accurately. In

KEY TERMS

Verbal communication is the exchange of information between participants using language skills.

Non-verbal communication is the use of facial expressions, eye contact, tone of voice and body posture to convey information or to reinforce verbal communication.

Qualitative information is data on individuals' opinions, tastes and preferences.

Body language is a person's gestures, poses, movements, and expressions. These help a person to communicate.

particular, one-to-one communications have the advantage of being personal and often face to face, allowing participants to engage and interact fully.

One-to-one discussions are often informal communications, involving activities such as making ad hoc progress checks, keeping people up to date and giving simple instructions. However, they can also be formal communications – examples here include individual staff appraisals and disciplinary meetings.

s t o p a n d **t h i n k**

Why might it be preferable for a business like McDonald's to use verbal communication for customer orders, whereas for a restaurant it might be better to write orders down?

2 Meetings

Meetings are formal communications. They are convened for specific purposes with a set format (or agenda) to follow. The purpose of many meetings is to provide information and allow discussion prior to taking business decisions, and they may often involve qualitative information that requires analysis and explanation. Through exploration and discussion, with all participants able to add their own views and interpretations, meetings help managers in assembling coherent information for decision-making.

Meetings also provide a key function in the communication exchange during negotiations. They help two, or more, parties to discuss differences and reach a consensus or agreement. A meeting is often a quicker way of reaching agreement than lengthy exchanges of documentation, although reports and background information may be presented as part of the negotiation process.

3 Interviews

Interviews are a form of formal verbal communication that are used extensively in recruitment and selection. While written applications can provide information about a candidate's qualifications and experience, verbal interviews generate more information about character and personality. Interviews can reveal:

- how a person reacts under pressure

- how a person would react to certain situations or handle key aspects of the job role

- a candidate's people skills, such as their verbal communication skills.

Non-verbal communication

Have you ever heard the saying "actions speak louder than words"? In person-to-person communications, messages are sent on two levels simultaneously – through verbal language and through non-verbal signals including facial expressions, eye contact, tone of voice, body posture and movement. Non-verbal communication also includes the way we wear our clothes, where we position ourselves in a group, and, sometimes, just keeping silent.

Non-verbal communications can help in reinforcing any verbal message and assist in putting across its meaning and importance. They can also help put customers and employees at ease. Somerfield trains its employees to use the acronym GUEST:

G - greet the customer

U - understand the customer's needs

E - eye contact

S - smile

T - thank the customer.

The positive use of non-verbal communications can enhance business performance. They can be used with both employees and customers to show interest, convey openness and trust, motivate, and display care and understanding.

1 Expression

It's not just the words that you say that are important, it's the way that you say them. Expression can mean two different things. It can mean tone. The way that words are spoken can suggest different meanings – for example, try saying "my God, that's brilliant" in a serious way and then sarcastically. The tone of voice can express interest, excitement or boredom. Saying the right words without the correct expression will send conflicting communications to the recipient.

Expression also means the shape and form our faces take while speaking or listening. This can take many forms, and a smile, frown, raised eyebrow, yawn and sneer all convey information. Facial expressions continually change during interaction and are monitored constantly by the recipient.

A major feature of facial communication is eye contact. It can be used to convey emotion, signal when to talk or stop talking, and indicate attraction or aversion. The frequency of eye contact may also suggest either interest or boredom.

2 Body language

We all use (either unconsciously or consciously) hand gestures, poses, movements and expressions while communicating. These aspects of communication can all be used to help the sender put across their message to the receiver. They can also be used by the receiver to encourage or discourage the sender, by displaying whether the receiver understands what the sender is trying to convey. It is important, therefore, to understand how body language impacts on communication. In particular, you need to consider posture, physical contact and gestures.

Posture

They way you are stood or seated conveys a degree of formality or of relaxation in the communication exchange. Are participants slouched or erect (alert)? Are their legs crossed or arms folded (defensive positions)? Are they leaning towards each other (showing interest) or away?

Physical contact

Shaking hands, touching, holding, embracing, pushing or patting on the back all convey messages. They reflect an element of intimacy and a feeling (or lack) of attraction.

Gestures

One of the most frequently used non-verbal communications is hand movement. Most people use hand movements regularly when talking. Common hand gestures include:

- pointing (to direct attention or emphasis)
- clenching fingers (anger)
- thumbs up signals (OK)
- fiddling with objects (boredom)
- scratching ears, nose or face (nervousness)
- clasping hands (fear).

Gestures that also make strong non-verbal signals include head movement (shaking or nodding for positive and negative responses) and general fidgeting (perhaps pacing up and down to indicate impatience).

3 Graphs, charts and pictures

A picture can convey in an instant what could take a long time to describe verbally. Graphs, charts and pictures can easily display large volumes of information in simple-to-understand formats.

Businesses use graphs, charts and pictures extensively because they are an efficient and cost-effective form of communication of information. For example, supermarket managers usually present information on work rotas in a chart that can be circulated to staff and placed on notice boards, rather than spend time individually informing each employee of their duties.

Similarly, communications with customers also use pictorial information. A company like Birds Eye puts big pictures on the front of its ready-meals packaging (sometimes labelled "serving suggestion") which allows customers to immediately identify the product. This is much more informative and accessible than reading a product description and a list of ingredients.

The key point in using graphs, charts and pictures is to consider which format would best convey information to the intended recipients. For example, monthly sales figures could be shown as row and column format numerical data in a table, but most managers would find it much easier to understand this information if it was presented as a bar chart.

Knowledge summary

- **Verbal communications are quick and can be used to exchange a large amount of information in a cost-effective way. They don't provide a permanent record of the exchange and so are not suitable for all communications.**

- **Any verbal communication is influenced by accompanying non-verbal signals. Non-verbal communications affect emphasis and influence the attitude of the receiver.**

- **Positive non-verbal communications can demonstrate characteristics such as interest, trust, care and understanding.**

quick **questions**

1 When might it be preferable to use written rather than verbal communication?

2 Give two examples of body language that could have a positive influence on communication exchanges.

3 What communication method would you use to inform staff about holiday dates?

Grantby Manor is a luxury spa and health resort hotel set in 20 acres of parkland. There is a driving range and facilities for horse riding and fishing. The hotel has 62 bedrooms ranging in size and cost from £185 per night for a single room to £340 for the four-poster bridal suite, although the hotel also offers special deals on spa weekend breaks.

The hotel has a spa, sauna, gym and swimming pool and offers beauty treatments, massage and aromatherapy sessions as well as personal trainer and dietician consultancy services. The hotel's management is committed to the ethos that guests at the hotel should find their stay either relaxing or invigorating, but all should leave feeling satisfied, happy and refreshed from their stay. "Happy customers are repeat customers," says Hannah Sole, the customer services manager, "and repeat customers are what a business wants."

Each customer is asked to complete a customer comment form as their bill is being prepared when they check out. Every six months, the information collected on the cards is collated and compared to the data on the previous six months to determine areas of improvement. Figure 5.4 has the latest data from the customer comment forms.

Figure 5.4: Responses to Grantby Manor's customer comment form

Services		Extremely satisfied	Satisfied	No opinion	Unsatisfied	Extremely unsatisfied	Total
Hotel facilities	This six months	3,321	2,110	1,134	746	354	7,665
	Previous six months	4,223	1,987	2,356	678	284	9,528
Cleanliness	This six months	2,978	1,687	1,453	985	468	7,665
	Previous six months	3,379	2,083	1,742	1,641	683	9,528
Condition of room	This six months	4,324	2,311	807	201	22	7,665
	Previous six months	4,734	3.162	1,142	432	58	9,528
Facilities in room	This six months	3,987	2,456	832	300	90	7,665
	Previous six months	4,247	3,865	913	411	94	9,528
Restaurant food	This six months	2,184	2,476	1,729	348	928	7,665
	Previous six months	1,549	3,167	2,760	712	1,340	9,528
Restaurant service	This six months	2,203	1,698	1,664	1,366	734	7,665
	Previous six months	3,430	2,018	2,113	1,245	722	9,528
Friendliness of staff	This six months	2,882	1,783	457	1458	1,085	7,665
	Previous six months	4,307	2,291	784	1,384	762	9,528
Helpfulness of staff	This six months	1,698	2,967	2,114	84	802	7,665
	Previous six months	1,815	3,420	3,116	179	998	9,528
Overall impression	This six months	2,948	2,185	1,275	659	598	7,665
	Previous six months	4,388	2,581	1,422	634	503	9,528

A Analyse the information in Figure 5.4 identifying two areas of strength and two areas of weakness.

B Convert the data in Figure 5.4 into a diagrammatic format so that it is easy to see areas of improving or worsening performance.

C Using your findings, explain two ways the hotel could improve results in the required areas.

Topic 4 Exchanging information

Setting the scene: sending the wrong message?

Communication is an essential element of any business activity – get the message wrong and the effects could be disastrous. This extract from an article by communications expert Jonathan Gabay provides some examples of ill-considered messages.

Consider the problems with the messages in each example of communication given the article. What might have been the financial consequences for each business?

Pardon my language

Clairol introduced a hair curling iron - the Mist Stick - into Germany, only to find out that "mist" means manure in German.

When Gerber started selling baby food in Africa it used the same packaging as in the USA. This had a picture of a beautiful baby on the label. Later, Gerber realised that African companies routinely put pictures on the label of what's inside the jar, since many people can't read.

Arcadia and Topman bosses were left red-faced after Topman brand director, David Shepherd, was interviewed by a trade magazine. David Shepherd said Topman customers only wore a suit for their first interview or their first court appearance.

Japan's second-largest tourist agency was mystified when it entered English-speaking markets and began receiving some unusual telephone calls. Upon finding out why, the owners of Kinki Nippon Tourist Co. changed the company's name.

Source: adapted from www.gabaynet.com

211

Choosing the best medium

The most important aspect of communication is that the recipient is able to understand the message, interpret its underlying tone and act on the communication accordingly. However, it is also important that the communication is made in the most efficient and cost-effective way, taking into consideration any need for speed, confidentiality and security. For example, a business couldn't assemble the entire workforce for a meeting every day to pass on simple instructions – think of the productive time that would be lost.

In this topic, we consider the medium used to send the communication and look at the advantages and disadvantages of various mediums. There are several factors to be considered when determining the most appropriate medium of exchanging communications:

- cost of the communication method
- ease of use of the method chosen
- accessibility of any information sent by the chosen method
- accuracy of the method
- time taken for the communication exchange
- confidentiality and security of the information.

Some methods of communication may be quick and cost effective, but they may not be suitable if the recipient cannot access the information – if, for example, not all recipients have access to e-mail or are comfortable using IT systems – or if the medium is not secure and confidential information could be leaked.

KEY TERMS

E-mail is a method of sending messages and computer files using the internet.

The **internet** is a worldwide communications system of linked computer networks.

Intranets are internal electronic communication systems linking computers within a single business.

Communication medium is the platform used to deliver a communication to its intended receiver.

1 Post

Post is a highly effective way of making sure hard copy documents reach their intended recipient. Figure 5.5 shows some of the advantages and disadvantages of post as a communication medium.

Post is suitable for internal (employees) and external (customers and other stakeholders) recipients. Post is also useful for sending bulk items that would exceed most e-mail data exchange limits or take an unacceptable amount of download time. Post is practical for some international communications as not all countries have reliable electronic data exchange systems or lack sufficient broadband, ADSL or ISDN phone line capacity.

Figure 5.5: Post as a communication medium

Advantages	Disadvantages
Very secure, particularly for special delivery and registered letters that have to be signed for by their intended recipient	Relatively slow compared to other mediums, especially for international mail
The only suitable method for some communications such as highly confidential information or signed contracts	Cost of deliveries especially for special guaranteed service (in terms of speed or security) can be very expensive
Does not require expensive outlay on IT equipment across a whole company	Security of normal post items can be compromised (damaged/lost)

2 E-mail

E-mail offers cost-effective and speedy communications but, as with any form of electronic communication system, there is a danger of excluding people who do not have ready access to the ICT network or who are not trained to use the e-mail system. As well as being widely used for much internal communication, e-mails are increasingly used by businesses to communicate with customers, such as through direct mailing or as part of campaigns to boost consumer awareness and company sales.

stop and think

Imagine how much it would cost a global company such as Ford to update its electronic communication systems so that its employees in all countries had compatible equipment. List some of the benefits that would persuade Ford to invest in a global IT system.

Figure 5.6: E-mail as a communication medium

Advantages	Disadvantages
Quick to send messages over any distance	Confidentiality – e-mail systems can be hacked into and communications copied
Very cheap and cost effective – saves on stationery as well as transmission costs	Network security – e-mails are often the vehicles for the transmission of viruses
Documents containing instructions (text, diagrams or pictures) can be attached	Cost of ICT equipment and software, plus any training for senders and recipients
Allows fast and efficient communication with customers – most businesses have a "contact us" section on their websites	Cost to the business of employee time spent sending and reading non-productive e-mails such as spam and personal communications
Group sending allows the same message to be sent to more than one person, ensuring all recipients get the same information	

3 Video conferencing

Video conferencing has similar problems and issues to e-mail with regard to communication exclusion and security of transmissions. Figure 5.7 shows some of the advantages and disadvantages of video conferencing as a communication medium.

Figure 5.7: Video conferencing as a communication medium

Advantages	Disadvantages
Allows interactive real-time voice and image communication between geographically separated parties	Expensive equipment required
Verbal information exchanges are the fastest way of communicating large volumes of information quickly	Only really works if all parties have high-speed broadband connections
Sender and receiver can also interpret some non-verbal communications, improving the accuracy of the communication method	Cost is relatively high compared to e-mail
Often cheaper than travel and time costs of assembling all parties for a physical meeting	

4 Internet

Most businesses use websites to interact with customers, and regard the internet as a key part of their external communications. However, although the internet is a convenient and relatively cheap method of sending and receiving communications it also provides access for hackers and viruses and so, unless a business takes proper precautions, the security and confidentiality of information can be compromised.

Figure 5.8: The internet as a communication medium

Advantages	Disadvantages
Quick access to large amounts of information	Expensive equipment required
Can be used to communicate to mass audiences 24/7, giving cheaper advertising and marketing communications	Website design, software and maintenance can be expensive
Allows multimedia presentation of information: text, pictures, sound, video and animation	Cost of ICT equipment and software, plus any training for senders and recipients

5 Intranets

Intranets can help a business improve its productive efficiency immensely. For example, they can be used to send orders from one department to another, to maintain company-wide information on products, services and procedures that can be accessed by all staff, and to hold a set of document templates for frequently used communication methods such as memos and letters. All this helps employees construct and use appropriate communications effectively.

Figure 5.9: Intranets as a communication medium

Advantages	Disadvantages
More secure than the internet as for internal use only, so can be used for confidential applications, and access can be managed by the business	Expensive equipment required
Cheaper than internet connections as they require no ISP (internet service provider) or phone line costs	Access to too much information can cause employee information overload, leading to slower decision-making
Data can be shared, cutting photocopying costs and improving communication speed between departments	Information management costs – intranets can quickly build up useless, inaccurate and outdated information unless maintained

6 Face-to-face communication

Face-to-face meetings and conversations possess many advantages over electronic forms. There are certainly customer relations advantages, as many consumers prefer to deal with people rather than interact with electronic systems, despite the fact that electronic systems may produce a faster response.

Figure 5.10: Face to face as a communication medium

Advantages	Disadvantages
Allows quick exchange of communications and can therefore be very cost effective	Can be expensive and time consuming if, for example, a meeting involves a large number of people
Allows for clear, accurate communication as written, verbal and non-verbal methods can be used simultaneously	Informal face-to-face communications provide no permanent record of the exchange
Can be used for a wide range of communications – formal, informal, feedback, instruction, confirmation and negotiation	
Generally secure as information is communicated only to the intended recipient(s)	

7 Telephone

The telephone is a cheap and cost-effective method, allowing quick and easy verbal communication exchanges. Many phone systems also offer various address book, answer machine and diary applications, all of which enhance communication capabilities. However, phones do have some drawbacks in terms of cost, security and limited level of data storage.

Figure 5.11: The telephone as a communication medium

Advantages	Disadvantages
Does not require expensive outlay on IT equipment across a whole company	Does not allow a permanent record to be available after the end of the conversation
Systems allow transmission of text, data, photographs and graphic images	Participants cannot interpret non-verbal signals, which can mean that there is a greater chance of confusion or misunderstanding
Compatible worldwide	There is a business cost in any time staff spend making personal calls

8 Print advertising

Many businesses buy advertising in magazines and newspapers. This communication medium allows businesses to target specific geographical areas or particular market segments (based on the readership of the publication). One major difference between print advertising and marketing through the business's own website is the direction of the communication. Advertising in newspapers and magazines is a way of sending messages out to consumers – the business initiates the communication. In contrast, to get website hits a business has to wait for consumers to initiate the communication.

Figure 5.12: Print advertising as a communication medium

Advantages	Disadvantages
Communications can be placed in specific publications to target particular market segments and consumer profiles	Adverts in national newspapers and magazines can be very expensive
Long and complex communication messages can be conveyed, such as financial adverts	There is no guarantee that the message will reach its intended recipient – readers may ignore the adverts
Newspapers and magazines allow flexibility in communications – specific messages and offers can be written for different geographical locations or publications	Communications in magazines and newspapers have a very short life – they may only be effective for the day or period that the publication remains current

Communication design

First impressions count – a recipient will be influenced by the type, design, layout and first visual impression of any communication. Companies therefore spend considerable time and efforts ensuring that the presentation of their business communications is as effective as possible.

From business letters to television adverts, the manner in which a communication is presented is vital in portraying the right image and emphasising the message it wishes to convey. Important consideration needs to be given to several factors. These include the use of font size, bold, colour and italics to highlight key points or to get the reader's attention. Magazines and newspapers, for example, use large, punchy headlines and striking colourful photographs to grab readers' attention.

Font types also give the recipient an idea of what's intended. Some bridal companies and magazines use script fonts; a company producing material aimed at teenagers may use a bubble appearance or high-tech presentation. The type of font helps convey the tone of the message such as serious or light-hearted.

Colour can be employed to bring attention to certain aspects of the message. Urgent communications, such as letters asking for payment of overdue bills, often use red – as do communications implying danger. Colour can also influence perception: look at the colours used on the packaging by detergent manufacturers such as Fairy, Persil and Surf – what message are they trying to put across?

It is worth noting here that some organisations deliberately use little colour – sticking primarily to black and white – to give a serious tone to their messages. Compare the presentation of tabloid and broadsheet newspapers or look at the advertising campaigns for charities such as the National Society for the Prevention of Cruelty to Children (NSPCC) which have deliberately stark presentations. Visit www.nspcc.org.uk for examples of NSPCC campaigns.

Companies don't just rely on print to get their message across, they also use other graphical devices including photography and other imagery. Logos are used extensively in company literature. The logos of companies like Kwik-Fit and Prontaprint convey more than just the name of the company: they also give an indication of what they do.

Finally layout – the structure of the communication – gives the final impression before the recipient actually reads the body of the communication itself. Again this can influence the receiver's perception and understanding of the message. Companies need to decide whether to present the communication formally or informally, in the way that recipients might expect or perhaps in an extraordinary manner.

stop and think

The Coca-Cola brand is known worldwide, from its name, colours and distinctive style. How does the way Coca-Cola presents itself suggest what its main target audience is?

Knowledge summary

■ The choice of communication medium affects the way the receiver interprets the message, the cost of the communication process and the speed at which it takes place.

■ Electronic communication methods involve initially high setup costs though the cost per communication thereafter is often relatively cheap.

■ Electronic communication methods can be fast and effective methods. However, they have connected risks of security and confidentiality.

■ An effective printed communication requires clear content and good presentation in terms of format, style and use of colour.

quick **questions**

1 Give two advantages of using standard postal systems.

2 Explain three dangers associated with the use of electronic communications.

3 What makes newspapers and magazines a more flexible communication medium than websites?

data **interpretation**
Tweenagers

This is an extract of an article written by Martin Lindstrom. It is based on a study investigating children's attitudes towards famous brand names such as Nike and Sony.

A Using the article, identify three reasons why tweenagers have become an important target audience for communication activities.

B Explain why the internet might be a more appropriate medium than television for communication activities aimed at tweenagers.

C Identify three examples of promotional activities aimed at tweenagers. Using these examples, prepare a five-minute presentation with the title: "What communication designs are used to influence a tweenager's buying behaviour?"

How tweenagers are taking over

Welcome to the world of tweens – children aged between 8 and 14. Almost every aspect of today's tweenager is different from what we have seen in past generations. They've grown up faster, are more connected, more direct and more informed. They have more personal power, influence and attention than any other generation before them.

No other generation has ever had as much disposable income as this one, and close to 80 per cent of all brands purchased by parents are controlled by their children.

Recent research shows that grammatically correct sentences in ads, on television or the internet are considered outdated. Tweens have an overwhelming preference to use the same language that they employ when texting with their friends.

New ways of communicating will most likely replace the traditional channels that we know today. It's already happening. About a third of all tweens prefer surfing the internet to watching television. And almost half would rather play a computer game than turn on a TV show.

Source: adapted from www.news.bbc.co.uk, 19 March 2003

In any organisation, information can flow downwards, upwards or horizontally across the different hierarchical or management levels.

Directors and management must be able to inform subordinates (junior managers and supervisors) of company aims, objectives and policies. Similarly, departmental heads, project managers and team leaders must send information and instructions to those within their span of control. These downward communications tend to be for giving instructions, keeping employees informed and up to date, and making checks.

Information also needs to flow in the opposite direction, as subordinates discuss matters with superiors. These communications tend to take the form of providing feedback on progress, confirmation of activities and tasks, and asking for clarification. It may also take the role of providing information to aid superiors in decision-making.

In reality, upward and downward communication often takes place at the same time, through face-to-face meetings and a variety of formal and informal exchanges.

Horizontal communication takes place across a business. Information and instructions often need to be passed from one area to another or from one department to another by employees on the same level of the hierarchy. This enables information to flow around as well as through a company.

Types of information

In order to establish appropriate and efficient systems, any organisation first needs to consider the type of information that has to be communicated and processed as this often determines how information is handled. It is important to understand the distinction between qualitative and quantitative information.

Qualitative information

Qualitative information cannot be expressed in numerical terms. Businesses can collect a considerable amount of qualitative information on issues such as customer opinions and preferences – for example, opinions on a product's taste or appearance – and their employees' attitudes and motivation.

This type of information helps a business understand its staff and customers and develop its products. It results from investigations into people's likes and dislikes and the motivation behind buying behaviour. It can also be used to explore employee motivations. Qualitative information may be generated through:

- consumer panels or focus groups
- observation of behavioural patterns
- surveys and questionnaires.

Due to its non-numerical nature, there are limits to the degree by which qualitative information can be manipulated and processed.

stop and think

The Kit Kat is evolving. In 2004 Nestlé launched some Kit Kat limited editions including Kit Kat White Lemon and Yogurt, Kit Kat White (covered in white chocolate), Kit Kat Dark (dark chocolate) and a Christmas Pudding flavour for Christmas. Other additions to the range include Kit Kat Chunky with a layer of caramel.

Consider what types of qualitative and quantitative information Nestlé would have gathered through research before launching any of these new variations.

Downward communication flows from higher to lower hierarchical levels. They are communications from superiors to subordinates.

Upward communications flow from lower to higher organisational levels. They are communications from subordinates to superiors.

Horizontal communications flow between employees on the same hierarchical level.

Qualitative information is data on individuals' opinions, tastes and preferences.

Quantitative information is measurable. It produces data that can be analysed in numerical form.

Quantitative information

In contrast, quantitative information can be expressed numerically – it has definite values that can be measured, such as the size of the population or the volume of sales in the market. Quantitative information is much easier to manipulate and process, especially by IT systems

Quantitative information can be processed and analysed to find historic trends, size of markets, seasonal variations or operational factors such as productivity rates or level of staff absences. Quantitative information can also be extrapolated to provide predictions of likely future outcomes.

Information processing

Information processing systems may be either paper based (manual) or IT based (electronic). They comprise both hardware and software. Information processing involves a number of specific functions.

1 Storing information

Once information has been generated or received, it first must be stored. To do this efficiently, it should be:

- stored in a logical manner – alphabetically, chronologically, numerically or by geographic area

- easily retrievable and accessible – able to be transmitted to the right places at the right times

- easy to edit – it should be possible to update and amend information and to remove out-of-date or incorrect information.

Figure 5.13 (see page 218) summarises some of the advantages and disadvantages of different types of data storage systems.

2 Processing information

Once gathered and stored, data can be processed (manipulated or developed) into useful formats. This might involve:

- text manipulation – edit, copy, formatting, spelling and grammar check

- mathematical manipulation – statistical analysis, trends, percentages, averages, extrapolation, totals

- classification – categorising data into type, time period or area, tabulating data, summarising

- graphical manipulation – line graphs, pie charts, bar charts, scatter charts

- diagrammatic manipulation – flow charts, critical path analysis, Gantt charts

- combination and synthesis – merging information, text and images, letters and a database of addresses (mail merge), graphics and sales by product category.

It is in the area of information processing that IT systems and software applications are far more efficient than manual systems. Not only is the processing quicker and correspondingly more cost effective, it is also more accurate – it reduces or removes the possibility of human error.

Of course the original data must be accurate. If it is inaccurate, any processing routine will fail to produce useful results. The acronym GIGO summarises this situation completely: garbage in, garbage out.

3 Retrieving data

Manual systems of information storage have a major disadvantage if there is only a single copy of information files and records. This means that the data can only be accessed and used by one person or department at a time. Retrieval of data is also slow as the file must be located, sent for or fetched. Of course, the information could be copied, but duplicating large paper-based files for multi-user access is very time consuming and expensive, and then the copied information needs to be stored – increasing the paper mountain and the demand for storage space required.

IT-based systems allow multiple users simultaneous access to the same information from differing or

Figure 5.13: Information storage systems

Manual systems		Electronic systems	
Ring binders, card indexes, document files, box files or filing cabinets		Removable media such as floppy discs, CD or DVD, Zip or Jaz drives, or magnetic tape	
		Permanent media such as random access memory (RAM), read-only memory (ROM)	
Advantages	**Disadvantages**	**Advantages**	**Disadvantages**
Not at risk from hacking or electronic data corruption	Requires large amounts of space	Speed of access	Volatile memory (RAM) loses its contents if power supply is lost
Access can be easily restricted	Easy to manually misfile	Automatic validation checks	Expensive to set up
Cheaper to set up	Data access can be slow	Less storage space required	Discs can become corrupted

remote locations. Access, compared to manual systems, is almost instantaneous (allowing for initialising or download time), but problems can arise if a file is being updated while the information is in use by another user – this user will be working with outdated information. Similarly, multi-user access can cause problems if all users are able to edit information – if this process is not controlled or managed, then errors can be introduced and go unchecked.

4 Information dissemination

All the communication methods and mediums that have been featured in this unit can be used to disseminate and distribute information throughout an organisation.

Manual systems have some advantages, as in many cases they consist of informal or verbal communications. IT-based communications, such as e-mail, can seem impersonal or distant. However, IT systems do have many advantages in information dissemination. Two features are particularly useful.

- **Automatic distribution routines** – these can be set to regularly send updates of information on preset schedules. For example, they can be used to automatically distribute latest sales figures to nominated receivers or schedule reminders of events and meetings to key personnel.

- **Automatic flagging routines** – these generate a flag (or warning) when a data field reaches a preset age or level (such as stock levels) so that users can take action. For example, the routines can be used to alert users to order more stock. Note that some sophisticated stock control systems automate this process, sending orders to suppliers when stocks hit specified minimum levels without the need for human intervention.

5 Validation and verification

There is little point gathering and storing information if the data is not accurate and reliable. Inaccurate information can result in major communication and decision-making errors. Therefore, an integral part of any information processing system (manual or IT) is a checking process to ensure that the information and data is trustworthy.

Validation and verification methods include:

- checking the original source of the information

- determining whether information stated is fact or opinion

- confirming who entered the data and when.

Judgements on the trustworthiness of an information source require human input. (The internet, for example, is a vast source of information but not all data found on the net is trustworthy, reliable or even true.) However, there are certain routines that can be incorporated by IT systems to reduce data errors on entry (data capture):

- **character checks** – only certain types of characters are allowed to be entered in specified files or fields, such as only allowing numbers in numerical fields

- **range checks** – this makes sure data lies within a specified margin, for example you might want all respondents to a market research exercise to be in a particular age group

- **presence checks** – this makes sure that a field or area has been completed, for example you'll quite often see website registration pages which insist that certain fields must be filled in before the registration is accepted.

- **check digits** – to ensure long numbers, such as bar codes, are entered correctly, the final number is a check digit – the check digit might be the final single number that results from the sum of all the preceding numbers, and if any number in the sequence is entered incorrectly, the resulting total will not equal the check digit and the entry will not be accepted.

As well as using these checks, a validation system might use a further range of error management techniques. This means identifying the cause of errors and taking steps to prevent them happening again. If, for example, it is found that manual input of data is generating many mistakes, an organisation might try to eliminate these errors by introducing automatic data capture technology like OMRs (optical mark readers).

Knowledge summary

- ■ Businesses rely on information, data and messages being able to flow upwards, downwards and across an organisational structure.

- ■ Qualitative information and quantitative data require different information management, storage and processing techniques.

- ■ Manual information storage systems have some advantages, but IT systems usually have much faster processing and retrieval times.

- ■ IT-based systems can also be designed with automatic validation and verification routines to help ensure data is up to date, relevant and accurate.

stop and think

Which is more likely to be an accurate source of information for UK businesses: the *Sun* tabloid newspaper, the *Financial Times* broadsheet or an internet search?

quick questions

1 Explain the difference between qualitative and quantitative information.

2 Discuss two benefits you might gain from using manual storage systems.

3 Describe three ways IT-based information systems can be used to process quantitative information.

data interpretation
Error sees overpayment of workers

Five hundred workers at Jersey's general hospital have been overpaid their wages by thousands of pounds. Because of errors with a new computer electronic payroll system, they have each been paid 100 times more than they should have been. It meant that, instead of a total amount of £168,000 going into accounts, £16.8 million was paid out instead.

The department responsible for the error has apologised and says it is speaking to every worker to ask them to repay the money. Policy and resources chief executive Bill Ogley has launched an inquiry into the incident. "I've asked external auditors to undertake a review of how it happened so I can find out why that error occurred."

Source: adapted from news.bbc.co.uk, 14 April 2005

A Explain two benefits of using an electronic payroll system.

B Discuss two methods that Jersey's general hospital could employ to prevent this mistake occurring again.

C Analyse the advantages and disadvantages of using manual information processing systems in this case.

Setting the scene: choosing software

Business Link, the government business support organisation, gives advice on how businesses can choose the right software on its website. Here is an extract.

Good software helps you to work more efficiently and to cope with more customers, but with fewer staff. It can help you keep control of your business and give you confidence that you'll be able to satisfy any regulators. In some cases, software can make a new way of working possible and advance your business ahead of its competitors.

In order to get the best out of software, you need to choose carefully. Investing in computer software for your business is an important process which will require financial commitment and time, and may involve your staff. It is important to approach the issue with care.

It is a good idea to carry out a "needs analysis" for your business before you choose to commit to software. This will involve analysing how your business processes work and deciding exactly what the software will be used for. These processes can help you avoid buying a software package that is unsuitable for your business.

Standardised packages, for example, are designed to accommodate any type of business accounting. Customising a package for your own business needs could mean employing software consultants, which could prove costly. Also, once the software has been upgraded, you will need to ask the consultants to revisit and rebuild your customisations.

Unnecessary financial outlay can be avoided through planning and research. If your business is of a specialist nature, you may find that a tailored software package is more appropriate. This may also ease the upgrading process and help you avoid having to use consultants. Even if you choose not to opt for a specialist package, researching software packages available on the market will pay dividends. For example, buying older software is a viable option as long as it meets the needs of your business.

Source: www.businesslink.gov.uk

IT in business

Most businesses, whether large or small, need to consider computerising aspects of their operations. When managed properly, computerisation provides:

- increased efficiency in work tasks and processes

- better communications with staff and customers

- improved financial management

- easier completion of tax returns and payroll.

There are some pitfalls to computerising systems. It can be easy to overspend by buying software the company doesn't need. There are unforeseen costs, such as IT advice, printing costs and training. There are legal requirements (covered in Topics 7 and 8), and businesses need to ensure that they comply with the Data Protection Act and other legislation.

To avoid these problems, the advice of Business Link (given above) is useful. It is important that companies analyse their IT needs accurately and then only purchase and use software applications that would be of real business benefit.

Spreadsheets

A spreadsheet is a software application designed to allow the user to enter and manipulate figures and to automate routine mathematical tasks. The user can enter numbers, formulae or text into individual cells laid out in a grid format on a sheet. Basically a computer-based calculator, spreadsheets can format and manipulate (process) the entered numbers, formulae or text to provide useful information. Most spreadsheet packages also allow:

- formatting of cell information, such as bold, italic or shading for emphasis

- automatic formatting of tables

- organising data in alphabetical or numerical order

- the ability to link into compatible packages such as word processors or databases.

Spreadsheets can be used for a wide variety of tasks including:

- holding records such as sales figures or details of expenses

- modelling "what if" situations such as the impact of changes in costs on profits

- monitoring job costs by allocating costs to a specific job, task or project

- financial planning and budgetary control, such as calculating variances

- producing statistics such as sales by area, product or person

- calculating subtotals, totals, percentages and averages in data

- producing forecasts

- converting currency transactions, particularly useful for import-export businesses

- producing timetables

- making tax, loan and investment calculations

- displaying numerical information in tables, graphs, charts and diagrams.

The flexibility of a spreadsheet is that if data is changed and updated, any calculations within the spreadsheet are automatically updated so that the impact of any changes (new calculation results) can be quickly shown. This cuts out the time and effort that would be involved in manually performing countless calculations or redrawing charts each time any factor changes. Spreadsheets are therefore a very powerful and useful tool for most organisations.

Word processing software

A very common and quite straightforward computer application, word processing provides for the basic IT communication and administrative needs of most business organisations. Word processing software is primarily used for the entry and manipulation of text and the production of business documents such as letters, memos, reports, agendas, minutes, forms, newsletters, invitations and references.

Most word processing applications allow the import (inserting) of graphs, charts, tables, symbols and pictures into text documents. This enables text to be formatted around images, allowing for the generation of more visual documents such as leaflets, brochures, notices and posters. Sophisticated systems have some desktop publishing facilities and simple drawing applications.

A key benefit of word processing software is the facility to link to databases via mail merge packages. This permits standard letters or information (direct mailing of a special offer, for example) to be easily produced and sent out to large groups of customers or employees.

Other features of many word processing applications include a facility to undertake simple mathematical functions, and the ability to insert a numerical table and use simple formula like "sum above".

Databases

A database is designed to act as a store for information, which can then be processed and interrogated to produce responses to user queries. Databases really equate to a form of electronic filing system. (In fact, many spreadsheet applications are highly modified and specialist databases.) Most business organisations would use a database to:

- collect and store information about customers

- collect and store information about suppliers

- collect and store information about products

- function as a stock control system

The key to databases is that information can be entered in the form of individual files or fields; these can then be linked together for analysis, for presentations or to answer specific queries. Some databases allow users to produce graphs and charts. Most can link with word processing applications (such as mail merge) to send letters to specific individuals.

Typically databases are used for these manipulations:

- **sorting** – unlike a spreadsheet, a database allows linking of different files, so a business may use a database to sort all products of a certain type, colour or price alphabetically, or produce lists of clients alphabetically

- **merging or combining information from several files into one file** – for example, a business may have data on customer names, addresses and contact details in one file and their customer account information in another, and by merging these together it can create a single customer file

- **field interrogation** – this involves extracting specific information from the database such as compiling a list of the names and addresses of all suppliers who stock a certain product, excluding all those who charge above a certain price limit and sorting in order of price

- **geographical analysis allowing users to determine information by location** – for example Tesco can use the database it builds up from information on the use of its club card to get the geographical locations of its customers, which can then be displayed on a map.

The capacity to undertake analysis, such as geographical sorting of data, shows the benefit of databases as a business tool. Geographical analysis, for example, can be used by many businesses to provide marketing information on customer density. Utility companies use it to show existing distribution networks; local authorities use geographical analysis for planning the provision of local services such as school catchment areas; bus companies use it to determine the most and least popular routes.

stop and think

What marketing advantage can Tesco's gain by knowing where the majority of its existing customers live (customer density)?

Graphics software

Documents often require – or can be aided by – the inclusion of graphics, such as pictures and images. Specialist graphics packages allow the creation, editing and manipulation of images to take place. Graphics software is particularly useful in industries that require a lot of technical drawing and design work such as engineering, architecture and publishing.

Graphics packages can be very cheap such as simple drawing and painting programs, mid range such as Smartdraw (a specialist diagram-drawing program), to very expensive such as tailor-made CAD/CAM (computer aided design/computer aided manufacture) systems. CAD/CAM systems enable a product to be designed onscreen using a software application, which then issues the specifications directly to machines that manufacture the product.

To have a useful graphics capability requires not just the appropriate software but also the right hardware in terms of the computer's processing speed and memory allocation.

Presentation software

A presentation package allows a business to prepare and display information using a computer-generated slide show. Each slide can contain text, drawings, graphics, photographs, video clips and sound.

Transitions between slides can be animated to give the presentation more impact. Presentations are very common in business and could be directed at customers, employees or other businesses. Common uses of presentations include:

- providing information in meetings
- putting forward business plans
- conveying product information to customers
- training sessions.

The use of presentation software allows communications to be more effective by combining the verbal messages of the presenter with the text, imagery and sound of the presentation. Variety also helps maintain the audience's interest.

Because of its many uses in business communications, presentation software has been one of the fastest growing areas of business software development in recent years. One development has been the introduction of plug-in programs to enhance presentation capability. One example is Proof Software's Graphicae application. Graphicae's main selling point is its ability to add extra diagram, table and map features to Microsoft PowerPoint, making it easier for business users to create flowcharts, tables, marketing analysis and other data graphics.

Knowledge summary

- **Software applications can enhance the operational and communications abilities of a company in many ways. However, businesses need to ensure they don't overload employees with information and only use applications that are of real benefit.**

- **Spreadsheet packages are specifically designed for storage, processing and communication of numerical data.**

- **A database mainly acts as a main filing system that can be questioned to provide information in useful combinations.**

- **Presentation software can aid business communications by enabling several different communication methods to be used in communicating one message.**

1 Explain three benefits that software packages can bring a business organisation.

2 List five business applications of a spreadsheet package.

3 Explain how presentation software aids the communication process.

data**interpretation**
Impaxt Gym

Impaxt Gym opened on Ecclesall Road near Sheffield city centre in January 2005. It was set up by Leon Heathers with backing from several ex-rugby league players. Leon had been a player and subsequently coach for Sheffield Steels RFC until 2004 when the club went into liquidation.

Leon's idea was to introduce a specialist gym environment for people who wanted to train for high-impact sports. Leon believed that this would provide him with a niche in the ever more competitive health club and fitness market. However, clients in this area are limited, so Leon has also deliberately targeted nearby office workers who may become concerned about insufficient exercise and weight gain through inactivity.

Leon offers an initial fitness assessment and a tailor-made training programme. However, as clients progress through their training they often want to develop their programme for themselves. Leon wants to produce an information leaflet, which he can also use for advertising, informing clients how many calories each type of exercise burns off. Figure 5.14 shows the basic information that the leaflet needs to contain.

A Enter the information in Figure 5.14 into a spreadsheet.

B Create a chart or graph displaying the calorific burn-up of various activities (try and organise this to show least to highest in order).

C Leon has been asked to give a five-minute presentation to the employees in a nearby large office block, detailing a 25 minute workout they could do at lunchtime without tiring them out. He believes this is a very good opportunity to attract new clients and so has asked you to help design the presentation. Design a professional presentation that Leon can use to attract more clients.

Figure 5.14: Gym activities, calories burnt per five-minute session

Activity	Calories burnt
Running machine: low impact	120
Running machine: high impact	168
Aerobics, step: 6–8″ step	204
Aerobics, step: 10–12″ step	240
Swimming	96
Cycling vigorous	168
Bicycling, stationary: vigorous, 200 watts	252
Callisthenics: vigorous, jumping jacks, push-ups, sit-ups, pull-ups	192
Callisthenics: moderate, sit-ups, back exercises	84
Circuit training	192
Elliptical trainer: general	173
Cycling moderate	96
Rowing moderate	168
Rowing vigorous	204
Weightlifting moderate	72
Weightlifting vigorous	144

Setting the scene: accountant fined £10,000 for data protection breach

On 20 October 2003 Mr Abdullah Dervish pleaded guilty to eight offences of obtaining, and two offences of disclosing, personal information contrary to Section 55 of the Data Protection Act 1998. In addition, the defendant asked for a further 165 offences of unlawfully obtaining and/or disclosing personal information to be taken into consideration.

Magistrates fined Mr Dervish £10,000 and ordered him to pay £5,000 costs. This is one of the largest financial penalties by a court on an individual for offences under the act.

Mr Dervish, a qualified accountant practising in Warley, West Midlands as A Dervish & Co had been an agent of Bradford & Bingley, providing a banking transaction counter service from his offices, and as such had access to some customer account data.

In December 2000 Bradford & Bingley gave him one month's notice terminating his agency contract. By February 2001 Bradford & Bingley had noticed that a number of accounts serviced by Mr Dervish had been placed on "notice to close". The court heard that Mr Dervish had placed a notice to close on the Bradford & Bingley accounts and had opened up new accounts for the same customers at another bank for which he had now become an agent.

In March 2001 Mr Dervish was warned not to take any further unauthorised actions in relation to Bradford & Bingley's customers. Nevertheless, the defendant continued to contact Bradford & Bingley customers to try to get them to switch banks.

For the protection and benefit of its customers, Bradford & Bingley reported the facts surrounding this isolated incident to the Information Commissioner's Office (ICO) and worked closely with the ICO to bring the case to court. The ICO investigated and prosecuted Mr Dervish under the Data Protection Act.

Offences under Section 55 (1) of the Data Protection Act 1998 include knowingly or recklessly, without the consent of the data controller, obtaining or disclosing personal data or the information contained in personal data.

Source: adapted www.informationcommissioner.gov.uk

Protecting privacy

Many organisations and companies hold personal information on their databases, such as medical histories, financial records and family details, that we would not wish to be freely available to everyone.

KEY TERMS

The **Data Protection Act 1998** limits the use of an individual's personal data by businesses and sets out principles for storing this information.

The **Information Commissioner** is the appointed official who supervises the enforcement of the Data Protection Act.

A **data controller** is a person or organisation that stores personal data.

A **data subject** is a person whose data has been collected and stored.

With global networks able to exchange vast quantities of information in seconds, people need legal protection to ensure that their personal data is not misused or mishandled by organisations.

The Data Protection Act's main function is to protect that right to privacy of every individual. It was first enacted in 1984 to ensure that an individual's personal data was managed and used correctly. The act was subsequently updated in 1998.

The Data Protection Act encompasses eight main principles (see Figure 5.15). It covers all personal data, whether held on IT systems or as paper-based records. Its provisions mean that a business can only obtain and hold your personal information for specific and limited purposes as registered with the Information Commissioner. The information must be accurate, processed fairly and lawfully, and stored securely. It cannot be transferred to any country that does not have an adequate data protection law.

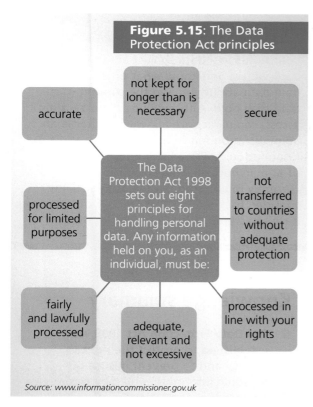

Figure 5.15: The Data Protection Act principles

accurate

not kept for longer than is necessary

secure

The Data Protection Act 1998 sets out eight principles for handling personal data. Any information held on you, as an individual, must be:

processed for limited purposes

not transferred to countries without adequate protection

fairly and lawfully processed

adequate, relevant and not excessive

processed in line with your rights

Source: www.informationcommissioner.gov.uk

Any organisation or person who needs to store personal information must apply and register with the Office of the Information Commissioner (www.informationcommissioner.gov.uk). Each application and register entry contains the following information:

- the data controller's name and address

- a description of the information that is to be stored

- the purpose for which the information will be used

- any plans to pass on the information to other people or organisations

- any plans to transfer the information outside the UK

- details of how the data controller will keep the information safe and secure.

stop and think

Many developing nations, such as India, are establishing data protection legislation. This will enable European businesses to set up offices and call centres overseas. Why do companies need data protection legislation in place before they can locate some functions and activities overseas?

What is covered by the legislation

Personal data is considered to be anything that allows a specific individual to be identified and an opinion about that individual to be formed based on that data. This includes areas such as:

- medical records

- bank details

- racial or ethnic origins

- religious beliefs

- sexual orientation

- political affiliations or beliefs

- trade union membership

- criminal records.

There are exemptions which allow for some situations in which personal data is not covered by the 1998 Act. These include personal data held for reasons of national security, and personal data held by private individuals for domestic purposes.

Some personal data has partial exemptions. For example:

- the Inland Revenue and HM Customs and Excise do not have to disclose information held or processed to prevent taxation fraud

- the police do not have to disclose information that is used to prevent crime, nor can convicted criminals see their police files

- there is partial exemption for data that is held for use in health, education or social work

- researchers have partial exemption for data being used for statistical, historical or research purposes that does not allow identification of individuals

- journalists and academics have partial exemption for data that is being held for use in research.

People whose personal data has been collected and stored by an organisation are called data subjects. They have several rights under the Data Protection Act. Data subjects are legally entitled to:

- a right of subject access – they can see a copy of data held about them

- a right of correction – data subjects can compel a data controller to correct any mistakes in the data held about them

- a right to prevent distress – an individual may prevent processing if they can demonstrate it would be likely to cause them damage or distress

- a right to prevent direct marketing – they can prevent their details being used for junk mail

- a right to prevent automated decisions – they can prevent the use of computers using data held to establish automatic routines such as point scoring on credit applications

- a right to compensation – an entitlement to financial recompense if personal data about them is inaccurate, has been lost or disclosed to third parties, or if its use has caused them damage or distress

- a right of complaint – individuals can complain to the Information Commissioner if they feel data controllers have misused their personal information.

Implications of non-compliance

In many cases companies who have breached the 1998 Data Protection Act do so out of ignorance rather than malicious intent. They perhaps do not possess the experience or knowledge to comply fully with all the data-handling regulations. In these circumstances, when a complaint has been received the Information Commissioner's Office will probably take one of two courses of action:

- informally advise the offending organisation of the breach and discuss with the data controller strategies for avoiding a repetition, perhaps improving systems, training and employee awareness

- issue a preliminary enforcement order instructing the organisation of the breach and how to comply.

Where non-compliance by organisations has been obviously intentional, or repeat offences have occurred, either private individuals or the Information Commissioner's Office can take unlawful companies to court. The courts have the power to impose fines of up to £5000 for each offence in a magistrates' court and unlimited fines in a Crown Court action.

stop and think

Your rights as a data subject are only applicable if you know what organisations hold data about you and the content of the data they hold. Although you have a right of access, companies are allowed to charge an administration fee for providing a copy of the information. Make a list (in groups if possible) of as many organisations you can think of that currently might hold data about you. Hint: consider, for example, the number of times you have registered with different websites.

Knowledge summary

- **The Data Protection Act 1998 was established to protect the right to privacy and to prevent misuse of personal information held by businesses and other organisations.**

- **The Data Protection Act covers all data whether held electronically or on paper.**

- **Organisations holding and using data must register with the Information Commissioner's Office and comply with the eight principles of data protection.**

- **Data subjects have rights allowing them some control over information held on them and how it is used.**

quick questions

1 What may happen to firms who do not comply with the Data Protection Act?

2 What types of information are exempt from data protection rules?

3 What is meant by the terms data subject and data controller?

Loyalty cards

The government wants ID cards containing biometric data such as fingerprints and iris scans to be compulsory by 2013. These would hold information on everything from medical details, benefits entitlement and criminal records, which could be accessed by police and other authorities. According to government ministers, there's no need for us to be scared of national identity cards as they will be no worse than the loyalty card schemes we sign up to voluntarily.

But how much information do loyalty cards really store about us? According to Loyalty Management UK, which runs Nectar – the country's biggest loyalty scheme – the cards collect strictly limited personal information and data on shopping habits and they are governed by the Data Protection Act 1998.

Basic data, such as name, address, gender and contact details, is provided voluntarily by Nectar collectors when they sign up. Members can also choose whether or not to provide additional information such as how many people there are in their household, how many cars they own and where they shop. What the data will be used for is explained on the Nectar registration form, and those who object can tick a selection of opt-out boxes.

After registration, each time the card is used to collect points, details of the date, location and points earned – but not what was actually bought – will be sent to Nectar. The information is stored in one of the country's largest databases but is not sold on or shared with companies outside the scheme. Instead, it is used to target Nectar collectors with offers designed to encourage them to collect more points and to tempt them into using the sponsors' shops and businesses.

Loyalty Management UK estimates Nectar is one of some 160 loyalty schemes operating in the UK – not all of which may be as scrupulous about what they do with the data they collect. Brian Sinclair, Loyalty Management UK's client services director, said: "We are the biggest in the marketplace and as such I think we have to be the most protective and careful about how we use our customers' information." He says the firm works closely with the Information Commissioner, who regulates data protection rules.

Source: adapted from news.bbc.co.uk, 19 November 2004

A Explain the role of the Information Commissioner.

B Outline what is meant by personal information under the provisions of the Data Protection Act 1998.

C Explain what data protection rules Nectar must follow in relation to managing and using one of the country's largest databases.

Legal and self-regulatory constraints

Setting the scene: software licensing

It is estimated that that the Western European software industry lost $2.7 billion in 2001 due to illegal use of software, and the situation is getting worse with worldwide piracy rates on the increase.

Part of the problem is due to software being counterfeited. However, the most significant problem lies within the business community, where the main issue is mismanagement of software licences.

In April 2002, individuals with responsibility for software management in 2,500 UK organisations, across all industry sectors, were invited to complete an online questionnaire on issues regarding software licensing and management. The survey found that:

- 54 per cent of organisations would find it difficult to prove that they are software compliant

- 69 per cent are aware of the high legal risk to their organisation if found to be non-compliant

- 40 per cent of organisations still do not have IT policies and procedures in place

- 80 per cent monitor internet use within their organisation

- 56 per cent now consider software compliance to be a board-level issue.

More than half said they would currently find it difficult to provide proof of ownership for all software in use in their organisation to their board, but they are evidently not taking adequate action to remedy the situation.

Despite the legal penalties for non-compliance, over three-quarters of respondents spent less than 4 per cent of their total desktop budget on managing and controlling the use of software, with many spending less than five man days per month on software management.

The survey was organised by FAST – the Federation Against Software Theft. FAST works to raise awareness of software management issues, advising and educating corporate UK on how to achieve and maintain a legally compliant and cost-effective IT environment. FAST encourages all organisations to implement clear policies to manage their IT assets. It is only through education that organisations and their employees can be made aware of the need for compliance and the repercussions of piracy.

Source: adapted from www.fast.org.uk/Software Licensing Survey 2002

The Computer Misuse Act 1990

The Computer Misuse Act was introduced to deal with a range of unlawful acts committed specifically by computer users. The act detailed three new crimes.

KEY TERMS

Computer Misuse Act 1990 defines crimes arising from inappropriate usage of computers such as hacking, fraud, data misuse and distribution of viruses.

The **Copyright, Designs and Patents Act 1988** includes provisions on the ownership and legality of copying and distributing software and manuals.

The **Health and Safety (Display Screen Equipment) Regulations 1992** was introduced to protect employees using computers in their work.

Hacking – accessing programmes or data without permission. Penalty is a maximum fine of £2,000 and/or a six-month prison sentence.

Computer fraud – accessing programmes or data with the intent to commit further criminal actions such as changing bank or credit records. Penalty is an unlimited fine and a maximum prison sentence of five years.

Unauthorised modifications – writing or deliberately spreading a virus. This also carries an unlimited fine and a maximum prison sentence of five years.

Computer misuse has become such a problem in global terms that many companies now hire hackers to deliberately try and break into their networks to test security. In a survey by Lloyd's of London insurance, three-quarters of UK businesses admitted to having no e-commerce insurance cover to protect against damage caused by hackers and viruses. The survey also showed that half the businesses surveyed had been affected by computer viruses, and 12 per cent have experienced problems with people hacking into their information technology systems.

Lloyd's also asked businesses to identify the cost to their organisations of dealing with viruses and hacker attacks. Of those affected by problems, one in ten respondents estimated damage to be in the range of £100,000 to £500,000 while the majority (25 per cent) said the bill was up to £100,000.

The Copyright, Designs and Patents Act 1988

Although not expressly set up for the prevention of crimes involving IT, the Copyright, Designs and Patents Act makes it illegal to copy software and/or use copied software. The law is designed to prevent the illegal copying, adapting, issuing, renting and lending of software to the public. The act covers:

- copying software and manuals
- using illegally copied software and manuals
- using legally purchased software without a correct licence – for example, buying a single-user licence for software that is networked throughout an organisation.

The legal penalties for non-compliance with the provisions of the Copyright, Designs and Patents Act that relate to software can result in an unlimited fine and up to two years' imprisonment.

stop and think

Is all the software you use on your home PC legal? List four ways illegal copying and downloading of software impacts on the company that should have received payment for the use of its programs.

Data security

Hardware, software and data needs to be protected in various ways from unauthorised access and misuse. Common protection procedures involve the use of password protection, which restricts access to information and programs to specified users or to particular workstations.

As well as controlling access, other restrictions can be put in place such as limiting a user's rights to modify information. This can be done by providing users (or specific files) with profiles that specify read, write, execute and delete restrictions. For example, individuals can be given a profile that allows them to run a particular program (execute rights) and use the information (read rights), but not to amend or change information (write rights) or erase information or remove the file (delete rights).

User protocols can also be set up that specify whether individual users are allowed to install hardware devices or new software. This provides additional protection by only allowing authorised personnel access to the administrative side of the IT system.

Virus protection

A virus is a program which is written with the intent to cause damage, disruption or harm to computers. Viruses can erase data or cause the system to crash completely. Special types of viruses that can cause problems include spyware and Trojan horses.

Spyware is a program that surreptitiously monitors your actions. Software companies have been known to use Spyware to gather data about customers and see if users are using software with or without licenses. A Trojan horse is a type of virus in which the malicious code is contained inside apparently harmless programming or data in such a way that it can get control and do its chosen form of damage, such as ruining your hard disk.

There are many of ways to protect a computer from viruses. Specialist protection software such as Norton AntiVirus and McAfee VirusScan can be installed on systems to scan for and block incoming viruses automatically. They can also be used to scan floppy discs and even run a complete check on a whole operating system. Other measures should include installation of a firewall (a device or program that stops people accessing a computer without permission while it is connected to the internet) as well as user policies.

Here is a four-step program to maintain the integrity of your IT system. It will provide protection for your files and data.

- First, choose an internet service provider or an e-mail service that offers online (server-side) virus, spam and content filters.

- Second, install a hardware router with a built-in firewall between your modem and your computer or network.

- Third, use personal firewall, anti-virus, anti-Trojan, anti-spyware, anti-spam and privacy software on your desktop computer and every computer on your network.

- Fourth, enforce user policies such as not allowing other users to use their own floppy disks on the system, only downloading files from reputable internet sites, write-protecting discs, and not allowing employees to take system discs home for use on less heavily protected domestic machines.

The final way to protect data is to prevent data loss or corruption by regularly backing up files. The question most businesses have to ask is whether the cost of protecting their systems and data is more or less than the expenses that would be incurred should their systems be hacked or crashed through a virus.

Health and safety legislation

There are many health problems associated with prolonged use of computers by employees. These include repetitive strain injuries (RSI) caused by constant typing, eyestrain from looking at VDU screens, and work-related upper limb disorders (WRULD) caused by protracted working on keyboards.

Any employer whose staff will be spending prolonged periods of time working with IT needs to be aware of these health issues. Employers also need to comply with the Health and Safety (Display Screen Equipment) Regulations 1992. These were introduced to protect employees who spend a significant proportion of their time using computer monitors at work. The regulations state that employers must:

- provide angle-adjustable screens

- provide anti-glare screens or fit anti-glare filters

- provide adjustable chairs (height and angle)

- ensure that lighting is suitable and causes no glare or reflections

- provide suitable heating and ventilation

- schedule frequent breaks

- pay for employee eye tests.

If these regulations are enforced – and employees take frequent breaks and are given the opportunity to change activities occasionally – then it should be possible to avoid RSI, eyestrain and WRULD injuries.

There are also other steps an employer needs to take to ensure that an IT environment is safe. These relate to handling and maintaining electrical equipment. Employers have a statutory duty to ensure that:

- wiring is safely installed and secured

- food and drink are not allowed near electrical appliances

- electrical supplies are properly earthed and each appliance fused

- electrical appliances are given regular safety tests and logged as tested.

stop and think

Ergonomics is the science concerned with designing safe and comfortable machines for humans. This science ranges from furniture design to the design of parts of the computer such as keyboards. Ergonomic keyboards such as the Goldtouch keyboard are more expensive than ordinary keyboards. But how might they save companies money in the long term?

Knowledge summary

■ The Computer Misuse Act outlaws hacking, computer fraud and the generation and distribution of viruses.

■ The Copyright, Designs and Patents Act is used to protect the rights of software manufacturers by aiming to prevent the unlawful copying and use of software.

■ Employers must respect health and safety legislation that aims to protect the wellbeing of employees who work a significant amount with computers.

■ Computer systems and data can be protected from viruses and other external threats. A secure system has several layers of defence and these can be costly to install and maintain.

quick questions

1 Why was the Computer Misuse Act introduced?

2 Explain two ways in which software may be used illegally.

3 Outline four health and safety factors that must be considered when using IT equipment.

data interpretation
Computer hacking "costs billions"

Three-quarters of UK companies have been hit by security breaches in their computer systems over the past year, costing billions to industry. Viruses, staff misuse and hacking are blamed in the survey by the Department of Trade and Industry (DTI) and accountancy firm PricewaterhouseCoopers (PwC).

Most businesses know there is a problem, PwC said, and virus-writing gangs are getting more sophisticated. UK businesses are being exposed to ever-greater threats to their information systems as use of the internet and wider connectivity increases. The average computer incident costs large companies £120,000 a time.

The DTI's information security breaches survey discovered that 74 per cent of all businesses and 94 per cent of large companies had an IT security incident in the year 2003/4, up from 44 per cent of all businesses in 2002 and just 24 per cent in 2000. The average UK business now has roughly one security incident a month and larger ones suffer around one a week.

The report recommended that companies invest more on security controls and that they make sure key security defences are robust and up to date. Unfortunately, no computer software is immune from criminal attacks, warned software giant Microsoft.

Source: news.bbc.co.uk, 27 April 2004

A Outline the three key components of the Computer Misuse Act.

B Analyse two ways in which computer misuse can cost UK businesses millions.

C Produce a leaflet that could be given out by the DTI demonstrating how companies can protect their IT systems.

Prioritising and planning

Setting the scene: vital Tube work "behind schedule"

Vital improvements to the Tube are months behind schedule, according to figures from Transport for London. A report shows just 10 out of 18 stations set to be refurbished by the end of the month are finished.

Metronet and Tube Lines took over responsibility for maintenance under the public private partnership (PPP) scheme in 2003. The firms have 30-year contracts worth £15 billion and combined profits of almost £100 million.

In the first seven years of the PPP contracts, 33 per cent of the tracks are meant to be replaced, but two years into the programme only 4 per cent of track has been replaced. The number of lifts and escalators planned for renewal has been "revised down" from 58 per cent to 44 per cent.

Transport union RMT's general secretary

Bob Crow said: "The only winners from the PPP scheme are the contractors, who are pocketing £2m a week in profits at our expense. Several reports have already shown that privatising work on the Tube infrastructure has brought nothing but delays, excuses and increasing safety concerns."

Roger Evans, deputy chairman of the transport committee said: "Obviously this is a 30-year contract so there is time to make up ground, but it's very important we catch these things early."

Story adapted news.bbc.co.uk, 8 March 2005

KEY TERMS

Work plans are lists of tasks that are necessary in order to complete a project.

Gantt charts are a diagrammatic method of scheduling tasks to complete an activity.

Critical path analysis is a method of scheduling tasks so a project can be completed in the minimum amount of time.

Planning tools

In order to meet corporate objectives and customer deadlines, businesses must be able to prioritise and plan work that needs to be undertaken to allow a project, job or task to be completed on time and to budget. For many simple tasks this is relatively easy to do. However, for large-scale projects, such as designing and building a new passenger plane like the

Airbus A380 (the largest passenger jet in the world, which was unveiled in January 2005), it can take years of planning and development, all of which needs careful co-ordination to deliver the finished product. In this topic, we look at the different types of planning tools and aids that organisations use to help them realise their objectives within a given timescale.

stopand**think**

Review the setting the scene article (opposite) on the delays to the Tube maintenance programme. **Describe the effects that falling behind schedule may have on the London Underground. Consider several areas such as costs, revenues and customer service.**

1 Work plans

Work plans are designed to help companies organise and prioritise tasks. They are used to help co-ordinate activities and save time. By detailing clearly defined tasks in order of priority, at any given moment managers and employees should know at what stage they are at and what needs to occur next. By monitoring the work plan, managers can see what has – and, as importantly, what hasn't – been done and should therefore be able to oversee the completion of a project more effectively.

There are several stages in work planning.

- First, managers need to determine the objective and timescale.

- Second, they need to identify and then schedule tasks. These tasks should be scheduled in order of priority, with set deadlines. They can be scheduled sequentially (one after the other) or simultaneously.

- Third, managers need to identify the resources needed for each task – people, equipment, materials and finance – and ensure their availability.

At this stage, it should be possible to produce the work plan. For example, this might be a printed schedule clearly showing the order of tasks and completion times.

During the project, managers should monitor – and, if necessary, revise – the plan. Long-term large-scale projects rarely go entirely as planned, and plans may have to go through several revisions as tasks and jobs fall behind or even get completed ahead of schedule.

Work planning has many benefits. These include:

- improves communications

- improves co-ordination of activities

- helps managers prioritise activities

- helps allocate resources effectively

- helps determine budgets

- helps to meet deadlines

- aids motivation by seeing each task as part of the overall plan.

Although work planning does have many benefits, it can be a costly and time-consuming process. The benefits must outweigh the cost of the management and employee time needed to create the plan. Because of this, work planning is not generally cost effective for small projects or jobs that only involve the combination of one or two tasks.

2 Creating schedules

A schedule is a list of planned activities or things to be done, showing the times or dates when they are intended to happen or be completed. This can be something as simple as a timetable, a planning list (such as work plan) or perhaps a wall planner. However, a range of more specialist tools exist for planning business activities.

Gantt charts

Gantt charts consist of a horizontal bar chart in which activities are shown in the order that they need to be completed, and the position of the bars indicate the date at which an activity needs to be started and the date by which it should be completed.

Figure 5.17 shows an example of a Gantt chart produced for the construction of a domestic residence. This way of planning can ensure that activities take place in the right order at the right time, as obviously some activities such as plumbing can't be undertaken until the actual building shell is completed. Planning in this way allows contractors to be booked in advance.

The vertical axis on a Gantt chart shows the tasks that need to be completed and the horizontal is the timescale, clearly showing projected start and finish times. Managers can use the chart to see how a project is progressing, by mapping actual time taken against the plan. This enables managers to determine if a task or the overall project is running behind or ahead of schedule and take steps to immediately rectify any problems that occur.

Figure 5.17: An example Gantt chart

TASKS	Start Date	End Date	March	April	May	June	July	August	Duration (days)	Cost
Contract writing	3/01	3/30 4/08							29 30	$50,000 $54,901
Contract signing	4/04 4/09	4/04 4/09							1	$400
Secure financing	4/04 4/09	4/10 5/04							6 25	$3,500 $6,234
Obtain permits	4/04 4/09	4/17 5/01							13 22	$1,200
Site work	4/10 5/01	6/28 6/07							79 37	$1,500,000 $1,200,000
Plumbing	6/28 6/07	7/20 7/03							22 26	$43,000
Electricity	6/28 6/07	7/20							22 43	$36,000 $91,050
Roof	7/20	8/10 8/05							21 16	$23,000 $22,548
Inspection	8/10 8/05	8/10 8/05							1	$1000
Move in	8/24	8/24							1	

LEGEND

- ▭ Planned duration
- ▨ Actual duration
- ⬔ Planned milestone
- ⬔ Actual milestone
- Planned
- Actual

Source: www.smartdraw.com/examples/gantt/construction.htm

stop and think

The Gantt chart in Figure 5.17 also shows budgeted and actual costs incurred at each stage of the project. How might this extra information help a manager co-ordinate a project?

Critical path analysis

Critical path analysis (CPA) is another method of scheduling activities, but this tool also takes into account the interdependence of various tasks. In any large project, some tasks cannot be undertaken before other tasks are completed. CPA prioritises the tasks upon which other tasks are dependent and so concentrates on creating a network of simultaneous activities that are scheduled in such a way that the time taken to complete a project can be minimised.

CPA analysis works on the basis that some tasks are critical to the completion of the project on deadline. If these critical tasks are delayed, the project will take longer than the projected minimum time; other tasks (that still need to be completed on time) are not critical – they have some float time, so that small delays in the completion dates of these activities will not actually delay the whole project. By identifying the critical activities in a project, managers can ensure that the critical tasks receive both the resources they require on time and closer scrutiny and monitoring to make sure they are achieved successfully.

Figure 5.18 shows a simple critical path analysis for the design and launch of a new game. It can be seen that some activities are key (critical) for the successful completion of the project such as path A, entering the computer coding to make the game engine work. Other activities such as designing and launching the website (paths L and M) are not critical to the successful game development. These can be undertaken simultaneously as other parts of the project proceed, but only after certain tasks have been completed. The website can be designed and launched while the final version of the game is being tested and the instruction manual written (path G). But the website could not have been constructed until after the game itself had been designed and written (tasks 1 to 6). However, the website must be completed to a deadline – it needs to be up and running before the actual game is released.

Critical path analysis can be combined with a Gantt chart or work plan to ensure that all the tasks take place at their scheduled time. The benefit critical path gives is that it tries to ensure the project is completed in the minimum time possible.

stop and think

Most effective forms of scheduling tend to be highly visual in nature. Why is this a more useful approach than a simple written list or table like a work plan?

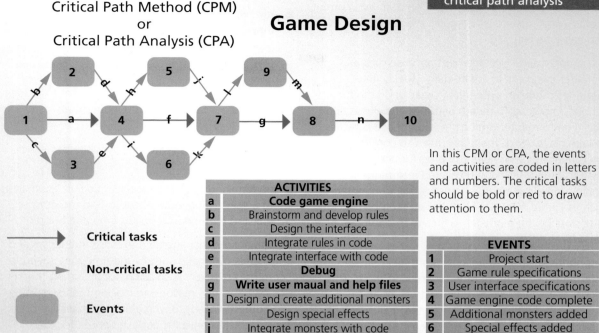

Figure 5.18: An example critical path analysis

Critical Path Method (CPM) or Critical Path Analysis (CPA)

Game Design

In this CPM or CPA, the events and activities are coded in letters and numbers. The critical tasks should be bold or red to draw attention to them.

→ Critical tasks

→ Non-critical tasks

▢ Events

	ACTIVITIES
a	**Code game engine**
b	Brainstorm and develop rules
c	Design the interface
d	Integrate rules in code
e	Integrate interface with code
f	**Debug**
g	**Write user maual and help files**
h	Design and create additional monsters
i	Design special effects
j	Integrate monsters with code
k	Integrate special effects
l	Design and write website
m	Launch website
n	**Package game, produce CDs**

	EVENTS
1	Project start
2	Game rule specifications
3	User interface specifications
4	Game engine code complete
5	Additional monsters added
6	Special effects added
7	Quality assurance testing
8	Documentation
9	Website design
10	Release

Source www.smartdraw.com/examples/cpm/gamedesign_full.htm

3 Time management techniques

Many employees will have multiple demands placed upon them by departments, senior managers, directors, employees and customers. With so many areas to be addressed, managers and employees must ensure that not only do they manage their objectives and projects successfully but also their own time. This involves being able to prioritise and order their own activities to enable them to complete routine and non-routine tasks as they occur.

Many activities, such as responding to e-mails, letters and general enquiries, are routine predictable activities that happen daily and can be given specific time allocations such as first thing in the morning and after

Figure 5.19: An example task priority table

Tasks	Deadline	Urgent	Not urgent	Current status/ comments	Priority
Order stocks	13 April	✓		Need price confirmation	1
Staff appraisals	30 August		✓	Four out of seven complete	5
Project progress report	15 April	✓		In progress	2
Budget update	15 April	✓		Needs project progress report	3
Subcontractor queries on stage 3 design	10 May		✓	Request original plans from files	4

lunch. This means that routine activities have definite periods each day when they will be dealt with, keeping employees on top of and abreast with current events. Meetings are also regular events and so can also easily be planned.

The simplest time management approach for a manager to take is to create daily, weekly and monthly schedules, entering in dedicated time for various (known/anticipated) activities and protecting that time from interruptions to allow those activities to take place. Next, managers need to consider all the other tasks that need to be performed. These need to be prioritised and ordered into sequence. Again a simple method is to use a task priority table such as Figure 5.19. These tasks can then be allocated time slots by the manager to ensure that priority areas get addressed.

By prioritising tasks, managers are thinking ahead and considering activities before undertaking them. This allows managers to make the best use of any planning and preparation time as they can focus on the future tasks that really need their attention. By considering tasks in terms of their priority, complexity and importance, managers can also determine which areas could be effectively delegated – saving the manager more time to focus on critical areas – or which tasks should be allocated to each employee.

Other techniques to improve time management and work efficiency include:

- reviewing the work environment – layout of IT, office equipment and files

- logging the time individual activities take – making future time allocations more accurate

- protecting allocated time – constant interruptions can make a task take much longer than anticipated

- using templates as much as possible for reports, schedules, minutes and standard letters

- undertaking time and motion studies – an analysis of a specific job in an effort to find the most efficient method in terms of time and effort.

As a final time management exercise, managers and employees can make a list of the time they spend in "comfort activities" such as chatting, surfing the net (for non-business reasons), e-mailing friends, sorting out domestic needs, daydreaming or excessive breaks. These activities have no positive benefit for the organisation and should be restricted, again creating more usable time.

stop and think

Consider one working day you spend at college, school or a place of employment. How much of your time is spent in comfort activities? Keep a time log of one day if possible.

quick questions

1. Give two advantages a company could gain from using work plans.

2. What is the major advantage of critical path analysis as a planning tool?

3. Explain two techniques managers could employ to improve their own time management.

Knowledge summary

- **Formal work planning can help a business run more efficiently and meet deadlines effectively.**

- **Highly visual schedules like Gantt charts and critical path analysis are easy for employees to understand and help a business to manage a project successfully.**

- **Time management techniques can assist managers and employees in ensuring routine and non-routine tasks are completed and in focusing employee energies on priority activities.**

- **Work plans and schedules not only help the organisation of tasks and projects, but also significantly aid monitoring of progress.**

Bow Wows

Bow Wows produces a range of goods for dogs such as treats, toys, baskets, training aids, and a small selection of specialist diet foods. The company's marketing manager has recently hit upon the idea of visiting regional and national dog shows with a glossy brochure advertising its products and inviting customers to order goods via mail order or through the company's website. Although this could be an expensive activity, it is hoped that increased sales will more than offset any initial costs.

The marketing manager is keen that the tone, look and feel of the brochure should appeal to the relatively select market of pedigree owners. The manager wants to research the competition and get the presentation of the brochure just right. The first major show is due to take place in ten weeks' time. The manager has estimated the time it will take to complete each of the activities needed to produce the brochure.

Printing the brochure	**2 weeks**
Gathering materials such as product pictures, pricing and description details	**4 weeks**
Researching competitors	**3 weeks**
Writing text	**10 days**
Editing and proofreading	**1 week**
Design and layout	**3 weeks**

A Using the information given, prioritise the tasks in the order that they need to be undertaken.

B Design a schedule clearly showing the order of tasks – and task start and finish times – that will enable the brochure to be produced in time for the first major show.

C Write a report to the marketing manager presenting your schedule and setting out the benefits to be gained from work planning.

Topic 10 · Business in practice: an organic business environment

Guidance

This topic does not attempt to replicate the external assessment for this unit. Instead, it is designed to be used to help you build the skills you will need to employ in the actual assessment itself.

Toft Priory Farm is located in the heart of the Devon countryside. Its 1,500 acres of land have been farmed by the same family (the Grants) for over five generations. Figure 5.20 shows the farm business's organisational structure.

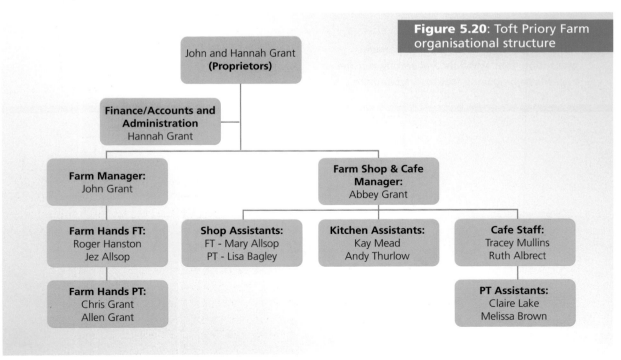

Figure 5.20: Toft Priory Farm organisational structure

- **John and Hannah Grant (Proprietors)**
  - **Finance/Accounts and Administration**
    Hannah Grant
    - **Farm Manager:**
      John Grant
      - **Farm Hands FT:**
        Roger Hanston
        Jez Allsop
        - **Farm Hands PT:**
          Chris Grant
          Allen Grant
    - **Farm Shop & Cafe Manager:**
      Abbey Grant
      - **Shop Assistants:**
        FT - Mary Allsop
        PT - Lisa Bagley
      - **Kitchen Assistants:**
        Kay Mead
        Andy Thurlow
      - **Cafe Staff:**
        Tracey Mullins
        Ruth Albrect
        - **PT Assistants:**
          Claire Lake
          Melissa Brown

The farm is primarily a commercial sheep farm with little land given over to arable use. There is some other livestock (chickens, ducks and pigs) but these are not kept for mass commercial farming purposes. These subsidiary ventures are used to provide produce for the family itself and its own farmshop and café.

John took over the running of the farm in 1984 when his father retired. John has always been forward-thinking and looking for new opportunities, so he has always kept an eye on developments of farming techniques, produce markets and prices. He introduced the first major change in 1989 when he had the idea of using a piece of land for a tea shop and a small car park. The impetus behind this came from John's realisation that he could tap into the growing local tourist trade: Toft Priory, that lay half a mile from his farm, was becoming increasingly popular with visitors since it been taken over by the National Trust and had been included in National Trust guides and brochures.

Originally, the tea shop had started as a small outlet serving hot and cold drinks, sandwiches, cakes and other snack items, and was run by Hannah, John's wife. However, the operation was taken over in 1994 by his daughter Abbey. Since then it has expanded to encompass a café serving hot and cold meals, and a farmshop. The shop stocks not only Toft Priory Farm's own products as it has agreements with several other local producers to sell their goods. John advised his daughter to start advertising and marketing the farmshop locally. This paid dividends, and generated sales all year round rather than limiting them mainly to the tourist season.

Keeping his eye on the press and the markets, John forecast a massive rise in demand for organic produce. In 1997, he began to convert his agricultural techniques to organic production, starting with a small flock of pedigree Lleyn sheep to provide organic lamb for sale. He now provides a wide range of produce for the shop.

Vegetables

The shop sells seasonal produce, offering a good range of organic fruit and vegetables at all times from its own 15-acre organic market garden.

Meat

All the pork and lamb in the shop has been reared at Toft Priory Farm. The organically reared animals benefit from a safe additive-free diet, homeopathic medicine and good pasture in fields which are not overstocked. The meat is butchered to an extremely high standard by a registered master butcher.

Dairy products

Local dairy farmers supply a range of organic milk, cheeses, yoghurts, creams and butter.

Eggs

Supplied by Toft Priory's small free-range flocks of Black Rocks.

Groceries

The shop also stocks bread, cake, jam, marmalade, honey and chutneys. Also available are pulses, herbs, juices and icecream. Everything is sourced locally and is fairly traded.

The shop has now outstripped the café in terms of success. Abbey is now regularly contacted by organic producers asking if the shop wants to stock their products. Toft Priory Farm now has two contracts with local restaurants to provide and source organic produce. As ever, John has kept his eye on developments, and a news item on the BBC and the Soil Association's *Organic Food and Farming Report 2004* have got him thinking again.

> # Booming trade
>
> Direct sales of organic fruit, veg and other foods have boomed in recent years in the wake of food scares and obesity scandals. And with the government promoting healthy eating, awareness about nutrition and the environment has grown. Even celebrity chefs are trying to turn children's hearts and minds to good nutrition.
>
> Sales at farmers' markets – where producers sell directly to the customer – were up from £4 million in 2000/1, to £8 million the following year. In 2003/4, the number of farmers' markets increased from 450 to 500.

news.bbc.co.uk. 3 March 2005

Figures 5.21, 5.22 and 5.23 are taken from the Soil Association's *Organic Food and Farming Report 2004* with additional information from previous editions. The Soil Association is the UK's leading campaigning and certification organisation for organic food and farming.

John's new idea is to convert his entire flock to organic methods over the next few years, particularly as organic produce tends to attract higher prices in the marketplace and higher profit margins. He has some concern about increasing competition – there has been an increase in the number of organic

Figure 5.21: Retail value of organic food in the UK 1993–2004

Year	Market value (£m)
1993/4	105
1994/5	121
1995/6	140
1996/7	200
1997/8	260
1998/9	390
1999/0	605
2000/1	802
2001/2	920
2002/3	1,015
2003/4	1,119

Source: www.soilassociation.org

Having asked the family for their ideas, he was surprised when Allen, the youngest member, spoke up advocating that they reject all four options but set up a website instead. This would be a cheap method that would allow the farm to sell its lamb and all the other products that are currently sold in the shop. They could then expand their range easily and make even greater profits, perhaps also acting as an agent for some local producers.

John, Hannah and Abbey were all interested in this idea, but being somewhat computer illiterate were really unsure of how it would work. John's older son Chris, however, was not so uninformed and immediately voiced several concerns, starting with how the internet would be unsuitable as the farm sold perishable goods not CDs, DVDs or books (the only things that sell well on the internet, he stated). A website could invite problems from hackers and viruses and it was not as cheap as Allen thought – the website business would need to comply with several laws as well.

producers, farmshops and farmers' markets in the area, and John is grateful that his location near to Toft Priory increases his number of customers significantly.

John was so convinced that organic is the way ahead that he called a family meeting to discuss how to proceed. He considers that there are four options available to Toft Priory Farm:

- expand the existing shop and invest in additional local marketing

- negotiate with individual independent butchers to stock the farm's lamb products

- negotiate a contract with upmarket grocers, such as Greenway and Sons, a chain with 12 branches

- negotiate a contract with a large supermarket.

John could see pros and cons with each option ranging from organisation and communication advantages (and some disadvantages) to drawbacks such as the fact that the likely demand, distribution and profit margins would differ in each market.

Figure 5.22: Number of registered organic producers in the UK

	Producers	% change
April 1997	828	-
April 1998	1064	29
April 1999	1568	47
April 2000	2865	83
April 2001	3691	29
April 2002	3865	5
April 2003	4104	3
March 2004	3995	–2.7

Source: www.soilassociation.org

Figure 5.23: Estimated UK retail value of organic food by outlet

	Sales (£m) 2002/3	Sales (£m) 2003/4	Annual growth (%)
Supermarkets	821.0	899.4	9.5
Direct sales	93.0	108.4	16.2
Independent retailers	101.0	111.2	10.0
Total	1,015.0	1,119.0	10.2

Source: www.soilassociation.org

activities

1 Insert the information in Figures 5.21, 5.22 and 5.23 into a suitable software application. Then:
  a) calculate the percentage growth in organic food sales each year
  b) insert a formula that uses average growth to predict sales for 2005
  c) calculate the percentage market share of supermarkets, direct sales and independent retailers for 2002/3 and 2003/4.

2 Explain the communication advantages and disadvantages of dealing with supermarkets as opposed to independent retailers.

3 Using word processing software, draft a report evaluating the pros and cons of setting up a website.

4 Using the information from the case study, explain two communication mediums suitable for reaching Toft Priory Farm's possible target market.

5 Explain how John Grant could communicate the change in company direction to the rest of the farm's employees.

6 Produce a schedule that Allen could use to show John what activities would need to be undertaken to design and launch a website. As part of the schedule, show the priority in which tasks would need to be completed.

THIS UNIT EXAMINES HOW BUSINESSES COMBINE resources to provide goods and services. You will explore all the factors that businesses take into account when developing new products. These include product features – the quality, functions and appearance of the product – as well as the safety issues that must be considered in producing any new good or service.

You will become familiar with the raw materials as well as the physical (factories and machinery, for example) and human resources used in production. You will also investigate the financial resources a business might access to develop a new product, as well as studying how businesses cost new products.

Finally, the unit considers how businesses reach decisions on the exact characteristics and specification of new products. Costs – and forecast revenues and profits – are very influential here.

Developing a product

Intro

Intro | Introducing product development

Setting the scene: a mobile phone to meet the needs of the elderly

The Vitaphone 1100 is designed for elderly people who hate technology in general and mobile phones in particular. It has just three buttons.

- **The red button connects the owner to Vitaphone's medical centre, offering the reassuring presence of medical help without having to remember different numbers.**

- **The green and yellow buttons can be programmed to dial two emergency numbers, a favourite son or daughter or the family doctor, for example.**

The other functions of the phone have been designed to suit elderly people who might be forgetful. It has extra long-life batteries so that it will work for more than 100 hours without being recharged. It has a cord so that it can be worn round the neck, making sure it is available when needed and won't get lost.

Mobile phone companies have tended to concentrate on the needs of young customers rather than the elderly. Vitaphone's Benjamin Homburg commented: "Everyone has their own needs – older people are less interested in sending text messages, but more interested in knowing that they can contact relatives or a doctor."

Developing the Vitaphone 1100 involved little research and development as it only required a simple adaptation of existing mobile phone technology. More importantly, market research played a part in establishing the exact needs of the elderly target group of consumers and ensuring that their needs were met by the new product.

Developing a new product

Developing a product entails a range of activities including finding out customers' needs, conducting scientific research and deciding upon the appearance and features of the new product.

KEY TERMS

A **product** is a general term for a good (such as a television) or a service (such as health care).

A **product's characteristics** comprise its appearance and its function – in other words, what it looks like and what it does.

Resources are the human and non-human assets used in production. These include raw materials, fuel, factories and offices as well as the contribution of the workforce.

1 Finding out customer needs

Before starting to develop a new product most businesses will conduct some market research to find out the needs of existing and potential customers. Unless a business knows exactly what its customers want, it will be unlikely to provide a product that will meet their needs fully and, therefore, satisfy them.

In Unit 4, you looked at some of the ways businesses undertake customer research. A business's market research may discover:

- what product features or functions customers would find desirable

- what level of quality they expect from the good or service

- whether the product's appearance is important and, if so, in what ways.

In addition, market research may also reveal important data about acceptable price levels and what after-sales service is expected.

2 Research and development

Knowing what the market wants allows businesses to set about designing a new product. For some businesses this may entail serious scientific research. For example, many computer manufacturers know that consumers want small and light laptops, but also that they want a full range of functions. Companies such as Hewlett Packard are investing in research in order to attempt to develop a suitable product that meets customers' needs.

Research and development attempts to create a product that has the characteristics that its consumers desire. However, research and development can be expensive. In an effort to control these costs, Hitachi and Matshushita Electric are joining forces to develop technology for flat-screen televisions. Both companies will use the results of the common research to develop new products.

Much research and development is unsuccessful. It can result in products that do not work properly, do not meet consumer needs or cannot be produced economically. Some products may not be legal or, if they are, they may not be considered safe enough to sell to consumers. For example, although mini motorcycles are not illegal in the UK, some British businesses are refusing to develop and sell them because they have appalling accident records in other countries such as the United States.

3 Resource issues

Even if a business comes up with a good product idea – and, crucially, one that consumers want – they might still decide not to produce it. The company may not be able to manufacture a product which contains all the characteristics that consumers want and to sell it at a price that consumers will find acceptable. If only a small number of consumers will buy the product, it may not make the company a profit. In this case they may decide not to go ahead with it.

As part of the development process, companies estimate the resources they will need to supply the product, calculate the costs of producing a new good or service, and judge whether it has the potential to make a profit.

stop and think

Researchers at Warwick University have developed a biodegradable mobile phone which starts to decompose within weeks of being composted. An additional feature of this mobile phone is that it contains a sunflower seed which germinates within the disintegrating phone and flowers later. Do you think this might be a successful new product? Explain your reasoning.

Setting the scene: Smarties have change of image after 68 years

In 2005 Nestlé Rowntree, one of the world's major manufacturers of chocolate products, decided to replace the traditional round tube it had used for Smarties with a hexagonal (six-sided) packet.

The familiar tube has been associated with Smarties since the product was launched in 1937. However, Nestlé Rowntree hopes to attract young consumers by repackaging Smarties, one of its most familiar products.

Nestlé said the revamp was needed to ensure the brand remained "fresh and interesting" to youngsters. Neil Ducray, director of marketing at Nestlé Rowntree, said that the company had decided to change the design of the product's packaging following research amongst children, who are the main consumers of the product. "We decided on the hexatube because it has a tactile feel with lots of edges."

He said that the new tube was functional too, in that the top doesn't come off too easily and so the sweets are less likely to spill on the floor. He denied that the redesign of the pack was intended to reduce the company's costs.

Source: adapted from news.bbc.co.uk, 18 February 2005

How businesses make products desirable

Businesses make their products appealing by including characteristics or features which many consumers (or potential customers) are likely to find desirable.

1 Appearance

Many consumers will choose a particular product because they are attracted by its looks. For some types of product appearance or form is perhaps the most important (but not the only) element influencing consumers' purchasing decisions.

Shoe manufacturers, for example, will have the design of the product at the forefront of their mind when developing a new range. It must attract customers as the initial appeal will be visual; only later will more practical matters such as comfort come into question. Unless the shoe's appearance is right, customers will not try it on.

KEY TERMS

A **product** is a general term for a good (such as a television) or a service (such as health care).

A **product's characteristics** comprise its appearance and its function – in other words, what it looks like and what it does.

A **product's function** is what it does and how well it does it. For example Apple's iPod should store and play music clearly; a kettle should boil water (hopefully quickly).

The **aesthetic appeal** of a product relates to its beauty rather than other features.

Marketing is discovering and meeting the needs of customers to give satisfaction while fulfilling the business's objectives.

A **unique selling point (USP)** is a feature or function that distinguishes a business's product from those supplied by its rivals.

Appearance (sometimes called form) is a vital element in the manufacture and sale of shoes. Can you think of four other types of product in which appearance is important to customers and is likely to have a big influence on their purchasing decisions?

Decisions about appearance are not only taken in relation to new products. The appearance of existing products may be changed too, especially if sales are declining. It is important to consider not just the product but the way in which it is sold. For example, a manufacturer may decide to change the design of the packaging on some goods. The basic product may be fine, but the manufacturer might feel that the packaging needs freshening up to appeal to new consumers.

Companies such as Mars, Nestlé and Cadbury Schweppes that manufacture confectionery pay great attention to the product packaging. Many people make impulse decisions at the point of sale – where the product is sold – and chocolate manufacturers seek a distinctive appearance for their products to encourage consumers to select them in the shop. However, packaging alone is not enough – the chocolate must taste nice too.

The aesthetic appeal of a product relates to its beauty rather than other features. Some products may be chosen solely because of their aesthetic appeal. It is the beauty that the consumer sees in pottery, paintings and other works of art that leads to the decision to purchase. This element is difficult to judge when developing a new product. It is necessarily subjective – a product that one person considers beautiful, another may find unattractive. Function is not a factor for goods that are judged solely on their aesthetic appeal. Note that this is not the case for products such as shoes and chocolate bars, where although appearance is important it is not the only factor that influences and concerns consumers.

In 2004, a pair of Martini glasses designed and manufactured by the artist Damien Hirst sold for £4,800. This was far above expectations, and the buyer may have seen the glasses as an investment. The point to note is that the glasses were valuable solely because of their aesthetic appeal, not because of their functional use.

2 Function

If you see a new product that interests you, you will want to know exactly what it does and how well it does it – in other words, you will want to know about its function. Consumers expect products to meet their needs as fully as possible. A consumer buying a refrigerator may look for a product that is environmentally friendly, offers plenty of storage space, easy access and, perhaps, comes with drink dispensers.

Function applies to services as well as goods. For example, a person dining in a restaurant might expect a wide choice on the menu, the food to be tasty and freshly cooked, and the waiting staff to be attentive to their needs.

In general, when assessing the functionality of a product, consumers consider two main issues: its range of functions and its quality.

- **Range of functions** – this is what the product does. Take an MP3 player as an example. Potential purchasers will want to know how much music will it store, does it have an FM radio, is it compatible with all recent versions of Windows? If a product has unique features, then the business is likely to use this to promote the product. Famously, James Dyson based his advertising around the fact that the suction power of his cyclone vacuum cleaners was much greater than conventional machines.

- **Quality** – it is not sufficient to have a range of functions; purchasers want to consider how well the product performs. Continuing with our example of the MP3 player, a potential customer might want to assess the quality of the sound reproduction or find out how quickly it will transfer files. A high-quality product is more likely to meet consumers' needs fully.

Why characteristics are important

Why do businesses expend so much time, effort and energy in determining the characteristics of products? One key reason – as noted above – is to develop products that meet customers' needs fully. But businesses have other objectives, and businesses take decisions on product characteristics to help them meet their goals – for example, to maximise profit or to increase market share.

1 Marketing reasons

Businesses frequently set out to design a product that is distinctive from those offered by rivals. It may be distinctive in a number of ways. For example a new product might:

■ be very different in its appearance

■ have functions that existing products do not have

■ meet consumers' needs more fully than rival products

■ be higher quality than rival products.

If a product is distinctive in any of these ways it is often described as having a unique selling point or proposition. This is normally shortened to USP.

Having a USP helps a business to market its products. Its advertising and promotional activity simply draws attention to the characteristics that its products have which are unique – its USP. This product differentiation can help to attract new consumers as well as to gain the loyalty of existing buyers.

In the 1990s, the management team of the Co-operative Bank decided to adopt an ethical position. This meant that the bank takes ethical and moral issues into account when taking decisions, and it does not simply follow the course of action which would result in the highest profits. For example, the bank will not lend money to businesses that damage the environment or supply weapons, even if these transactions would be highly profitable. This has given the Co-operative Bank a USP and helped it to attract new customers who want to deal with a bank that has a social conscience. This has helped the Co-operative Bank to succeed in a market containing much larger competitors such as Barclays and HSBC.

Having a product with unique characteristics also has a further advantage – it might allow a business to charge higher prices because its product is differentiated from those of rivals. The Dyson vacuum cleaner is substantially more expensive than most of its competitors. This ability to charge high prices can generate large profits for the company.

2 Controlling costs

A further reason for specifying in detail the appearance, functions and quality of a product is that this enables a business to estimate the likely costs to be involved in its supply. This allows the business to control its costs and increase its chances of making a profit. For example, a baker making meat pies may use cheap cuts of meat to ensure that the costs of production do not exceed the price at which the pies can be sold.

Knowledge summary

- A product's characteristics comprise what it looks like and what it does. This is often referred to as appearance and function.

- Appearance is an important characteristic for many groups of products (clothing, footwear, furniture) and crucial for others such as paintings and porcelain.

- A product with more functions than rival products is generally desirable, but consumers will also want to know how well it carries out those functions (its quality).

- Businesses are concerned about making their product characteristics distinctive, because this allows them to base their marketing around a USP.

quick **questions**

1 Explain why appearance is an important element of the product characteristics of fashion clothes, but not so important for a wheelbarrow.

2 What is the difference between a product's range of functions and its quality?

3 How might giving careful attention to a product's characteristics help a business to control its costs?

data **interpretation**
The iPod

Apple's iPod made the digital music player a very desirable, even sexy, product. The company has benefited hugely. By the end of 2004 Apple had sold more than 10 million iPods (they were launched in 2001), and had enjoyed significant increases in profits as a consequence.

With an award-winning design and a high price, iPods were launched using a global marketing campaign. Consumers were desperate to buy them.

The iTunes music download store is also the market leader, and although it now faces strong competition from the likes of MSN and Napster, this has helped to boost the Apple brand.

However, Apple has not been content to rest on its success and allow competitors to catch up. The latest iPod model is able to store more music and can store and display colour photos. This new iPod is being sold at a higher price.

A What are the key product characteristics of the Apple iPod?

B Examine the benefits that Apple has received as a result of producing a product with such distinctive characteristics.

C What is more important in your view: the product's appearance or its functions? Justify your answer.

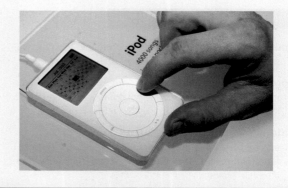

Setting the scene: Marriott Hotels

Marriott Hotels is a chain of franchised hotels previously owned and managed by the Whitbread group. Whitbread sold the hotels back to Marriott International in 2005. Marriott Hotels is the company's premier brand. It has considerable customer loyalty from guests throughout the UK and overseas.

UK & Ireland

| Find & Reserve | Specials & Packages | Destinations | Meetings & Events | Marriott Rewards |

Liverpool Marriott Hotel City Centre Home
View All Photos
Guest Rooms in Detail
Hotel Specials & Packages
About This Hotel ⊞
Area Information
Maps & Transportation ⊞
Plan Events & Meetings ⊞
Use Marriott Rewards Points
Printable Hotel Fact Sheet

Liverpool Marriott Hotel City Centre

Marriott Hotels and Resorts is the company's flagship brand trusted by guests the world over to enhance their travel or meeting experience with knowledgeable service, genuine care and gracious attention to detail. Our thoughtfully designed hotels feature spacious and comfortably appointed guest rooms; pools and fitness centres; superb restaurants and room service; and for the business traveller looking to enhance productivity, guest rooms with convenience and functionality, business centres, and Concierge and Executive Levels.

Source: http://marriott.co.uk/

The hotels boast a wide range of facilities. The Marriott Hotel in Liverpool, for example, has a bar, two restaurants, a health club with swimming pool, a whirlpool, a sauna and a fitness room. It also has seven conference rooms, parking facilities and a baby-sitting service. The hotel offers "deluxe accommodation". Each room has a bathroom, telephone, voice mail, data port, radio, television, mini-bar, hair dryer, trouser press, air conditioning and work desk with lamp.

Marriott aims to supply a product that is characterised by quality. This is achieved by a combination of high-quality service and using materials (for example, in meals) which are also of the highest quality.

Imagine you are about to stay the night in a relatively cheap hotel. What differences might there be between this hotel and a Marriott hotel?

KEY TERMS

Inputs are the resources – materials, components and labour services – that are used to supply goods and services.

A **product's characteristics** comprise its appearance and its function – in other words, what it looks like and what it does.

Materials are physical inputs used in supplying goods and services. Examples include the ingredients in a restaurant meal or the components used to manufacture a mobile phone.

Factors that determine product characteristics

A product's characteristics – the way that it looks and the ways in which it satisfies consumers' needs – are determined by several factors. However, these factors can be categorised into two groups.

■ **Quality of materials**. If a product is made using high-quality materials, it is more likely to exhibit luxury characteristics.

- **Quality of service**. Some products are characterised by high-quality service that meets the varying needs of individual consumers. This contrasts with a standard service that does not cater for differences in customers' needs.

1 Quality of materials

A wide range of materials can be used in making goods or supplying a service. Nissan and Café Rouge give diverse examples of the types of materials used by businesses.

- Nissan, the car manufacturer, uses glass for windscreens and other windows, rubber tyres, fabric to make seats, and steel for the body shell of its cars. It also buys oil products as lubricants and fuel.

- Café Rouge operates 80 restaurants throughout the UK. The company buys beers, wines and spirits to stock in its bars as well as a wide range of teas and coffees. In addition, as Café Rouge has an extensive menu, the company purchases a wide range of foodstuffs from suppliers.

stopand**think**

The British Airways fleet flies on routes throughout the world. Make a list of the materials that this company uses to supply its service.

The quality of materials used in supplying a product is an important factor in shaping a product's characteristics and therefore consumers' perceptions of the product.

Häagen Dazs is the premier maker of luxury ice cream in the world. Its products are superior to many standard ice creams because the company uses high-quality ingredients. The ice cream is creamier than many rival brands because a high proportion of fresh cream is used in its manufacture. The company also ensures less air enters the product to achieve a smoother taste. The quality of the product is maintained by using interesting flavourings such as Bailey's Irish Cream and Belgian chocolate fudge.

2 Quality of service

All businesses offer some form of service as part of the product that they supply to consumers. This is true of businesses supplying manufactured goods, as well as those that only supply services. By meeting (or exceeding) customers' expectations, businesses can improve their image and establish a reputation for supplying products with high-quality characteristics. The features of quality service include:

- making sure the customer is safe

- delivering good customer service

- improving the quality of the product

- making sure the customer is not kept waiting

- demonstrating good after-sales care.

To see how businesses offer service in practice, let's look at some real examples. Dell Computers is a manufacturer and online retailer of computers. It supplies computers tailor-made to match customers' precise requirements, and this means that the quality of components and materials is vital in creating its product characteristics.

Dell also offers a variety of services as part of its provision to customers. The company can provide installation services to make sure computers are set up correctly. It also offers online courses, insurance against theft or accidental damage, and after-sales support including repairs.

It is this combination of materials and components together with a range of services that is important in shaping and determining Dell's reputation, the distinct characteristics of its products and the company's competitiveness.

stopand**th**i

Why might Häagen Dazs have created a brand image that is characterised by its reputation for luxury?

The quality of service can shape a product's characteristics and how it is rated by buyers. Consider these two contrasting examples of quality of service when buying clothes.

A bespoke tailor

Tony Lutwyche is a bespoke tailor, which means he makes individual clothes to order for each customer. He is based in Soho in London and works with a team of expert tailors dedicated to providing customers with high-quality service and attention to detail.

Customers can visit the workshop to choose a design and the material and to be measured for their clothes. Alternatively, Tony offers a home visiting service for customers who live within London.

It is measure of Tony Lutwyche's success that 85 per cent of his customers return to order more suits.

A high street retailer

Next plc sells a range of men's suits online and through its high street shops. The company has a good reputation for the quality of its clothing. However, the quality of the service provided by the company arguably does not match the quality of the material used in its clothes.

A linen suit costs around £100 but it only comes in a selection of standard sizes. This means that the suit may not be a perfect fit for many potential purchasers. Although Next may use the same type and quality of material as Tony Lutwyche, the ability to provide a made-to-measure garment for each customer means that the bespoke tailor provides a better-quality service, and this helps to define the product's characteristic.

Knowledge summary

- A product's characteristics are shaped by two major factors: the quality of materials used and the quality of service provided.

- Manufacturers as well as firms that solely provide services need to pay attention to the quality of their service inputs as this will impact on their products' characteristics.

- The quality of materials used in production helps to shape a product's characteristics.

quick**questions**

1 Rolls Royce cars are highly regarded. What inputs have created this reputation?

2 In what way might the quality of service help to determine the product characteristics of McDonald's food?

3 Why don't all businesses aim to create products that are appealing in appearance and have high-quality functions?

data**interpretation**
Paul's Burgers

Paul Hills sells burgers, sausages, pizzas and chips. He operates his business from a van, which he drives to the villages near where he lives. Paul's business is very popular with lorry drivers who pass through on their way to the Channel Tunnel.

Paul sets low prices. He chats with customers while cooking meals and often offers free refills of tea or coffee to encourage people to come again. Paul's food is cheap and cheerful: he doesn't buy the most expensive ingredients, but customers do not complain.

A What part might quality of service play in Paul's business?

B Discuss the ways in which Paul might improve his customers' perceptions of his products.

C Do you think it is possible for Paul to provide "best value" and "best quality"? Justify your opinion.

Setting the scene: the Sudan 1 scare

Sudan 1 is a red dye which is commonly used to colour solvents, oils, waxes, petrol, and shoe and food polishes. There is some evidence to show that Sudan 1 can increase the risk of cancers if consumed in sufficient quantities, and it has been banned from use in foodstuffs throughout Europe since July 2003.

The 2005 Sudan 1 scare began when the dye was found in a chilli powder which was used by Premier Foods to make Worcester sauce. The sauce was then added to 350 different foodstuffs, including soups, sauces and ready meals. Many of these were ready meals sold by supermarkets.

The UK Food Standards Agency identified 474 products that contained the contaminated Worcester sauce. The affected foodstuffs were removed from sale almost immediately. This led to the biggest food recall ever to take place in the UK, at an estimated cost of £100 million.

Premier Foods, the company at the heart of the Sudan 1 scandal, blamed its supplier for the crisis because it had allegedly certified that the chilli powder was free of Sudan 1. Since the ban on the use of Sudan 1 in foodstuffs, importers must have certificates to show that chilli powder has been tested and found to be free from Sudan 1.

Premier Foods revealed that its profits were not affected by the controversy. The Sudan 1 scare caused a lot of work and worry for the company, but the financial implications were limited because it had taken out insurance to cover this type of situation.

Safety legislation

Businesses must work within existing legislation – the laws passed by Parliament and regulations enacted by the European Union. New and existing products have to conform with safety laws. These are designed to protect all people involved in the manufacture, distribution, delivery and consumption of products.

Consumers are highly vulnerable to goods or services that are unsafe, and residents living near to businesses can also be harmed by unsafe products and processes. Employees can be at risk from dangerous production processes. Firms must therefore ensure that:

■ their goods and services are not harmful to consumers – this applies both to products they manufacture and deliver and to products made by other businesses which they sell

■ production processes are not harmful – this means protecting both their own employees as well as

stop and think

Kingswood Baby Products pleaded guilty in 2004 to selling a pushchair that failed to comply with British safety standards. The pushchair was found to have problems with stability and the effectiveness of its brakes. The company was fined £9,500. Apart from the fine, why might this episode have been very damaging for Kingswood Baby Products?

any other people that may be involved (directly or indirectly) in bringing the product to customers.

There are many safety regulations which govern the ways in which businesses can produce and supply products. In this topic, we look at some of the main Acts of Parliament that cover safety.

1 Health and Safety at Work Act 1974

The Health and Safety at Work Act focuses mainly on protecting employees at work and during the production process. It makes it a legal obligation for employers "to safeguard all their employees' health, safety and welfare at work". Clearly a business would be unable to supply any product if its production processes may cause harm to employees.

The Act covers a range of business activities. It requires employers to:

- install and maintain safety equipment and provide safety clothing
- maintain workplaces at reasonable temperatures
- give employees sufficient breaks during the working day
- provide protection against dangerous substances.

The Act also places some responsibility on employees. It requires employees to follow all health and safety procedures and to take care of their own and others' safety.

Businesses are required to protect the health and safety of their employees "as far as it is reasonably practicable". This means that a business must provide protection appropriate to the risks. A chemical manufacturer, for example, would be expected to provide considerable protection for its employees because of the risk of contamination and the dangers inherent in chemical processing.

The Health and Safety Executive (HSE) oversees the operation of the Act and carries out inspections of business premises. The HSE also carries out detailed and thorough investigations following any serious workplace accident, particularly those which result in bad injuries or death.

2 Food Safety Act 1990

The Food Safety Act is a wide-ranging law that makes it illegal to sell food which has been contaminated or adulterated, or is unfit for human consumption, or is labelled or advertised in a way that misleads the customer. The Act aims to ensure that any food produced for sale is safe to eat, of high quality and not misleadingly presented. The Act, therefore, influences and constrains the characteristics of food products.

The Food Safety Act 1990 revised, strengthened and extended the Food Act 1984 which, with the Food and Drug Act 1955, enforced the hygienic preparation and sale of food and also set guidelines for labelling foodstuffs. However, the 1990 Act not only covers food but also brings farmers and growers within legislation for the first time. It also covers articles which come into contact with food, such as wrappings and factory machinery.

Other key stipulations of the Food Safety Act 1990 are that:

- premises selling food must register with the local authority
- training must be provided to all staff who handle food.

Local authority enforcement officers who find a business in breach of the Act can issue improvement notices or, in certain cases, order the business to cease trading.

stop and think

Workers in the chemical industry are subject to many dangers. To what risks might employees in retailing and the hotel industry be subject?

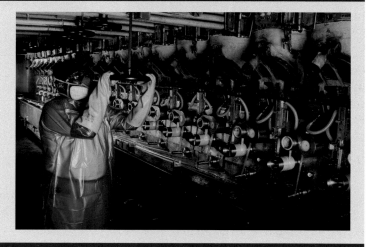

3 Consumer Protection Act 1987

The Consumer Protection Act was introduced to bring the UK into line with other European Union countries. The Act made it a criminal offence for a business to supply unsafe goods. Businesses became liable under the Act for any damages that defective products may cause. Consumers can sue businesses for an unlimited amount if a product causes personal injury or damage to personal property.

In 2005 Christine Peckham from Lancashire started a legal action to sue the pharmaceutical company Merck, Sharpe and Dohme. She alleged that one of the company's drugs that she had been taking caused her to become ill and, as a result, she suffered two strokes. Mrs Peckham is seeking "a six-figure sum" as compensation.

The damage to consumers does not have to be physical. In 2005 the budget airline Ryanair was fined £24,000 for six breaches of the Consumer Protection Act. The company was found guilty of misleading customers about the prices that they would have to pay for flights.

Failure to comply

Businesses have to be aware of laws that can affect their operations. Ignorance of the law is not an acceptable defence. If a business launching a new product that infringes the law in some respect, it can suffer two adverse consequences.

First, it can be prosecuted or sued. Fines and damages can be substantial. This could have a huge impact on a business as it attempts to launch a new product. It may impact on the firm's cash flow – the business may find that it is short of cash – and the profitability of the project is bound to be reduced.

Second, and as important, its image can be damaged. When a new product is launched, businesses seek positive publicity to help to boost sales. Receiving media coverage for breaking laws – and possibly posing a threat to consumer or employee safety – is unlikely to enhance a business's reputation or its sales.

Knowledge summary

- A product's characteristics are constrained by laws relating to the safety of employees and consumers.

- The Health and Safety at Work Act 1974 is designed to protect employees in the workplace.

- Consumer protection legislation makes businesses liable for any damage suffered by the users of their products.

- Business can suffer financial penalties as well as damage to their public image for infringing safety laws.

1 How might the Health and Safety at Work Act help to ensure that the paints produced by a chemical manufacturer are safe for consumers?

2 Why should manufacturers pay attention to product labelling and packaging as well as the products themselves when considering safety issues?

3 Peter Masters is about to open a café. How does the Food Safety Act 1990 affect his business?

data**interpretation**
AB Scaffolding Ltd

In 2004 Hugh Morris and Dave Childs launched AB Scaffolding. The business provides scaffolding for people repairing and building houses. Hugh and Dave had many years in the trade and knew that it was a competitive market in which price is an important factor.

The duo intended to provide a low-price service and to meet customers' needs by assembling and dismantling scaffolding quickly. In this way, they hoped to win customers and to retain their loyalty.

Five employees were taken on in the first few months and, after some brief training, were sent out on jobs across London. AB Scaffolding began to win contracts from rival firms. The owner of one of the more established scaffolding businesses commented that the new company was cutting corners and likely to face trouble soon.

A Why is quality of service important in winning customers in the scaffolding business?

B What dangers might AB Scaffolding's business pose to its employees?

C Assess the extent to which relevant safety legislation might affect the characteristics of AB Scaffolding's product.

Topic 4 Physical and human resources

Setting the scene: Zopa – online loans exchange

Zopa Limited was launched in March 2005. It is a lending and borrowing exchange – a new type of bank, in other words. It trades through a website designed to bring together people who want to borrow money with people who want to lend it. Zopa puts the two parties in contact for a fee equal to 1 per cent of any loan that is finally agreed.

Zopa launched with just two offices, one in London and one in the West Midlands. Trading online means that the company does not need large amounts of physical resources. This is one reason why Zopa charges low fees.

Lenders are able to set their own rates of interest – possibly set according to how risky the loan seems to be – and can choose whether to take on any particular borrower. Lenders do not face a high degree of risk because Zopa stipulates that any single lender makes loans to at least 50 borrowers and does not make any single loan for more than £200.

Zopa was founded by the creators of online bank Egg and has a management team, led by Richard Duvall, that is experienced in online banking. It is financed by the venture capital company that backed eBay in its early days.

Zopa is a term taken from business theory. It stands for zone of possible agreement. This is the overlap between one person's bottom line – the lowest price they're prepared to receive for something – and another person's top line – the most they're prepared to give for something. If there is no Zopa, there is no deal.

Source: adapted from www.zopa.com

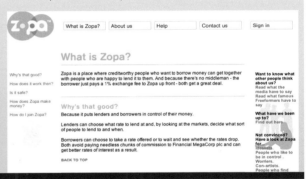

Business resources

In Unit 3 (see Topic 4, page 122), we looked at resource management issues. As Figure 6.1 shows, all businesses require resources to be able to trade and serve their customers.

Manufacturers need materials and physical resources such as factories, machinery and vehicles to produce and deliver their products. Businesses supplying services need resources such as offices, shops, computers and stationery. Every business also needs

two other types of resource: people and money. Without human resources to manufacture goods or to supply services, it is impossible for a business to trade. Without financial resources, it would be impossible to establish the business in the first place and to ensure that sufficient cash is available for its day-to-day operations.

When developing and launching a new product, a business's requirements for resources may change. This topic considers the particular resource needs that may accompany the development of a new product.

KEY TERMS

Resources are the human and non-human assets used in production. These include raw materials, fuel, factories and offices as well as the contribution of the workforce.

Human resources are the people who work within an organisation, from shop floor employees to senior managers and directors.

Physical resources are tangible items used in production such as buildings and vehicles.

Components are manufactured parts used in the production process.

Raw materials are items bought by a business in a relatively unprocessed state. Flour and sugar beet, for examples, are raw materials used in the food processing industry.

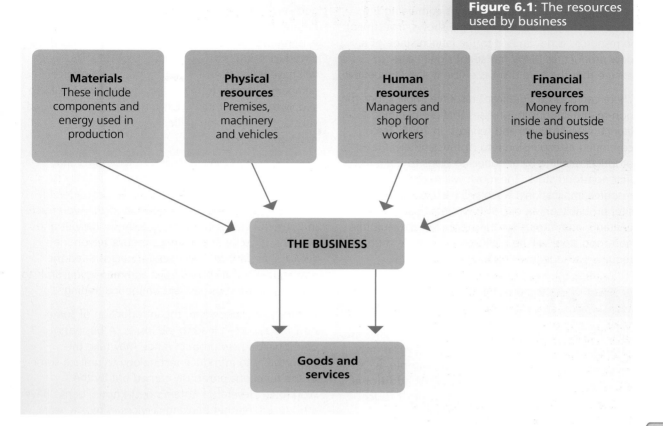

Figure 6.1: The resources used by business

Materials	Physical resources	Human resources	Financial resources
These include components and energy used in production	Premises, machinery and vehicles	Managers and shop floor workers	Money from inside and outside the business

THE BUSINESS

Goods and services

stop and think

Make a list of the resources that Zopa (see opposite) would have needed before it started trading in March 2005.

1 Raw materials and components

When businesses develop new products, they may require additional raw materials and components. When Cadbury launched Dairy Milk Bubbly, it could simply use its existing range of raw materials to manufacture the new chocolate bar. However, when Microsoft developed its new Xbox games console, the Xbox 360, the company needed to source a range of new components and materials for use in production.

The Xbox 360 contains a new chip with a vast amount of built-in memory and a revolutionary liquid cooling system (as opposed to a fan). These components are new and, even within an enormous company like Microsoft, posed a set of problems for managers. It needed substantial research to produce suitable components, and then significant time and effort in testing to confirm that they would function effectively and reliably within the new product.

This Xbox example illustrates how any new product which requires different materials and components can use up valuable resources, placing demands on staff time as well as on financial resources.

2 Physical resources

New products inevitably create a demand for physical resources. This demand may be greater for manufacturing rather than service industries. If, for example, a car manufacturer decides to produce a new model, it is likely that either an existing factory will have to be substantially adapted to make the new model or a new factory will need to be built.

If the manufacturer decides on the first option – of redeveloping, and possibly updating, the production line to enable the new car to be produced – it will incur substantial expenditure on new production line equipment as well as having the costs of remodelling the factory layout.

However, it is not uncommon for manufacturers to decide to build brand new factories to produce a new product range. By the end of 2006 BMW will have invested £1,280 million in its Oxford plant where it first started producing the new Mini in 2001. The company has responded to booming demand for its new car by tearing down old factories on the site and replacing them with new buildings containing the latest technology. As this example shows, investment in resources is not limited to the launch stage of a new product, as BMW has spent significantly to ensure that the Mini plant is efficient and competitive.

There can also be significant resource implications for non-manufacturing businesses that are planning to launch new products and services. In 2005, Tesco continued its expansion into clothes and electrical products retailing by announcing plans to open its first non-food store. The move will have significant resource implications. Tesco will require an accessible site, probably on an out-of-town retail park, a modern building, and fittings for the store. If successful, this non-food store will be replicated across the country, requiring a huge investment by the company.

stopand**think**

In 2005 easyJet, the budget airline, announced that it was introducing flights on several new European routes including, for example, a service from Belfast to Rome. What additional resources might easyJet require to introduce these new flights?

3 Human resources

A business's human resources are all the people who work for the organisation, including office staff, operational and shop floor employees, supervisors and managers. The human resource impact of developing and launching a new product will depend upon the nature of the product. A minor expansion of the existing product range, such as Cadbury's decision to introduce a white chocolate version of its Flake bar, will have little effect on the company's workforce. The company already has staff with the necessary skills to supply this new product. Only if the product achieved substantial sales might it become necessary to recruit additional employees.

However, the introduction of a new product that requires new skills in the workforce, or is likely to achieve high levels of sales, will have a considerable impact on the size and composition of the workforce. In 2005 the easyGroup (best known for easyJet and easyCar) launched its cut-price mobile telephone service, easyMobile. This decision necessitated the appointment of technical sales and managerial staff to enable the new business to commence trading.

Contrary to expectation, the introduction of some new products can lead to job losses. A business developing a new product range may take the opportunity to introduce technology to replace some of the functions previously carried out by the workforce. Several of Britain's best-known banks have introduced internet banking services in recent years. As many customers have preferred to use the online banking service, this development has, over time, enabled the banks to reduce their branch networks and to cut jobs. New technology does not always lead to job losses, and you might consider ways in which the introduction of new technology into a business that is launching a new product can create new jobs.

stopand**think**

This robot is part of the production facility at a factory in Sweden. By using the robot, the factory estimates it can cut production costs by 75 per cent. What are the human resources implications – the number of staff employed and their skill levels – that arise from the business installing this robot?

Knowledge summary

■ Businesses combine physical resources, materials and components, human resources and financial resources as part of the production process.

■ New products may require a firm to source new components and materials.

■ A new product usually creates demand for additional physical resources, and can require ongoing investment in physical infrastructure and technology.

■ Human resources are a vital asset for many businesses, although not all product launches boost employment.

quick**questions**

1 Explain, with the aid of examples, why businesses supplying services might need to purchase materials and components.

2 A restaurant has decided to launch a new range of "healthy eating" meals. Assuming the launch is successful, what might be the resource implications for the business?

3 What are the resource implications for the BBC of a decision to produce a television adaptation of a Victorian novel?

data**interpretation**
SpeedDater: a successful new business

Speed dating is designed for single young people. It offers participants the opportunity to meet up to 30 potential partners in a single evening. Speed dating allows two people the chance to chat briefly before each moves on to meet someone else. If a couple "click", they can exchange details and meet up later.

SpeedDater was founded by Simon Prockter and Ben Tisdall in 2002. Simon had tried internet dating. After experiencing a couple of blind dates going wrong, he heard about speed dating. Simon loved the concept, and SpeedDater was launched to offer speed dating in a non-pressurised environment to the kind of people who probably wouldn't consider contacting a dating agency.

SpeedDater uses upmarket bars to host events for professional single people. By the end of 2004 SpeedDater was running more events in more cities than any other company, and had quickly become Europe's leading speed dating company and a commercial success. SpeedDater charges between £20 and £25 to each person attending one of its events. There are more than 30,000 people registered with the company.

More information can be found at www.speeddater.co.uk.

A Describe the resources that Simon Prockter and Ben Tisdall might have needed before starting their new business.

B Explain why human resources might be very important for the company.

C SpeedDater was able to expand quickly because it needed relatively few resources. Do you agree with this statement? Justify your view.

Topic 5 | Financial resources

Setting the scene: Microsoft's first ever dividend

Microsoft is one of the world's largest companies. It employs 57,000 people in sites scattered across the world. In the 2004/5 financial year, it expected sales revenue to be nearly £20,000 million and profits to be in the region of £6,000 million.

Most companies use their profits in two ways: they retain a proportion of profits within the business and they pay the balance to shareholders. These payments are called dividends. Yet despite Microsoft's enormous wealth, for years the company did not pay a dividend and pass any of its profits onto its shareholders.

Microsoft preferred to keep its profits within the business and to invest them in developing new software and new products such as the Xbox. However, the company overestimated how much money would be needed for its investment plans. It steadily accumulated a huge reserve of cash as its retained profits amounted to more than it invested in new products.

By 2004 Microsoft's cash holdings were about £30,000 million. At this point, Microsoft decided to distribute some of these cash reserves to its shareholders. In December 2004, Microsoft's shareholders received a dividend of $3 per share (about £1.60) and the company announced plans to distribute more of its cash mountain to shareholders over the next four years.

Bill Gates, the company's founder and current chairman, hoped to achieve high rates of growth by reinvesting the company's profits in new products. This proved to be a successful strategy and even in 2004, when dividends were paid to shareholders, the company's growth rate was over 6 per cent.

Sources of finance

There are several sources of finance available to a business, but essentially they can be divided into two broad categories:

■ internal sources of finance – funds that are already available within the business

■ external sources of finance – funds supplied by individuals, organisations and financial institutions outside the business.

We looked at finance in detail in Unit 3, Topic 2 (see pages 114–17). In this topic, we consider the financial sources available to businesses contemplating developing a new product.

Internal sources

The major internal sources of finance are retained profits which can be reinvested in the business, and the working capital that comes from the owner's own funds or from initial share capital.

1 Retained profits

Retained profits are that part of a business's profits that managers decide to keep within the business for investment purposes. Profits are a significant source of finance for new product development. In 2005 Virgin Atlantic Ltd announced profits of £68 million, the highest figure it had achieved since 1999. At the

KEY TERMS

Resources are the human and non-human assets used in production. These include raw materials, fuel, factories and offices as well as the contribution of the workforce.

Financial resources are the funds available to a business to establish itself and to carry out its commercial activities.

An **internal source of finance** is one that exists within the business such as retained profits.

An **external source of finance** is supplied by individuals and organisations outside the business.

Capital is money invested into a business in the form of shares or loans.

same time the company confirmed that it will be operating new routes (from the UK to Jamaica and Dubai) from 2006. The company is in a position to fund some of the costs of the new routes, such as aircraft and staff, by reinvesting some of its profits.

Reinvested profits are also used by small businesses for growth and investment. Some more risky small businesses have difficulties raising finance from external sources and must use past profits to fund new goods and services. In 1993 Tom Bloxham founded Urban Splash, a company which redevelops derelict urban property to a high level of design. Tom Bloxham has consistently funded new projects by reinvesting profits. He argues that this has allowed him to keep control of the company as it has grown. Its turnover was £25 million in 2005.

There are other benefits from funding new product development through reinvested profits. There are some tax breaks – the first £10,000 of profits reinvested back into a business are exempt from corporation tax (the tax companies pay on profits). By using profits for investment in new products, rather than taking out loans, a business also avoids the tricky position where it has to pay interest on loans before the new product generates an inflow of cash.

stop and think

The cosmetics manufacturer, L'Oreal, uses some of its profits to finance the development of new products aimed at Asian and Hispanic women. Why do you think that the company chooses to finance the new products in this way? What other sources of finance might the company use to develop these new products?

2 Owner's funds

Owner's funds is simply capital put into a business by its owners. In the case of sole traders or partnerships, this is in effect a loan to the business on which interest is not charged. With private and public limited companies, owners invest money in return for shares – this is called share or equity capital.

Many small businesses finance the development of new products through the use of their own money. In 2002 Thea Vandeputte took out a loan against the value of her flat in London. She rented the flat out to pay the mortgage, and used the money she had raised to open a children's clothes shop in Ibiza. Thea had no clear business plan and would have had difficulty in attracting finance from external sources.

Some companies finance product development through their initial working capital. However, larger businesses also have the option of raising funds for product development through new share issues – though this, in effect, is an external source of finance as the company is inviting other people to invest in return for a stake in the business. Shed Productions, the television production company which makes *Footballers Wives*, has announced that it is to sell shares in the company by listing on the Alternative Investment Market, a subsidiary of the London Stock Exchange. It wants to raise capital to allow it to "attract and retain the best creative talent" with the aim of expanding its range of programmes. Selling shares is an important source of funds for businesses that seek to grow organically through new product development. It is also a means of raising large sums for an expensive programme of product development.

External sources

When other businesses or financial institutions provide capital to a business, this is termed an external source of finance.

1 Leasing

Leasing is a means to acquire assets. It allows a business to rent (or lease) an asset (for example, a vehicle or a photocopier) rather than actually buying it. The ownership of the asset remains with the finance company, and the rent is sufficient to provide the finance company with a level of profit.

Airbus, the European aircraft manufacturer, has an order for A380s (its latest aircraft) from International Lease Finance. This company will lease the aircraft to airlines, allowing them to operate on new routes without having to invest huge amounts on aircraft. In the airline industry leasing is an important element in financing new product development.

Smaller businesses often lease assets such as cars and photocopiers rather than purchasing them outright because this avoids the need for a large outlay of capital. This would, for example, be an appropriate source of finance for a small estate agent considering opening new offices.

stop and think

Consider the arguments for and against using leasing as a means of financing new product development for airlines such as Qantas.

2 Hire purchase

Hire purchase is a credit agreement enabling a business to purchase an asset by putting down a proportion of the asset's price as a deposit and paying the remainder in instalments over an agreed period of time. In any hire purchase arrangement, the purchaser only owns the asset when the final instalment is paid.

The benefits of hire purchase for new product development are similar to those of leasing. Assets can be acquired without a large outflow of capital, and this can improve the cash position of the business, possibly at a time when cash is scarce due to the expenses of launching a new product.

3 Bank loans

It is common for businesses to raise loans from banks when planning to introduce new goods and services. The financial institution advances a set figure and the business makes repayments over an agreed period of time. The interest rates charged on bank loans can either be fixed or variable. Some businesses prefer fixed rates because they find it easier to plan and manage the business's finances with a fixed interest payment and loan repayment schedule.

stopandthink

Why might an entrepreneur launching a new business prefer to negotiate a fixed rate of interest on a loan?

Bank loans are not an option for some entrepreneurs, as the banks may consider the new business venture to be too risky. Some small businesses seeking to expand through product development may not meet all the lending criteria of high street banks. However, some banks, such as the Bank of Scotland, do claim to investigate each loan application on its merits.

The Small Firms Loan Guarantee scheme has made it easier for small businesses to raise a loan for expansion or new product development. The scheme guarantees loans from the banks and other financial institutions for small firms that have viable business proposals but which have failed to get a loan from a bank. Loans are available for periods of between two and ten years on sums from £5,000 to £250,000. The scheme guarantees 75 per cent of the loan. In return for the guarantee, the borrower pays the Department of Trade and Industry a premium of 2 per cent a year on the outstanding amount of the loan.

4 Venture capital

There are a number of organisations in the UK that specialise in providing venture capital to small and medium-sized firms. Since 1983, the UK venture capital industry has invested around £40 billion in over 20,000 companies. Venture finance is a mix of direct loans, which must in time be repaid, and share capital. Venture capitalists often provide relatively small amounts of finance, but because they will invest in risky projects, this source of finance can be important for more unusual new products.

Three Cambridge graduates started Innocent Drinks, a company selling fruit smoothies, in 2000. By 2005 the company was selling over 80,000 drinks a day in a wide range of outlets including Sainsbury's, Waitrose and Boots. However, without a £250,000 loan from an entrepreneur when the company first launched its fruit drinks, the enterprise would have been unlikely to succeed, as the founders of the company had little capital. Maurice Pinto, a wealthy US businessman, decided to back the project at a vital time.

5 Government grants

Businesses in designated areas of the UK can benefit from several schemes offered by the government or by agencies on its behalf.

Selective Finance for Investment

Selective Finance for Investment normally takes the form of a grant or occasionally a loan. In each case the amount offered will be the minimum necessary for the proposed project to go ahead. Applications must be for at least £10,000. Scotland, Northern Ireland and Wales have slightly different systems.

The scheme is ideal for businesses launching a new product, as bids for funding are expected to include expenditure on assets such as buildings and machinery. However, one drawback is that the project will be expected to create skilled jobs. This may represent a substantial hurdle for some ambitious businesses.

Business start-up scheme

This scheme provides training and financial assistance to those who were previously unemployed and who wish to start businesses. These schemes vary from area to area, but applicants are normally expected to make a substantial investment into their business and, in return, receive a weekly wage and some support in running their business. This source of finance is limited to people launching small businesses, but it is an important source in that many businesses at this stage often lack access to other financial resources.

Knowledge summary

■ Businesses can use both external and internal sources of finance to raise capital and fund product development.

■ Internal sources of finance are especially important for larger businesses planning new product development.

■ External sources of finance are not always readily available to small businesses. However, the government has set up schemes to give smaller firms greater access to external finance.

quick questions

1 What are the benefits to a small business of using internal sources of finance to develop a new product?

2 Why might an established business choose to use external sources of finance to provide the capital for a large investment project?

3 Katie Shilling is about to start a business repairing and installing computers for local people and businesses. She has saved £10,000 but needs another £20,000 to start her business. Identify and describe two sources of finance that she might use to raise the outstanding £20,000.

data interpretation

AmpleBosom

Sally Robinson had managed a successful bed and breakfast and holiday cottage business for some years. In 1999 she decided to branch out into the underwear world.

The result is AmpleBosom – a business which sells larger-size bras. The idea was first put into Sally's mind by an employee desperate to find good underwear for her wedding day, but unable to do so.

The business – launched from a barn on her Yorkshire farm with an £80,000 bank loan – originally offered only larger-size bras, but it now sells a wide range of underwear and swimwear in all sizes.

Sally is proud of her business and its success, but admits to facing problems along the way. One of the biggest difficulties, she says, has been paying interest charges on the bank loan.

Sources: www.amplebosom.com and news.bbc.co.uk, 28 June 2004

A Outline two other sources of finance that Sally might have used to start AmpleBosom.

B What were the possible advantages and disadvantages of Sally taking out an £80,000 bank loan to start the business?

C Do you think that it is always easier for an existing rather than a new business to raise finance? Justify your answer fully.

Topic 6 | Deciding on the right mix of resources

In March 2005 Simon Fuller sold his 19 Entertainment company to an American entrepreneur, Robert Sillerman, for an estimated £81.5 million. Sillerman will absorb 19 Entertainment into his company, which is called CFX.

Fuller is perhaps best known for creating and launching the Pop Idol television programme in 2001. This was so successful that a US version (American Idol) followed. However, his company has also played a role in the careers of many recording artists, including Madonna, U2, Craig David, Kylie Minogue and Britney Spears. It has been involved in the creation of 106 number one singles and 83 number one albums. The company also manages the Beckham brand on behalf of David and Victoria Beckham. In 2003, its sales turnover exceeded £53 million.

19 Entertainment is a business based on human resources. The company is heavily dependent upon the skills of its employees, from Simon Fuller downwards. It has attracted a unique collection of people with the expertise to integrate, develop and nurture talent and with skills in television, music publishing and recording, film, sponsorship and brand promotion.

Source: adapted from www.19.co.uk

Factors influencing the choice of resources

A business planning to develop a new product may require human, physical and financial resources. However, businesses do not use the same combinations or mix of these resources to achieve their aims. Sally Robinson, the founder of AmpleBosom (see page 265) needed significant financial resources (£80,000) to develop her business. In contrast, someone launching a window-cleaning operation would require limited financial and physical resources. This business would depend primarily on human resources.

KEY TERMS

Resources are the human and non-human assets used in production. These include raw materials, fuel, factories and offices, as well as the contribution of the workforce.

A **resources mix** is the combination of materials and human, financial and physical resources used by a business to supply its products.

Mass production takes place when a business produces relatively similar products on a large scale.

stopandthink

Ravenwood Hall Hotel is set in seven acres of grounds three miles from Bury St Edmunds in Suffolk. It has 14 bedrooms. The hotel offers guests luxurious surroundings, including a heated swimming pool and conference facilities for businesses. It has a first-class restaurant. What resources are necessary to operate this hotel?

A number of factors influence both the quantity of resources used by a business and its resources mix.

1 The complexity of the product

Businesses that supply complex products are likely to require diverse resources. The quantities of the resources required will depend upon the scale of the operation. Let's look at some contrasting examples:

- British Energy plc
- a dental practice
- a painting and decorating business.

Hinkley Point is one of British Energy's nuclear power stations. It is located on a 26 hectare site in Somerset. It employs 326 people. Building and maintenance costs have exceeded £1,000 million since 1970. Hinkley Point uses a range of resources. Is this because of the scale of the operation or the nature of Hinkley Point's product?

British Energy plc

British Energy's principal business is the nuclear generation of electricity. The largest generator of electricity in the UK, the company produces about 20 per cent of the country's electricity, employing around 5,200 staff, many of whom are highly skilled. British Energy owns and operates eight nuclear power stations in the UK. These power stations contain very sophisticated equipment to deliver high-volume electricity production. Environmental considerations are critical, and the company takes careful steps to protect the safety of employees and the public. The production process is extremely complex and it uses a large amount and a wide variety of resources.

A dental practice

Dental practices care for people's teeth. They undertake a range of activities, from providing simple advice on dental hygiene to extracting teeth and other dental surgery. Dentists provide a complex product. Dental surgeries can only operate with the right human resources. They cannot practise without fully trained and qualified dentists and dental nurses, and they need receptionists and other administrative staff. The practices must be stocked with materials such as anaesthetics and mouthwashes. Suitable premises are needed, equipped with appropriate machinery such as drills, X-ray equipment and specialist lighting. Even a small dental surgery requires this range of resources.

A painter and decorator

Painting and decorating is not a highly complicated product. The job involves preparing (inside and outside) walls, windows and doors prior to painting and/or hanging wallpaper. It is not untypical for a painting and decorating business to have only one employee. Limited physical resources are required, although a van and a ladder are essential. Decorators use materials such as paint and white spirit.

Many painters and decorators use a limited range of resources. Name three other types of business that may use relatively few resources.

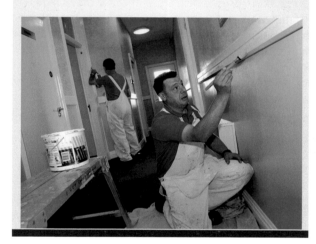

2 Capital-intensive and labour-intensive products

Some products can only be supplied by using an extensive array of machinery and production equipment. For example, even a relatively small car repair and maintenance business will use a wide range of tools, electronic equipment for testing engines and exhaust emissions and hydraulic ramps for lifting cars. Skilled labour and materials are a vital part of the mix of resources, but repairing motor vehicles uses a disproportionate amount of machinery.

Other businesses require an entirely different mix of resources. This can be because the product is labour intensive. House Angels is a domestic and commercial cleaning company. It undertakes house and carpet cleaning as well as other domestic services such as washing and ironing clothes. The business relies heavily upon its human resources and uses relatively few other resources.

stop and **thin**

What materials and physical resources would House Angels require? Would it be possible to establish a cleaning business such as House Angels with relatively limited financial resources? Explain your answer.

Houseangels.me.uk
Domestic & Commercial Cleaning

3 The scale of operations

Some businesses require considerable resources because they supply products in large quantities. This may not mean that they require diverse resources, just larger amounts of the same resources.

Some businesses remain small because they sell to a limited market. A corner shop is a good example of a small business – its market is limited geographically and so the resources it employs are limited. In contrast, supermarkets such as Tesco operate in a global market and demand far more resources.

Tesco sells food, clothing and electrical items in stores across the UK. It also has shops in many other countries including China, Taiwan, Poland and the Czech Republic. Its resource needs are much greater than a corner shop partly because of this global scale. Tesco buys enormous quantities of fresh, frozen and tinned food every day. However, its scale of operation also means that it requires additional human resources (a large workforce) as well as far more physical resources (delivery lorries, superstores, smaller Metro stores, and thousands of fridges and freezers) and financial resources.

stop and **think**

What human resources might Tesco use that a corner shop would not? You should think about different types of employees, rather than numbers. What financial resources is Tesco able to access that would not be available to a corner shop?

4 Technology

Advances in technology have changed the ways in which many businesses operate. For example, technology allows some businesses to use mass production techniques and alter their resources mix. In

general, technology enables businesses to use different mixes of resources.

The way that books are sold in the UK provides a clear example of the impact of technology on the resource mix. Traditionally books were sold in bookshops – and many still are. Some bookshops are independently owned; others are part of national chains such as Waterstones. The major resources used in this type of business are high street premises, offering consumers ready access. The shops hold a large stock of books.

stop and **think**

Amazon's fulfilment centre in Milton Keynes supplies books to consumers throughout the UK. How might Amazon's resource mix differ from that of Waterstones?

Technology, however, is changing the way in which books are sold. One of the largest booksellers in the UK is the online retailer Amazon. The company sells books (and an increasing range of products) on the internet. Amazon has the UK's most visited retail website and has achieved rapid increases in sales. In 2004, Amazon's global sales reached £3,650 million and its profits were £310 million.

Other businesses have used technology to replace labour, thereby altering their mix of resources. This has been common in UK manufacturing businesses as they have sought to respond to intense competition from low-cost and low-wage foreign suppliers.

Knowledge summary

- Businesses use different mixes and different quantities of resources to produce and supply goods and services.

- The scale of operations affects the mix of resources and the amount used. Businesses that mass produce are more likely to use technology.

- The nature of some products forces businesses to be labour intensive; others rely heavily on machinery and equipment.

- New technology is changing the product mix in service industries as well as manufacturers.

quick**questions**

1 Why might a larger scale of production result in a more diverse mix of resources being used?

2 What are the resource mix implications of switching from labour-intensive to capital-intensive production?

3 Does an increase in the use of technology always mean that businesses will use less human resources?

data**interpretation**
EasyJet gains market share

The budget airline easyJet was founded by Stelios Haji-Ioannou in 1998. The airline keeps costs low by eliminating the unnecessary costs and frills which characterise its more traditional competitors. This is done in a number of ways.

Use of the internet to reduce distribution costs. Approximately 95 per cent of seats are sold online, making easyJet one of Europe's biggest internet retailers.

Maximising utilisation of assets. By keeping each aircraft in the air for as much time as possible (earning sales revenue), easyJet makes the most of its costly assets and significantly reduces costs.

Ticketless travel. Passengers are not issued with tickets – they receive an e-mail containing their travel details and booking reference when they book online.

No free lunch. Everybody always jokes about airline food – so why provide it. Eliminating free catering on-board reduces costs and unnecessary bureaucracy and management.

Efficient use of airports. EasyJet gains efficiencies through rapid turnaround times (30 minutes or less), and progressive landing charges agreements.

Paperless operations. EasyJet has simplified its working practices by introducing the paperless office. The management and administration of the company is undertaken entirely on IT systems.

A Does easyJet provide a product with complex or simple characteristics?

B How might easyJet's mix of resources change as the company grows?

C Is easyJet's use of resources the most important factor behind its rising sales? Justify your view.

Figure 6.2: EasyJet passenger numbers

Year	Passenger numbers (000s)
1998	1,880
1999	3,670
2000	5,996
2001	7,664
2002	11,400
2003	20,300
2004	24,300

Source: www.easyjet.com

Setting the scene: Nissan's decision

Nissan has announced that the production of the Tone, a small people carrier, will be carried out at its factory in Sunderland, starting in 2006. The decision by the company's management team has secured the jobs of 1,000 employees at the factory.

The chief executive of Nissan had threatened to produce the car overseas. He was concerned that the UK's reluctance to adopt the euro would incur extra costs for the company. Changing from one currency to another incurs transactions costs, and changes in the pound-euro exchange rate can increase the cost of components and other imported materials.

Nissan recognised that establishing a new factory overseas could be costly. There are many costs associated with setting up a car manufacturing plant. On the plus side, opening a new car plant in, say, the Czech Republic would lower wage costs. Average hourly wage rates in the Czech Republic are less than £2.50 (compared with over £10 in the UK). Other costs such as fuel and transport costs may also be lower.

However, Nissan's managers recognised that to move a factory even to a low-cost location such as the Czech Republic could result in the company paying higher costs in other areas. Nissan would face far greater costs in developing a new factory in the Czech Republic than in expanding its existing plant in Sunderland.

In the end, Nissan's board of directors decided to stay in Sunderland because, when all costs were considered, it was the cheaper option.

KEY TERMS

Fixed costs are costs that do not alter when a business alters its level of output. Examples of fixed cost include rent and rates.

Variable costs vary directly with a business's level of output.

Semi-variable costs are expenses incurred by a business that have fixed and variable elements.

Total cost is the sum of fixed and variable costs.

Direct costs can be attributed to the production of a particular product and vary directly with the level of output. Examples include the costs of raw materials.

Indirect costs cannot be allocated to the production of a particular product, but relate to the business as a whole. Indirect costs are sometimes termed overheads and include the costs of marketing and administration.

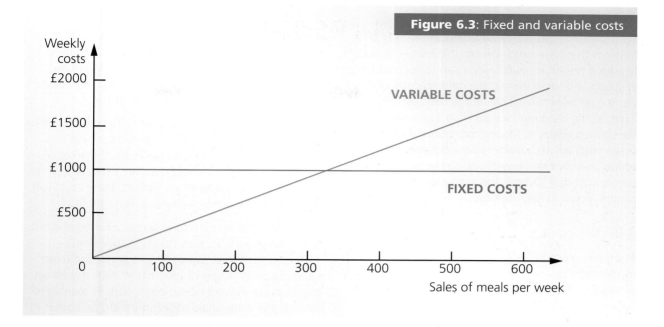

Figure 6.3: Fixed and variable costs

Weekly costs

£2000

£1500

£1000

£500

0   100   200   300   400   500   600

Sales of meals per week

VARIABLE COSTS

FIXED COSTS

Business costs

What is a cost? It is simply expenditure that a business makes as part of its trading and operations. The expenses or costs that firms incur include payments for raw materials, fuel and components as well as labour costs (in the form of wages and salaries).

When starting a new enterprise or developing a new product, businesses have to pay many costs. Some occur before the business commences trading – there are, for example, some legal costs which have to be met in setting up a company – while others have to be paid to supply the product to customers before a business is able to generate revenue through sales.

The costs faced by a business can be classified in a number of ways, though the most common way of understanding costs is to divide business expenses into fixed and variable costs.

1 Fixed costs

Fixed costs do not change when a business alters its level of output. The rent a business pays on its premises – or its business rates – do not vary if there is an increase or decrease in the level of production.

Figure 6.3 shows the costs of a restaurant serving fast food. The fixed costs line shows that, regardless of whether the restaurant sells 100 or 500 meals each week, the weekly fixed costs faced by the business will remain the same at £1,000. The reason that these costs do not alter is that the restaurant has to pay for its facilities regardless of the number of customers: it simply uses the facilities more fully when it is busier.

When a business develops a new product it may incur a number of fixed costs. Initially it will have to pay any research costs incurred in developing a new product. For a small business, this could simply be the cost of one person's time and any materials used to develop a product. A business developing a new service may have to pay market research costs – it might, for example, commission a survey to find out consumers' opinions on the proposed product. Other fixed costs could be the cost of advertising the new product and the fees charged for registering patents.

2 Variable costs

Variable costs vary directly with the level of output. If a business increases output, it will have to pay higher costs – the cost of producing each additional unit of output. If a firm reduces output, it will expect costs to fall because it will use fewer raw materials and other inputs. Examples of variable costs are expenditure on fuel, raw materials and components.

Figure 6.3 shows the variable costs for the fast-food restaurant. It faces variable costs of £3 for each meal it prepares. This is necessary to pay for expenses such as the ingredients and cooking oil. To prepare and sell 500 meals each week costs £1,500 (£3 x 500). It is usual to illustrate variable costs as a straight line as in Figure 6.3. This suggests that expenditure on items such as fuel, labour, raw materials and components rises steadily along with output. Variable costs are drawn this way for simplicity. In the real world, the line may gradually flatten out as businesses are frequently able to negotiate lower unit prices when placing large orders.

3 Semi-variable costs

Semi-variable costs are those expenses incurred by a business that have fixed and variable elements. If our fast-food restaurant purchases a van to supply burgers at sports and social events, the running costs of the van would be semi-variable. Some costs would be fixed, as the restaurant would have to tax and insure the van regardless of the number of events it attends. Other costs will be variable – for example, the amount of fuel used will be proportional to the number of events attended. Overall, the van's running costs may be considered as semi-variable.

4 Total costs

Although in practice some costs are semi-variable, many firms assume that all their costs are either fixed or variable. This means total costs can be calculated by simply adding all the fixed and variable costs.

The total cost of production is an important piece of information for a business. Managers can use this information in deciding whether to launch a new product. For example, our fast-food business may find that it will face high fixed costs to establish a mobile operation. These may be higher than expected and may result in the project not going ahead.

Costing is of fundamental importance to businesses launching a new product. Most businesses introduce new products to make a profit. They can forecast their likely income, using market research to identify sales and selling prices. If the costings indicate a loss may be incurred, managers may decide not to go ahead with a project or may alter it in some way.

5 Direct and indirect costs

Another way of classifying the costs is to divide them into direct and indirect costs. Direct costs can be attributed to the production of a particular product and vary directly with the level of output. Examples include the costs of raw materials and fuel.

Indirect costs cannot be allocated to the production of a particular product, but relate to the business as a whole. Indirect costs include the costs of marketing and administration. Indirect costs are often difficult to control. Unless managers are vigilant, these costs can increase rapidly and reduce a business's profits.

Nissan, like any manufacturer, incurs a range of direct and indirect costs. Its direct costs include direct materials, such as steel and engine parts, and direct labour, such as wages of production staff. Its indirect costs include indirect labour costs, such as managers' salaries and wages paid to security staff, and other indirect costs, such as the cost of distribution.

Indirect costs are sometimes called overheads. They are always fixed costs. Direct costs tend to vary with the level of production and are normally (but not always) variable costs.

Calculating costs

Businesses monitor their costs to ensure that they are producing efficiently and not using too many resources. They also calculate costs to assist in pricing decisions. So long as the total costs of producing a product are lower than the price it is able to charge,

Figure 6.4: Monthly production costs for the Grower 3 greenhouse

Level of production (Grower 3 greenhouses per month)	Fixed costs(£)	Variable costs(£)	Total costs(£)
0	4,000	0	4,000
10	4,000	800	4,800
20	4,000	1,600	5,600
30	4,000	2,400	6,400
40	4,000	3,200	7,200
50	4,000	4,000	8,000
60	4,000	4,800	8,800
70	4,000	5,600	9,600
80	4,000	6,400	10,400

the company will make a profit. Any business developing a new product therefore needs to check that the production costs are not going to exceed any price that it would be able to charge.

Figure 6.4 shows the monthly production costs of the Grower 3, a new model of greenhouse that Colby Products is considering launching. From this data, managers at Colby can see that if they produce, say, 40 Grower 3 greenhouses a month, the total costs of production will amount to £7,200. The data in Figure 6.4 can be used to work out the cost of one unit of production (one Grower 3 greenhouse) – this is referred to as average or unit costs. Unit costs can be calculated by dividing the total cost of production by the total level of production. Say Colby produces 30 Grower 3 greenhouses in a month, then its total costs are £6,400 and the unit cost – the cost of a single greenhouse – is £213.33 (£6,400/30).

stop and think

What would be the unit cost of a greenhouse if Colby produced (a) 20 Grower 3 greenhouses per month and (b) 80 Grower 3 greenhouses per month? Why do you think that the unit cost figure falls?

Knowledge summary

- ■ Costs can be classified as direct and indirect or as fixed and variable.

- ■ Most new projects incur fixed and variable costs, though sometimes these are difficult to classify.

- ■ Costing is a vital element in deciding whether a new product development project should go ahead.

quick questions

1 A new garden centre's costs include plants bought for resale, wages of sales staff, heating costs for greenhouses, rent for fields, the manager's salary, and business rates. Which of these are fixed costs?

2 Why might a brewery calculate the fixed *and* variable costs of a new beer product?

3 Why might a business want to calculate the unit costs of a new product?

data interpretation
Mina's figures

Mina Patel is a highly skilled artist who plans to start a one-person business making a range of attractive glass paperweights, which are always in demand. She thinks that she could make a profit from selling paperweights. She reckons that she could make and sell 1,000 paperweights in her first year of trading.

Mina sat down and looked at the figures in front of her (see Figure 6.5). She knew that it would be helpful if she could work out how much it would cost her to produce a single glass paperweight, but wasn't sure how to do it.

A Assume that Mina make 1,000 paperweights in her first year of business. What would be the total costs of production for the year?

B What is the average cost of production for a single paperweight? How would this change if she doubled her output without taking on any staff?

C Discuss whether it is worth Mina calculating her average cost of production.

Figure 6.5: Mina's forecast costs

Item	Cost
Annual rent	£5,000
Annual lease on equipment	£800
Materials per paperweight	£1.50
Mina's salary	£10,000
Advertising costs	£750
Business rates	£1,000
Packaging per paperweight	£0.20
Fuel costs per paperweight	£0.50

Research and development

James Dyson, the man who invented the "bagless" vacuum cleaner, showed enormous determination in turning his idea into a commercial success. In 1978, he noticed how vacuum cleaner bags clogged with dust, and he determined to resolve the problem. It took five years and 5,127 prototypes before his G Force Dual Cyclone had become a product that was saleable.

Dyson then sought a business to produce his product under licence. It was two years before a Japanese company took up the idea. The vacuum cleaner became a huge success in Japan and sold for a premium price. This generated enough profit to provide the finance for Dyson to start manufacturing in the UK.

His first cleaner, the DC01, became the fastest selling vacuum cleaner ever in the UK. Not satisfied with this, he carried on his research and introduced the Root Cyclone vacuum cleaner and later the Dyson DC06 robot, which cleans automatically without human intervention.

Dyson's vacuum cleaners, characterised by their bold colours, have achieved sales in excess of £3,500 million globally. The Dyson company has achieved sales of over £3,000 million worldwide, with profits in excess of £40 million in 2003.

James Dyson is the company's chairman and sole shareholder, and with an estimated fortune of £700 million he is one of Britain's richest men.

What is research and development?

Research and development (R&D) is often necessary to develop and make new products available to consumers. Some research and development involves scientific investigation. This may take the form of brainstorming ideas or work in a laboratory.

As Figure 6.6 shows, firms in industries such as pharmaceuticals and computer software spend enormous sums on research and development. The intention is to gain a competitive advantage by offering products that are better designed and more technologically advanced, and that meet consumer needs as fully as possible.

Good ideas are at the heart of the R&D process. Ideas lead ultimately to new products, which can underpin new businesses – as in James Dyson's case – or give a substantial boost to existing businesses – as was the case with the iPod which helped transform Apple's fortunes. The iPod and the Dyson bagless cleaner are good examples of innovation – good ideas which are turned into products that are wanted by consumers.

So how are these product ideas generated? Some are the result of an inventor working alone and developing a product proposal from an initial insight or clever idea. Other new products are the result of expensive research by a team of employees. For example, Viagra, the anti-impotence drug, was the result of 10 years' research and development by a team at Pfizer.

KEY TERMS

Research and development is the scientific, technological and customer research necessary to develop and make new products available to consumers.

Innovation is the process of introducing novel ideas to develop new products or new methods of production.

	1986	1991	1993	1995	1997	1998	1999	2000	2001
Pharmaceuticals	11.8	15.8	25.7	28.0	32.6	34.2	32.4	35.9	34.6
Aerospace	9.3	8.5	10.9	11.3	7.6	8.0	8.8	8.5	10.7
Electrical machinery	5.4	3.9	5.6	3.5	3.8	4.0	3.7	3.8	4.9
Motor vehicles	2.5	2.5	2.8	2.5	3.0	2.9	3.3	3.2	3.4
Mechanical engineering	1.1	1.1	1.9	1.6	1.5	1.6	1.5	1.7	2.3
Chemicals	2.3	2.9	3.1	2.5	2.7	2.8	2.9	2.6	2.0
Other manufacturing	0.5	0.4	0.5	0.5	0.5	0.6	0.6	0.6	0.6

Source: Association of the British Pharmaceutical Industry website (www.abpi.org.uk)

R&D and product characteristics

Research and development can influence the characteristics of a product in a number of ways.

1 Technologically advanced

Research and development can help a business produce a product that is ahead of the competition. One of the most successful new products of recent years is the iPod, which was first introduced by the US technology company Apple in 2001.

The original research that went into the iPod created a product with unique characteristics that has fuelled extraordinary levels of demand. The iPod weighs less than 170 grams and can store up to 5,000 songs. It can play a variety of forms of music, and later versions can store photographs and images.

Apple has a reputation for being innovative and developing products for technology connoisseurs rather than mass markets. Apple's commitment to research and development has imbued its products with quality, high-tech characteristics.

stop and think

Most Apple products have a slightly exclusive feel, achieving limited rather than mass-market sales from a loyal customer base. However, the iPod has been a phenomenal success. By January 2005 Apple had sold more than 10 million iPods. Has iPod's success changed the image of the company?

2 A unique design

Some products are noted for their unique designs. They may not be the most advanced products available on the market, but may appeal to consumers aesthetically. Some companies pride themselves on excellent design: developing products which have good rather than the most advanced functions but which look stylish and distinctive and work effectively. Good design may be the outcome of many years of research and development.

In 2004, Sony won an award for the design of one of its laptops. The company was credited for its focus on design rather than simply concentrating on adding more functions or using advanced technology. Sony's PCG-X505/P Vaio laptop has been described as a "stunning piece of engineering". According to *PC Pro* magazine, the laptop has "ultra-sleek design, solid build quality and dashing good looks". It is also a very expensive product.

3 Original products

Sometimes research and development results in goods and services that are genuinely unique. The pharmaceutical industry spends huge amounts on researching and developing new products. Pfizer, the world's largest pharmaceutical company, stumbled on Viagra almost by accident. The company was researching a drug to counteract the effects of angina – a form of heart disease – when it noticed that the prototype version of what was to become Viagra appeared to cure male impotence. After further research, Pfizer found it had a product with unique characteristics and for which there was enormous worldwide demand. By 2004 the company's sales of Viagra exceeded £1,500 million.

Research and development costs

Research and development incurs a range of costs for businesses. First, a company needs to establish research facilities. Large businesses may have extensive research facilities containing workshops and laboratories. These can cost millions – for example, in 2005 the US company Inverness Medical Innovations invested £60 million in a new research centre in Stirling. The company specialises in diagnostic health products, including pregnancy tests and blood clot monitors.

Most research and development also requires highly specialist and highly paid staff. Inverness Medical Innovations will employ 500 people in its new research facility in Stirling. Many will have scientific qualifications, and they will command relatively high salaries.

Not all research needs to take place in expensive facilities, however. Sir Clive Sinclair, famous for inventing the ZX Spectrum computer and the C5 electric car, originally worked from a single room and now uses a small workshop above his flat.

Once research has generated the basis for a new product, further expenditure is required to turn it into a saleable product. Several prototypes are likely to be developed and tested. A prototype is a sample that is produced to see if the product idea will work in practice as well as theory. Potential customers are often invited to test the prototypes through a programme of market research.

Boeing, the US aircraft manufacturer, used to produce wooden prototypes of its aircraft to ensure they could be assembled successfully and to iron out any design errors. Since 2000, the company has used computer software to simulate this process. Developing prototypes should result in fewer errors, better-quality products and more satisfied customers.

Limiting R&D costs

Britain's pharmaceutical companies spend more than £10 million each day on research and development. How do businesses with limited budgets compete with companies that have huge sums to spend on research and development? They can follow one – or a combination – of three main strategies.

"Me-too" products

Me-too products are simply copies of other goods. Although patents offer the original producers some protection, competitors are often able to produce similar products without infringing patent laws. This can save expenditure on research and development. Walls Cornetto was a me-too copy of a Lyons Maid King Cone, and has arguably become more popular than the original.

Contracting out research

Smaller organisations can avoid the high costs of maintaining research facilities by paying other organisations to conduct research on their behalf. They can, for example, use some of the research expertise in universities. Manchester Metropolitan University has recently invested £42 million in new research facilities at its Dalton Institute, which will carry out some work on behalf of private businesses.

Relying on quality of service

Some smaller businesses may not be able to supply the most up-to-date goods or services. Instead, they rely on providing a very high-quality service to maintain customer loyalty. Some companies supply to niche markets to avoid competing in mass markets with businesses that invest heavily in research and development.

stop an d **t h i**

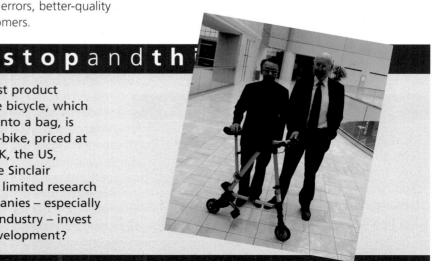

One of Sir Clive Sinclair's latest product innovations is the A-bike. The bicycle, which weighs just 5 kilos and folds into a bag, is aimed at city dwellers. The A-bike, priced at £170, will be on sale in the UK, the US, Singapore and Japan. Sir Clive Sinclair developed this product using limited research facilities. Why do other companies – especially those in the pharmaceutical industry – invest so heavily in research and development?

Knowledge summary

- Some firms invest heavily in research and development to gain a competitive advantage by introducing new products to the market.

- Research and development can influence product characteristics through design, originality and technological sophistication.

- Research and development can be expensive, requiring expenditure on buildings, highly specialised equipment, and highly paid and high-skilled staff.

- Small businesses avoid spending large amounts on research and development by producing "me-too" products or by contracting out research.

quick **questions**

1 Explain two ways in which a business might reduce its expenditure on research and development.

2 Why do you think that pharmaceutical and medical research and development is so expensive?

3 Many small-scale manufacturers survive despite spending little money on research and development. How is this possible?

data **interpretation**
Dummy tests crumbs

Experts have invented a mannequin with a motorised mouth to test the amount of crumbs biscuits produce. Staff at the McVitie's laboratory in High Wycombe designed the Crumb Test Dummy to test which baking techniques produce the most crumbs.

The motorised mannequin has plastic teeth and is designed to replicate human eating. A McVitie's spokeswoman said the crumbs produced by a biscuit show if it has been cooked to perfection.

"Eating lots of biscuits is obviously an enjoyable prospect for most people, but we haven't yet found a human who can test on this scale," McVitie's brand manager Liz Ashdown added.

Sources: news.bbc.co.uk, 8 March 2005

A What costs might McVitie's incur in maintaining its High Wycombe laboratory?

B How might the tests carried out by the dummy help to define the product characteristics of McVitie's biscuits?

C Small firms that manufacture biscuits could not afford to conduct this type of research. Does this mean that small biscuit manufacturers are unlikely to be able to launch new products to compete with those supplied by McVitie's?

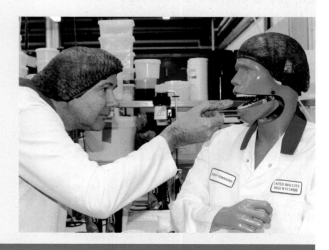

Topic 9   Deciding on product characteristics

Setting the scene: Falcon's new cooker

Falcon Foodservice Equipment (which is owned by the Aga Foodservice Group) is very optimistic that the Infinity Fryer will be a winner. This new product – a deep-fat fryer – emerged from the company's continuous research and development programme.

Designed for use in kitchens in restaurants, hotels, pubs and cafés, the Infinity Fryer has a number of unique features that provide it with a USP:

- up to 69 per cent reduction in energy costs
- up to 68 per cent less oil required
- 37 per cent quicker heat-up times
- double oil life expectancy and improved quality
- fewer oil changes offering real savings on disposal costs
- low noise and reduced heat emissions.

Falcon Foodservice Equipment thinks that the new product is going to be a winner. Already the Whitbread Group (which owns Premier Travel Inn, Brewers Fayre, Beefeater and TGI Friday's) has the product on trial and believes that it will help the company to show that it cares about the environment. The Infinity Fryer's fuel efficiency makes it a very environmentally friendly product.

Falcon Foodservice Equipment has forecast significant orders for the new fryer. The high level of expected sales has allowed the company to research the product intensively and to ensure that it meets the needs of customers fully, as it expects to recoup development costs through sales revenue.

Source: adapted from www.infinityfryers.com

A product's final characteristics

In any product development process, there comes a stage when a company has to decide on the product's final characteristics. In considering its options – and in determining the exact specifications of the new product – it will be influenced by several factors.

1 Costs

The design, quality and functions of a new product will be limited by cost considerations. There are two major cost elements in bringing any new product onto the market.

First, the cost of research and development. Even the smallest businesses will incur some expenditure on

---

KEY TERMS

Profit arises when a firm's revenue is greater than its total expenses.

Projected profit is a forecast of the expected surplus of revenues over costs during some future trading period.

Revenue is the income a business earns from selling its products.

Costs are expenses incurred by a business in its day-to-day operations.

A **product's characteristics** comprise its appearance and its function – in other words, what it looks like and what it does.

researching and developing a new product. For example, they may pay for some market research to see if an idea for a service is sufficiently popular. Larger firms can incur substantial costs in researching new products.

Second, the costs of producing the product. A business needs to estimate the fixed and variable costs of production to arrive at an average or unit cost for the product.

A business cannot allow the costs of developing and producing a product to become too great. Managers are normally aware of the prices that can be charged for particular products, either as a result of market research or through informal discussions with customers. If the costs of production are too high – perhaps because the product has many features or is made to a very high specification – then a business may be forced to set too high a price for the market. This would mean that it would not be able to sell the product in sufficient quantities to make a profit. In this case, it may be forced to reconsider the design and characteristics of the product in order to ensure that it could set a price more in line with consumer expectations.

Fashion designers produce enormously expensive and extravagant clothes for the annual round of highly publicised fashion shows. The prices that would have to be charged to recover the costs of producing these clothes would deter even the most fashion-conscious shopper. However, the fashion ideas and designs are incorporated into more modestly priced products using cheaper materials and mass production techniques by businesses that sell to high street clothes retailers. They produce clothes that are fashionable, but keep costs down so that the prices do not deter too many buyers.

2 Expected revenue

Any business considering a new product launch will forecast its expected earnings from the product as part of its financial planning. The anticipated level of earnings will help to shape the final specification of the new product. If a company is selling into a luxury market where it can set high prices and expect solid revenues, its product characteristics will reflect this in terms of quality and functions. It may also focus heavily on design, confident that the future income will cover the development costs.

Sony Ericsson, the Japanese-Swedish mobile phone manufacturer, enjoyed rising sales of its range of mobile phones with cameras in 2004, and forecast strong sales growth in 2005. As a consequence, the company decided to launch two new camera phones with more advanced functions. The company also expected to be able to sell the new camera phones at a premium price, boosting its sales revenue further.

stop and think

How might Sony Ericsson attempt to forecast its sales revenue? Why might this forecast prove to be inaccurate?

Many hotels offer luxury packages for guests over the Christmas period. They design the Christmas breaks to provide guests with high standards of comfort and care, including seasonal food and presents for children. Hotels offering a Christmas break package can provide a quality product, safe in the knowledge that they can charge high prices because they know there is always high demand in the festive season.

stop and think

Why do fashion designers such as Stella McCartney prepare very expensive clothes for models to wear at their shows, knowing that they will be too expensive for most consumers?

3 Projected profits

A vital part of the financial planning of a new product is drawing up a profits forecast or projection. A product will make a profit for a business if its revenue over a period of time exceeds the expected costs of production. Most businesses aim to make a profit – or avoid making a loss – so these forecasts are examined with particular interest.

If the projected profits look acceptable, a company is likely to go ahead with the product launch. If the projected profits are poor, or if a loss is forecast, a business may decide not to go ahead with the launch. It may decide to alter the product's characteristics to produce a more profitable product, or it may drop the project altogether and decide to focus on its existing product range.

The US online marketplace eBay has forecast steady increases in profits from its trading activities. As a result, the company has expanded the number of countries in which it operates. Indeed, it expects to make more profits from its overseas operations than in the US. It is this expectation that has driven the company to launch its product in countries such as South Korea, China and India.

Forecasting profit

It can be difficult for a business to forecast the projected profits of a new product. This is because product characteristics and profits are interrelated. Profit levels are determined by forecast revenues and costs – and both sales (and hence revenue) and costs are determined in part by the product's characteristics. However, the projected profits also determine to some extent the characteristics of the product, and a business may alter the new product's design, quality and range of functions to achieve a more acceptable profit forecast.

Profit forecasts rely on sales estimates – a business can usually estimate its costs fairly accurately – and it is not always easy to forecast the demand for a new product. Sometimes the product's characteristics prove much more appealing than expected, fuelling consumer demand and resulting in much higher sales than forecast.

Toyota's new Prius model has proved to be a phenomenon. It is a hybrid car: the car runs on an electric motor, but the motor's battery is recharged by an electric generator which is powered by a petrol engine. The petrol engine provides extra power for the car when required. The car is environmentally friendly and has been endorsed by celebrities such as Leonardo di Caprio, Harrison Ford and Susan Sarandon.

The Prius has become a "must-have" product. It was voted car of the year for 2005 in Europe, and received a similar award in the United States. The car's surprise success is expected to change for ever the design and product characteristics of cars. Toyota has been unable to produce enough cars to meet demand, though it is planning a huge increase in output over coming years.

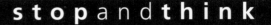

stop and **think**

How might the unexpected success of the Prius have affected the projected profits for the product? How might it affect the unit costs of producing the Prius in future years?

Knowledge summary

■ When introducing new products, businesses have to pay attention to development and production costs.

■ Both the estimated costs of producing a new product and its expected revenues are likely to influence its design, quality and functions.

■ Most businesses aim to make profits. Decisions on whether to proceed with a new product will be informed by the level of projected profits.

quick **questions**

1 Why might a confectionery manufacturer decide to produce chocolate Easter eggs even though they are expensive to manufacture?

2 How might a business forecast its expected revenue from a new product?

3 What actions might a film production company take if it appears that the projected profits from a planned new movie will be lower than it would want?

data **interpretation**
The restaurant

Polly looked at the profits forecast she had nearly completed for her restaurant for the next three months. The months after Christmas were always difficult. However, this year Polly wanted things to be different. Surely, she thought, I must be able to do something. "Perhaps I should change the menu," she mused out loud. "Many ingredients are more expensive in late winter."

Figure 6.7: Polly's forecast costs and revenue

	January £	February £	March £
Sales revenue	21,070	19,575	20,250
Total costs	19,840	17,945	18,880

A How much profit is Polly expecting to make over the three months?

B Explain why Polly might need to alter her menu in the winter months when some ingredients are more expensive.

C Discuss the factors Polly might take into account before introducing an entirely new menu into her restaurant.

Business in practice: Alpha1 Airways

Martin Halstead had been keen on planes and flying since childhood, and by the age of 18 was training as an airline pilot. Martin was keen to pursue a career as a pilot, but it is an unstable job market with few opportunities as there are more pilots than jobs. Martin joked with a friend that the only way to be sure of getting a flying job was to set up his own airline.

As sometimes happens, a chance remark led to a big idea, and Martin started to think seriously about the options. Not surprisingly, the finance available to Martin to start his business was limited. However, he was able to use money left to him by his grandmother plus what he had managed to save from a series of part-time jobs.

Planning the business

Martin investigated several business plans, ranging from air taxi firms to a transatlantic airline operating from Scotland. By November 2004, he had chosen a business model. Martin's plan was to operate Alpha1 Airways out of his home town airport, and the airport where he trained, at Oxford. The airport hadn't seen any scheduled passenger flights since a summer service to Jersey in the early 1990s, but it was keen to get into the scheduled airline market.

About a year before Martin started drawing up his business plan there had been talk of an Oxbridge shuttle between Oxford and Cambridge. Transport links between the two cities are infamous: despite only being 65 miles apart as the crow flies, it takes over two hours by car and even more by train, including two changes in London.

An Oxford-based company AirMed had been talking about starting the operation between the two cities for some time, but it had been unable to find a suitable marketing partner. AirMed was very content to operate the service, but it wanted another business to promote the service and to organise the booking and selling of tickets by telephone and through a website.

AirMed is an established business offering a range of services including:

■ air charter, air taxi and air ambulance

■ flying cargo by air

■ offering aerial photography for businesses.

The company appeared to have just the experience and skills that Martin was looking for. Discussions began between Martin and AirMed in late 2004. By January 2005, Martin and AirMed had reached agreement and the planning process continued.

Figure 6.8: Transport connections between Oxford and Cambridge

Road: 82.7 miles (2 hours 9 min)

Plane: 65 miles (20 min)

Train: 170 miles via London (2hours 32 min)

20 miles

To Paddington

To King's Cross

M1 Bedford Cambridge A428 Milton Keynes A421 M11 M40 M25 Oxford

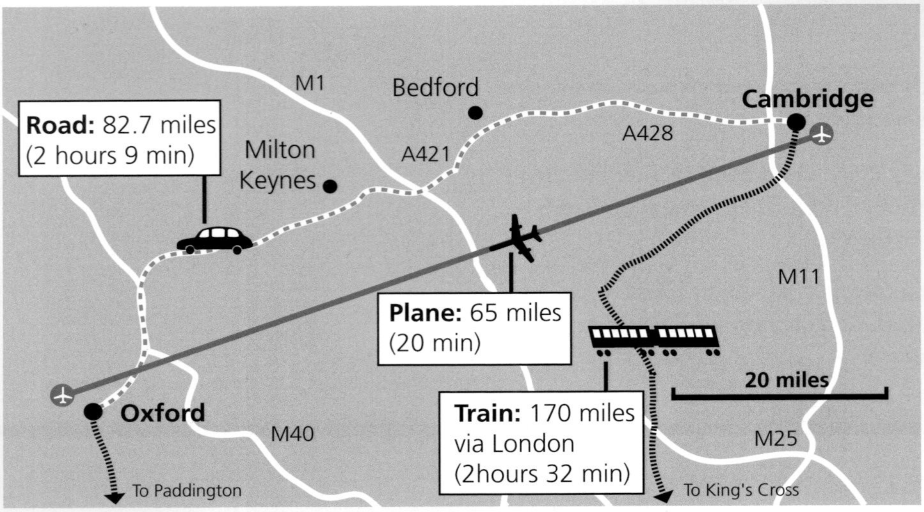

The business

Alpha1 Airways was formally founded in June 2004 by entrepreneur Martin Halstead, although it hasn't begun trading at the time of writing (May 2005). Alpha1 expects to operate its scheduled AirMed services between Oxford and Cambridge using eight-seater Piper Navajo Chieftains.

Throughout its planning stages, the business had the support of some important stakeholders. These included James Dillon-Godfray, the head of marketing and development at Oxford Airport. In backing Martin Halstead's plans, he said: "There has not been a direct air link between Oxford and Cambridge since the late 1930s. We were looking at the idea of running a scheduled service when Martin knocked on our door. He is a very dynamic young man."

Mr Dillon-Godfray said dozens of academics, business people, students and tourists travelled between the two cities each weekday. A journey by car or train takes more than two hours but will be just 20 minutes by air, with single fares costing up to £49.

The product

Alpha1 Airways only plans to operate between Oxford and Cambridge initially. The flight time is less than 30 minutes and the company has scheduled two flights in each direction every day. Figure 6.9 shows the proposed timetable.

The flights have been planned to arrive in the two cities before 9 o'clock in the morning and to return after 5.30 in the afternoon. This aspect of the product's design is intended to encourage business travellers to use the service.

The Piper Chieftain aircraft used by Alpha1 Airways can seat up to seven passengers. It is fully carpeted, has leather seats, and cruises at about 200 miles per hour. It contains the latest all-weather technology.

The customer experience

Alpha1 Airways has set out features of the customer experience it plans to offer.

- All Alpha1 passengers are free to use our executive lounges at selected airports. Relax with a complimentary newspaper and a cup of coffee, or get that last-minute work done in a quiet corner. Most of our lounges have e-mail, telephone, fax and internet facilities as well as satellite television.

- Coffee, tea and light refreshments, newspapers and internet access are all included in the price of your Alpha1 ticket. We really are the executive's choice!

- Our fleet of eight-seater PA-31-350 Piper Chieftain commuter airliners is ready to transport you quickly and comfortably to your destination. Relax in the knowledge that you are being flown by some of the best pilots in the industry in one of the most popular and safest aircraft ever built.

- Sit back and enjoy our in-flight magazine *1World* packed with exciting articles, interviews, and guides to our destinations, or relax and watch the world pass by 10,000 feet beneath you as you cruise along at 200mph. We'll get you to your destination in no time!

Figure 6.9: Cambridge–Oxford timetable

To Oxford Kidlington

Flight number	Departs	Arrives	Flight time	Stops	Aircraft type	Days
ALF102	0815	0845	30 minutes	0	PA-31-350 Chieftain	M T W T F
ALF104	1800	1830	30 minutes	0	PA-31-350 Chieftain	M T W T F

To Cambridge City

Flight number	Departs	Arrives	Flight time	Stops	Aircraft type	Days
ALF101	0730	0800	30 minutes	0	PA-31-350 Chieftain	M T W T F
ALF103	1720	1750	30 minutes	0	PA-31-350 Chieftain	M T W T F

Fares

As with most airlines, Alpha1 intends to offer a selection of services and fares. Single fares cost from £39 to £49.

Cheapest (non-flexible)

This is the base fare and is non-changeable and non-refundable. Name changes are also not allowed with this fare. This fare includes:

- light refreshments and lounge access at selected airports

- optional online check-in

- up to 10 kg of hold baggage and 4 kg of hand baggage

Semi-flexible

This fare allows ticket changes up to 24 hours prior to departure but is non-refundable. Name changes are not allowed with this fare. This fare includes:

- light refreshments and lounge access at selected airports

- optional online check-in

- up to 10 kg of hold baggage and 4 kg of hand baggage

- the option to make changes to reservations up to 24 hours before departure.

Fully flexible

This fare allows ticket changes up to one hour prior to departure and is fully refundable. Name changes are also allowed on this ticket. This fare includes:

- light refreshments and lounge access at selected airport

- option online check-in

- up to 14 kg of hold baggage and 6 kg of hand baggage

- full ticket changes up to one hour before departure, including name changes

- free bus transfer on arrival to the city centre of your destination (at selected airports).

Student fare

This fare is available only to students in full-time education and in possession of an NUS card. It is non-changeable and non-refundable. Name changes are not allowed on this ticket. This fare includes:

- Light refreshments and lounge access at selected airports

- Up to 10kg of hold baggage and 4kg of hand baggage.

The future?

If the Cambridge Oxford service is successful, the company hopes to expand its route network using larger aircraft. The Beech 1900D, BAe Jetstream 31 and Embraer 110 are all possibilities for the future expansion of Alpha1 Airways services.

Martin Halstead aims to manage his business with a very modern and open working culture and to benefit greatly from developing excellent relationships with all the airports and suppliers it uses. He hopes that the Alpha1 brand will become a symbol of quality and service.

Martin Halstead

Postscript

At the time this book went to print Alpha1 had not launched its air service between Oxford and Cambridge. Martin Halstead had posted an announcement on his website (www.flyalpha1.com) explaining that delay was due to an additional injection of capital enabling the business to expand on its original plans. The details of the new service have yet to be revealed, but the delay highlights the uncertainty and risk associated with launching a new product.

Sources

The Daily Telegraph (http://portal.telegraph.co.uk), Alpha1 Airways and AirMed.

activities

1 Aurigny (www.aurigny.com) and Eastern Airways (www.easternairways.com) are similar operations to Alpha1 Airlines. What decisions have these companies taken about their quality of service and the resources that they will use?

2 How might researching competitors' products have helped Martin decide on his product's characteristics?

3 To what extent was the type of customer Martin was hoping to attract vital in determining the product his company planned to offer?

4 What safety issues might Martin encounter supplying this service and how might this affect the product he supplies?

5 Was Martin right in (a) the mix of resources that he chose to run his airline and (b) designing his product in the way he did? You should justify your answer.

6 Despite the delay in its launch, do you think that Martin's product has the potential to be successful? Explain and justify your answer.

THERE IS A WIDE RANGE OF CAREERS, BUT HOW do you choose a career or a job that suits you? Perhaps you already have a "dream job" in mind, or maybe you want to run your own business. However, do you know what is needed for you to be able to achieve these goals?

This unit is designed to help you explore the types of career that are available. It will assist you in finding out the job opportunities that exist, and deciding on which are likely to suit you.

By developing a personal skills profile, you can investigate what training and development opportunities you may need for your chosen occupation. At the end of your investigations, you should be able to produce a personal career plan which describes suitable career paths that you may follow.

Career planning

Setting the scene: job profiles

Events of the magnitude of the Reading and Glastonbury festivals are not easy to organise or to promote. The number of different job roles involved in these events is considerable. Two of the behind-the-scenes roles are public relations and health and safety. The festivals need public relations staff to manage and minimise their impact on other stakeholders such as the local communities, and they need health and safety specialists to ensure the wellbeing of all those involved in the festival, from the artists to the fans. Have you ever considered what it takes to build a career as a public relations officer or health and safety adviser? Look at these two job profiles.

job profile: Public relations officer

Job description

A public relations (PR) officer uses communication mediums and methods to build, maintain and manage the reputation of organisations or individuals. In other words, PR is a planned attempt to establish and maintain goodwill and effective relationships between an organisation and its stakeholders.

Responsibilities can include:

- undertaking market research using focus groups or surveys to gauge the perception of the organisation among stakeholder groups
- writing press releases, speeches and articles
- planning and organising PR campaigns
- producing publicity brochures, promotional videos and other media
- developing relations with newspapers, magazines, radio and television
- organising events, such as press conferences, public open days and corporate sponsorship activities.

Qualifications and entry requirements

Public relations uses knowledge and skills drawn from areas like management, journalism, politics, marketing and psychology. Entrants come from a wide variety of academic backgrounds. There are no set or easy entry points into this very competitive industry, although a good first degree is increasingly considered essential. Previous experience in the media and communications industry is desired by many companies. Potential PR officers will need to show evidence of:

- good communication, interpersonal and writing skills
- self-discipline and motivation
- individual and team management skills
- creativity and imagination.

job profile: Health and safety adviser

Job description

Health and safety advisers help businesses to generate, promote and maintain a safe working environment. They are responsible for ensuring that businesses adhere to all safety legislation and adopt good health and safety policies and practices. They help plan, implement, monitor and review the protective and preventive measures that companies are required (or choose) to put in place. They work to minimise occupational health problems, accidents and injuries. They may provide training to employees about health and safety issues and risks.

Qualifications and entry requirements

Health and safety is a discipline in its own right. Some experience working in scientific and technical fields at an operational level, gaining an understanding of industrial processes, is also extremely useful. The recommended route into the profession is to use this industrial experience to develop an interest in health and safety before moving into an advisory role.

Much health and safety work involves an appreciation of operational processes as well as the use of instruments and electronic monitoring equipment. It would be expected that advisers would either have an accredited postgraduate degree, degree or HND in occupational safety, life science, engineering or health studies, or a National Examination Board for Occupational Safety and Health (NEBOSH) diploma and level 4 of the vocational qualifications for occupational health and safety practice.

Applicants will also need to show evidence of good written and spoken communication skills, negotiating skills, patience, and diplomacy and administration skills.

Health and safety advisers should be corporate members of the Institution of Occupational Safety and Health. Corporate membership is increasingly used by employers as a standard for recruitment and pay. Three years' professional experience are required before you can become a corporate member. Graduates from a relevant discipline can join at non-corporate level while they accrue the experience to upgrade to full corporate status.

Why career planning is important

There is a wide choice of occupations, and most people have no idea of the full range of job and career options that are available. Moreover, most people are unaware of what jobs would suit their talents, interests and ambition.

By getting information on jobs and careers, you will be in a better position to look at what skills and qualities you may already be able to offer, and begin to think how you might gather the experience and qualifications that you are currently lacking for any jobs or roles that you are interested in pursuing.

You need to be able to identify your own personal skills profile, determine what occupations suit or match the skills that you possess or can develop, consider which ones match your expectations, needs and wants, and then choose an appropriate career route.

What this unit covers

Career pathways

In order to establish a direction – a career path – it is necessary to appreciate and explore the wide range of available occupational options. This will involve using a wide range of sources to investigate different occupational alternatives and, in each case, to learn about the required skills, qualifications, experience and expected personal qualities required, the training and development offered by the sector or employer, and possible career progression routes.

Training

It is important to understand the different methods of training provided by businesses and the type of skills

base gained from each method. This unit also helps you develop an awareness of alternative pathways available through national training initiatives such as apprenticeships, Investors in People and New Deal.

Developing a personal skills profile

It is possible to develop a profile of the skills you already have to offer potential employers. These may include team working, influencing, risk-taking, training at work, self-confidence and motivation, interpersonal skills, communication, leadership and supervisory skills. You will learn how psychometric tests and personality tests can be used in order to identify your skills and describe your personality traits. These can be helpful in establishing the right type of occupation for you.

Qualifications

There is a wide range of qualifications. This investigation will help to establish the opportunities by looking at the various study options open to individuals, including higher education, training at work, apprenticeships, voluntary work, and study and work abroad.

Funding and budgeting

In order to follow a career route, it is necessary to look at the various types of funding that may be available to help finance the cost of getting the necessary qualifications and experience. Information about funding will help you to construct a personal budget, identifying the costs associated with your chosen career plan and the sources of income that will enable you to follow your chosen pathway.

Topic 1 Career pathways

Setting the scene: careers at Cadbury Schweppes

The Cadbury Schweppes website (www.cadburyschweppes.com) has a whole section devoted to careers, with several job profiles showing the range of roles available within the firm. Here is a small extract, with two example career profiles.

Within Cadbury Schweppes you can expect a career with plenty of challenges. At the same time you can look forward to the satisfaction that comes from achieving your ambitions – you will never be held back from realising your potential.

We encourage our people to move around the business, so you'll have every opportunity to broaden your skills and experience, either in your own country or abroad. With over 100 locations around the world, there really are no limits as to where your career can go.

Whatever your area of expertise, there will always be the chance to build on it and develop new skills. We have a variety of opportunities in areas ranging from strategy, finance and IT to supply chain, commercial and HR. We look for people with the initiative to make change happen and the credibility to influence people at all levels. Of course we're interested in a proven track record of achievement. However, we also value your determination, your commitment and your passion for success.

The eventual destination of a career is up to each of our employees, anything can happen. We provide the opportunities and resources, our employees provide the motivation and energy to make the most of the opportunities we provide.

profile: Olatunde Falase

Current role: Value-based Management Manager

After graduating with BSc in management and accounting, she spent a year as a clearing clerk at the Union Bank of Nigeria before joining Cadbury Schweppes as a management trainee in 1990. Subsequently worked in a lot of different areas: as export processing manager, treasurer, then company treasurer in Nigeria; as financial accountant and acting finance manager for Cadbury Ltd (UK); then back to Nigeria as general manager IT. As business development controller, she contributed to strategy formulation relating to new business initiatives and the subsequent translation of strategy into activity programmes. In October 2001, she moved back to the UK as business development manager for the Africa, India and Middle East Region. Now her role is as value-based management manager for that region.

profile: Louise Munton

Current role: Global Marketing Manager, Group Commercial

Joined in 1993 on the Graduate Trainee Programme. Subsequently worked in a number of roles: as sales support representative, assistant product manager, product manager and senior product manager. In 1999, as part of the Accelerated Development Programme, she did an international assignment as new product development manager for Cadbury Chocolate Canada in Toronto, then as group product manager for Moulded and Bars. Between October 2000 and February 2001 she took a leave of absence to travel around the world. Currently she's global marketing manager, group commercial.

There are many other job and career profiles from the Cadbury Schweppes website. How many different job roles are mentioned? Why do you think Cadbury's encourages its employees to move around the company?

Career choices

In order to make an informed career choice, it is essential to use a range of sources to investigate a variety of suitable occupations that might be of interest and that would be appropriate choices for us to make.

One way of looking at different career choices is to investigate what individual companies offer. This can be done by researching their websites or writing to their personnel departments. Many people start their careers in the knowledge that they want to work in a particular industry or type of company; however, there are also individuals who don't have a clear idea of where they want to work, and they need to establish possible occupational pathways.

stop and think

Is there any information on career choices on the Cadbury Schweppes website that might appeal to potential applicants? Explain what factors would influence your decision.

Finding an occupational pathway

There are many factors that determine what occupation, job role or career suits each individual person. People have different desires, wants and needs, and they possess varying strengths, weaknesses, skills and responsibilities. You need to find out what occupations are likely to suit you.

Establishing a range of potential career pathways involves a great deal of research and investigation. Even if you have an idea of a dream job or a long-term interest in a particular occupation, it is important to gather information on a range of alternative options to keep the career pathways open.

The Department for Education and Skills publishes *Occupations*, a careers book listing over 3,000 occupational areas. This book is a very useful tool for

KEY TERMS

A **career plan** sets out what an individual needs to do in order to achieve the qualifications and experience required for the type of job that they want.

Job profiles describe the nature of particular jobs, including what they involve and the requirements of the job role.

Aptitude is a measure of the ability of an individual to develop particular skills or knowledge.

finding out detailed criteria for specific occupational areas, but it's too detailed for an initial broad search. So how do you begin to explore your options? In order to help pinpoint occupational areas that may be of interest, there are several areas that you can investigate.

Location – are you looking for a career locally, nationally or internationally? The smaller the geographic area, the more restricted will be your choice of jobs and careers.

Job adverts – look in newspapers, specialist magazines and at the jobcentre to get a feel for the variety of opportunities available and the type of jobs that might be of interest.

Careers resources – access one of the many career software programs and explore the information on a wide range of occupations.

Work experience – use any work experience you undertake to get an insight into jobs. Work experience can highlight areas that provide stimulation and motivation, thus pinpointing them as possible career choices, but it can equally reveal jobs that wouldn't suit you, allowing some occupational routes to be discounted.

Friends, relations and contacts – draw on other people's experience. Ask people what jobs they do? What is involved? What do they enjoy? What are the less enjoyable aspects?

Observation – identify possible career options by observing people at work. This can be done by simply watching television and by looking around you as you go about life.

The key to a successful investigation is to gather as much information from as many sources as possible. A folder should be kept collating examples of the specific jobs and occupational areas that are found to be of interest. This helps to narrow down the search, as it will start to point in the direction of careers that are appealing at this stage.

In many cases, though, you may still need to narrow down your options further. At this point, it is often

There are many trade magazines that focus on specific industries or occupations. For example, *The Grocer* reports on the UK's food and drink sector. Some companies only advertise job vacancies in these trade publications. What advantages do they gain by doing so?

Figure 7.1: A job profile matching sheet

	Personal profile			Job profile		
	Well developed	Developing	Not yet developed	Essential	Desired	Not required
Core skills						
Oral communications						
Written communication						
IT skills						
Numeracy skills						
Organisational skills						
Researching information						
Collating information						
Problem solving						
Time management						
Personal skills/qualities						
Work independently						
Work well in a team						
Leadership skills						
Reliability						
Motivation						
Accuracy						
Responsible						
People skills						
Other skills required						
1:						
2:						
3:						

helpful to start to explore ideas with a careers adviser. This can usually be organised through the Connexions service (www.connexions.gov.uk) – appointments can be arranged through local offices, or the service can be contacted online. If you are over 19 years old, you can also arrange to see an adviser through your local learning and skills council.

Careers advisers can offer information on a wide range of careers, and assist in helping to develop a career plan. They provide resources, books, videos and internet access to help people research training opportunities, college courses, voluntary work, work placements, gap years, apprenticeships and developing or changing careers, as well as how to prepare for interviews and work experience.

Online help

There are many websites that can help you explore career choices. Some of these provide short questionnaires which help to direct you to the type of career that you will find appealing. For example, www.findspot.com/free-career-tests.htm offers a free career test. The website http://quiz.ivillage.co.uk looks at what type of career suits differing personality profiles. The website www.prospects.ac.uk provides career advice for graduates with many quizzes and activities to help work out which career areas are most suitable.

There is a wealth of online advice on jobs, training opportunities and careers. Sites to explore include:

- www.worktrain.gov.uk
- http://jobsadvice.guardian.co.uk/
- www.careers.lon.ac.uk/links
- www.careersa-z.co.uk
- www.totaljobs.com
- www.topjobs.co.uk
- www.voluntarywork.org.uk

Remember there are many other sources of advice, from the many publications on careers, to videos, television programmes and advice centres – you will need to look around and make wide and thorough investigations. Finding your ideal career starts with these exploratory steps.

Job profiles

Having narrowed down the options and established a range of occupations which may be of interest, the next step is to consider each occupational area in more depth. This is done to establish:

- the required skills, qualifications and experience
- the personal qualities looked for by employers
- the training and development opportunities that may be offered
- the type of career progression that is available.

It is useful to build up these job profiles. By establishing the key requirements of any job role, you can then examine whether particular job options are actually realistic, suitable and obtainable – and you can decide on the options to follow up. The most accurate way to do this is to try and match the skills, qualifications, experience and personal qualities required with those you already possess. It may be helpful to use a job profile matching sheet (see Figure 7.1).

Testing your aptitude

Many job roles require successful applicants to undertake further qualifications and training. The employing organisation may offer training, or potential applicants may have to look at ways of gaining further qualifications prior to applying for employment in that occupational area.

Testing your aptitude is about assessing whether you have the basic abilities to develop particular skills or knowledge in the future. This will also help you when completing a job profile matching sheet. There are several different ways to test a person's aptitude.

General aptitude

There are a whole range of general aptitudes, such as hand-eye co-ordination, dexterity, spatial ability, numeracy, word-fluency and critical thinking. General aptitude tests may be used by an employer to determine a candidate's suitability for a job role.

Intelligence

To some extent, intelligence forms part of our aptitude. However it may not be directly related to the qualifications we hold; it relates to a whole range of abilities that form part of our make-up. An intelligence test measures an individual's ability to understand and interpret information and to co-ordinate, assimilate and synthesise information from different areas.

Trainability tests

Trainability tests attempt to measure actual performance and learning ability. For example, job applicants can be given instruction on how to do a specific task or small part of a job, and then tested to see the extent to which they can carry out that task.

Knowledge summary

- To make an appropriate career choice, you need to research a range of suitable occupations that might be of interest and that would be suitable, realistic options.

- There are a large number of information sources on careers, including the internet, the press, careers publications, job centres, television programmes, friends and family, and careers advisers.

- To build up a job profile, you need to establish the key requirements for the role. Job profile matching sheets and aptitude tests can help determine whether an individual is suitable for a particular occupational pathway or job role.

quick**questions**

1 How might observation be used to help determine potential career opportunities?

2 What is the point of completing a job profile matching sheet?

3 Explain two ways in which work experience can help an individual determine an occupational pathway.

data**interpretation**
Unit manager post

The job advertisement for a unit manager position shown opposite was posted on an online recruitment site. Read the advert carefully and then answer the questions below.

A Describe the skills, qualifications and experience that you feel might be needed for the role of unit manager with RPS Ltd.

B What personal qualities are required?

C What training and development opportunities does the company provide?

D Is there any career progression – what is available to employees?

E The company offers a range of benefits. Explain why the business is offering these incentives to its staff.

Position:	**Unit Manager**
Salary:	**£22,000**
Location:	**Cambridgeshire**
Company:	**RPS Ltd**
Date:	**1 June 2005**

Our client has a history dating back to 1961 and a turnover that exceeds £1.7 billion. It is active in 35 countries, and employs over 30,000 people, focusing on food service for the road, rail, air, marine and bus business channels. It aims to deliver the quality and consistency of branded offers, combined with local flavour from around the world.

We are looking for strong, creative and customer-focused people to help achieve the vision by having a can-do attitude, sharing success, fostering teamwork, having a passion for quality and embracing diversity. To be successful you will:

■ do whatever it takes to create a better experience for customers

■ constantly aim to develop more efficient and productive ways of working

■ help to implement changes to products and services by monitoring market trends and evolving consumer needs

■ believe in providing customer-focused products and services that make the business a success

■ help create and be involved in incentive programmes that encourage a sense of ownership

■ help develop and reward great ideas that lead to innovations in any products and brands

■ assist in creating opportunities to share

■ implement great practices across the business

■ be a strong communicator

■ put the customer first in everything you do

■ work with customer information to help influence product ranges

■ strive to continuously improve the development, training and measurement of the operational, brand and service standards

■ create a positive working environment and recognise, respect and value the uniqueness of your employees, customers and clients, and believe that this enriches the working environment

■ build multicultural teams that provide a real point of difference and competitive advantage in winning and sustaining new business

■ encourage the development of products and brands to cater for the many different tastes of our international customers and clients.

You will be currently working as a food manager, store manager, assistant manager, deputy manager, general manager, unit manager, trainee manager, department manager, section manager, restaurant manager or pub manager, and you will be ideally located in Cambridge, St Ives, Godmanchester, Huntingdon, Eaton Socon, Royston, Saffron Walden, Haver Hill, Ely or Newmarket.

If you are successful, benefits for working for this company are a competitive salary, an investment/pension scheme after three months, a bonus scheme based upon sales performance, turnover and profit margins, 20 days' holiday which increases to 23 after two years' service, privilege card, incentive scheme, and discounts across many brands

There is great emphasis on personal development, and appropriate training and development will be utilised to bring out the best in you, ensuring you have the correct tools to do the job. Our client will create an environment in which you can progress to your full potential within the business. Its internal training programmes – Training Tracks and Internal Trainee Management Development – have been recognised as part of the National Training Awards in the UK.

If you have a can-do attitude and you thrive on new challenges, you enjoy working in a team within a diverse environment and appreciate the value of shared success, apply now!

Source: www.totaljobs.com

Setting the scene: management training at McDonald's

MacDonald's takes training seriously, and as this extract from the company's website illustrates, it offers opportunities for all employees to develop their skills.

Running a McDonald's restaurant is commercial management in its fullest sense. As a restaurant manager, you'll set targets, plan budgets, control stock, recruit and inspire your team, create and drive marketing campaigns, and build bridges with the local community.

Whatever you are working, from a few hours a week to full time, McDonald's will provide all the training you need. There is a structured training programme to ensure you have all the skills you need to prepare the world-famous food and provide that unbeatable customer experience.

The training offered is the best in its field – 60 per cent of current managers started their careers as crew in the restaurants. The training and opportunities cater for all levels of ambition. You could make restaurant manager within two or three years. Equally, the only constraint on how far you rise will be your own talents.

However, the first step involves entry to the intensive 19-week management development programme as a trainee business manager. This will involve a thorough grounding in the McDonald's business and help you to build a whole raft of skills. Training will focus on:

- developing leadership skills
- team-building
- people development
- decision-making

- creating a positive working atmosphere
- business development
- generating profit.

As well as learning about the operational side of the restaurants, you will become an expert in finance, marketing and human resources. Step by step, you'll develop the talents you need for a long-term management career.

Once you become a restaurant manager, you have access to a wide range of internal and external training, including the chance to get a Diploma in Management from Nottingham Trent University. You'll also benefit from specific training such as the business leadership practices course, which helps managers with 12–18 months' experience think more creatively, plan more effectively, manage change and build community links.

Source: www.mcdonalds.co.uk

KEY TERMS

Training is the process of imparting new skills.

Development is the process of consolidating new skills and building them to greater levels.

On-the-job training takes place in the normal work environment.

Off-the-job training takes place away from the normal work environment.

Accredited training is endorsed in some way by an independent and recognised awarding body.

Developing skills

Personal development and training is something that should happen throughout people's working lives. As such, training and qualifications should form part of any career plan structure – and it should be seen as an ongoing process, not merely a period of initial training to get the qualifications needed to find a first job. As Figure 7.2 illustrates, people in all age groups engage in job-related training, and the trend from 1995 to 2003 is for increasing numbers to be involved in training.

Figure 7.2: Participation by employees in job-related training ('000)

	1995	1999	2003
All employees	5,559	6,740	7,360
By age			
16–19	288	472	448
20–24	694	799	855
25–29	925	1,008	934
30–39	1,619	1,957	2,092
40–49	1,382	1,551	1,836
50–64	651	953	1,194

Note: Counts all employees that have participated in job-related training (including both on-the-job and off-the-job training) in the last thirteen weeks.

Source: Labour Force Survey, Spring 1995, 1999, 2003

1 Training

It is likely that, whichever career path you choose, you will need or require some form of training. It is useful, therefore, to be aware of the specific skill requirements that are needed in particular occupational areas and the training and career development opportunities that are offered by particular businesses.

If, for example, a particular company only offers very limited training, it may deter you from applying as you may feel that there will be little chance of getting the skills to develop your career. Most people want to join a business that encourages training and development, as this enables them to become more proficient within their job role and advance through promotion or through career opportunities with other firms.

Many businesses offer staff training and development in order to ensure that they keep the staff they have recruited and to encourage staff that excel in their work to gain promotions. These businesses see a direct benefit in developing and retaining the skills and experience of their staff. In this way, the investment a business makes in training and development pays rewards in terms of a motivated workforce, high staff retention and efficient productivity.

By establishing what training and development is offered, potential applicants can assess its merits against their own career plan and goals. Initially, at the start of a career, it is very important to take into account the training a potential employer will provide. If there is no training and development on offer, then

you will need to identify how and where you can undertake the training needed in order to progress in the industry sector.

Businesses can offer training in various ways. Not all training will take place away from the job at a college or training centre. It might be useful to look again at Unit 2, Topic 2, which sets out in detail the different forms of on-the-job and off-the-job training provided by business organisations (see pages 64–68).

stop and think

Look again at the article on management training at McDonald's (see opposite). What methods of training are being used by McDonald's? Explain why the company has its own trainee management schemes. Given that it provides so much training in-house, explain why McDonald's might decide to send some staff on external training to get Diploma in Management qualifications?

2 Qualifications

One of the key issues with career plans is to look at what qualifications employers want at different levels (stages) of employment – what, for example, is the criteria for moving from a supervisor or team leader's position to a trainee or junior manager's role. By identifying these gaps between qualification and experience requirements at different employment levels, you should be able to identify the training, qualification and skills that need to be acquired before the next step of the career plan can be achieved.

For example, banks like Barclays, NatWest and Lloyds TSB may stipulate that they want potential management trainee candidates to be qualified to degree level. If you have just completed your GCE examinations, it may be that part of your career plan will involve exploring a suitable pathway to achieving the degree-level qualifications that you will need to find a management trainee position with a bank.

Career planning involves exploring the various ways of achieving required qualifications. There is often more than one route or option – for example, degree-level qualifications can be achieved through a full-time or part-time course at university, through a distance learning programme with an institution such as the Open University, or through vocational pathways leading to NVQ level 4 awards. This flexibility can be important – distance learning, for example, gives you the option of working full-time while studying.

Industry-led qualifications

Some industries and disciplines make obtaining relevant qualifications a key requirement of working in the sector. To work in personnel it is necessary to take qualifications that are accredited by the Chartered Institute of Personnel and Development (CIPD), the professional body for human resource practitioners. Career opportunities within the human resource field are dependent upon obtaining these qualifications.

This does not necessarily mean that entrants to professional areas have to go to college or university first to obtain appropriate qualifications. Some businesses will support employees through day release, evening or distance learning courses in order to obtain the qualifications required. For example, it is possible to start work after leaving school or college in a personnel department and study for the Certificate of Personnel Practice, which will give you a lead-in to further CIPD qualifications.

Many professions offer their own formal qualification pathways. Sometimes the qualifications are simply known by the initials of the awarding body – and Figure 7.3 provides a quick guide to some professional institutions that offer qualifications to help people progress in their respective industries.

Figure 7.3: Some professional institutions that offer qualifications

AAT	Association of Accounting Technicians
CIMA	Chartered Institute of Management Accountants
CIM	Chartered Institute of Marketing
CIPR	Chartered Institute of Public Relations
CIB	Chartered Institute of Bankers
IFS	Institute of Financial Services
SEO	Society of Event Organisers
NCTJ	National Council for the Training of Journalists
ILM	Institute of Leadership and Management
CILT	Chartered Institute of Logistics and Transport UK
IOM	The Institute of Operations Management
CIPS	Chartered Institute of Purchasing and Supply

3 Transferable skills

A key issue to consider when career planning and looking at training and qualifications is whether any awards, such as certificates, or any aptitudes and skills gained can be considered as transferable skills.

Transferable skills can be used in many different situations – and usually have wide application beyond the demands of a specific job role or business. They often encompass key skills such as communication, IT, numeracy, working with others, problem-solving, and improving own learning and performance. Many employers expect staff (and job applicants) to have competence in key skills. These skills can be learnt throughout life and to any level. They are as relevant on the shop floor as they are in the boardroom and, as such, they are regarded as being transferable between one business or job role and the next. Attaining transferable skills is valuable in maintaining options and keeping a flexible careers path.

In contrast, non-transferable skills are narrow competences that are job or company specific. This means that non-transferable skills can only be used in the particular firm or for the specific job role. These skills may help you progress in the company or job role for which they were acquired, but they may not be useful or even recognised if you decide to look for work elsewhere.

The same distinction – between transferable and non-transferable awards – also applies to qualifications. Nationally recognised qualifications are regarded as being transferable – they are recognised by all employers – but some in-house training schemes and certificates provided by employers may not be acknowledged by other companies and would not be regarded as accredited training.

Knowledge summary

■ **Each business takes an individual approach to staff training and development, often providing training which is directly appropriate to the needs of the business.**

■ **It is essential to investigate the training and development opportunities that are on offer by businesses in establishing which career pathway may be suitable.**

■ **Some occupations and businesses set minimum qualification requirements for specific job roles. You need to establish whether these qualifications can be gained after starting work or whether you need to obtain them in advance of seeking employment within that industry.**

In Unit 2, Topic 2 (see page 70), we looked at the training approach adopted by Corus, the international steel producer. Let's look in more detail at some of the training opportunities it provides.

Corus places importance on people development, stating that: "The ambition to achieve managerial, technological and operational excellence demands high and sustained levels of competence and skill. This is the driving force behind our recruitment policy and our investment in the training and development of all employees."

Corus has its own management training college, but also ensures that people are trained and developed on-site, which enables them to relate their learning back to their everyday role. Corus believes that school leavers who join the company should continue their education. It has a dedicated website coruseducation.com designed for both students still in school, as well as those who have left school, or are due to leave education and are considering their future.

Every graduate at Corus joins the talent development programme at the start of their career. This provides them with opportunities for development, encouraging all graduates to pursue their area of interest within their career. It is up to the individual to decide what they want from their career and the path to choose.

Corus offers apprenticeship schemes which lead to vocational and academic qualifications. Recruits are provided with first-class training programmes, including day release or blocks of time at an FE college. Apprentices have the opportunity to achieve senior levels in the company.

Corus has its own training unit that provides training to personnel both on-site as well as through off-the-job training at the training college. The training is a variety of experimental role play and activity-based learning, aimed at inspiring managers to gain higher levels of performance. Key training areas include:

- career and leadership development
- commercial (sales, marketing and finance)
- team development
- people management
- project and change management
- safety improvement
- personal development
- NVQs in management.

Source: www.corusgroup.com

A Explain why Corus believes in investment in the training and development of its employees.

B Describe the types of training it offers, and split this into on-the-job training and off-the-job training. Explain why it offers a mix of these two training approaches.

C Give one reason why you think it is important to Corus to have its own management training centre.

D What accredited qualifications does Corus offer? Explain why it might offer these to its employees.

E Using the recruitment section of the Corus website (www.corusgroup.com), find out what qualifications are required for any advertised jobs that interest you. For example, do you need previous qualifications to join the apprenticeship scheme? What other types of vacancies are there? What are the key requirements for these posts?

The government promotes several initiatives to encourage businesses to provide training. The programmes and schemes change over time, but the underlying aims remain fairly constant – to provide incentives to ensure that people have the right skills to help UK industry improve competitiveness.

When career planning and exploring career pathways – when considering how to obtain the experience, qualifications and training necessary to reach each stage in employment or to attain a career goal – it is important to see if any national training schemes and initiatives could be useful. The different schemes provide training and experience – either for employees or for people out of work – which can help you gain employment or career advancement.

1 Apprenticeships

There are different levels of apprenticeship available (see Figure 2.5, page 68). They all lead to national vocational qualifications (NVQs), key skills qualifications and, in most cases, a technical certificate such as a BTEC or City & Guilds.

Apprenticeships are mainly used to help individuals gain particular skills in a vocation. They focus on training and developing transferable skills in particular professions such as accounting, business administration, insurance services, retailing and, even, hospitality and events. The key aspect of an apprenticeship is the fact that skills are gained while the trainee is in paid employment.

Apprenticeships are now open to adults, scrapping the previous 25-year-old age limit, and lead to qualifications equivalent to A-level studies. Further details of individual apprenticeship areas can be found at www.apprenticeships.org.uk

2 Learning and Skills Council

The Learning and Skills Council (LSC) was set up to make England's employment base better skilled and more competitive. It has a single goal: to improve the skills of England's young people and adults to make sure that the workforce is of world-class standard. The LSC is responsible for planning and funding high-quality vocational education and training for everyone. One of the LSC's key roles is to provide funding and support for employers who want to offer apprenticeship programmes. In Wales, ELWa (Education and Learning Wales) has similar functions and responsibilities. You can find out more about both bodies from their websites, www.lsc.gov.uk and www.elwa.ac.uk.

3 Investors in People

Businesses benefit from having a well-trained workforce – indeed, a business risks failure if its staff lack the right skills. Investors in People (IIP) uses a powerful business model as the basis of a process that

stop and think

Why is so much money being invested in apprenticeships? What advantages are there in taking an apprenticeship as a start to a career pathway rather than following traditional academic routes to further education and university?

Source: LSC press release, 31 March 2005

Additional £38 million for apprenticeships

The Learning and Skills Council (LSC), the organisation that exists to make England better skilled and more competitive, is making available an additional £38 million in response to the growing demand from employers for apprenticeships.

Part of the money will fund new apprentice places and will be directed to employers and training providers that deliver high-quality apprenticeship programmes. It will help the LSC meet its commitment to increase the number of young people starting an apprenticeship in the current year to 175,000.

helps businesses to link staff development to meeting the needs of the business. The National Employers Skills Survey 2003 commissioned by the Learning and Skills Council reported that 16 per cent of businesses were Investors in People.

If you are applying for a job, it is worth noting if your prospective employer has achieved (or is working towards) the IIP award. Businesses that have Investors in People status have made a long-term commitment to provide funding and opportunity for employees to undertake personal development, training and study toward qualifications. This can be vital in helping to achieve a career plan, and certainly the support of the employer (as IIP status indicates) can make the attainment of each step or stage much easier.

4 New Deal

The New Deal comprises a number of schemes for people who are out of work and claiming benefit. The intentions of this programme are to help people who have been out of work for a period of six months or over. At various stages, a career plan can become stalled or need to be changed or adapted – sometimes individuals can be the victim of circumstances outside their control: they might be made redundant in an economic downturn or their company might go into liquidation.

In these circumstances, programmes like the New Deal can be a useful aid to getting a career plan back on track or perhaps to switching to a different pathway. New Deal provides intensive help and support in finding work, guided by a personal adviser, or helps participants find employment with a New Deal employer that receives a subsidy for six months for taking on a trainee.

5 Learndirect

Learndirect has a remit from government to provide high-quality post-16 learning. Developed by the University for Industry, it operates a network of more than 2,000 online learning centres in England, Wales and Northern Ireland, providing access to a range of e-learning opportunities. Learndirect offers more than 550 different courses covering a range of subjects, including management, IT, skills for life, and languages, at all levels. Most courses are available online, allowing people to learn wherever they have access to the internet – at home, at work or at a learndirect centre. This means that:

- courses can be accessed at any time, so learners are not restricted to waiting for the next course date or for the start of the academic year

- there is no requirement to commit to a regular time to study, which means that this type of e-learning is very flexible.

Online study is a particularly useful tool in career planning as it means that many gaps in skills and qualifications can be bridged even if your employer doesn't provide training or if there is no suitable education and training centre available locally. Learndirect courses can be accessed at any stage in a person's working life, and offer the chance to address specific skills gaps or take longer-term programmes leading to established qualifications.

Learndirect

There are over 700 different job profiles available on the learning advice section of the learndirect website. Have you, for example, considered a career as a:

- dog handler
- chimney sweep
- image consultant
- cinema projectionist
- air cabin crew

Each profile has details of what the job involves, the hours you can expect to work, what qualifications you need, and anything else you might want to know. Find out more at www.learndirect.co.uk.

stop and think

Although online study can provide some advantages, what disadvantages might also be associated with this style of learning?

6 Other training incentives

Although many government schemes are actually directed at helping people find work or encourage training through employers, there are a several other training initiatives which can be used to develop skills and useful experience.

Help for disabled people

Every jobcentre has a disability employment adviser (DEA) as part of a disability service team (DST) that can provide specialist advice to disabled people and actual or potential employers. The DEA can advise on practical help through the Access to Work scheme, the Job Introduction Scheme and supported employment.

National Skills Strategy

The National Skills Strategy provides unskilled or low-skilled adults with the skills they need for sustained and productive employment. Examples of what is offered through this strategy (which may vary regionally) are:

- free tuition for a first full level 2 qualification
- adult learning grant for adults on low incomes
- employer training pilots – help for improving skills at work
- free information and advice, covering courses and qualifications
- learner support funds – extra help with costs of transport and childcare
- business support services for small and medium-sized enterprises.

Worktrain

Worktrain is a national online jobs and learning site (www.worktrain.gov.uk) provided by the Department for Work and Pensions. It provides up-to-date details on over 300,000 jobs, as well as information on different types of jobs, training opportunities, childcare (including local provision) and a news service.

Work in Europe

The Employment Service belongs to the European Employment Services organisation (known as EURES), an association of EU government bodies dealing with employment matters. It allows job vacancies and information on living and working conditions across Europe to be advertised in all EU member countries. Vacancies on the EURES system are sometimes advertised in jobcentres. If you are interested in working in the EU, you should ask your local jobcentre for an overseas search for suitable vacancies.

Knowledge summary

- **There is a wide range of national training initiatives, include apprenticeships, Investors in People, the New Deal programme and learndirect.**

- **Schemes are subject to change over time. The government might review, cancel or adapt any of the initiatives.**

- **It is important to investigate whether any current training initiatives could support your career plan. There may be a programme which will help you gain the experience and training you need in order to apply for the type of job that interests you.**

The run-up to Christmas is always a busy time for supermarkets, but Tesco found time to celebrate a new award. As well as being Britain's biggest grocer, the group has become the first retailer to have its in-house training accredited by the exams watchdog, the Qualifications and Curriculum Authority. It is now authorised to run its own apprenticeship scheme and award nationally recognised qualifications.

Clare Chapman, Tesco's personnel director, visited apprentices on the shop floor to celebrate the success of the firm's new approach to staff training. Tesco's trial of the apprenticeship scheme started this year with 20 young people in three supermarkets. It plans to expand the scheme to a further 480 employees in 60 stores.

Chapman believes the business benefits from investing in staff skills. "Some employees are attracted by curiosity, others by the ability to earn as they learn, and many by the chance to prepare for promotion to management," she says. "Whatever the motivation, there is a lot of satisfaction with the apprenticeship programme, and staff retention improves."

The group also plans a pilot scheme of apprenticeships for those over 24, as the government is extending apprenticeship training to workers aged 25 and above. Chapman says: "Apprenticeships could help to build the confidence of older workers and encourage those returning to work after a career break."

Tesco is one of 26 companies in an industry taskforce that has been set the challenge of raising the profile of apprenticeship schemes among individuals and employers. Stephen Gardner, director of work-based learning for the Learning and Skills Council, says: "Apprenticeships are employer-focused, providing the skills that companies really need. The fact that Tesco, the biggest private employer in the country with 237,000 workers, has had its training accredited in this way gives apprenticeships an even greater level of credibility."

Teresa Bergin, head of sector skills at the Qualifications and Curriculum Authority, says: "Big employers already make a huge investment in staff training. If those programmes are sufficiently strong to allow the adoption of external awards, it can benefit both employees and the organisation itself."

Source: Mail on Sunday, 19 December 2004

A Explain the key features of the apprenticeship programme. Explain the benefits you think that employees gain from the apprenticeship scheme.

B What benefits do you think that Tesco might gain now it has become an accredited in-house training centre?

C Explain the input of the Learning and Skills Council to the apprenticeship scheme.

D Consider other national government training initiatives, such as the New Deal programme, learndirect and Investors in People. Would these programmes motivate you to train and develop your learning? What are your views on the government's training initiatives?

Topic 4 Personal skills profile

Setting the scene: customer service assistant at Norwich Union

The extract below sets out the key skill requirements for a full-time post as a customer services assistant in a Norwich Union office in Bristol.

NORWICH UNION
an AVIVA company

Customer Services Assistant

About the role
The personal lines, customer services division has an opportunity for an administrative role. This section of Norwich Union deals with car, motorbike and van insurance policies.

The job entails supporting the customer services manager. You will also review administrative processes and paperwork within the office.

Skills, behaviours, personality traits
The successful applicant will possess the following abilities:
- good telephone manner
- ability to work on their own initiative
- effective planning and organisation skills
- good working knowledge of Word and Excel is desirable.

The key skills and behaviours for the role are:
- making things happen
- working with others
- personal development
- customer responsiveness.

Why has Norwich Union listed the skills required to carry out this job successfully? Which of the listed skills do you think that you possess? How might you acquire those that you don't have?

Personal skills

For each occupation that interests you, it will be necessary to establish the range of skills that are important in getting selected and succeeding in the job. You will then need to match these requirements against the skills that you currently have.

In this topic, we review some of the key personal skills that are important in many business and occupational roles. Many skills overlap with one another – and this emphasises their integrated nature.

Team working

Many modern jobs entail working as part of a team on a daily basis. To work effectively in a team, you may need to be able to negotiate with other team members – for example, to decide who is to complete certain tasks – and you will need time management skills to ensure that the team's project is completed by the agreed deadline. You may need to monitor the

KEY TERMS

Leadership is the function of ruling, guiding and inspiring other people within an organisation in pursuit of agreed objectives.

Communication is the transfer of information between people or organisations.

A **supervisor** provides a link between a manager and operatives and support staff.

team's performance and achievements against set targets and discuss these with other team members. It is also important to be able to recognise and work to and around your strengths and weaknesses (as well as those of others). So if you are good at planning tasks, this might be your special contribution to the team's effort.

2 Influencing skills

If you are working in public relations you will need to be able to influence and persuade people. These skills are also important for all managers and for a variety of other roles. Influencing skills can be very subtle: they may take the form of gaining support from colleagues (both senior and junior), persuading other people to become your supporters, and creating relationships with important groups such as colleagues, suppliers and customers.

Influencing skills require a delicate balance between tact and assertiveness. They are not about bullying people, rather they require you to be:

- a good listener so that you appreciate what motivates others and are able to affect their views

- able to put across your views, hopes or aspirations in a way that might inspire others to adopt them.

3 Risk-taking

Risk is common in many businesses. Traders on the London markets buy company shares and commodities such as gold in the hope of selling them later at a profit. The risk is that the prices might fall, and the traders incur a loss for their companies. A decorator may quote a high price to a potential customer for wallpapering a room and take a risk on whether this will be acceptable. The key risk-taking skills include the ability to make judgements about the likelihood of a decision succeeding, to estimate the likely costs of failure, and to learn to accept that taking risks does sometimes result in mistakes.

stop and think

In 2003 two Romanian inventors, Marian Gavrila and Garbriel Patulea, came up with the idea of putting smoke detectors into mobile phones. This, they argued, would save thousands of lives. What personal skills might the Romanians need to turn this idea into a viable business proposition?

4 Self-confidence and motivation

Self-confidence is freedom from doubt: it is about possessing faith in yourself and your abilities. Successful employees, managers and entrepreneurs demonstrate this skill. For example, they are calm when approaching difficult situations, think positively (not negatively), and project an assured image when dealing with other people. Motivation (the will to do something) often accompanies self-confidence. If you are sure about an idea or a decision, then it is more likely that you will be committed to work hard in support of it.

5 Communication skills

Communication is the transfer of information between people or organisations. In a technological age this can be done in many ways, ranging from face-to-face communication, perhaps as part of an interview for a job, to communicating to thousands of people through a website. You need a wide range of skills to communicate effectively. They include:

- using information technology (computers and relevant software such as PowerPoint)

- the ability to deliver presentations, write reports, lead meetings and respond to questions

- being a good listener (so as to be able to respond appropriately and effectively)

- displaying appropriate body language when communicating – such as making regular eye contact with an audience and maintaining an open body posture.

Good communication skills underpin many of the other personal skills examined in this topic.

stop and think

Polly has just started work as a shop assistant at Marks & Spencer. With whom might she need to communicate? In what ways might she be able to perform her job more effectively if she has good communication skills?

6 Leadership skills

Leadership is the functions of ruling, guiding and inspiring other people within an organisation in pursuit of agreed objectives. Leadership is an important element within a successful organisation. A good leader needs a number of skills. Although the exact list might be debatable, the necessary skills include:

- possessing a positive self-image and associated self-confidence

- being informed and knowledgeable

- having the ability to think creatively and innovatively

- having the ability to act quickly and decisively

- possessing an air of authority

- displaying first-class communication skills

- having the ability to solve problems, often under pressure.

7 Supervisory skills

Supervisors provide a link between a manager and operatives and support staff. They are classed as the first line of management and, in many cases, their jobs have become more demanding recently.

The responsibilities of supervisors are varied and require a range of skills including:

- communication skills to deal with staff over day-to-day issues, such as how to cover an employee absence

- decision-making skills to resolve minor problems – for example, which customer orders to complete first or which decisions to pass up to more senior managers

- negotiation skills to resolve a dispute between junior employees

- information technology skills to record employee attendance at work or production data.

8 Interpersonal skills

Interpersonal skills help you to develop and use many of the other skills discussed in this topic. For example, effective interpersonal skills will help you to communicate effectively with other people and assist you in influencing their views and decisions and in persuading them to accept your leadership or supervision. The term interpersonal skills also encompasses communicating and listening, resolving conflict, dealing with criticism of oneself, being assertive when appropriate, and being honest with people. Some people naturally have good interpersonal skills; others may need training to develop them. Either way, they are a vital element of a successful working life.

stop and **think**

You should investigate the personal skills required for certain jobs. You can find general information from the job profiles on the learndirect website (www.learndirect.co.uk). Then you will need to get information from individual businesses to see their specific requirements for the job roles they have.

Different skill sets

Each occupation you may consider will require a different set of skills. Similarly, each level of post within a given business will require a different skill set. It is likely that you will develop these skills over time. If you are working as a manager, for example, you will need a specific set of skills.

Consider the requirements that McDonald's sets for its managers which we introduced in Topic 2 (see page 296). The company has a focus on leadership skills, providing training that covers team-building, people development, decision-making, creating a positive working atmosphere, business development and generating profit. It doesn't expect people joining the company to work in a junior capacity to have all these attributes, but it is prepared to give them the opportunity to develop these skills through training and work experience.

stop and **think**

Dave Wallwork, Steve Cooper and Chris Wright are all in their early 30s. They have two other things in common: in the autumn of 2001 they gave up their jobs with Coca-Cola, and they jointly established The Feel Good Drinks Company. This new company sells fruit drinks intended to appeal to those seeking health-promoting products.

The trio spent nine months planning their business. They wanted to create a brand that was different: it had to be fun, fast-moving and designed to make consumers feel good. Three years on, the company is on track to attain annual sales in excess of £10 million.

What personal skills might Dave, Steve and Chris have required to set up and operate a successful business?

Knowledge summary

- Everybody requires a range of personal skills to carry out their jobs effectively.

- Personal skills are wide-ranging including communication, interpersonal and leadership skills.

- Some people naturally have effective personal skills; others acquire and hone them through training.

- Different occupations and even different jobs within the same occupation require different sets of personal skills.

data**interpretation**

Job research

This task requires you to research two jobs in which you might be interested. You should use local newspapers, a jobcentre or the internet to identify two jobs for which you could apply and in which you have a genuine interest. Once you have identified the jobs, and obtained some information about the particular job requirements, complete these activities.

A List the main duties associated with each job.

B Using the information in this topic, outline the major skills you think that you would require to be able to carry out each job effectively.

C Select the job to which you are best suited, giving reasons for your decision.

Setting the scene: psychometric tests in job selection

Many employers now use psychometric testing to assess the personalities of potential employees. There are several kinds of test, but usually candidates have to answer questions on their preferences, relationships with other people and interests.

Many people are wary of psychometric tests. Sam had completed an MA in investigative journalism when she applied for a job as a reporter on her local newspaper in the Midlands. At the interview, she was asked to complete a psychometric test. "I have a real suspicion of these tests because I don't like being pigeon-holed," she explains, "but I went along with it. I found the questions way too simplistic. There were things like, 'Do you like being with people? All the time, some of the time or hardly ever?' It was difficult to answer because I'm different at different times."

Sam didn't get the job and when she received the test results, she was shocked. "It wasn't flattering," she says. "I was described as decisive, aggressive and impatient, among other things. It seemed to be about someone who wouldn't be able to work with other people but I work hard to get on with people."

Disillusioned, she sought help from a professional careers adviser who also used psychometric testing. This time, it was a more positive experience. "I was given a different test which had been designed for professional, highly educated people," she says.

"The consultant talked about the findings in depth and gave me a lot of useful insights. He confirmed, for example, that I couldn't work alone and that I'm motivated by a need for social change." One of the suggestions made by the consultant was that Sam might be suited to working in the voluntary sector. She now works as a co-ordinator for community advice centres in the Midlands and enjoys her job.

Sam's experience is a common scenario. Many people find psychometric testing very useful for careers advice but have had bad experiences with job interviews. The problem is that tests are often used in the wrong way. Psychometric tests should only be one part of the recruitment process, and employers should spend at least fifteen minutes elaborating on the test results. Feedback is crucial.

If you are given a test at an interview, don't be tempted to fill in the answers you think the interviewer is looking for. If you're too perfect, they'll smell a rat. And if you have to misrepresent yourself, is it really the job for you? If you try and fit the profile of their ideal candidate, there might be problems if you get the job because there could be things you won't be able to do.

Source: Adapted from http://jobsadvice.guardian.co.uk/

What are psychometric tests?

A psychometric test is a way of assessing a person's ability or personality in a measured and structured way. Psychometric literally means measuring the brain. Some tests are used by employers to help them in their recruitment process, while other tests can help people with career decision-making.

Psychometric tests are used by many employers across most sectors, including IT, engineering, energy, banking, consultancy, accountancy, the civil service and the retail industry.

There are three main types of test.

1 Measuring personality

Most tests that focus on personality consist of a series of written statements – for each set of statements, you are asked to indicate, as spontaneously as possible, the one with which you most readily identify. (For an example, see Figure 2.18, page 100.) Upon completion of the test, the results are plotted on a chart, or personality profile, to show the shape of your personality.

Interpreted correctly, this can be a useful indicator, both to the employer as a predictor of the extent to which this personality profile matches the person specification for the job, and to you in examining the type of person you are and the extent to which this matches the personal characteristics required within various jobs and occupations. There is not a right answer to these types of psychometric test, as they are designed to assess whether a person will fit into a specific job and be able to work with a particular group of employees.

2 Assessing general abilities and aptitudes

Some test are designed to assess your overall or "general" intelligence, or particular types of intelligence, such as your logical reasoning or thinking performance. Many tests are designed to measure a particular skill such as verbal and numerical reasoning, and diagrammatic and data interpretation. Aptitude tests frequently aim to identify your potential to learn to do a new task rather than set out to describe the abilities you already have. This is important to many employers. These tests frequently have to be completed within a given time period, usually between 30 and 50 minutes. A common format is to ask you to select the correct answer from a choice of three or four possible answers.

3 Measuring and assessing specific abilities

If you are applying for careers in say IT, science or engineering, you might be asked to take more specialised tests to assess some specific occupational requirements. The questions here are similar in structure to other tests but require some knowledge and understanding of the relevant occupational area.

Together these three types of psychometric test can help to identify whether you have some of the personal skills that we discussed in Topic 4. They can uncover whether you have the ability to influence others or to communicate effectively, or have the aptitude to take risks as part of your job.

Did you think the tests accurately reflected your personality and skills? Would the results be useful to a potential employer?

Use of psychometric tests by employers

There are a number of different types of psychometric test used by employers. These include the Occupational Personality Questionnaire (OPQ), the 16PF (16 Personality Factors) and the Myers-Briggs Type Indicator (MBTI).

Psychometric tests are increasingly used by employers as part of the recruitment process. The recruitment process can be costly; the average direct cost is estimated to be in the region of £4,300, however this rises to £6,800 when recruiting at manager level. Hence any technique, such as psychometric tests, which can help to recruit the right people is likely to be welcomed by employers.

Psychometric tests may be used as an initial filter in the selection process, to determine whether you will proceed to the next stage (usually an interview). In this case, there is a fixed cut-off score (pass/fail). They can provide a reasonably cost-effective method of reducing the number of applicants for a job to manageable proportions. Psychometric testing specialists can be hired at a daily rate of £350–£500 plus expenses.

Alternatively, and perhaps more commonly, psychometric tests may be used at the final stage of selection, as part of an assessment centre. In this case,

---

stop and think

If you want to tackle some sample questions and receive some feedback, they are available through www.shldirect.com. You will need to follow the links to "help on assessment", "practice test and feedback" and "practice real tests and get feedback".

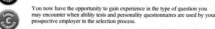

Practice & Feedback

Practice and get Feedback on the Ability Tests used by Employers

You now have the opportunity to gain experience in the type of question you may encounter when ability tests and personality questionnaires are used by your prospective employer in the selection process.

Today most selection procedures, even for graduates, involve ability tests and/or personality questionnaires as well as an interview. Here you can choose to:

- try some free examples of ability test questions and see what a personality questionnaire involves.
- do real timed practice tests with feedback on how you compare to other applicants
- Take part in a test we are currently trialling and receive feedback

Example Questions | Practice Real Tests and get Feedback | Test Trial

the tests may not carry any more weight than the other elements of the selection procedure.

Any tests used by employers have to be reliable and valid if they are going to be of effective use in selection. It is essential that those involved in the selection process are trained in the use of personality tests – in particular, the interpretation of outcomes of the test results – to be able to use test results effectively in the selection of candidates.

There are some practical benefits of using psychological tests in helping to select suitable candidates to job posts. While it is not actually possible to "test" someone's personality, these psychometric tests can be used to examine personality traits – that is, the way we tend to behave or how we

tend to think. It gives employers an insight into personality and, correctly interpreted, can be a useful addition as part of the selection decision.

There are drawbacks to using psychometric tests. First, these tests are not infallible; some people are nervous when taking tests and this may cause them to answer incorrectly; others may try to "cheat" and provide the answers they think are wanted. Second, the results from psychometric tests may contradict the information gleaned through other parts of the selection process such as interviews. Third, the results can be unhelpful without expert interpretation, and there is a need for those interpreting tests to be fully trained, and for effective feedback to be provided to candidates.

Unit 7 Career planning

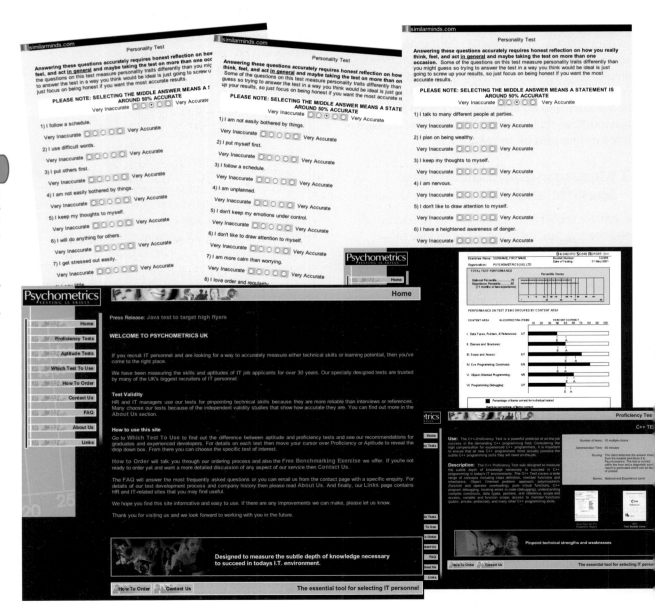

Knowledge summary

- Psychometric tests are used by employers to make better selection decisions within the recruitment and selection process.

- There are generally three types of test they use in selection: measures of personality, measures of mental and general ability, and measures of specific aptitudes.

- Personality tests measure self-reported typical behaviour patterns or traits.

- A personality test does not contain any right or wrong answers. It aims to present a picture of how a person will behave, given particular circumstances.

data interpretation
Psychometrics UK

Psychometrics UK has been supplying IT-specific skills and aptitude tests to blue-chip clients since 1987. Its tests are trusted by many of the UK's largest recruiters of IT personnel. The company's goal is to help its clients find the people with the best technical skills for the job.

Recruiters use the tests year on year to maintain the high technical standards they have established. This is often achieved by benchmarking the tests across an IT department and setting qualifying scores for new recruits.

HR and IT managers use Psychometrics UK's tests for pinpointing technical skills because they are more reliable than interviews or references. Independent validity studies show that they can accurately measure technical skills and learning potential.

Source: adapted from www.psychometrics-uk.com

A What skills is Psychometrics UK attempting to assess using its tests?

B Why do you think Psychometrics UK's tests have proved popular with many IT businesses?

C Visit the Psychometrics UK website and learn more about the company's operations. Assess the case for and against an employer using Psychometrics UK's tests as a major part of its selection procedure.

Setting the scene: teleworking

The 2003 Labour Force Survey reports that more than 2 million or 7.5 per cent of the working population are opting for some form of teleworking. This figure has risen from less than 1 million in 1997.

Teleworkers undertake their work from home and link to the outside world via computer, telephone, internet and fax. Occupations range from those you might expect, such as journalists, to those you would not. Solicitors, radio presenters, audio typists, architects, travel agents and accountants can fulfil their roles outside the office as long as they have the right equipment.

This all sounds very inviting, but are you really suited to this way of doing things? "It's important to know yourself very well," says Linda Doe, a chartered psychologist who advises companies such as BP, Nationwide and Microsoft on effective teleworking strategies.

"You need to know if you can maintain your self-motivation and, just as importantly, know what demotivates you." You should also consider your style of interaction. "Think about how you like to work and the type of communication you enjoy, that is, face to face or on the telephone," says Doe.

"Do you prefer working things out on your own or swapping ideas with a team? And do you

deal with problems or decisions alone or seek the input of others?" It is still possible to get others involved in your work when you're based at home, she says, it just requires organisation.

According to the Department for Education and Skills, teleworkers should exhibit particular characteristics if they are to operate successfully. The department listed six important personality traits for teleworkers:

- mature
- trustworthy
- self-sufficient
- self-disciplined
- good time managers
- good communicators.

These personality traits help teleworkers to be successful, but many managers would argue that they are the sort of characteristics they seek in all employees.

Source: adapted from http://jobsadvice.guardian.co.uk/

Personality tests and occupations

Topic 5 looked at how tests of our personality may be used by employers as part of their assessment process. In this topic, we explore how you can use psychometric tests to identify and describe the main

features of your own personality (known as personality traits). These can then be used as part of the information needed to develop your personal development and career plan.

Not all people have the personalities to carry out all types of jobs. It is an important part of your career planning that you identify your personality traits or features and use these to help determine the type of career that you might follow. One way in which to do this is to use a personality test. However, before doing so, it is important to be aware of how they work.

Personality tests can identify the traits or features that make up your personality. Different tests are designed to identify aspects of your personality. For example, some tests might uncover how you view yourself, while others will assess your relationships with other people. A personality test might help you to assess these traits:

KEY TERMS

A **personal development plan** (also called a **personal career plan**) is a plan of action setting out your aspirations and intentions for your future career.

Personality traits are the elements that comprise a person's character. For example, they might be decisive or a very effective communicator.

Personality tests are a type of psychometric test.

- self-discipline – can you motivate yourself to meet targets and goals on time, even if this means working long hours?

- assertiveness – are you confident in dealing with other people, can you put across ideas and defend your arguments?

- self-reliance – are you confident in your own abilities and are you able to take decisions on your own without asking for advice and guidance?

- independence – do you like working on your own, making plans and following them through with little support and contact from others?

Personality traits can play a significant part in helping you choose a career. By identifying your personality traits, you can better judge which occupations are best suited to your personality.

stop and think

What personal traits do you think might be appropriate for:

- a college lecturer

- a shop manager

- a website designer?

Personality tests also have some weaknesses. They only tell you how people like to approach things differently, and you should use them with caution.

- The scores are subjective, and can change depending on your mood, attitude and mindset when completing the test. You might get different results if you take the same test two or three times.

- The results are not infallible, or even highly reliable. Research shows even the best personality type questionnaires produce an incorrect result in, on average, 25 per cent of cases.

This has important implications if you are thinking of completing a personality test. You should be prepared to challenge the results if you think they are wrong, and not base any important judgements solely on the personality test. It may be useful to contact a careers adviser to ask for advice about tests. They may offer to help you in the process and provide additional feedback.

Many psychologists advise businesses that they should not use personality tests as a sole instrument for selecting employees. The same advice applies to you.

They are a useful part of your personal development plan, but should not be given undue weight.

Skills and occupations

Personality is merely one factor to take into account when choosing a possible career. You should also consider the personal skills that you have and how these might help to prepare you for particular careers. We considered a range of personal skills in Topic 4 of this unit.

As the following two profiles – of Gary Stevens and Carol Harvey – illustrate, matching your personal skills as well as your personality to a possible career increases your chances of success.

profile: Gary Stevens, GS Computers

In 2003 Gary Stevens established his own business resolving IT problems faced by businesses and individuals in his area. He installed new equipment, undertook minor repairs and helped people link up to broadband internet services as they became available. He gave up a well-paid job with British Telecom to set up his business. By 2005 he had over 300 customers and was considering taking on staff to help with his growing workload.

Gary believes that, apart from the obvious technical skills, it was important that he was efficiently organised and able to plan his working day to meet the needs of as many customers as possible. He also relies heavily on his interpersonal and good communication skills, as much of his work is face-to-face. If his business continues to expand, Gary recognises that he will also need to develop supervisory and leadership skills.

stop and think

How might Gary develop the necessary supervisory and leadership skills if his business continues to grow?

313

Topic 6 Personality traits

Carol is a community or district nurse. Community nurses provide care for people of all ages in a variety of non-hospital settings including patients' homes, doctors' surgeries and residential nursing homes. Carol is part of a team that aims to respond quickly and intensively to patients' medical needs. This means that many patients do not have to be admitted to hospital and they can stay in their own homes for longer when they are elderly or unwell.

Carol loves her job, but thinks that it requires very definite personal skills to carry it out successfully. "Community nursing care is provided by a team, and it is vital to be a team player to give patients consistent care and support. I also have to persuade patients to follow particular courses of treatment and they can be very reluctant. Sometimes I have to argue with managers to provide more resources for a specific case. You have to be very persuasive."

"However, communication is possibly the key skill. Dealing with patients who are often frightened and sometimes verbally aggressive (because they are afraid) requires tact and diplomacy, combined with a degree of assertiveness."

Your personal development plan

Your career or personal development plan is best built up over a period of time. The structure and contents of these plans can vary, but they should contain some key common elements.

- Your curriculum vitae (CV). This should be as up to date as possible to provide a clear picture of where you are at any moment in time.

- Job descriptions of any work that you have already undertaken. This provides evidence of your skills and how you have developed.

- Set out what motivates and demotivates you. Try to analyse your strengths and weaknesses. In this section, you might choose to include the results of personality tests and assessments of your personal skills.

- Collect job advertisements that interest you. This will help you to identify the skills and qualities you may need in the future.

- Be ambitious and set yourself targets or objectives. Where do you want to be in, say, three years and five years time? This should help to motivate you as well as providing a sense of direction.

Several websites allow you to take personality tests online. You can use these to provide you with an understanding of your own personality traits.

Use one of the resources listed below to get a profile of your own personality and record the results. This will assist you in establishing the types of career or occupation that you might find suitable.

www.testingroom.com/beginHtmlTest.do

The Testing Room site is run by Psychometrics Canada. It gives you three test options:

Career Interest Profiler – aimed at helping you to discover the type of work that is most suitable and enjoyable to you.

Career Values Scale – aimed at identifying key elements in your work that make you satisfied or dissatisfied, this test looks at your career values in a number of key areas such as team orientation and influence, career development, and excitement.

The Personality Index – aimed at providing an objective measure of different traits and facets of your personality, the test helps you to understand a little more about yourself.

www.prospects.ac.uk

This is the official graduate careers site. However, it has some useful test profiles which may help in the search for suitable career choices. By logging into the prospects planner, you can access tests which will provide you with a skills profile and an interests and motivation profile.

www.bradleyscvs.co.uk.htm

This website provides advice and help on getting a job, including interview preparation and compiling a CV. It allows you to take a practice psychometric test.

www.findspot.com/free_career_tests.htm

This website provides links to a number of sites which offer free career assessment tests, interest tests, career placement tests, career quizzes, etc. A useful start for establishing what type of person you are, and what types of career might interest and motivate you.

A Use one or more of the websites to complete a personality test.

B Consider the results carefully. Discuss them with friends and family to discover whether they are an accurate summary of your personality traits.

C Add the results to your personal development plan, but make sure they are only part of the evidence used to determine you future occupation.

Setting the scene: three contrasting job profiles

Consider these three profiles. Each individual required different types of training and post-school education, and took a different route to get the qualifications and experience required for their current job role.

profile: Lynn Buchanan

Lynn Buchanan works for the Samaritans. She manages the organisation's website.

Qualifications/experience: Lynn did a first degree in psychology, a masters in information technology, then worked for two years at IBM as an IT specialist before joining the Samaritans. To do her job, you need to be good with words as well as computers. She suggests you get some marketing and administrative experience, and perhaps contribute to or edit your school, university or work newsletters. You can also progress through the technical route, which involves gaining some web technology experience. In addition, it's a good idea to set up your own website or a website page you've written for someone else. This will show you have got some direct experience.

Source: www.bbc.co.uk/radio1/onelife/

profile: Emma Rich

Emma Rich decided she wanted to enter teaching or lecturing as a career, and is now a lecturer at the University of Loughborough.

Qualifications/experience: most lecturers are now expected to have a PhD (a postgraduate degree) in their specialist subject. In addition to educational qualifications, it's important to keep in touch with some of the key professional bodies in the subject area. In Emma's case, this involved membership of the International Olympic Academy Participants Association. She did some part-time teaching as a postgraduate student before lecturing full time.

profile: Dany Cotton

Dany Cotton was the first female station officer in a fire brigade in the country. Now promoted to assistant divisional officer, she's the highest-ranking female officer in the fire service.

Qualifications/experience: O-levels and A-levels. There are no formal qualifications needed to join the fire service. Training is given to new recruits on a 16-week course at a training centre.

Post-school pathways

There will often be more than one pathway to achieve the training, qualifications and experience you need for your considered career choice. This choice will depend on what suits you individually, and which routes are more readily available to you at the time you are developing your career plan.

In this topic, we explore the advantages and disadvantages of the different options for continuing training and education post-school. These include:

- higher education
- apprenticeships
- employment and training at work
- voluntary work
- study and work abroad
- self-employment.

1 Higher education

If you want to achieve advanced qualifications, one of your main options is to enter higher education. This may mean applying to university to take a full-time course leading to a degree and postgraduate qualifications. You can also apply for foundation degree courses, which have lower entry requirements than first degree courses. This will enable you to access a degree course if you are taking one or two A levels, or do not achieve the target entry level for the first degree course.

You will need to consider how you will fund yourself through university. You will need to pay fees, and you will need to finance your living expenses during what can be several years of study. You will need to examine whether you can obtain some assistance with funding through, for example, sponsorships, student loans or help from your local education authority.

2 Apprenticeships

Rather than continue in full-time education, you may decide that you want to join a company and undertake training while in work in order to gain the appropriate skills and experience for your career choice. Apprenticeships offer one structured means of gaining vocational skills and qualifications while working. Information on apprenticeship schemes is available from your local learning and skills council and from your careers service.

Taking part in an apprenticeship scheme means you will work towards accredited NVQs. NVQs are available at different levels, from level 1 through to level 5, and you will be placed on the level suited to the access point of your apprenticeship. You do not necessarily start at level 1 and then progress through each level. Each NVQ identifies a range of skills or competences you need to possess in order to effectively meet the skill requirements of the job. For example, if you are training to be a supervisor on your apprenticeship, it may not be necessary for you to progress through to the higher level 5 qualification; you may only need to be competent to level 3.

The benefit of this approach is that you are getting paid work experience throughout your apprenticeship, and any off-the-job training – at a local college, for example – will be funded by your employer. You should obtain the experience and qualifications that may help you secure long-term employment with the firm with which you have undertaken your apprenticeship, or help you to apply for jobs with other firms.

Further information about apprenticeship schemes is available from:

- www.realworkrealpay.info
- www.lsc.gov.uk
- www.jobcentreplus.gov.uk
- www.employmentservice.gov.uk

3 Work

You may choose to go directly into work instead of continuing full-time education or taking an apprenticeship. This will enable you to gain experience in the career of your choice – providing you have the requirements to get on the first rung – and your workplace may offer you on-the-job training which will help you to develop the skills and knowledge you require in order to carry out the job effectively.

In general, any training will be suited to the needs of the employer, and directed towards the acquisition of the skills and knowledge required of their employees. On-the-job training will be directly relevant to the job requirements. You will be trained to be able to perform your job competently. Some organisations, such as the fire service and the armed forces, provide their own training, as the occupation requires such specialist skills.

However, an employer might fund you to attend a day-release course at a local college to gain essential qualifications for your job role. For example, a health and safety officer would be sent on an external course in order to obtain necessary certification for the job role. Your employer may also fund you through a distance learning course. Additional development could be offered if the organisation believes you have promotion potential.

4 Study and work abroad

You may decide that you want to look at opportunities for study and/or work abroad. Working and living abroad will bring a wide range of opportunities for your self-development. It can provide a useful route towards your career pathway.

Experience of living abroad will expand your personal skills, and any work experience – whether paid or on a voluntary basis – will add to your personal profile.

It may be that you are interested in taking a gap year – a year out of your normal work or study in order to work overseas. gap years can provide you with the opportunity of gaining valuable experience, building your personal profile and adding to your personal bank of skills. There are many opportunities, although you will need to fund the costs unless you can get paid work or some financial assistance. If you wish to study abroad, you will need to research university sites and find out information about the country in which you wish to study.

You can get further information on working and studying abroad on the support4learning website (www.support4learning.org.uk). From the home page, click on "jobsearch", and then choose "working abroad (overseas) from the UK" in the menu. The website has advice and information on job opportunities, CVs, interviews and presentations, specialist agencies, relocation information, voluntary work and work experience.

The support4learning website also has links to other useful sites which give further information about overseas work and study opportunities. You might usefully investigate the websites of:

- Voluntary Service Overseas (VSO)
- AdventureJobs4u
- jobscentreplus
- oneworld.net
- idealist.org
- i-to-i.

5 Self-employment

You may decide that, rather than working for someone else, you would like to set up your own business. This will take a lot of determination and effort, and it will require a great deal of advance planning. Consider whether you have the strengths to follow this option. Are you self-motivated? Do you have belief in your own abilities? Have you conducted thorough research into whether there is a market for your idea?

There is plenty of support and advice to help you examine the potential of your business ideas and to consider in more detail the opportunities and the challenges of self-employment. These websites are worth investigating:

- www.businesslink.org
- www.princes-trust.org.uk
- www.shell-livewire.org
- www.lsc.gov.uk
- www.sbs.gov.uk
- www.chamberonline.co.uk
- www.projectdynamo.com – for students in Wales.

Local careers services can also advise you on contacts in your area that may offer you advice in setting up your own business, and any potential sources of funding to assist in setting up your own business.

Figure 7.4: Pros and cons of self-employment

Pros	Cons
You're in charge of your own destiny	It can be lonely to have to make decisions on your own
You can stick to your principles and set out your own rules and philosophy	You have to provide your own job perks, such as pensions and paid holidays
You have flexibility in your work	You do not have a regular income
	You have total responsibility for the business

Source: www.bbc.co.uk/radio1/onelife/

Knowledge summary

- **There are many options open to you in order to gain training, education and work experience. It is useful to investigate a range of options to help you to plan the most effective pathway for you.**

- **It may be possible to achieve the qualifications or work experience you need by several different pathways. You need to consider which option might be more preferable and accessible for you to take, given your current circumstances. The route you choose will be that which best fits your individual career development plan.**

data**interpretation**
The Fubra Group

Brendan McLoughlin set up The Fubra Group (www.fubra.com) with his mates Paul Maunders, Phil Glanville and Ben Kennish straight after their A-levels.

What is The Fubra Group? We're an e-business solutions provider – we help businesses use the internet to improve their efficiency. Our most recent success story is a mail-order business whose profits increased by 50 per cent after our help.

How'd you start your business? We borrowed money from my dad and used money I'd earned from building computers at sixth form to buy computers, software and a networking unit. Our office was my old bedroom and we negotiated relationships with other businesses to keep us going – for example, we arranged a deal with a local sandwich shop for lunch. When we moved, our internet connection didn't work for four months, which could have ruined us, but we'd saved enough money to keep going for six months. We learnt not to rely on third parties – we would have been useless without a fast, reliable internet connection.

How much research do you do for your products? A lot! We look for markets with high technical entry barriers, poor competition and bad practices, and shake them up with innovative new products or services.

Who do you talk to for advice? We talk to each other, the advisory people on our company board and, more recently, Business Link, as they can help with sales and marketing. Plus, we spent about £250 on books, and we've learnt to do things ourselves anyway.

What about money? Money is a goal, but our main reward has been experience – in fact we take home less than a part-timer at McDonald's! We plough everything back into research and development. We've never had outside investment – we're not short of offers, but we want to look back and attribute any money we make to our hard work. Our turnover was under £100,000 for our first year, but we expect our second year's turnover to be higher.

What's your advice for others who want to start their own business? Remain positive! Have end goals and keep aiming to reach them. Narrow your focus and match it with demand in the marketplace. Make sure you really want to do it – the biggest costs will be your time and effort.

Source: www.bbc.co.uk/radio1/onelife/

A What do you think motivated the owners of The Fubra Group to want to become entrepreneurs?

B Setting up in business takes a great deal of effort and determination. Explain the amount of planning and research conducted prior to opening The Fubra Group. Why do you think this is necessary when setting up your own business?

C Discuss the alternative routes that the owners of The Fubra Group could have taken in order to gain the skills, qualifications or experience needed for self-employment.

Setting the scene: career development loans

A career development loan helps you pay for vocational learning or education. It is a deferred payment bank loan, enabling you to borrow between £300 and £8,000 to fund up to two years of learning, and up to one year's practical work experience if this forms part of the course.

Career development loans have helped tens of thousands of people to give their careers a lift. Bryn Allcorn, for example, used a career development loan to help him pursue an acting career.

Bryn came to acting after an HND in media studies, which whetted his appetite for performing. He spent time training at Farnborough Theatre but was keen to get a formal acting qualification which would launch his career. He knew about the "company course" at The Academy in Whitechapel – but he would need to pay fees of around £5,800 and he faced substantial transport costs in making the two-hour journey each way every day.

"My career development loan enabled me to go from just wanting to act to being able to act. In fact, I've been working almost non-stop since leaving drama school. Some of my friends who didn't take out loans haven't been able to progress their acting careers because they've had to do temporary jobs to make ends meet."

Bryn completed his drama course in July 2001 and gained his Equity card in September. He has since clocked up an impressive number of acting roles, including two feature film leads, a schools tour in the south-east – even a part in a corporate video.

Source: www.lifelonglearning.co.uk/

Lifelong Learning

Your independent voice for lifelong learning

Financing education and training

There is a wide range of funding available to help people get the educational qualifications, training and experience that they need to obtain their career goals. In this topic, we explore some of these funding sources.

At the outset, you should be aware that these grants and funding schemes are frequently amended – and the sums available and the eligibility requirements are particularly subject to change. It is essential, therefore, to undertake your own research and find out the current position. For this reason, some useful web links are provided to help you in your investigations.

1 Higher education: student support and grants

As a student, your two main costs will be tuition fees and living expenses – and it is possible to get financial help for both of these costs. If you decide to enter higher education in order to gain qualifications for your chosen career, there are several sources of funding opportunities to explore.

Detailed information is available on the Department for Education and Skills website (www.dfes.gov.uk/studentsupport/). Students in further education, higher education and training in Wales should visit the Education and Learning Wales (ELWa) website (www.elwa.ac.uk/).

Student loans

Student loans are the way most students part-finance their living and study costs while they are in full-time higher education. In 2004/5, the scheme offered loans of up to £4,095 (£5,050 for students studying in London, and £3,240 for those living at home). These rates will be raised from September 2006.

Everybody is eligible for a student loan, though the total amount that will be loaned depends on your and your household's income. You only start repaying your student loan when you've left university and earn more than £15,000 a year. Repayments are collected through the tax system, directly linked to an individual's earnings, so the less you earn, the less you pay; the more you earn, the more you pay.

Higher education grants

From September 2004, new full-time students from lower-income households were eligible for a non-repayable higher education grant of up to £1,000 a year to help meet the costs of going to university or college.

This amount is likely to change in the future and, from September 2006, new full-time students from lower-income households will be eligible for a new income-assessed non-repayable maintenance grant of up to £2,700 a year.

Learner support and hardship funds

Learner support funds – sometimes known as access, hardship or contingency funds – provide help for students who are on low income and may need extra financial support for their course and to stay in higher education. These funds are administered by individual colleges and universities, and the eligibility criteria vary from institution to institution. Payment is usually given as a grant, so it does not have to be repaid.

In Wales, there are financial contingency funds designed to help students facing financial hardship to meet the cost of things like books, travel, childcare, accommodation and general living expenses. Colleges and universities again set their own criteria, but you could get, depending on your income and circumstances, between £100 and £3,500.

Help with other costs

There is a range of extra help available for students with particular needs. Students in full-time education with dependent children can get a childcare grant. How much help you get will depend on your circumstances, such as your income, and whether you are classed as a dependent or independent student.

There is a parents' living allowance, an adult dependents grant and a range of disabled students allowances which can provide help with the extra costs you have as a result of attending your course and/or as a direct result of your disability.

2 Other support for higher education

There are several other sources of funding, such as bursaries or scholarships, that may be available to you to help you through higher education or college.

These need careful investigation because they are not always prominently advertised and details change frequently.

Educational charities and trusts

Educational charities and trusts usually have specific criteria that they try to meet when awarding funds. They generally support first-time students rather than postgraduates. Awards often have very restricted or specific eligibility criteria. You may have to be:

- following a particular course
- below a certain age
- from particular parts of the country or the world
- working towards jobs in particular professions or industries.

If a charity or trust does decide to help, you may only receive a few hundred pounds – for example, £300 is not untypical – and the money may be awarded for a particular purpose, such as purchasing tools or equipment. Payments may also be made because the charity thinks the funds will make the difference between non-completion and completion of a course.

Professional study loans

Some high street banks offer professional study loans for courses in medicine, dentistry, law, veterinary science and architecture. Loans of up to £10,000 are available. Contact a branch of the major banks for further details.

Business school loan scheme

The business school loan scheme is run by the Association of MBAs in partnership with Barclays and NatWest banks, and provides loans for people studying for an MBA in a full-time, part-time or distance learning capacity,

3 Support for 16–19 year olds

In general, there is little financial support for students in full-time education in the sixth form or at college. However, the government wants to encourage more people to stay on in full-time education, and two schemes have been introduced to provide some help for students who might need financial help to complete courses.

Education maintenance allowance

This is a means-tested benefit which is paid to those aged between 16 and 19 who start or remain on full-time courses up to NVQ level 3 (A level equivalent).

Childcare grants for teenage parents

The government wants to increase the number of teenage parents taking A-levels, so it has set up a pilot scheme which will give up to 400 young parents in England free childcare to enable them to study. The childcare places are worth up to £120 a week.

4 Benefits

Depending on your particular circumstances, you may qualify for general benefits. It is important that you find up-to-date information on these, as they often change.

Jobseeker's allowance

Jobseeker's allowance is a benefit for people who are unemployed and are looking for work. There are several conditions that you need to meet in order to claim this allowance. You may still be able to claim jobseeker's allowance if you are studying part time and still actively seeking work, or if you are doing voluntary work.

New Deal

If you are aged 18–24 and have been claiming jobseeker's allowance for more than six months, you can access the New Deal programme. A personal adviser will give you careers advice and guidance and help you find a job, or a subsidised job, work and training with a voluntary or environmental group, or you can study full time for a qualification. New Deal also exists for those over 25 who have been claiming jobseeker's allowance for 18 months or more.

Housing benefit and income support

These benefits are means tested, so any income will be taken into account when assessing your eligibility. Some benefits cover a 52-week year, not just term time – and this will be taken into account when assessing benefit entitlement during the summer vacation.

Child benefit and other benefits

Students may qualify for child benefit, council tax exemption and a range of health benefits if they are on a low income.

5 Other sources

There are a range of other possible sources of special funding, ranging from awards for dance and drama to support from charities and trade unions. You will need to investigate what is available, given what you are trying to achieve.

If you are in paid work, your employer may be willing to subsidise and support you through a course or qualification. For example, the National Health Service offers bursaries for NHS employees. An employer may make a contribution towards the cost of a course, or provide reduced-rate loans to help to subsidise your course costs.

Of course, you may have to self-fund, relying on any savings you have or paying out of your wage or salary if you are employed. It is helpful, however, to investigate any sources of funding that you can access. These websites may help your research:

- www.careerswales.com
- www.connexionscard.co.uk
- www.support4learning.org.uk
- www.dfes.gov.uk/studentsupport
- www.elwa.org.uk
- www.lsc.co.uk

Knowledge summary

- **There is a wide range of funding that may support you while you are obtaining qualifications and undertaking training.**

- **You will need to investigate which sources of funding may be available to you, given your circumstances and what you are trying to achieve.**

- **Establishing suitable sources of funding will help you evaluate which career pathway may be the best option and help you construct a workable career plan.**

- **Funding schemes change frequently, and it will be essential that you keep your information up to date.**

For 39 year old Sally Sadler, a career development loan proved to be the key that unlocked the door to a whole new future.

Sally took out a career development loan to cover the £2,000 course fees she needed to complete the approved driving instructor qualification. Now qualified, she has launched her own business in Bournemouth, the Zodiac School of Motoring. Only a few months on, Sally – a single mother with four children – is starting to reap the benefits of self-employment. She can be flexible and choose how many hours she wants to work, which helps her to combine her new career with her responsibilities at home.

The story began when Sally lost her job when the mobile phone shop where she had worked for eight years closed unexpectedly. She found herself claiming benefit and contemplating applying for a job in a local supermarket to help her support her children. "I sat down and made a list of all the things I enjoyed. I knew that I liked working with people – and that I enjoyed driving. Becoming an instructor was a natural choice, but I didn't see how I could afford to make it happen."

Undeterred by the apparent financial obstacles, she went to talk to a tutor at the Southampton Instructors' College. Here she learned that if she worked hard she could complete the course quickly. She was also told about career development loans as a way of financing her training: "I read the information pack, and the great thing was that I wouldn't have to start making repayments until shortly after I had completed my training. I knew that if I worked really hard and qualified, I'd be generating an income by the time I had to start making repayments."

She applied to Barclays, and just two weeks later heard that the loan had been agreed. Nine months later she had completed the course and emerged as a fully qualified instructor. When the first repayment became due she was already making a success of her new business. Sally is so enthusiastic she is already planning to use a second loan to finance the next stage of her career development: the HGV instructor's qualification.

Source: www.lifelonglearning.co.uk/

A Research the alternative sources of funding that might be available to Sally to help her through her driving instructor course.

B Discuss whether this was the only way Sally could have undertaken this change of career. In your answer, consider alternative training and education routes she may have taken.

The career plan

Having worked through the process of developing your possible career options, you will need to draw this information together in order to construct your own career plan. The career plan is a working document. It will need to include a personal budget, which will help you to evaluate the feasibility of your chosen career pathway. It should also include:

- a personal skills profile and personality traits
- a list of training and development opportunities
- your proposed career pathway and training and education route
- an action plan for the next three years.

Personal skills profile

Your personal skills profile should set out your personal qualities, your skills and achievements, and any qualifications you have achieved to date.

Personal qualities

A psychometric test (see topics 5 and 6) will help you to identify your personality traits and personal qualities. Your personal qualities are a description of you as a person.

Skills and achievements

You also need to include a summary of your achievements and skills. Some of these may have been gained from a period of work experience. In your achievements, record things you have done which you are proud of, and back these up with evidence.

It will be useful to keep an account of any key skills you may have gained. Employers are often looking for people who have a positive attitude to work, and who are flexible. You need to consider what skills you have to offer, and how you have developed these attributes. Remember you will need to keep these up to date. It would be useful to keep a log.

Qualifications

You need to include a record of the qualifications that you have obtained (as well as those that you are

expecting to get). This should include school and college examinations with (achieved or expected) grades, and a brief note of where you studied.

SWOT analysis

SWOT is an acronym: it stands for strengths, weaknesses, opportunities and threats. To identify key elements of your personal profile, consider your strengths and weaknesses and identify any opportunities and threats that may influence your eventual career plan.

Career goals

By establishing your ambitions and what you want to achieve, you will have a focus and direction in which to take your career plan.

Use the information you gained from your investigation into career paths to establish what you actually want to achieve in terms of your career. It may be that you are already in work, and wish to change your career direction. It may be you are yet to enter your first career. You will need to make sure that the choices you make are realistic. Consider the training, experience, skills and qualifications, and personal qualities that the new career requires. Is it possible for you to achieve these, given your circumstances? You will need to reflect on the various career options and the routes available to you to achieve these options.

In this section, examine the training and development routes you may wish to take. Again, by exploring all the options, you will ensure that you put together a robust and workable plan, and that you begin to make choices that best suit your eventual goals.

Budget

Whichever route you plan to take, you will need to establish what financial support will be required, and what sources of funding may be available to you. This will help you to determine whether your planned career path will be realistic given your personal circumstances, and help you to justify why the route you actually choose to take is right for you.

To construct your personal budget, you will first need to make a record of your expenditure (money you

Figure 7.5: Sample personal budget (per month)

Income	£	Expenditure	£
Salary/wage from work		Accommodation (rent/mortgage)	
Grants, scholarships		Utilities	
Student loan		Childcare costs	
Benefits (housing, jobseeker's allowance, any other)		Entertainment (such as going out, gym, travel)	
Other income: (state source)		Education (books, trips, fees)	
		Personal (mobile phone, toiletries, clothes, etc.)	
Subtotal		**Subtotal**	
Additional income sources (list potential sources and amounts)		Additional expenses associated with course or training	
Total income		**Total expenditure**	

have to pay out) and of any income (money you have coming in). Figure 7.5 shows a format that you could use to help you think through and set out your budget. You will need to look at the costs associated with the proposed career route you wish to take. How does this affect your budget?

You will need to then explore the various funding sources to establish whether these will provide ways to increase your income. It will be necessary for you to ensure that your expected income at least equals, or is more than, your anticipated expenditure. If not, then it would not appear to be a feasible route to take. You may need to consider an alternative career route that does not have such a major impact on your expenditure.

Action plan

Your action plan should provide you with a systematic and achievable approach to help you achieve your ambitions and goals.

Development plans

Having established where you want to get to in terms of your career, you will need to match this against where you are now. For example, compare the key requirements of the career you want with what you are actually able to offer as a person now. The gap – between what you have and what you need – is your personal development needs.

Targets

In order to reach your goal, you will need to set SMART objectives, which will detail the action you intend to take, with targets and time limits. You will need to monitor and review your action plan regularly, to keep yourself on track.

Consider the training, experience, skills and qualifications you will need for the career of your choice. How will you approach these? Set yourself development targets, and make realistic plans for obtaining these goals. You may need to consider your plans in the short term (during the next year), and the longer term (during the next the years). For example:

Goal

Get advice about IT-related courses, including the costs of study for each option.

Target

Speak to colleagues who work in IT, get advice from my careers adviser and from local colleges.

By when

Make an appointment with the careers adviser within the next two days. Be in a position to collate all the advice regarding courses within the next two weeks.

stop and think

Describe the targets involved, and suggest suitable "by when" dates for each of these goals:

a) gain work experience within the NHS

b) improve skills in team-working

c) obtain a degree

d) improve key skills in application of number

e) build my self-confidence.

Consider some of your personal goals. Describe targets that may form part of your action plan.

Be flexible

It is no longer realistic to expect to be in the same job for your working lifetime. There may be many reasons why you need or want to change career. You may decide to make a radical change to a completely different occupation, or you might be forced to seek an alternative career because job functions change, or your employer goes into liquidation, or because you decide to move abroad. You may need to consider these eventualities within your career plan. Keeping your options open and allowing yourself choices later on in your career is sensible, as it will provide you with flexibility in your career.

data interpretation
Connexions Direct

Connexions Direct is an advice service for young people aged 13–19 that offers quick access to information on a wide range of topics through one easy-to-use website.

You can also speak to Connexions Direct advisers by telephone, web chat, e-mail or text message. They are there to listen to you, but can offer confidential advice and practical help too. And if you need even more specialist help they know all the right people.

Connexions personal advisers can give you information, advice and practical help with all sorts of things, like choosing subjects at school or mapping out your future career options. They can help you with anything which might be affecting you at school, college, work or in your personal or family life. All advice is confidential, and you don't have to give a name and address if you don't want to.

Connexions Direct advisers are available to take your call from 8:00 am to 2:00 am, seven days a week.

Call 080 800 13-2-19

Text on 07766 4 13-2-19

Web chat or e-mail from www.connexions-direct.com

A Using the www.connexions-direct.com website, identify the advice Connexions Direct can provide in your investigation into possible career choices.

B Explain the guidance Connexions Direct can give you to help construct your personal profile.

C Discuss the other sources of advice available to you when constructing your career plan.

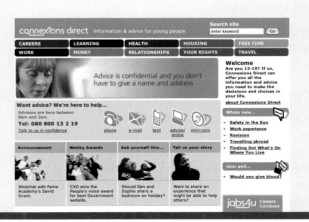

Topic 10 · Career planning in practice: Klaudia's choices

Klaudia Darbinova is 17 and is in the sixth form at a school in East Anglia. Klaudia is from St Petersburg in Russia and has been at school in the UK since she was 14. Klaudia's English is very good; she speaks the language fluently and has opted to take English A-level as well as studying business and other subjects. She thinks that speaking two languages will be a significant advantage when she is looking for a job. Klaudia was successful in her GCSE examinations achieving seven passes at grade C or better, including English and mathematics.

Klaudia has never taken a psychometric test, but has a good idea of her personal strengths and weaknesses and the personality traits she possesses. She sees herself as:

- a highly confident person, able to take decisions and work with minimal supervision

- well-motivated and keen to achieve her personal targets

- a good communicator both verbally and in writing

- more suited to working alone rather than as part of a team

- someone with effective interpersonal skills that she uses in social and working environments

- having the characteristics to be a leader, and she would relish the opportunity to set goals and take decisions.

Klaudia comes from an entrepreneurial background. Her father is a highly successful businessman. He owns and manages a family business that manufactures handbags and small cases. The business has factories in Russia, China and the Czech Republic, and sources many components such as zips from factories in China. Its products are sold in many European countries. Klaudia has spent some time working with her father in the business. She has therefore been used to the language of business from an early age, and this has shaped her attitudes and abilities and, of course, her career aspirations.

Klaudia has had further experience of the business world. In 2004, she had a period of work experience as an administrative assistant for HarperCollins in west London. She carried out a number of duties including taking telephone messages, conducting minor pieces of research, reorganising filing systems and assisting in preparing the substantial amounts of mail sent out from the office. Klaudia's supervisor during her work placement was hugely impressed by her performance, as the following brief report shows.

work experience report

Klaudia was different from many of our previous work placement students; she was very presentable, confident, mature and well organised. She carried out her tasks quietly and efficiently and was 100 per cent reliable. Colleagues were impressed by her cheerful and positive nature and her willingness to help others. It was easy to forget that her first language is Russian, as she spoke and wrote English so well.

Although she seemed to prefer working on her own, she joined in the office banter at times. However, what set Klaudia apart from many other students was her approach to her work. She was motivated throughout and did not sit doing nothing when she had finished a task. Either she would ask colleagues if she could help them or she would use her own initiative to do something helpful. Few students have been able to work so effectively unsupervised.

Klaudia's possible career paths

Klaudia's interests lie in business. She hopes to eventually work in a European business where she can use her languages as well as her business knowledge and skills. She thinks that a career in marketing is one possibility, and another idea is working in human relations. She is not confident about her numerical skills and would not, for example, wish to train as an accountant. Although she is sure of two general areas in which her future may lie, she remains unsure about precisely what route to take over the next three to five years.

Option 1: marketing

Klaudia enjoyed the marketing sessions that she has completed on her business course, and she has researched the possibilities of a career working in marketing. She says that there are two choices if she opts for a career in this area. "I could go to university and study marketing. In some ways I would like this, as it would allow me to gain all the necessary knowledge of marketing and other business subjects before starting work. Some courses also have a year out in industry, which I think I would like".

The alternative route is for Klaudia to enter work straight away as an 18 year old with level 3 (A-level and equivalent) qualifications in business and other subjects. This would allow her to get hands-on experience, but she would need to train on the job to gain relevant and more advanced qualifications.

Figure 7.6 summarises Klaudia's research findings and shows the different options and opportunities offered by the two routes she has identified to a career in marketing.

Figure 7.6: Routes to a career in marketing

	University	Work
Description of proposed route	Completing a three-year course in marketing (maybe with Russian [at Strathclyde University?]) possibly with an additional year in industry. This year could be overseas. Then seek employment.	Enter employment directly on leaving school at 18. Seek first-level marketing job, though hopefully in company with clear progression routes.
Job possibilities	Research revealed: 1. Marketing promotions executive with BBC. Implementing marketing strategy. 2. Marketing assistant with Global Resourcing Solutions Ltd. Maintaining websites, reviewing marketing activities, writing follow-up reports.	Research revealed: 1. Marketing assistant with smallish firm in Bristol. General marketing duties supporting marketing dept. 2. Marketing assistant with Fingershield Ltd in Manchester. Designing mail shots and managing marketing databases.
Skills identified	Verbal and written communications, creativity, time management, IT skills, data analysis and presentation, managing budgets, basic supervisory.	Telephone skills, written and verbal communication, website maintenance, creativity, care and accuracy.
Other issues	Many jobs require experience. Some want professional qualifications (Chartered Institute of Marketing) rather than marketing degree.	Some salaries are very low and not all firms offer training. Will career be limited if no degree? Need to discuss with careers adviser.
Salaries	From £16,500–£25,000 (varies with location).	Very variable £13,000–£18,000 depending on location.
Financial implications	Student fees for overseas students are high: a selection of universities showed annual fees from £8,750 to £11,500 for 2005/6 academic year. On top there would be living costs.	Possible cost of Chartered Institute of Marketing examinations is £200 per year rising to £450–£500 for more advanced courses.
Possible sources of funding	Bank loans, parents, gap year at work to provide some finance.	Employers may pay for training – at least in part – bank loan, parents.
Training	Expectation would be to take Chartered Institute of Marketing exams (though marketing degree would remove need to study for lower-level qualifications).	Chartered Institute of Marketing courses, including introductory certificate and the professional diploma in marketing. This could possibly take five years. Also need to check out the ISMM (Institute of Sales and Marketing Managers) courses.

Personnel management is about making sure organisations get the best from the people who work for them. Professionals in this role are involved in selecting the right sort of staff and promoting practices which ensure they are managed effectively.

The terms personnel and human resources are largely interchangeable, although the latter does imply more of a strategic approach. There are a range of specialisms, but those starting out often take generalist roles assisting with all aspects and may move into specialist areas after a promotion.

Recruitment and selection

Working alongside staff in various departments, drawing up job descriptions, preparing advertisements, checking application forms, interviewing and sometimes testing applicants. There may also be involvement in redeployment and redundancy programmes.

Employee development

This includes induction for new staff, developing appraisal systems, analysing training needs and evaluating the effectiveness of what is delivered. Some personnel staff are involved in producing and presenting training materials.

Employee relations

Dealing with all the tricky bits like grievances, disciplinary proceedings, redundancy and resolving differences between staff members. This can also include responsibility for developing equal opportunities policies, writing staff handbooks and advising on contractual issues.

Pay and benefits

Job evaluation is a major role, ensuring salaries are a fair reflection of the demands of a job.

Human resource planning

Predicting future staffing needs and ensuring development and training policies reflect the long-term needs of the organisation.

Specialist and senior posts may require wide-ranging experience, often in roles other than personnel such as law, accountancy, general management and administrative work.

Employee services

Putting together staff perks and benefits – anything from private health cover or cheap holidays to social events or counselling services.

Qualifications

The professional qualification for personnel management is the Chartered Institute of Personnel and Development's (CIPD) Professional Development Scheme. This can be studied part-time, full-time or through flexible learning schemes. Full-time normally takes a year, part-time is two to three years. Many universities offer the full-time course as part of a postgraduate diploma or masters course in human resource management.

The majority of students are funded by employers on part-time courses. Full-time students have to fund themselves, and course fees vary between institutions. The CIPD website has details of all accredited institutions and can provide information and advice on the difference between courses.

Study covers four fields. Students completing one field are normally eligible for licentiate membership of the CIPD. This is of great advantage when applying for posts with employers who are willing to consider applicants working towards the qualification. Students taking the part-time or distance learning option do not have to be employed in a personnel role, but it would be difficult to complete some of the assignments without having access to a personnel department.

Prospects

This is a profession that can be hard to break into without experience. Other office or administrative work can provide a useful background. Many HR departments recruit graduates into assistant posts and will sponsor staff through the CIPD course. Good sources of vacancies include www.jobs.ac.uk for assistant and professional posts in universities, and the vacancy section of www.cipd.co.uk for professional posts generally.

Source: prospects.ac.uk

Option 2: human resource or personnel management

Klaudia has enjoyed the "people" aspects of her business course and is considering a career in this area. She envisages herself in a few years' time working as a personnel manager for a medium-sized or large-sized company. Klaudia's research on employment in this area has not progressed far, but she has obtained a clear idea about the nature of personnel work from the www.prospects.ac.uk website (see job profile on page 329).

activities

1 How might taking a psychometric test help Klaudia to plan her career? Do you think she needs to take a psychometric test? Explain your answer.

2 What personal skills do you think that Klaudia possesses? Apart from the career routes that Klaudia has investigated, to what other occupations do you think that Klaudia is suited? Explain your reasoning.

3 In what ways would a personal or career development plan help Klaudia at this stage?

4 Use the internet to research jobs in personnel and human resource management for which Klaudia might be able to apply now, or after taking a relevant degree. Do you think that Klaudia is suited to employment in this occupation?

5 What training do you think she might need to achieve her possible aim to become a personnel or human resource manager in a medium-sized or large-sized company?

Index

Applied Business AS

Applied Business AS